Project Flexibility, Agency, and Competition

Project Flexibility, Agency, and Competition

*New Developments in the Theory and
Application of Real Options*

Edited by

MICHAEL J. BRENNAN
LENOS TRIGEORGIS

New York   Oxford
OXFORD UNIVERSITY PRESS
2000

Oxford University Press

Oxford New York
Athens Auckland Bangkok Bogotá Buenos Aires Calcutta
Cape Town Chennai Dar es Salaam Delhi Florence Hong Kong Istanbul
Karachi Kuala Lumpur Madrid Melbourne Mexico City Mumbai
Nairobi Paris São Paulo Singapore Taipei Tokyo Toronto Warsaw

and associated companies in
Berlin Ibadan

Published by Oxford University Press, Inc.
198 Madison Avenue, New York, New York 10016
http://www.oup-usa.org

Oxford is a registered trademark of Oxford University Press

Library of Congress Cataloging-in-Publication Data

Project flexibility, agency, and competition : new
   developments in the theory and application of real options
   / [edited by] Michael J. Brennan, Lenos Trigeorgis.
       p.   cm.
   Includes bibliographical references.
   ISBN 0-19-511269-5 (paper)
   1. Capital investments—Decision making.   2. Resource allocation
—Decision making.   3. Capital budget.   4. Corporations—Finance.
5. Options (Finance).   I. Brennan, Michael J.   II. Trigeorgis, Lenos.
HG4028.C4P757   1999
658.15'2—dc21   98-40655

                                                          CIP

Printing (last digit) 9 8 7 6 5 4 3 2 1

Printed in the United States of America
on acid-free paper

Contents

Contributors

Petter Bjerksund
Department of Finance and Management Science, Norwegian School of Economics and Business Administration

Svetlana I. Boyarchenko
Graduate School of Arts & Sciences, University of Pennsylvania

Kjell Arne Brekke
Division for Resource and Environmental Economics and Statistics, Norway

Kirt C. Butler
Department of Finance, The Eli Broad Graduate School of Management, Michigan State University

Peter Carr
Vice President, Morgan Stanley & Co. Inc.

Jaime Casassus
Ingeniera Industrial y de Sistemas, P. Universidad Catolica de Chile

Joseph A. Cherian
School of Management, Boston University

Gonzalo Cortazar
Ingeniera Industrial y de Sistemas, P. Universidad Catolica de Chile

Avinash K. Dixit
Department of Economics, Princeton University

Steven R. Grenadier
Graduate School of Business, Stanford University

Domingo Castelo Joaquin
Department of Finance, Michigan State University

Ilya Khripko
School of Management, Boston University

Bart Lambrecht
Judge Institute of Management Studies, University of Cambridge

Sergei Z. Levendorskiĭ
Rostov Academy, Russia

David C. Mauer
Edwin L. Cox School of Business, Southern Methodist University

Robert L. McDonald
J.L. Kellogg Graduate School of Management, Northwestern University

Kristian R. Miltersen
Department of Management, Odense Universitet

Alberto Moel
Harvard Business School

Mark Moon
Heidt Capital Group

Steven H. Ott
School of Management, University of Kentucky

Jay Patel
School of Management, Boston University

Robert S. Pindyck
Sloan School of Management, Massachusetts Institute of Technology

Jean-Daniel M. Saphores
Department of Economics, Université Laval

Bjarne Schieldrop
Department of Mathematics, University of Oslo

Eduardo S. Schwartz
The John E. Anderson Graduate School of Management, University of California, Los Angeles

Gunnar Stensland
Department of Finance and Management Science, Norwegian School of Economics and Business Administration

Peter Tufano
Harvard Business School

Jostein Tvedt
Den Norske Bank ASA (also of the Norwegian School of Economics)

1

Real Options

Development and New Contributions

MICHAEL J. BRENNAN
LENOS TRIGEORGIS

Given the basic premise that the financial objective of the corporation is to maximize the wealth of the investors in the corporation,[1] investment project analysis is synonymous with investment project valuation: investment projects should be accepted if and only if their value exceeds their cost, so that their acceptance increases the wealth of shareholders.

The practice of project valuation is a good illustration of the Keynesian adage that "practical men, who believe themselves to be quite exempt from any intellectual influences, are usually the slaves of some defunct economist."[2] Where once the payback criterion reigned supreme, the discounted cash flow techniques that owe their origins to John Hicks and Irving Fisher gradually gained acceptance and now tend to have pride of place;[3] as yet, only a few corporations are beginning to employ the real options paradigm that is derived from the classic financial option pricing paradigm of Black-Scholes and Merton.[4] The chapters in this book are concerned with the further development and application of this paradigm. Before discussing them individually, we shall place them in perspective by reflecting briefly on the historical evolution of the different approaches to corporate and project valuation.

It is useful to distinguish three stages in the evolution of the valuation models used in project analysis. We shall refer to the models corresponding to these stages as (1) static, or mechanistic models, in which an investment project is completely

[1] This standard objective function is appropriate only under certain assumptions. See De Angelo (1981) and Makowski (1983).

[2] Keynes (1936, p. 383).

[3] The proportion of *Fortune 500* corporations using discounted cash flow for investment appraisal has risen from 38% in 1962, to 64% in 1977, to 90% in 1990–93 (Segelod, 1998).

[4] "To Wait or Not to Wait," *CFO Magazine*, 13 (May 1997), 91–94.

described by a specified stream of cash flows whose characteristics are given; (2) controllable cash-flow models, in which projects can be managed actively in response to the resolution of exogenous uncertainties about output price and other variables; and (3) dynamic, game-theoretic models, in which it is assumed that projects can be managed actively to take into account not only the resolution of exogenous uncertainties but also the (re)actions of outside parties, in particular of competitors in the product market. It is interesting to observe that these three stages in the development of valuation models find their counterparts in the development of the theory of corporate financial structure.

The first-stage, static, mechanistic, models treat projects as inert machines that produce specified streams of cash-flows over time whose joint probability distribution is given exogenously; the analyst must value these projects by discounting the exogenously given expected cash flows at an appropriately determined but exogenous risk-adjusted discount rate. This is the familiar "discounted cash-flow" approach to valuation whose procedures are now widely programmed into electronic calculators and spreadsheets. A similar mechanistic point of view is apparent in the early theory of corporate financial structure, as represented by the Modigliani–Miller propositions. Here, the whole firm is treated as a machine that produces cash-flows over time whose joint probability distribution is given exogenously, and the only role for financial structure is to allocate different components of the cash-flow stream among different classes of security holders. In this early stage of the development of financial theory, decision makers or agents do not play a significant role in either the model of asset valuation or of financial structure. If individual decision makers or agents appear at all, it is as idealized, ethereal creatures who act without consideration of their own interest and always maximize the value of the firm.[5]

The second stage of development in the theory of project valuation recognizes that the cash flows are, at least partially, controllable: the agent making the investment decision may be able to act in the future to influence the probability distribution of cash flows generated by the project, and will generally wish to do so as more information becomes available. The contingent future actions of the decision maker must be taken into account when the project is initially analyzed, since they will affect the expected value and the risk of the future cash flows of the project under consideration. This controllable cash-flow model of project valuation parallels the agency theory of corporate financial policy stemming from the insight of Jensen and Meckling (1976) that financial structure not only serves to divide up a given stream of cash flows but also affects the size of the cash flows available for distribution through the incentives it creates for the agents who now have control over the probability distribution of those cash flows. One difference perhaps is that the controllable cash-flow model of project analysis generally assumes that the decision maker's objective is to maximize the net value of the firm's cash flows, whereas the agency theory of financial structure focuses on the conflicts of interest between managers and investors and among different classes of investors.

Recognition of the importance in project analysis of the ability to manage or control project cash flows is not new. Hertz had shown as early as 1964 that

---

[5] For example, see Fama and Miller (1972).

Monte Carlo analysis could be used to value a project when the future decisions could be related to a set of stochastic state variables whose values could be simulated, while in the same year Magee (1964) had shown that decision trees could be used in more complex cases in which the optimal future decisions must be determined by taking into account subsequent stochastic events and decisions. The practical importance of such future decision contingencies was soon recognized by scholars such as Robichek and Van Horne (1967) who analyzed the value of being able to abandon a project early if it became unsuccessful. In this second stage of the development of project valuation, project cash flows are treated as endogenous because they are under the control of the decision maker. Thus, it is appropriate to label this stage the "controllable cash-flow stage" of project analysis development.

However, although decision tree analysis and Monte Carlo simulation are useful techniques for estimating the probability distribution of future project cash flows, they offer little guidance as to how future decision possibilities or contingencies affect project risk and therefore project discount rates. Thus, so long as the problem of risk, and therefore the appropriate discount rate, remained unsolved, the second stage of theory development remained stagnant and incomplete, so that it was not possible to integrate Monte Carlo analysis and decision trees into the value maximization framework of neoclassical corporate finance. The discount-rate problem was eventually solved by Black and Scholes (1973) and Merton (1973) in the context of claims on financial assets; in showing how to value a claim whose payoff is contingent on the value of another asset, they developed the technique of risk-neutral, or equivalent martingale, pricing [later formalized by Cox and Ross (1976), Constantinides (1978), Harrison and Pliska (1981), and others]. The far-reaching implication for project analysis is that if the expected rates of change in the underlying cash-flow drivers or stochastic state variables are risk adjusted, the resulting "expected" (risk-adjusted) cash flows can be discounted at the *risk-free* interest rate, regardless of the types of future decision contingencies inherent in the project or of the nature of the relation between the stochastic state variables and the cash flows of the project.[6]

Brennan and Schwartz (1985) and McDonald and Siegel (1985) were the first to actually employ these insights in the valuation of real assets, thus helping to complete this second stage in the development of project valuation, which has become known as "real options" analysis. The term "real options" recognizes both the similarities and the differences between the valuation of rights to controllable cash flows and the valuation of financial options. The similarities arise not only because the ability to control or manage a cash-flow stream represents an option, but, more importantly, because equivalent martingale pricing techniques are appropriate to both real and financial options. The major difference is that although financial options are almost always options on traded assets,[7] the rights to controllable cash flows typically cannot

---

[6] In particular, whether the relation is linear or not. The simplest type of nonlinearity arises from the tax code that taxes positive profits but does not allow tax rebates for losses.

[7] This is not always the case: an option on a constant-maturity treasury bond or an option on a foreign stock index converted to another currency at a fixed exchange rate are examples of financial options on nontraded assets.

be reduced to claims on traded assets; this often makes the determination of the equivalent martingale measure or risk adjustment more problematic than is the case for financial options.

Nonetheless, the real options approach provides a much more satisfactory method of taking account of the effects on project risk caused by the controllability of project cash flows than does the mechanistic discounted cash-flow approach, which essentially ignores future decision contingencies. The real options approach, which is able to capture the risk-reducing effects of cash-flow controllability through the equivalent martingale risk adjustment, can be thought of as bringing discipline and analytical rigor to the older techniques of Monte Carlo simulation and decision tree analysis for valuing claims to controllable cash flows, by correctly adjusting for risk. In fact, Monte Carlo analysis is often a simple and convenient alternative to solving partial differential equations or using lattice methods to value European-style financial options,[8] and the lattice methods themselves bear more than a passing resemblance to simple decision trees.

The third stage in the development of the theory of project analysis takes account of the fact that the cash flows from an investment project are influenced not only by agents within the firm who can react as new information becomes available, but also by the actions of agents outside the firm, such as competitors and suppliers, and that these actions can in turn be influenced by—as well as influence—the actions of the agents within the firm. From this perspective, the cash flows from a project (and therefore the value of the project) can be seen as the outcome of a game, not just between the inside agent and nature, as recognized in the earlier, second-stage models, but among the inside agent, outside agents, and nature. Therefore, we refer to these as game-theoretic models, although not all take an explicitly game-theoretic perspective. Dixit (1989) and Williams (1993) were among the first to consider real options within an equilibrium context. More explicit game-theoretic approaches can be seen in Trigeorgis (1991), Smit and Ankum (1993), Smit and Trigeorgis (1993), Trigeorgis (1996), Grenadier (1996), and in several of the chapters in this book. Game-theoretic models appeared somewhat earlier in the theory of financial structure. Brander and Lewis (1986), Maksimovic (1988), and Maksimovic and Zechner (1991), among others, have considered the relation between financial structure and product market competition. In these models the firm's financial structure affects the payoffs to the equityholders who control the firm's decisions, and thereby affects their incentives; this allows them to use financial structure to make credible precommitments about their output policy.

Actually, the analytical distinction that we have made between the theory of asset valuation and the theory of financial structure is more one of convenience than of substance. The value of an asset may depend not only on its cash flow stream but also on who owns and controls it, and on their ability to switch it to alternative uses or to sell it if necessary. Shleifer and Vishny (1992), for example, show that the value of an asset depends not only on the capital structure of the firm owning it

---

[8] As a forward-looking technique, however, standard simulation is limited in valuing the early-exercise feature of American-style options. Boyle (1977) was the first to use Monte Carlo methods to value financial options.

(which determines when it has to be liquidated), but also on the capital structure of other firms in the industry (which can affect the degree of competition in the market for liquidated assets). Similarly, Parsons and Mello (1992) and Mauer and Ott (this volume) show how the firm's capital structure can affect the policy used to control the cash flows from an asset, and therefore its value.

The chapters in this book fall into one or the other of the later two stages in the development of project valuation. The first part of the book, focusing on the valuation and exercise of real options, corresponds to what we have called the second stage in the development of valuation theory, and is concerned with situations in which future cash flows are at least partially controllable, but the uncertainty is exogenous and the firm is not concerned about the reactions of other decision makers. The last part, on strategic options and product market competition, corresponds to our third stage of theory development and focuses on game-theoretic or equilibrium valuation models.

Part I deals with the determination of optimal contingent policies and the value of flexibility. A standard conclusion of real options analysis is that uncertainty about the future profitability of an investment project makes it optimal for a firm to postpone commitment to the project relative to a setting in which there is no uncertainty. The first three chapters are concerned with different aspects of the timing of project commitment. McDonald (Chapter 2) analyzes the extent to which commonly used heuristics, such as the setting of hurdle rates above the cost of capital or minimum profitability index criteria, approximate the optimal rules for the timing of investments under uncertainty. Somewhat surprisingly, he finds that simple heuristics yield a large proportion of the value attainable by the optimal rule. Brekke and Schieldrop (Chapter 3) examine how operating flexibility, in the form of the ability to choose between alternative fuel inputs with uncertain future prices, affects the optimal timing of investment. In general, uncertainty leads to delay in the optimal timing of an irreversible investment, just as increased volatility tends to postpone the optimal exercise of financial options. The authors show that operating flexibility, by making the investment less irreversible, tends to offset the effects of uncertainty and leads to earlier optimal investment. They also demonstrate that the ability to choose between gas and oil fuels leads to substantial cost savings in present value terms for reasonable parameter values. Dixit and Pindyck (Chapter 4) are also concerned with the effects of flexibility on the timing of investment, but from a new perspective. They distinguish between *expandability*, the firm's ability to add capacity, which is akin to a call option, and *reversibility*, the firm's ability to undo its previous investments, which is akin to a put option, and argue that it is the lack of reversibility that leads a firm to postpone its investment commitment when there is uncertainty about cash flows, and not the call option per se. They analyze the optimal capacity choice of a firm whose investment opportunities exhibit limited expandability as well as reversibility, generalizing their earlier work.

The Black–Scholes (1973) and Merton (1973) roots of the real options paradigm are evident in the virtually universal assumptions that trading and decision making take place in continuous time and that the underlying sources of uncertainty follow Brownian motions, even though these assumptions may well be unsuitable in many corporate contexts. Boyarchenko and Levendorskii (Chapter 5) relax these assumptions and show how to analyze the investment timing decision in a discrete-time setting under quite general assumptions about the underlying probability law.

Their principal result is that the non-Gaussian assumption leads to postponement of investment relative to the Gaussian case with the same variance. However, when investment is partially reversible, the effect of the non-Gaussian assumption on the exit strategy is ambiguous.

Schwartz and Moon (Chapter 6) show how real options analysis can be applied to projects that are characteristic of the pharmaceutical and other research-intensive industries. They focus on the valuation of an R&D project and the optimal rules for abandoning a project in progress. Like Pindyck (1993), they take account of uncertainties about the cost of project completion and learning as the project proceeds about this cost, as well as about the value of the completed project. They also introduce a Poisson probability of project failure, and show how the analysis can be adapted to the multistage character of modern drug development.

Part II deals with agency, contracts, and incentives in a real options context. The papers by Bjerksund and Stensland (Chapter 7), Moel and Tufano (Chapter 8), and Mauer and Ott (Chapter 9) are concerned with the agency problems that arise in a dynamic setting when cash flows are controllable and the decision maker has private information about the underlying state. Bjerksund and Stensland (Chapter 7) analyze a situation in which there is joint production between two firms, but one party has private information about its costs and determines the level of joint production. They construct a contract that specifies the range of output prices for which production occurs, and the compensation for the firm with private information, that leads to the maximization of the joint market value of the two firms. Moel and Tufano (Chapter 8), in an unusually detailed and thoughtful analysis of a real case, study an auction for rights to explore and develop a mining property in Peru. The case presents a classic problem of valuing the development option. More interesting, however, is the nature of the bidding rules that bidders were required to follow. Each bid was required to specify not only a price for the right to explore and develop the property, but also the minimum amount that the bidder would spend on developing the property if they decided to go ahead. This is equivalent to allowing the bidders to specify the exercise price of the development option, and the authors show that this aspect of the bidding rules could induce the successful bidder to make uneconomic investments. The authors also analyze the default option possessed by the successful bidder, the possibility of renegotiation with the government, and the type of firm that is most likely to bid aggressively. Mauer and Ott (Chapter 9) present a parametric analysis of the classic Myers (1977) underinvestment phenomenon caused by the agency problem created by a debt overhang. They show that outstanding risky debt causes a firm that is run in the interest of the shareholders to postpone investment relative to an all-equity firm, and quantify the effect of this agency problem on the wealth of stockholders and the yield on the debt. They also analyze the effects of debt maturity, more lenient bond indentures, and product market competition on the magnitude of the agency costs.

Part III deals with the determination of optimal policies, and the valuation of flexibility, in natural and environmental resource investments. The earliest papers on real options were concerned with analyzing projects for which the underlying state variable was a commodity price.[9] The reason for this is that the existence of forward

---

[9] See Brennan and Schwartz (1985) and McDonald and Siegel (1985).

or futures markets for many commodities allows a simple and direct calculation of the equivalent martingale measure. The equivalent martingale measure for commodity prices is obtained in the same way as in the Black–Scholes model for stock prices, except that the "convenience yield" on the commodity plays the role of the dividend yield on the stock. Although the early models assumed a constant rate of convenience yield, subsequent work has allowed the convenience yield to be stochastic.[10] Miltersen (Chapter 10) builds on earlier work with Schwartz to value commodity contingent claims when interest rates are stochastic and the convenience yield follows a Gaussian process; the basic framework is adapted from the Heath–Jarrow–Morton model of the term structure of interest rates.[11] Miltersen shows how this model may be used to value the option to develop a resource project when the project contains discrete production options, and demonstrates that the stochastic nature of the convenience yield has important implications for valuation. Cortazar and Casassus (Chapter 11), although retaining the constant convenience yield assumption, focus instead on how to choose the optimal production policy and how to value a commodity resource project when the production process has several stages and intermediate goods inventories are held. Such multistage processes are a typical feature of mineral resource projects. Cherian, Patel, and Khripko (Chapter 12) analyze a further characteristic of natural resource projects, the tendency of costs per unit to rise as more of the resource is extracted. They determine the optimal extraction policy and compare it with the myopic policy of maximizing the instantaneous profit rate, demonstrating that ignoring the cumulating costs can lead to a significant loss of project value. Finally, Saphores and Carr (Chapter 13) consider the timing problem for an environmental investment whose benefits depend on the stock of the pollutant. They analyze a model of an environmental pollutant that decays at an exogenous but stochastic rate, and causes social costs that are incurred at a rate that increases quadratically in the level of the pollutant. They show that a small level of uncertainty in the decay process may either advance or delay the timing of an investment that will reduce the pollution rate; however, when the uncertainty is sufficiently high the expected environmental costs become the dominant consideration and it becomes optimal to reduce emissions immediately. Interestingly, the optimal policy when the uncertainty is small is quite different from the deterministic case (when it is zero).

Part IV is concerned with what we have called game-theoretic models, in which strategic interactions between agents are important. Grenadier (Chapter 14) analyzes the equilibrium in a perfectly competitive real estate market with stochastic demand in which new capacity takes time δ to build.[12] The time-to-build and continuous-time features of the model mean that the state space is infinite since it must include the volume of construction started at each instant over the past δ periods. Despite this, Grenadier is able to characterize the optimal construction policies as well as provide closed-form expressions for asset values and the density function of prices, by constructing an artificial economy with a finite state space in which the equilibrium

---

[10] See Brennan (1991), Gibson and Schwartz (1990), and Schwartz (1997) among others.

[11] Cootner (1961) appears to have been the first to recognize the analogy between futures markets for bonds and for commodities.

[12] In models in which the two firms have identical costs the order of entry is indeterminate.

construction strategy is identical to that of the true economy. An interesting feature of the model (which contrasts with the usual results in the real options literature) is that competition forces exercise of the new construction option when the net present value of new construction is precisely zero: thus the value of the option is zero and there is no exercise delay. This analysis points to the importance of analyzing the full industry equilibrium before offering prescriptions about optimal firm investment timing under uncertainty.

Lambrecht (Chapter 15) is concerned with the optimal timing of investment when there are two competing firms. The difference is that here the cost structures of the firms are private information and the investment project involves two stages— the first stage yields a *patent* that allows the first firm to complete the stage to acquire the sole right to continue to the second stage of commercialization. Without strategic considerations, the firm would undertake both stages at the same time as in Dixit and Pindyck (1994, Chapter 10) and the investment timing would exhibit the delay phenomenon that is characteristic of many real option problems; however, the possibility of preempting the rival leads to the advancing of the first-stage investment relative to the monopoly case. The first firm to complete the first stage then acts as a classical monopolist with respect to the timing of the second-stage investment; the result is that the patent acquired in the first stage may be left to "sleep" for a random period before being exploited in the second stage. Lambrecht shows that when the threat of preemption is low, the first-stage investment policy approaches the monopoly solution of Dixit and Pindyck; when the threat of preemption is high, the policy approaches the classic rule that the investment should be undertaken as soon as its net present value is positive, as in Grenadier (Chapter 14).

Following Smit and Trigeorgis (1993), Trigeorgis (1996), and Dixit and Pindyck (1994), Joaquin and Butler (Chapter 16) deal with the issue of the timing of investment when there is competition in the product market. In this chapter randomness is introduced into the cost and revenue functions by assuming that costs and revenues are subject to exchange risk, while the initial investment is fixed in terms of the home currency; one competitor has lower costs than the other, and the price in the product market is determined by Cournot competition between the two firms. It is shown that output flexibility and strategic considerations lead the low-cost firm, which enters first,[13] to invest earlier than it would if it could not adjust its output when the competitor enters. This illustrates the general principle that increased postcommitment flexibility leads to earlier investment commitment. As a further illustration of the importance of industry equilibrium considerations for project valuation, Tvedt (Chapter 17) analyzes the value of a ship in a competitive shipping market in which different ships have different operating costs and ships may be laid up temporarily if it is unprofitable to operate them. The dynamics of the freight rate process depend not only on the dynamics of demand, but also on the distribution of operating and lay-up costs that influence the lay-up decisions of ship owners, and hence the aggregate supply of shipping services. Thus the value of the lay-up option to any individual shipowner depends on the distribution of the costs of its competitors.

---

[13] Grenadier (1996) analyzes a related model in which there are only two developers.

The chapters in this book illustrate how the principles of real options analysis can contribute to an understanding of the effects of flexibility, the role of agency, and the importance of strategic considerations in the analysis of investment projects. For many investment projects, these are crucial aspects that are not taken into account by traditional discounted cash flow analysis. We hope that these chapters, by placing project analysis in a broader context, will stimulate interest and lead to further developments and applications of what has come to be known as the real options paradigm.

REFERENCES

Black, F., and M. Scholes. (1973). The Pricing of Options and Corporate Liabilities. *Journal of Political Economy* 81, 637–659.

Boyle, P. (1977). Options: A Monte Carlo Approach. *Journal of Financial Economics* 4, 323–338.

Brander, J. A., and T. R. Lewis. (1986). Oligopoly and Financial Structure: The Limited Liability Effect. *American Economic Review,* 76, 956–970.

Brennan, M. J. (1991). The Price of Convenience and the Valuation of Commodity Contingent Claims. In D. Lund and B. Oksendal (eds.), *Stochastic Models and Option Values.* Amsterdam: North-Holland.

Brennan, M. J., and E. S. Schwartz. (1985). Evaluating Natural Resource Investments. *Journal of Business* 58 (2), 135–157.

Constantinides, G. (1978). Market Risk Adjustment in Project Valuation. *Journal of Finance* 33 (2), 603–616.

Cootner, P. H. (1961). Common Elements in Futures Markets for Bonds and Commodities. *American Economic Review* 51, 173–183.

Cox, J., and S. Ross. (1976). The Valuation of Options for Alternative Stochastic Processes. *Journal of Financial Economics* 3 (1/2), 145–166.

De Angelo, H. (1981). Competition and Unanimity. *American Economic Review* 71, 18–27.

Dixit, A. (1989). Entry and Exit Decisions under Uncertainty. *Journal of Political Economy* 97, 620–638.

Dixit, A., and R. Pindyck. (1994). *Investment under Uncertainty.* Princeton, NJ: Princeton University Press.

Fama, E., and M. H. Miller. (1972). *The Theory of Finance.* Hinsdale, IL: Dryden Press.

Gibson, R., and E. S. Schwartz. (1990). Stochastic Convenience Yields and the Pricing of Oil Contingent Claims. *Journal of Finance* 45, 959–976.

Grenadier, S. R. (1996). The Strategic Exercise of Options: Development Cascades and Overbuilding in Real Estate Markets. *Journal of Finance* 51, 1653–1679.

Harrison, J. M., and S. Pliska. (1981). Martingales and Arbitrage in the Theory of Continuous Trading. *Stochastic Processes and their Applications* 11, 215–260.

Hertz, D. B. (1964). Risk Analysis in Capital Investment. *Harvard Business Review* 42, 95–106.

Jensen, M., and W. Meckling. (1976). Theory of the Firm: Managerial Behavior, Agency Costs, and Ownership Structure. *Journal of Financial Economics* 3, 305–360.

Keynes, J. M. (1936). *The General Theory of Employment, Interest and Money.* London: Macmillan.

Magee, J. (1964). How to Use Decision Trees in Capital Investment. *Harvard Business Review* 42, 79–96.

Makowski, L. (1983). Competition and Unanimity Revisited. *American Economic Review* 73, 329–339.

Maksimovic, V. (1988). Capital Structure in a Repeated Oligopoly. *Rand Journal of Economics* 19, 389–407.

Maksimovic, V., and J. Zechner. (1991). Debt, Agency Costs and Industry Equilibrium. *Journal of Finance* 46, 1619–1644.

McDonald, R., and D. R. Siegel. (1985). Investment and the Valuation of Firms When There Is an Option to Shut Down. *International Economic Review* 26, 331–349.

Merton, R. C. (1973). The Theory of Rational Option Pricing. *Bell Journal of Economics and Management Science* 4, 141–183.

Myers, S. C. (1977). Determinants of Corporate Borrowing. *Journal of Financial Economics* 5, 146–175.

Parsons, J. E., and A. S. Mello. (1992). Measuring the Agency Cost of Debt. *Journal of Finance* 47, 1887–1904.

Pindyck, R. S. (1993). Investments of Uncertain Cost. *Journal of Financial Economics* 34, 53–76.

Robichek, A., and J. Van Horne. (1967). Abandonment Value and Capital Budgeting. *Journal of Finance* 22, 577–589.

Schwartz, E. S. (1997). The Stochastic Behavior of Commodity Prices: Implications for Valuation and Hedging. *Journal of Finance* 52, 922–973.

Segelod, E. (1998). A Note on the Survey of Project Evaluation Techniques in Major Corporations. *International Journal of Production Economics* 54, 207–213.

Shleifer, A., and R. W. Vishny. (1992). Liquidation Values and Debt Capacity: A Market Equilibrium Approach. *Journal of Finance* 47, 1343–1366.

Smit, H. T. J., and L. A. Ankum. (1993). A Real Options and Game-Theoretic Approach to Corporate Investment Strategy under Competition. *Financial Management* 22, 241–250.

Smit, H. T. J., and L. Trigeorgis. (1993). Flexibility and Commitment in Strategic Investment. Working paper, Boston University and Tinbergen Institute, Erasmus University.

Trigeorgis, L. (1991). Anticipated Competitive Entry and Early Pre-emptive Investment in Deferrable Projects. *Journal of Economics and Business* 43, 143–156.

Trigeorgis, L. (1996). *Real Options*. Cambridge, MA: MIT Press.

Williams, J. (1993). Equilibrium and Options on Real Assets. *Review of Financial Studies* 6, 825–850.

Part I

Optimal Contingent Policies and the Value of Flexibility

2

Real Options and Rules of Thumb in Capital Budgeting

ROBERT L. MCDONALD

Most firms do not make explicit use of real option techniques in evaluating investments. Nevertheless, real option considerations can be a significant component of value, and firms that approximately take them into account should outperform firms that do not. This chapter examines whether the use of seemingly arbitrary investment criteria, such as hurdle rates and profitability indexes, can proxy for the use of more sophisticated real options valuation. We find that for a variety of parameters, particular hurdle-rate and profitability index rules can provide close-to-optimal investment decisions. Thus, it may be that firms using seemingly arbitrary "rules of thumb" are approximating optimal decisions.

2.1 INTRODUCTION

Suppose that a manager must decide whether to invest $500 million for a manufacturing facility that can be built today or at some later time. If the present value of cash flows from the facility is estimated at $500.001 million, net present value (NPV) is $1000; hence by the NPV criterion the investment should be undertaken. Finance students often find the decision to invest $500 million to earn $1000 troubling, though they are often unable to articulate a reason. This lack of comfort may extend to managers: it appears common for firms to use investment criteria that do not strictly implement the NPV criterion.

Anecdotal evidence suggests that firms making capital budgeting decisions routinely do a number of things that basic finance textbooks say they should not do:

- Projects are taken based on whether internal rates of return exceed arbitrarily high discount rates (often called "hurdle rates").
- Hurdle rates are sometimes higher for projects with greater idiosyncratic risk.

13

- Project selection is sometimes governed by a "profitability index," i.e., NPV (investment cost) must be sufficiently high.

- Otherwise acceptable projects go untaken, i.e., firms engage in capital rationing.

Summers (1987) surveyed corporations on capital budgeting practices and found that 94% of reporting firms discounted all cash flows at the same rate, independently of risk; 23% used discount rates in excess of 19%. This behavior is suggestive of the use of hurdle-rate rules, and certainly is at odds with textbook prescriptions for how to do capital budgeting.

This chapter examines whether these seemingly "incorrect" capital budgeting practices might serve as proxies for economic considerations not properly accounted for by the standard NPV rule. It is well known by now that the NPV criterion has serious shortcomings. In particular, the project in the example above could be delayed. Under uncertainty, the decision about when to invest is analogous to the decision about when to exercise an American call option, and the firm should generally invest only when the project NPV is sufficiently positive. Obviously, most managers do not formally perform this calculation as a routine part of capital budgeting.[1] Nevertheless, although managers may not use formal models to evaluate the options associated with an investment project, these options can be economically important and their effects grasped intuitively. Firms that make decisions ignoring these options should on average be less profitable than firms that somehow take them into account. This raises the following question: Is it possible that firms can make investment decisions that are *close* to optimal by following simple rules of thumb?[2]

We consider the extent to which observed investment decision-making behavior might be justified as an informal way to account for real options considerations, and in particular, investment timing. We take as a benchmark case the investment timing model of McDonald and Siegel (1986). In the context of that model, a firm should delay investing in a project until the NPV of the project is sufficiently positive, with the specific investment hurdle determined by inputs such as the volatility of the project, and the cash flows foregone by deferring investment. We focus on investment timing flexibility, since it is a simple option to evaluate and one that is likely to be important in a wide variety of real-world investment problems. We ask whether simple investment decision rules can approximate the optimal investment deferral implied by the investment-timing model.

It is obvious that in the simple case where the value of the project follows a time-homogeneous process, for any particular set of project characteristics there is a corresponding hurdle-rate or profitability index rule that will give the correct decision about when to invest. For an investment project with a known and constant drift, variance, and required rate of return, investment in the project is optimal when the

---

[1] "To Wait or Not to Wait", *CFO Magazine*, Vol. 13, No. 5 (May 1997), pp. 91–94, reports on companies that have adopted explicit option valuation methods.

[2] Although we show that some intuitively plausible rules of thumb can be reasonable decision rules, we do not try to explain how firms arrive at these particular rules.

project value reaches a particular level which strictly exceeds the investment cost. This project value in turn can be expressed in terms of an IRR, so there is always a correct investment rule of the form: "invest when the IRR reaches r^*."[3] A more interesting question is whether simple rules are relatively robust to changes in project characteristics. For example, suppose that a firm has projects with a wide variety of characteristics, including discount rate and volatility. Can a single hurdle-rate rule yield approximately correct decisions for these projects?[4]

We perform experiments in which we fix the investment rule and vary project characteristics, such as the project discount rate and expected growth rate of cash flows. We find that for a wide range of project characteristics, fixed hurdle-rate and profitability index rules can provide a good approximation to optimal investment timing decisions, in the sense that the *ex ante* loss from following the suboptimal rule is small; it is possible to follow the wrong investment rule without losing much of the *ex ante* value of the investment timing option.[5] In fact, as the investment timing option becomes worth more and it becomes optimal to wait longer to invest, the option value becomes less sensitive to errors in investment rules.

We also consider the effect of the project abandonment option, discussed by Brennan and Schwartz (1985) and Dixit (1989), and show that permitting nontrivial reversibility (for example being able to scrap the project for 50% of the investment cost) does not significantly alter the conclusions. There are, of course, other options besides the investment timing option that affect the value of projects and the optimal investment strategy: multistage investments, which allow the firm to abandon the project before completion, options to shut down production, strategic options, switching options, etc. In addition, while we focus on cash-flow uncertainty, a valuable investment timing option can also be generated by interest rate uncertainty (Ingersoll and Ross, 1992). Thus the findings here are only suggestive, and not intended to imply that particular rules of thumb should be universally adopted.

The results in this chapter can help to assess the relative value of knowing different characteristics of a project, and thus in principle help managers to allocate their time in investment decision making. For example, knowledge of the project discount rate is extremely important for a standard NPV calculation. Nevertheless, it sometimes turns out to be unimportant for the investment timing decision, in the sense that a given rule of thumb might work well for projects with a variety of discount rates. Raising the project discount rate lowers the value of the project, but also lowers the value at which investment becomes optimal, so that a decision rule of the form "invest when the project has an internal rate of return of 20%" might in fact be appropriate for a wide variety of projects.

---

[3] Dixit (1992) shows how to compute the hurdle rate for a given real option, and Boyle and Guthrie (1997) show that there is always an equivalent payback rule.

[4] If a firm does not understand well the economics underlying investment decisions, there might be an advantage to specializing in projects of a particular type and applying an appropriate investment rule, compared to a conglomerate applying a "one-size-fits-all" rule to various projects.

[5] Cochrane (1989) poses a similar question in the context of consumption models, and finds that the loss from following nonoptimal consumption rules is small.

Section 2.2 presents the basic investment timing problem and explains the procedure we use for evaluating investment rules of thumb. A key result here is that as the investment option becomes more valuable, it also becomes less sensitive to errors in investment rules. Section 2.3 explores different investment rules in more detail and examines the loss associated with different rules under various parameter values in the basic investment timing model. Throughout the chapter we use as benchmarks two somewhat arbitrary rules: a 20% hurdle-rate rule and a 1.5 profitability index. Section 2.4 examines robustness of the results to different assumptions about the evolution of project value, such as a negative growth rate and the possibility of a jump to zero in project value, and also considers the impact of adding a scrapping option. Section 2.5 concludes. The general conclusion is that the rules of thumb considered here generally capture at least 50% of a project's option value, and often as much as 90%.

2.2 THE INVESTMENT TIMING PROBLEM

In this section we review the basic investment timing problem and explain how a given rule of thumb may be assessed in this framework.

2.2.1 The Basic Problem

Suppose that C_t, the instantaneous cash-flow rate from an irreversible investment project, follows the diffusion process:

$$\frac{dC_t}{C_t} = \alpha \, dt + \sigma \, dZ(t) \tag{2.1}$$

where α is the expected growth rate of cash flows and σ is the standard deviation of the cash-flow process.[6] Note that with α and σ constant, the project value is time homogeneous. If the project is infinitely lived, the present value of the cash flows—conditional on the project being undertaken—is given by

$$V_t = \frac{C_t}{\rho - \alpha} \tag{2.2}$$

where ρ is the required rate of return on a project with the risk implied by Eq. (2.1). Note that since V is proportional to C, dV/V also follows a stochastic process of the same form as Eq. (2.1). The model can be expressed either in terms of C or V, but since we are interested in the effects of varying ρ and α, it is useful to specify the relation between C_t and V_t. We will be agnostic about the determination of ρ, although in practice it could be determined by the Capital Asset Pricing Model (CAPM) or some similar equilibrium model. Investment in the project costs I.

Let $\delta = \rho - \alpha$ be the difference between the required return on the project and the actual rate of appreciation in value, α. Note that $\delta \equiv C_t/V_t$ is a measure of the

---

[6] This process assumes that net cash flows are always positive. Essentially the same model can be derived when C_t represents gross cash flows and there is a cost. See Dixit (1989).

proportional cash flows foregone by not investing in the project. For this reason we will refer to δ as the dividend yield on the project. The risk-free rate is given by r, so that the project's risk premium is $\rho - r$.

The basic investment timing problem with risky cash flows is analyzed in Brennan and Schwartz (1985), McDonald and Siegel (1986), and Dixit (1989).[7] The firm can acquire the project, worth V, by investing I. This raises two questions: when is it optimal to invest, and what is the value of following the optimal investment rule? The general solution is outlined in Appendix A. Consider the special case in which the project is completely irreversible (i.e., the scrap value is 0) and we follow the rule to invest when the value of the project is at an arbitrary threshold level, $V_A > I$.[8] Prior to undertaking investment, the value of the option to invest in the project, assuming that the firm invests when project value reaches a trigger value V_A, is

$$W(V, V_A) = (V_A - I) \left(\frac{V}{V_A} \right)^{b_1} \tag{2.3}$$

where

$$b_1 = \left(\frac{1}{2} - \frac{r - (\rho - \alpha)}{\sigma^2} \right) + \sqrt{\left(\frac{r - (\rho - \alpha)}{\sigma^2} - \frac{1}{2} \right)^2 + \frac{2r}{\sigma^2}} \tag{2.4}$$

The optimal policy is obtained by maximizing (2.3) with respect to V_A. This yields

$$V_H = \frac{b_1}{b_1 - 1} \cdot I \tag{2.5}$$

We shall refer to $W(V, V_A)$ as the value of the investment timing option and V_H as the *optimal* trigger value for investment. An important feature of the solution is that it is optimal to invest only when V is strictly greater than I.

It is useful at this point to recall some basic intuition about the value of the investment timing option. The option value W and the optimal trigger value V_H depend on the parameters r, ρ, α, and σ. As we vary these parameters, the option value W and the optimal trigger value V_H change in the same direction: when V_H increases, $W(V, V_H)$ also increases.[9] The comparative statics of W are well known. First, deferring investment is valuable because the expenditure I is delayed and interest is earned, hence as r increases, optimal deferral of investment increases. Second, deferring investment is more valuable the greater the uncertainty, σ: the option to wait to invest implicitly provides insurance against declines in the value of the investment project. Third, deferring investment is less valuable when the cash flows lost by deferral, $\delta = \rho - \alpha$, are greater.

[7] Ingersoll and Ross (1992) analyze the case of risk-free cash flows and stochastic interest rates.
[8] If the scrap value of the project is positive, optimal scrapping is easily accommodated with a numerical solution.
[9] This is easily verified in general by noting that V_H is decreasing in b_1 [from Eq. (2.5)] and $W(V, V_H)$ is decreasing in b_1 [from Eq. (2.3)). By the envelope theorem, dV_H/db_1 can be ignored in evaluating $\partial W(V, V_H)/\partial b_1$. Hence since $V < V_H$, W is decreasing in b_1.

Figure 2.1 depicts the value of the investment timing option as a function of the project discount rate, ρ, and illustrates the effects of varying the cash-flow growth rate, α, and project volatility, σ.[10] Each point on the graph should be thought of as a separate project with a different discount rate, each of which currently has a zero NPV, i.e., $V = I = 1$. A firm that invests immediately at zero NPV would therefore lose the full value of the investment option depicted in Figure 2.1. Holding V fixed, the value of the option is an increasing function of the cash-flow growth rate, α, and the volatility, σ, and a decreasing function of the difference between the project discount rate, ρ, and the cash-flow growth rate, α.

Figure 2.2 shows how the optimal trigger value V_H varies with ρ, α, and σ. V_H declines as ρ rises, and increases with σ. In all cases, V_H asymptotes to infinity as ρ approaches α, i.e., as the project dividend yield, δ, approaches 0. This corresponds to the well-known result that an American call option on a nondividend paying stock will never be exercised prior to expiration.

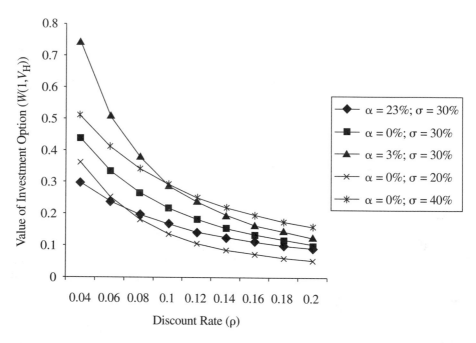

Figure 2.1 Value of the investment timing option, $W(1, V_H)$, as a function of the project discount rate, ρ. *Note:* Each point represents the value of the investment timing option for a different project with a zero NPV. Computed using Eq. (2.3) with $I = 1$: $W(1, V_H) = (V_H - 1)(1/V_H)^{b_1}$. Assumes the risk-free rate $r = 8\%$.

[10] For a given V, the option value is a function only of $\delta = \rho - \alpha$. However, the capital budgeting rules we will later consider do sometimes depend separately on ρ and α, hence we consider them separately in the figures.

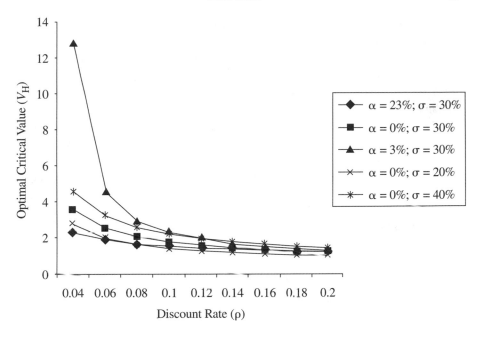

Figure 2.2 Optimal trigger value, V_H, as a function of the project discount rate, ρ. Optimal critical value V_H, computed as $b_1/(b_1 - 1)$. Assumes project value, V = investment cost, $I = 1$, and $r = 8\%$.

2.2.2 Measuring the Cost of Suboptimal Investment

In the typical real options problem we are interested in the optimal investment decision rule and the value of following that rule. However, Eq. (2.3) permits us to assess the option value associated with any arbitrary investment decision rule. For a given α, σ, and ρ, the use of a particular investment decision rule—for example, the hurdle-rate or profitability index—is equivalent to the choice of some investment trigger V_A. The central question in this chapter is whether various approximations to the optimal rule given in Eq. (2.5) are "good enough" for practical purposes. In other words, if a manager does not explicitly calculate Eq. (2.5), is it possible that a seemingly arbitrary investment rule comes close, in the sense that the value lost from the approximation is small?

   The value of following a nonoptimal investment policy is depicted by Figure 2.3, which shows how the value of the investment option, $W(1, V_A)$, varies as we vary the investment trigger, V_A, from 1 to 7, assuming that $r = 8\%$ and $\alpha = 0$. In each case, V_H is the level of V_A at which the option value W attains a maximum. For example, at $\rho = 12\%$ and $\sigma = 30\%$, $V_H = 1.63$ is the level of V at which investment is optimal. Also displayed are the results for discount rates of $\rho = 5$ and 20%, and a 40 vs. 30% volatility. Several points are clear from Figure 2.3. First, the *worst* investment decision is to invest when $V = I = 1$, i.e., when NPV is zero. Second, the loss from selecting the wrong investment rule is asymmetric: it is usually better to wait too long to invest (i.e., to select too high a V_A) than to invest too soon. Finally, the conclusion is not that the investment rule does not matter (clearly it does), but rather that a broad range of rules gives roughly similar (albeit suboptimal) outcomes.

Table 2.1 is a counterpart to Figure 2.3, showing precisely what range of trigger values V_A will provide a specified minimum percentage of the optimal option value for a given set of parameters. For example, in the case where $\rho = 0.05$ and $\sigma = 0.3$, an investment trigger value range of 1.91 to 5.52 preserves 90% of the optimal option value, while a range of 1.28 to 23.71 preserves 50% of the optimal option value. In general, the greater the option value when the optimal critical project value is chosen, the wider the range of V_A at which a given percentage of the option value can be obtained. Put differently, for more valuable options, a given deviation from the optimal rule generates a smaller loss in project value. This is evident in Figure 2.3, where $W(1, V_A)$ is flatter in the vicinity of V_H when the option value is greater. This property is true in general, as can be seen by differentiating Eq. (2.3):

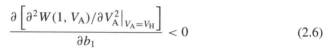

$$\frac{\partial \left[\partial^2 W(1, V_A)/\partial V_A^2 \big|_{V_A = V_H} \right]}{\partial b_1} < 0 \qquad (2.6)$$

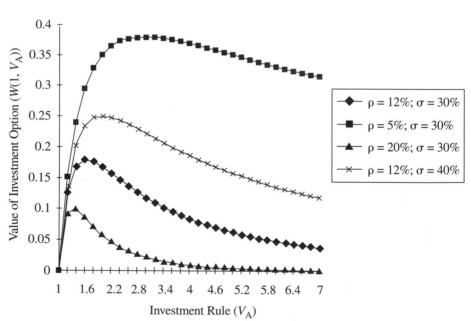

Figure 2.3 Value of the investment option, $W(1, V_A)$, as a function of the critical project value that triggers investment, V_A. *Note:* $W(1, V_A)$ computed using Eq. (2.3) with $I = 1$: $W(1, V_A) = (V_A - 1)(1/V_A)^{b_1}$. Assumes project value, $V =$ investment cost $I = 1$, and risk-free rate $r = 8\%$.

Table 2.1
Ranges of Critical Project Values, V_A, over Which Investment Option Attains at Least a Given Percentage of Its Maximum Possible Value[a]

Option value obtained when V_A is set equal to specified low and high values (%)		$\rho = 0.05,$ $\sigma = 0.3$	$\rho = 0.12,$ $\sigma = 0.3$	$\rho = 0.20,$ $\sigma = 0.3$	$\rho = 0.12,$ $\sigma = 0.4$
	$W(1, V_H)$	0.38	0.18	0.10	0.25
100	V_H	2.96	1.63	1.32	2.00
90	Low / high	1.91 / 5.52	1.35 / 2.12	1.19 / 1.53	1.52 / 2.92
75	Low / high	1.56 / 9.29	1.23 / 2.63	1.12 / 1.75	1.33 / 4.00
50	Low / high	1.28 / 23.71	1.12 / 3.81	1.07 / 2.09	1.17 / 6.83

[a] For example, if $\rho = 0.05$ and $\sigma = 0.3$, the investment option attains at least 90% of is optimal value if $1.91 < V_A < 5.52$. Assumes investment cost $I = 1$, project value $V = 1$, risk-free rate $r = 8\%$, and cash-flow growth rate $\alpha = 0$. All examples are computed using Eq. (2.3): $W(1, V_A) = (V_A - 1)(1/V_A)^{b_1}$.

Equation (2.6) is verified analytically in Appendix B. This characteristic of option value proves important when we later assess approximations to the optimal investment rule.

Of course, Table 2.1 depends on the assumption that cash flow follows geometric Brownian motion. If cash flows instead followed a mean-reverting process, the range over which a given fraction of the option value is preserved would be smaller, and the upper values of the range would not be as great.

2.3 ASSESSING "RULES OF THUMB"

In this section we examine the effect on investment value of using different ad hoc investment rules. Since we wish to investigate approximations to the optimal rule, we fix the investment rule and vary the assumptions to see how well a given investment rule performs in a wide range of situations. Here we consider variations in the cash-flow growth rate, α, the project volatility, σ, and the project discount rate, ρ. Varying the discount rate is a particularly interesting experiment since discount rates are hard to estimate in practice. Further, academics do not agree on an appropriate equilibrium model even for estimating firm-level discount rates, for which stock returns are observable; estimation of project-level discount rates is even more problematic. Thus it seems likely that there is a great deal of uncertainty associated with estimating project-specific discount rates. We next examine three rules: hurdle-rate, profitability index (V/I), and payback.

2.3.1 Hurdle Rates

As Dixit (1992) points out, for time-homogeneous cash flows the optimal investment rule can be expressed as a constant hurdle-rate rule. For a given level of current project cash flow, C_t, the internal rate of return on the project, R, is

$$R = \frac{C}{I} + \alpha$$

A hurdle-rate rule calls for investing when the project's internal rate of return exceeds the hurdle rate, which we will denote as γ. A hurdle-rate rule, γ, is equivalent to a cash-flow rule in which the cash flow trigger, C_γ, is given by

$$C_\gamma = I(\gamma - \alpha) \qquad (2.7)$$

or, in terms of project value, since from Eq. (2.2), $C = V(\rho - \alpha)$, we would invest when project value is

$$V_\gamma = \left(\frac{\gamma - \alpha}{\rho - \alpha}\right) I \qquad (2.8)$$

For an arbitrary trigger value, V_A, the corresponding hurdle-rate rule would be to invest when the internal rate of return, R, equals γ_A, where

$$\gamma_A = \alpha + (\rho - \alpha)V_A/I$$

The zero-NPV rule is to invest when $V_A = I$, hence $\gamma = \rho$, i.e., when the internal rate of return equals the cost of capital. Since the optimal investment trigger under uncertainty is $V = V_H$, the optimal hurdle-rate rule is

$$\gamma_H = \alpha + (\rho - \alpha)b_1/(b_1 - 1) \qquad (2.9)$$

This is similar to the expression in Dixit (1992).

Although it is not obvious by inspection of Eq. (2.9), comparative statics for the optimal hurdle-rate, γ_H, mimic those for the optimal trigger value, V_H. First, an increase in the project discount rate, ρ, increases the optimal hurdle rate, γ_H. Second, an increase in the project cash-flow growth rate, α, decreases γ_H. Third, an increase in σ raises the optimal hurdle rate. These results can be verified by differentiating Eq. (2.9).

To get a sense of magnitudes, Table 2.2 reports γ_H for representative parameters. The optimal hurdle rate, γ_H, is sensitive to changes in ρ and σ and relatively less sensitive to changes in α. Obviously if one were to adopt a fixed hurdle rate for all projects, say 20%, there would generally be errors in the timing of investment. For example if $\rho = 8\%$, $\sigma = 30\%$, and $\alpha = 3\%$, the correct decision is to invest when project cash flow, C, satisfies

$$C/(0.178 - 0.03) = 1,$$

or $C = 0.148$. A 20% hurdle-rate rule would entail investing when

$$C/(0.2 - 0.03) = 1$$

or $C = 0.17$. Although investment generally occurs at the wrong time using a 20% hurdle rate, the question Table 2.2 does not address is whether the use of the wrong hurdle rate creates a significant loss of value. Our earlier analysis suggests that the

Table 2.2
Optimal Hurdle Rate, γ_H, for Representative Paramaters[a]

Cash flow volatility, $\sigma(\%)$	Cash flow growth rate, $\alpha(\%)$	Project discount rate, ρ 8%	12%	16%
20	−3	12.2	15.5	19.1
	0	13.1	16	19.4
	3	14.5	16.7	19.8
30	−3	15.8	19.1	22.5
	0	16.7	19.6	22.9
	3	17.8	20.3	23.4
40	−3	20.2	23.5	26.9
	0	20.9	24	27.3
	3	21.8	24.7	27.8

[a] Computed using Eq. (2.9): $\gamma_H = \alpha + (\rho - \alpha)b_1/(b_1 - 1)$. Assumes risk-free rate $r = 8\%$.

loss in *value* is not necessarily large, even if the investment decision is made at the wrong time.

Figure 2.4 depicts the fraction of project value, $W(1, V_\gamma)/W(1, V_H)$, obtained by using a 20% hurdle-rate rule for the cases depicted in Figures 2.1 and 2.2 (also considered in 5 of the 9 rows in Table 2.2). To see how the figure is constructed, consider the case where $\rho = 12\%$, $\alpha = 0$, and $\sigma = 40\%$. The optimal hurdle rate from Table 2.2 is 24%. From Table 2.1, following this rule gives an option value of 0.25, and we should invest when $V = 2$. By following a 20% hurdle-rate rule, we invest when C is such that $C/0.2 = 1$, or $C = 0.2$, which implies a trigger value of $V_A = 0.2/0.12 = 1.67$. This in turn yields an option value of 0.24, 96% of the optimal option value of 0.25. For those cases with optimal hurdle rates γ_H below 20%, the effect of the 20% hurdle-rate rule is to delay investment beyond the optimal point, while it accelerates investment when γ_H exceeds 20%. The 20% hurdle-rate rule works quite well as long as the true project discount rate is 16% or below: in almost all cases, the project is worth at least 80% of its maximal value.

The 20% hurdle-rate rule works least well in the low volatility case, i.e., when $\sigma = 20\%$. When project volatility is low, the investment option is worth the least, and it is optimal to invest at relatively low project values. In this case the 20% hurdle-rate rule leads to excessive delay. Since the optimal trigger, V_H, is declining in volatility, performance of the rule would be even worse for lower volatilities.

Figure 2.4 is intentionally constructed to show that the hurdle-rate rule provides zero value if the true project discount rate is 20%. This occurs for the following reason: if we adopt a hurdle rate equal to the true project discount rate, then we are back to following the NPV rule. In that case we lose all value from the investment timing option. The potential gain with a hurdle-rate rule comes from selecting a hurdle rate that is higher than the true discount rate, in order to delay investment under uncertainty.

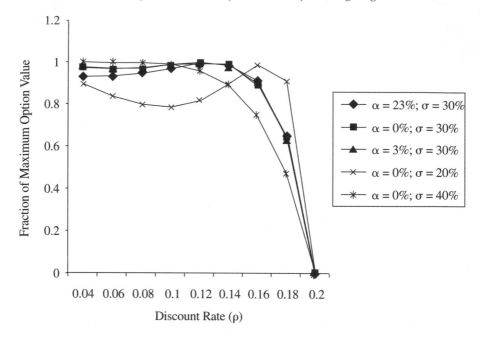

Figure 2.4 Fraction of maximum option value obtained by basing investment decisions on a 20% hurdle-rate rule. Computed as $W(1, V_\gamma)/W(I, V_H)$, the ratio of option value when investment trigger value is computed using Eq. (2.8), i.e., $V_\gamma = I(\gamma - \alpha)/(\rho - \alpha)$ with hurdle rate $\gamma = 20\%$, to the option value when the investment trigger is optimal. Assumes risk-free rate $r = 8\%$.

2.3.2 Profitability Index

The profitability index criterion entails investing when the ratio of the gross project value per unit cost, V/I, reaches some preselected level, which we will denote by Π. The profitability index is usually presented in textbooks as a criterion used to rank projects when investment funds are limited. It may also be, however, that the profitability index has survived as a capital budgeting practice because in some situations it produces better results than the NPV rule, even though the textbook rationale for its use is spurious. The operational difference between the hurdle-rate rule and the profitability index is that with the hurdle-rate rule, the trigger value V_A implicitly changes as the true underlying parameters change. The profitability index, on the other hand, explicitly specifies a fixed V_A/I. Obviously, setting $\Pi = V_H/I$ yields optimal investment decisions; here we are interested in how a given profitability index performs across different projects.

Suppose we set $\Pi = 1.5$. Figure 2.5 depicts the fraction of the maximum option value obtained by following this investment rule for projects with different characteristics. By definition the rule performs best in those cases where V_H/I is close to 1.5. For the project with $\sigma = 20\%$, the profitability index rule works best for lower discount rates. As σ increases, the rule works better for progressively higher discount rates, reflecting the movement in V_H as the project parameters change. The

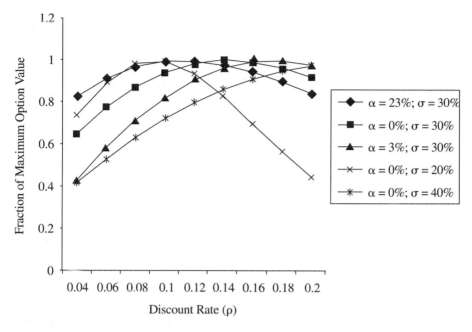

Figure 2.5 Fraction of maximum option value obtained by investing when the project is worth 1.5 times the investment cost, i.e., $\Pi = 1.5$. Computed as $W(1, 1.5)/W(I, V_H)$, the ratio of option value when the investment trigger value is 1.5 to the option value when the investment trigger is optimal. Assumes risk-free rate $r = 8\%$.

profitability index rule works best, relative to the hurdle-rate rule, when discount rates are very high. Where the hurdle-rate rule provides insufficient project delay (because the hurdle rate is close to the true project discount rate), the profitability index rule provides at least some delay.

2.3.3 Payback Rules

Payback rules are also useful to examine in this framework.[11] Payback is defined as the time until the sum of expected future cash flows equals the investment cost. Cash flows in this calculation can be either discounted or undiscounted; we focus on the latter. The payback period is the horizon T such that

$$
I = C_t \int_t^{t+T} e^{\alpha(s-t)}\, ds
$$

$$
= \frac{C_t}{\alpha}(e^{\alpha T} - 1)
$$

(2.10)

If we set an arbitrary payback period, then the payback criterion is satisfied when $V = V_P$, where V_P is given by[12]

---

[11] Boyle and Guthrie (1997) examine payback in a similar context.

[12] With discounted payback, the critical project value is given by $I/(1 - e^{(\alpha-\rho)T})$.

$$V_P = \begin{cases} \left(\dfrac{\alpha}{\rho - \alpha}\right) \dfrac{I}{e^{\alpha T} - 1} & \alpha \neq 0 \\[2ex] \dfrac{I}{T\rho} & \alpha = 0 \end{cases} \qquad (2.11)$$

Note first that when $\alpha = 0$, from Eqs. (2.8) and (2.11), the payback rule with payback period T is equivalent to a hurdle-rate rule with hurdle rate $\gamma = 1/T$. Thus, the behavior of the two rules differs only when $\alpha \neq 0$. For the parameters reported in Figure 2.4, the differences between the hurdle rate and payback calculations are mostly slight and hence are not reported here. The material differences occur for high discount rates: when α is positive, the payback rule generates a critical project value that is greater than 1, and hence this rule avoids the sharp drop-off in value generated by the hurdle-rate rule of Figure 2.4 as ρ approaches 20%.

2.3.4 Comparison of Profitability Index and Hurdle-Rate Rules

In comparing Figures 2.4 and 2.5, the hurdle-rate and profitability index rules tend to be most inaccurate for different sets of parameter values. The profitability index rule $\Pi = 1.5$ works least well for low discount rate projects, when it is optimal to wait until V reaches a substantially higher critical value. The 20% hurdle-rate rule works least well when project discount rates are close to the hurdle rate. This suggests constructing a third rule as a hybrid of the two rules, for example, selecting the maximum critical project value implied by the two rules. By implementing this rule, we generate high threshold Vs from the hurdle-rate rule when discount rates are low, and threshold Vs significantly above 1 when discount rates equal or exceed the hurdle rate.

Such a hybrid rule can prevent the large errors at extreme discount rates generated by either rule alone. For the cases we have examined, in all but the $\sigma = 20\%$ case, the hybrid rule captures at least 85% of the value of the optimal rule in all cases, and captures 95% or greater in the vast majority of cases. Although this example stretches the concept of a "rule of thumb" a bit, it demonstrates that firms in practice might find it useful to consider multiple rules at once, perhaps using a rule that best justifies making intuitively plausible investment decisions.

2.4 ROBUSTNESS TO ALTERNATIVE PROJECT ASSUMPTIONS

We have so far assumed that projects are irreversible and that cash flows, and hence project values, follow geometric Brownian motion. In this section we briefly consider the effect of alternative assumptions about the project characteristics. One objection to the prior analysis is that it does not accommodate cases in which there is an intuitive sense that the project will be lost if it is not taken quickly. We consider two ways to model this: negative expected cash-flow growth rates, and the possibility that project value can take a Poisson jump to zero. Finally, we also examine the effect of scrapping, which amounts to permitting costly reversibility of the investment.

2.4.1 Negative Cash-Flow Growth

Suppose project cash flows are high but are expected to decline quickly. This is expected in an industry in which competitive entry is anticipated. A *ceteris paribus* reduction in the growth rate reduces both the value of the investment timing option, W, and the optimal trigger value, V_H. Figures 2.1 and 2.2 confirm that even a small negative cash flow growth rate, α, noticeably lowers the value of the timing option and V_H.

   With a cash-flow growth rate, α, of -20%, the value of the timing option falls below 0.15 per dollar of investment cost and V_H is below 1.45 for all cases we have previously considered. The 20% hurdle rate rule performs better than the 1.5 profitability index rule, in this case, because the trigger value implied by the hurdle rate, V_γ, declines as the growth rate α declines. The profitability index, by contrast, specifies a fixed trigger value, which is too high. For example, if the hurdle rate, γ, is 20% and the cash flow growth rate $\alpha = -20\%$, then from Eq. (2.8) the trigger value for the 20% hurdle rate is $V_\gamma = [0.2 - (-0.2)]/[\rho - (-0.2)]$. For ρ between 8 and 16%, V_γ ranges from 1.42 (when $\rho = 8\%$) to 1.11 (when $\rho = 16\%$), while V_H ranges from 1.36 to 1.06. Although the 20% hurdle rate induces excessive delay, nonetheless, for volatilities of 30 and 40%, the loss from following the 20% hurdle rate rule with $\alpha = -20\%$ is similar to the $\alpha = -3\%$ case depicted in Figure 2.4. When volatility is 20%, however, the 20% hurdle-rate rule performs significantly worse, particularly at low discount rates. The 1.5 profitability index rule, on the other hand, induces even greater delay, causing a greater percentage loss in the value of the investment option than with the 20% hurdle rate.

   In the cases considered here, the percent loss in value due to following rules of thumb is greater as the growth rate becomes more negative. However, the timing option is worth less to begin with in these cases.[13] The net effect is that the rules of thumb we consider, especially the 20% hurdle rate, preserve much of the value of the investment timing option, even for growth rates as large in absolute value as -20%.

2.4.2 Probability of the Project Becoming Worthless

In practice there may be first-mover advantages from early investing, which the standard investment-timing model ignores. One way to incorporate this effect is to model a random chance that the investment option will become worthless, for example, due to preemption by a rival. Following Merton (1976), this is modeled as a Poisson process in which the option value can jump to zero with instantaneous probability λdt. Permitting the value of the project to jump to zero reduces the value

---

[13] This is partly a consequence of Eq. (2.6); as the option has less value, the loss from following a suboptimal investment policy is greater.

of the option and accelerates investment. McDonald and Siegel (1986) show that the investment-timing model in this case is modified by replacing r with $r + \lambda$ and δ with $\delta + \lambda$.[14] An increase in λ lowers the optimal trigger value V_H and the option value W, but has less of an effect than an identical change in α.[15]

Introducing a moderate probability of a jump to zero, for example 20% per year (i.e., an average of one jump every 5 years), improves the performance of the 1.5 profitability index rule at low discount rates relative to the accuracy shown in Figure 2.5. The reason is that the possibility that the project will become worthless eliminates those cases in which it is optimal to wait until V_H is very high, so setting $\Pi = 1.5$ provides a reasonable approximation to the optimal trigger values. In cases in which the investment option has little value, i.e., for high discount rates and low volatility, even 1.5 is too high a trigger value, and the performance of the profitability index is poor, capturing as little as 20% of option value in the worst case. Otherwise, the profitability index rule performs at least as well as in the no-jump case.

Regarding the hurdle rate, the main issue is how managers evaluate the hurdle rate when there is a possibility of a jump. If managers incorporate the jump probability by increasing the discount and hurdle rates, from Eq. (2.8) the effect on the hurdle rate is algebraically equivalent to a decrease in the cash-flow growth rate α, the case analyzed in the previous section. If, on the other hand, the jump probability is ignored in computing the hurdle rate, then a jump to zero can lead to a substantial error when using the hurdle rate. The reason is that in many cases the hurdle rate induces waiting when it is no longer optimal to do so. This is a problem particularly with very low discount rates and positive growth rates.

2.4.3 Impact of Scrapping (Abandonment) Option

The analysis thus far has assumed that the scrap value of the project is zero, i.e., the investment is completely irreversible. A positive scrap value has two effects: the value of the investment timing option increases, but the firm should invest at a lower project value. The option to scrap raises the value of the investment option because it increases the value of insurance against a decline in the value of the asset—investing creates both project cash flows and a put option to scrap the project. At the same time, the existence of the scrapping option creates partial reversibility that makes the firm less willing to lose cash flows by deferring the project.[16]

---

[14] The intuition is that if there is an instantaneous probability λ that the project value can jump to zero, this increases the instantaneous discount rate by λ. Since the discount rate is increased by λ but the expected cash flow and α are unchanged, the dividend yield, $\delta = \rho - \alpha$, is also increased by λ. This differs from the standard result for an option on a stock, in which case only the risk-free rate is increased by λ (see Merton, 1976).

[15] The difference in derivatives for the two parameters is proportional to $b_1 - 1$, which is positive.

[16] See Trigeorgis (1996), Chapter 7, for a discussion of option interactions along these lines.

In practice, scrapping does not significantly alter the optimal trigger value V_H as long as the scrap value is not close to $I = 1$.[17] This can be understood by considering the solution of the investment problem with scrapping, presented in Appendix A. If V_H is large and the scrap value as a fraction of the investment cost is significantly less than 1, then the value of the option to scrap, which is acquired along with the project when $V = V_H$, will be the value of a deep out-of-the-money put option. The value of this option will be small, hence the optimal critical investment level V_H will not be affected very much.

Table 2.3 illustrates the effect on the profitability index and hurdle-rate rules of different project scrap values. To provide a benchmark, entries in the column with scrap value equal to zero (full irreversibility) correspond to points depicted in Figures 2.4 and 2.5. Consider first the profitability index rule. When the project discount rate ρ is 8%, the optimal trigger value V_H is generally above 1.5. In that

Table 2.3
Fraction of Investment Option Obtained by Using 1.5 Profitability Index and 20% Hurdle Rate, under Different Assumptions about Scrap Value of the Project.[a]

	Project discount rate, ρ	Cash Flow Growth Rate, α	Scrap values as fraction of investment cost			
			0	0.25	0.5	0.75
1.5 Profitability	0.08	−0.03	0.965	0.978	0.997	0.991
index		0	0.868	0.883	0.919	0.966
		0.03	0.712	0.721	0.750	0.803
	0.12	−0.03	0.999	0.989	0.943	0.818
		0	0.983	0.993	1.000	0.967
		0.03	0.908	0.923	0.956	0.992
	0.16	−0.03	0.947	0.894	0.765	0.545
		0	0.992	0.974	0.907	0.752
		0.03	0.995	1.000	0.991	0.928
20% Hurdle	0.08	−0.03	0.947	0.936	0.903	0.838
rate		0	0.975	0.972	0.960	0.937
		0.003	0.993	0.993	0.991	0.987
	0.12	−0.03	0.995	0.981	0.928	0.799
		0	0.999	0.996	0.976	0.914
		0.03	1.000	1.000	0.998	0.982
	0.16	−0.03	0.920	0.984	0.981	0.792
		0	0.908	0.962	1.000	0.918
		0.03	0.893	0.932	0.987	0.990

[a] Profitability index panel computed as $W(1, 1.5)/W(1, V_H)$; 20% hurdle-rate panel computed as $W(1, V_\gamma)/W(1, V_H)$, where $V_\gamma = (\gamma - \alpha)/(\rho - \alpha)$ and $\gamma = 20\%$ is the hurdle rate. W is computed as described in Appendix A. Assumes risk-free rate, $r = 8\%$, and cash-flow volatility $\sigma = 30\%$.

[17] A similar finding is in Abel and Eberly (1995). They study the effects of a difference in the purchase and sale price of capital, showing that a small difference in the purchase and sale price of capital leads to an investment rule that is close to that with full irreversibility.

case raising the scrap value reduces the optimal trigger value and hence improves the performance of the profitability index. By comparison, when the discount rate is 16%, V_H is generally below 1.5. The profitability index then performs more poorly with a higher scrap value.

In the case of the hurdle-rate rule, the hurdle rate declines with the project discount rate, ρ, tracking the similar decline in the optimal trigger value V_H. Except when scrap value reaches 75% of investment cost, the use of the 20% hurdle rate captures at least 90% of the value of the optimal investment timing option. In general, the introduction of scrapping does not significantly alter our conclusions about the performance of either rule of thumb.

2.5 CONCLUSION

We have suggested that seemingly arbitrary investment rules of thumb can proxy for optimal investment timing behavior. This is so because when the timing option is most valuable, it is also least sensitive to deviations from the optimal investment rule. Thus, managers may use approximately correct investment timing rules without losing much value. We do not suggest that managers *should* use these rules of thumb, but rather that their use in practice might stem from the success of apparently arbitrary rules that are revealed over time to be close to optimal. Managers likely observe the capital budgeting practices in their own and other companies, and in many cases probably mimic what seems to work.

One problem with analyzing firm investment decisions is that we do not know very much about how managers actually behave. We know that hurdle-rate and payback rules are used in practice, but it must be the case that managers adjust these rules in extreme situations, for example, when an investment is strategic and expiring. One might guess that managers also think differently about projects with different volatilities, even though textbook finance is of little guidance in this regard. A project with no volatility is intuitively like a bond, and standard NPV analysis would be appropriate. In fact, the rules of thumb we consider here work least well for low-volatility projects. A project with high volatility, on the other hand, may intuitively seem to call for a higher discount rate, which is how the use of hurdle rates might have arisen. The interesting finding is that this intuition may in fact be justified, since projects with high volatility have higher optimal trigger values, justifying investment only at a higher hurdle rate.

There are certainly several caveats attached to the specific examples used in this chapter. For many kinds of projects, for example natural resources, it is plausible that output prices and hence NPVs might evolve as mean-reverting processes. This would lower long-run volatility and the value of the timing option (Schwartz, 1997) and, if mean reversion is ignored, can lead to excessive delay. Investment decisions may also involve strategic options that can alter these results. It is also unclear how managers evaluate "platform investments," i.e., investments that generate the possibility of profitable investments or other options in the future. Excessive waiting (induced by a hurdle-rate rule) could be detrimental for such investments. Of course, if the investment decision is based on cash-flow projections that presume the future option is profitably exercised, then the value of the future option may in practice be overstated. The critical issue is how firms actually make these decisions, which is not yet well understood.

It would be interesting to see if industry characteristics are correlated with capital budgeting practice. For example, are industries with strong mean reversion in project values likely to display less use of rules of thumb, since there would be a smaller gain to deviating from standard NPV calculations? One might also expect to see hurdle-rate rules used for low cash-flow, long-lived, nonstrategic projects (for which significant delay is optimal), and profitability-index type rules used in other cases. The challenge is to find data that could be used to test these kinds of predictions.

Appendix A

The Investment-Timing Option

Let W_0 denote the value of the initial investment option, and W_1 the value of the scrapping option that may exist once the investment is undertaken. Following standard arguments (see, e.g., Dixit and Pindyck, 1994), the values of these two options are described by the partial differential equations

$$\frac{1}{2}\sigma^2 V^2 W_{i,VV} + (r - \delta)V W_{i,V} = r W_i \qquad i = 0, 1 \qquad (2.A1)$$

where r is the risk-free rate. A general solution to this equation is

$$W_i(V, \sigma, r, \delta) = A_1 V^{b_1} + A_2 V^{b_2} \qquad (2.A2)$$

where

$$b_1 = \left(\frac{1}{2} - \frac{r - (\rho - \alpha)}{\sigma^2}\right) + \sqrt{\left(\frac{r - (\rho - \alpha)}{\sigma^2} - \frac{1}{2}\right)^2 + \frac{2r}{\sigma^2}}$$

$$b_2 = \left(\frac{1}{2} - \frac{r - (\rho - \alpha)}{\sigma^2}\right) - \sqrt{\left(\frac{r - (\rho - \alpha)}{\sigma^2} - \frac{1}{2}\right)^2 + \frac{2r}{\sigma^2}}$$

with A_1 and A_2 determined by appropriate boundary conditions.

The investment problem is further characterized by boundary conditions. In each case we need to solve for V_L and V_H, the trigger values at which scrapping and investment are optimal. There are two boundary conditions each for the options to invest or scrap, high-contact and value-matching conditions.

Value-matching

$$W_0(V_H) = W_1(V_H) - I$$

$$W_1(V_L) = K - V_L \qquad (2.A3)$$

High contact

$$W_0'(V_H) = W_1'(V_H)$$

$$W_1'(V_L) = -1$$

(2.A4)

To compute the value of the option for an arbitrary investment boundary, we simply omit the first high-contact condition and set $A_1 = V_A - I$, where V_A is the arbitrary investment level.

Appendix B

Verification of Eq. (2.6)

By differentiating Eq. (2.3) we obtain

$$\frac{\partial^2 W}{\partial V_A^2} = -b_1 V^{b_1} V_A^{-(b_1+2)}$$

(2.B1)

We want to show that the absolute value of this expression is increasing in b, i.e., that W is more concave as the option becomes less valuable. Without loss of generality set $V = 1$. Taking the log of the absolute value of the right-hand side and differentiating with respect to b we get

$$\frac{1}{b_1} - \ln\left(\frac{b_1}{b_1 - 1}\right) - (b_1 + 2)\left(\frac{1}{b_1} - \frac{1}{b_1 - 1}\right)$$

The behavior of this expression as b goes to 1 depends on the behavior of $1/(b-1) + \ln(b-1)$.

$$\frac{1}{b_1 - 1} + \ln(b_1 - 1) = \ln\left(\frac{\exp 1/(b_1 - 1)}{1/(b_1 - 1)}\right) = \ln\left(\frac{e^x}{x}\right)$$

(2.B2)

This has a limit of infinity as x goes to infinity. Thus the degree of concavity of W increases with b.

ACKNOWLEDGMENTS

For helpful comments I thank Jonathan Berk, Michael Brennan, Debbie Lucas, Lenos Trigeorgis, and seminar participants at Northwestern University, the Federal Reserve Bank of New York, and the conference "Real Options: Theory Meets Practice," held at Columbia University in June 1997.

REFERENCES

Abel, A. B., and J. C. Eberly. (1995). Optimal Investment with Costly Reversibility. Working Paper 5091, National Bureau of Economic Research.

Boyle, G. W., and G. A. Guthrie. (1997). Payback and the Value of Waiting to Invest. Working paper, University of Otago.

Brennan, M., and E. Schwartz. (1985). Evaluating Natural Resource Investments. *Journal of Business* 58(2), 135–157.

Cochrane, J. H. (1989). The Sensitivity of Tests of the Intertemporal Allocation of Consumption to Near-Rational Alternatives. *American Economic Review* 79(3), 319–337.

Dixit, A. (1989). Entry and Exit Decisions Under Uncertainty. *Journal of Political Economy* 97(3), 620–638.

Dixit, A. (1992). Investment and Hysteresis. *Journal of Economic Perspectives* 6(1), 107–132.

Dixit, A., and R. S. Pindyck. (1994). *Investment Under Uncertainty*. Princeton, NJ: Princeton University Press.

Ingersoll, J. E. Jr., and S. A. Ross. (1992). Waiting to Invest: Investment and Uncertainty. *Journal of Business* 65 (January), 1–29.

McDonald, R., and D. Siegel. (1986). The Value of Waiting to Invest. *Quarterly Journal of Economics* 101(4), 707–727.

Merton, R. C. (1976). Option Pricing When Underlying Stock Returns are Discontinuous. *Journal of Financial Economics* 3(1), 125–44.

Schwartz, E. S. (1997). The Stochastic Behavior of Commodity Prices: Implications for Valuation and Hedging. *Journal of Finance* 52(3), 923–973.

Summers, L. H. (1987). Investment Incentives and the Discounting of Depreciation Allowances. In M. Feldstein (ed.), *The Effects of Taxation on Capital Accumulation*. Chicago: University of Chicago Press.

Trigeorgis, L. (1996). *Real Options: Managerial Flexibility and Strategy in Resource Allocation*. Cambridge, MA: MIT Press.

3

Investment in Flexible Technologies under Uncertainty

KJELL ARNE BREKKE

BJARNE SCHIELDROP

We study the option to invest in a flexible technology that allows the firm to adapt to future changes in uncertain variables. We consider a firm with an option to build a plant producing a single good, using one of two input factors, with uncertain prices. The firm may choose either a pure technology that can use only one input factor or a flexible technology that allows switching between input factors. We demonstrate that the flexible technology can give a substantial reduction in expected fuel costs. If the flexible technology is not available, then the choice between inflexible technologies introduces an additional irreversibility that makes the firm more reluctant to invest than if only one technology were available.

3.1 INTRODUCTION

Flexibility is at the core of real option theory. The ultimate in flexibility is achieved if investments are fully and costlessly reversible. Firms can then reverse all investments that are not optimal for current economic conditions, and invest in the capital stock that is instantaneously optimal. When investments are irreversible and the economic environment is stochastic, the option value of maintaining flexibility is important.

Several studies have considered models in which the investor has some ability to adapt to future changes even after the investment option is exercised. Brennan and Schwartz (1985) study the starting and stopping of a mine. Brekke and Øksendal (1991, 1994) also consider a mine that switches between open and closed operating modes and develop sufficient conditions for the solution of such sequential stopping problems. Dixit (1989) studies entry and exit into a market (see also Dixit and Pindyck, 1994, Chapter 7). Arntzen (1995) extends the work of Kobila (1993) to solve a model in which capital equipment can be resold at a price below the purchasing price (see also

Abel and Eberly, 1996; Dixit and Pindyck, this volume). Kulatilaka (1995) develops a general real option model to describe all these forms of flexibility.

In the above models the degree of flexibility is given. Either capital can be resold or it cannot; the mine can be reopened or not. In this chapter we study a model in which the firm actively chooses the degree of flexibility, i.e., the firm must choose among capital equipment with different degrees of flexibility in the use of input factors. For concreteness, we can think of the example of a thermal power plant burning either oil or gas, where the plant can use either a pure technology that can use only either gas or oil, or a flexible technology that can switch between the two types of fuel. This is similar to Kulatilaka's (1993) study of dual-fuel industrial steam boilers. Our study differs from Kulatilaka's in several aspects. First, most of our discussion is analytical, as compared to Kulatilaka's numerical solution. Moreover, whereas Kulatilaka assumes a constant gas price, both gas and oil prices are stochastic in our model. This allows us to study further the effect of correlation between the two prices.

He and Pindyck (1992) also study a model with endogenous flexibility. Their main focus is on output flexibility, i.e., flexibility with respect to which of two products to produce, although they provide a brief discussion of how their approach can be extended to input flexibility, which is our focus here. They provide a concrete example, in which the prices of the two products are perfectly negatively correlated, whereas we allow for any degree of correlation.

A central insight gained from real option theory is that it may be optimal to delay an irreversible investment even when the net present value is positive. The reason for this is that irreversibility means that investment involves a surrender of some flexibility in the choice of capital stock. In this chapter we study how the introduction of endogenous flexibility affects the timing of investment. We also study how uncertainty and irreversibility affect the value of flexibility.

3.2 A MODEL OF FLEXIBILITY

Both gas prices P_t and oil prices Q_t are assumed to follow geometric Brownian motions of the form

$$\frac{dP_t}{P_t} = (\mu_p - \delta_p)\, dt + \sigma_p\, dB_{1t} \tag{3.1}$$

$$\frac{dQ_t}{Q_t} = (\mu_q - \delta_q)\, dt + \sigma_q\, dB_{2t}$$

where B_{1t} and B_{2t} are correlated Brownian motions, with $E(dB_{1t}dB_{2t}) = \rho dt$, with $|\rho| < 1$. We assume that there exist traded assets or portfolios perfectly correlated with P_t and Q_t, paying dividends at rates δ_p and δ_q. Assuming complete markets, the value of any contingent claim is given by the expectation with respect to an equivalent martingale measure. Under the equivalent martingale measure, the price processes will be as above, but with the drifts μ_p and μ_q replaced by the risk-free interest rate r (see Dixit and Pindyck, 1994, Chapter 4; Duffie, 1988, Section 17).

Consider a firm that is deciding when to build a new electric power plant, which may be either oil or gas fired. The firm must decide on both the time of investment

τ and the type of technology i to choose. Let $i = g$ denote the pure gas-fired plant and $i = o$ the pure oil-fired plant, while $i = f$ denotes the flexible technology. The choice of technology is made at the time of investment. Let $\pi(P_t, Q_t, i)$, denote the cash flow produced by an installed plant. We assume that the cash flow is zero before the plant is installed, and afterward the cash flow is

$$\pi(P_t, Q_t, i) = \begin{cases} A - P_t & \text{if } i = g \\ A - Q_t & \text{if } i = o \\ A - \min(P_t, Q_t) & \text{if } i = f \end{cases} \qquad (3.2)$$

where A is the cash flow from electricity generated by the plant, while the fuel cost is P_t if a pure oil plant is installed, Q_t if a pure gas plant is installed, and the cheapest of the two, $\min(P_t, Q_t)$, if a flexible plant is installed.

The problem facing the firm is to find the investment strategy that maximizes the present value of the expected cash flow net of investment cost. An investment strategy is a rule that specifies the stochastic timing of investment, τ, and the choice of technology i. The problem is thus to find

$$V^*(p, q) = \sup_{\tau, i} E^{*p,q} \left[\int_\tau^\infty \pi(P_t, Q_t, i)e^{-rt}dt - K_i e^{-r\tau} \right]$$

$$= \sup_{\tau, i} E^{*p,q}\{[V_i(P_\tau, Q_\tau) - K_i]e^{-r\tau}\} \qquad (3.3)$$

where $E^{*p,q}$ denotes expectations under the equivalent martingale measure, with the superscript denoting initial prices $P_0 = p$ and $Q_0 = q$; K_i is the investment cost of a plant of type i and $V_i(p, q)$ is the value of the plant when the process starts at prices (p, q):

$$V_i(p, q) = E^{*p,q} \left[\int_0^\infty \pi(P_t, Q_t, i)e^{-rt}dt \right] \qquad (3.4)$$

In what follows we first consider cases in which only a subset of the technologies discussed above is available, and then consider the case in which the full set is available.

3.3 OPTIMAL INVESTMENT BEHAVIOR

In the current model, the firm not only chooses when to invest, but also chooses the technology. If this additional choice is irreversible and made at the time of investment, the irreversible character of the investment becomes more important, and we would expect the firm to be more reluctant to invest. On the other hand, if the choice of fuel is reversible, i.e., the flexible technology is chosen, the firm will be able to adapt to future developments. If the firm chooses to invest in the gas technology at a time when the gas price is low, then it will be stuck with this investment even if the gas price should increase again. With a flexible technology the investment may still be profitable if the gas price happens to rise, provided the oil price is sufficiently low. The flexible technology thus has a lower risk, and we would expect firms to be less cautious about investing in them than in pure technologies. To develop this point, we analyze each case separately, first with only one pure technology, then with both pure technologies available, and then we consider the case in which only the flexible technology is available. Finally, we combine the above elements in an analysis of the complete problem in which all three technologies are available.

3.3.1 The Benchmark Case: Only One Fuel Type Available

Consider first the case in which only one pure technology is available. With only one fuel type, say gas, the problem is

$$V_g^*(p, q) = \sup_\tau E^{*p,q} \left[(V_g(P_\tau, Q_\tau) - K_g)e^{-r\tau} \right]$$

$$= \sup_\tau E^{*p} \left[\left(\frac{A}{r} - \frac{P_\tau}{\delta_p} - K_g \right) e^{-r\tau} \right] \tag{3.5}$$

where A/r is the present value of future revenues and P_τ/δ_p is the present value of future fuel costs. The solution to this problem, which has been analyzed by McDonald and Siegel (1986), is in the form of a trigger level on the fuel price. The firm invests once the gas price is at or below the level

$$p^* = \left(\frac{b}{b-1} \right) \frac{\delta_p}{r} (A - rK_g)$$

where $b = [1/2\sigma^2 - r + \delta_p - \sqrt{(r - \delta_p - 1/2\sigma^2)^2 + 2\sigma^2 r}]/\sigma^2 < 0$. The value of an option to build a gas-fired plant is

$$V_g^*(p, q) = a \, p^b \text{ for } p \geq p^*$$

where $a = [(A/r) - K_g]^{1-b}(1 - b)^{b-1}(-b)^b$. The trigger price q^* when only oil is available is similar.

As a benchmark for the discussion below, consider the case in which both types of fuel are available, and the firm behaves as if the cheapest fuel (in present value) is the only one available. Thus if $Q_t/\delta_q > P_t/\delta_p$, the firm ignores the availability of the oil technology and invests in a gas-burning plant if $P_t \leq p^*$, and similarly invests in oil if $Q_t/\delta_q < P_t/\delta_p$ and $Q_t \leq q^*$. This solution is illustrated in Figure 3.1. The process (P_t, Q_t) moves around in the plane as indicated. As long as $P_t > p^*$ and $Q_t > q^*$, the firm will not invest. But once it hits one of these trigger levels, the firm will invest and the choice of technology will be determined by whichever trigger level is hit first.

3.3.2 Investing in Pure Technologies

Now suppose that both fuel types are available, but only as pure technologies. This introduces a form of irreversibility. Once a plant is installed, the investment costs are sunk, and, in addition, the fuel type cannot be changed.

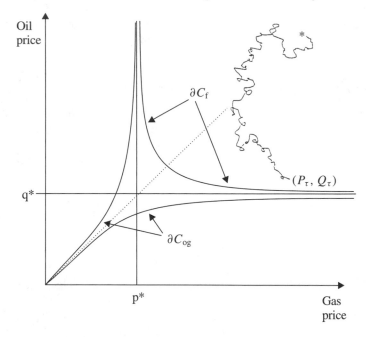

Figure 3.1 The border of different continuation areas. ∂C_f and ∂C_{go} are the borders of the continuation regions with the flexible technology and both gas and oil technologies available, respectively. p^* and q^* are the reservation prices for the pure gas and pure oil technologies.

If the firm invests at a state (p, q), then the optimal choice of technology will obviously be the one that maximizes the net present value of the plant, or equivalently the fuel type that minimizes the present value of cost. Thus the problem is

$$V_{og}^*(p, q) = \sup_{\tau \geq 0} E^{*p,q} \left[\max_{i=g,o} V_i(P_\tau, Q_\tau) e^{-r\tau} \right]$$

$$= \sup_{\tau \geq 0} E^{*p,q} \left\{ \left[\frac{A}{r} - \min \left(\frac{P_\tau}{\delta_p} + K_g, \frac{Q_\tau}{\delta_q} + K_o \right) \right] e^{-r\tau} \right\} \quad (3.6)$$

We shall show that when both fuel types are considered simultaneously, the firm is less willing to invest than in the benchmark case in which these two options are considered in isolation. To show this, we define the continuation region as the set of states in which it is optimal not to exercise the option. Since the exercise value at a state (p, q) is $A/r - \min[(p/\delta_p) + K_g, (q/\delta_q) + K_o]$ whereas the value of the option is $V_{pq}^*(p, q)$, the continuation region is the set

$$C_{og} = \left\{ (p, q) \in R^2 : V_{og}^*(p, q) > \left[\frac{A}{r} - \min \left(\frac{p}{\delta_p} + K_g, \frac{q}{\delta_q} + K_o \right) \right] \right\} \quad (3.7)$$

That is, the continuation region is the set of states in which the optimal policy is to continue waiting for a better investment opportunity.

Theorem 1. *The continuation set C_{go} includes the intersection of the continuation sets for the single technology cases, and also the line at which the present values of the cost of pure technologies are equal:*

$$C_{og} \supseteq \left[(p, q) \in R_+^2 : (p > p^* \text{ and } q > q^*) \text{ or } \left(\frac{p}{\delta_p} + K_g = \frac{q}{\delta_q} + K_o \right) \right]$$

Proof. The proof is given in Appendix C.

The solution is illustrated graphically in Figure 3.1. The trigger levels for the single technology cases are indicated as p^* and q^*. The firm will wait as long as the process lies in the continuation region, but once the process hits the boundary ∂C_{og} the firm will invest and the choice of technology will be determined by which part of the boundary is hit. If $P_\tau/\delta_p < Q_\tau/\delta_q$, where τ is the time of investment, the firm invests in gas technology; otherwise it invests in oil technology.

Note that compared to the benchmark case, in which each option is considered separately, the firm in this case is less willing to invest, since the continuation region has increased. Note that it is never optimal to invest when the present values of the cost are close. The intuition is that when the two alternatives are just about equally good $[(p/\delta_p) - K_g \approx (q/\delta_q) \quad K_o]$ there is much to be gained from waiting for more information, since one of the alternatives may soon appear distinctly better than the other.

3.3.3 Investing in the Flexible Technology

With the flexible technology, the fuel type can be changed anytime after the new technology is installed. We assume that there is no cost of switching between oil and gas, and the optimal policy at any time is to use the fuel type that is cheapest. The production cost at time t is thus $\min(P_t, Q_t)$.

To simplify the analysis, we assume that $\delta_p = \delta_q = \delta$ and $\sigma_p = \sigma_q = \sigma$, which makes the solution symmetric. Standard calculations (see Appendix B) show that the value of the installed flexible technology plant, evaluated at state (p, q), is given by

$$V_f(p, q) = E^{*p,q} \left\{ \int_0^\infty [A - \min(P_t, Q_t)] e^{-rt} dt \right\}$$

$$= \begin{cases} \frac{A}{r} - \frac{p}{\delta} + \frac{p}{\delta(2\xi+1)} \left(\frac{p}{q} \right)^\xi & \text{for } p \leq q \\ \frac{A}{r} - \frac{q}{\delta} + \frac{q}{\delta(2\xi+1)} \left(\frac{q}{p} \right)^\xi & \text{for } p \geq q \end{cases} \tag{3.8}$$

where $\xi = \left\{ -1 + \sqrt{1 + 4\delta/[\sigma^2(1 - \rho)]} \right\} / 2$.

The investment problem is then

$$\sup_{\tau} E^{*p,q} \left\{ [V_f(P_\tau, Q_\tau) - K_f]e^{-r\tau} \right\}$$

The form of V_f is too complex to allow an explicit solution of this optimization problem, and hence we apply an approximation technique.

Let $(\hat{p}, \hat{q})$ with $\hat{p} < \hat{q}$ be a point in the continuation region for the flexible technology case. By definition this means that

$$V_f^*(\hat{p}, \hat{q}) > \frac{A}{r} - K_f - \frac{\hat{p}}{\delta} + h_g(\hat{p}, \hat{q})$$

where

$$h_g(p, q) = \frac{p}{\delta(2\xi + 1)} \left(\frac{p}{q} \right)^\xi$$

In Appendix B, it is shown that

$$V_f^*(p, q) - h_g(p, q) \le V_g^*(p, q) \text{ for } (p, q) \in C_p \cap C_f \tag{3.9}$$

and hence

$$V_g(\hat{p}, \hat{q}) \ge V_f^*(\hat{p}, \hat{q}) - h_g(\hat{p}, \hat{q}) > \frac{A}{r} - K_f - \frac{\hat{p}}{\delta}$$

Hence $(\hat{p}, \hat{q})$ is in the continuation region of the single technology case. The same argument applies in proving the symmetric result for $q < p$. Thus, the continuation area has decreased compared with the benchmark case in which each fuel type is analyzed in isolation. The reason for this is that the irreversibility in some sense is reduced. Even if it turns out that oil becomes too expensive for the power plant to give positive profits, the gas price may develop more favorably. The investor thus takes less risk when investing in the flexible technology.

Note also that even when the investments are fully reversible, the firm will not invest unless the fuel cost, $\min(p, q)$, is less than revenues A net of user cost of capital rK_f. The area $\{(p, q) : \min(p, q) \ge A - rK_f\}$ should thus be included in all continuation regions, as indicated in Figure 3.1. An approximated boundary ∂C_f of the continuation area is shown in Figure 3.1. As we would expect, the value of flexibility is largest when $p \approx q$.

3.4 THE VALUE OF FLEXIBILITY

Thus far we have assumed that the firm faces either two pure technologies or one flexible one. If all the alternatives are present, and there is no additional cost with the flexible technology, the flexible technology clearly dominates. The interesting case, however, is when flexibility is costly. We consider two cases: first that in which the capital equipment is more costly, and second that in which the energy efficiency of the flexible technology is lower than that of the pure technology so that the plant will need more fuel to produce the same amount of energy.

3.4.1 Flexibility at Higher Cost

This section considers the first case in which flexible technology requires more expensive capital equipment. Let K_f denote the cost of investing in a flexible technology, and $K = K_g = K_o$ the cost of investing in a pure technology,[1] with $K_f > K$. If the firm decides to invest in state (p, q) it will chose the flexible technology if the net value of the flexible technology $V_f(p, q) - K_f$, exceeds the value of each of the pure technologies. It is readily seen from the results above that the flexible technology will be chosen if and only if

$$
K_f - K \leq
\begin{cases}
\frac{p}{\delta(2\xi+1)} \left(\frac{p}{q}\right)^\xi & \text{if } p \leq q \\[2ex]
\frac{q}{\delta(2\xi+1)} \left(\frac{q}{p}\right)^\xi & \text{if } p \geq q
\end{cases}
\tag{3.10}
$$

The right-hand side is the value of flexibility, the amount the firm will be willing to pay to purchase a flexible technology rather than a technology that can use only one fuel. This value depends on relative prices: if p and q are too different, then the most expensive fuel will not be an interesting alternative for a long time, and with discounting its value is negligible. In this case flexibility does not matter much. Note further that, given p/q, the value of flexibility is proportional to the price level of the fuel. This is reasonable since the more expensive the fuel is, the more is at stake in making the right choice of fuel type.

To get an idea of the value of flexibility, note that if a pure technology is chosen, the present value of the expected fuel cost is p/δ when $p < q$. With a flexible technology the expected costs are reduced by an amount which is the value of flexibility. Thus for $p < q$, the premium that the firm is willing to pay for flexibility, expressed as a proportion of the present value of the fuel cost of a pure technology, may be written as

$$
\frac{K_f - K}{p/\delta} = \frac{1}{2\xi + 1} \left(\frac{p}{q}\right)^\xi
$$

As an example, this cost reduction for specific parameters is shown in Table 3.1. Pindyck (1997) reports estimates of σ for oil in the range 0.15–0.20. We consider $\sigma = 0.1$ and $\sigma = 0.2$ for both oil and gas. The two prices are clearly correlated. To illustrate the importance of correlation, the cost reduction is computed for correlations of 0, 0.75 and 0.95. Oil prices are not expected to grow much in the near future, even though we would expect a risk premium on correlated financial assets. A growth rate in oil prices of 2% and a required equilibrium return of 7% gives a below-equilibrium return shortfall of $\delta = 5\%$; we also consider the case $\delta = 2\%$. The cost reduction is computed both with $p \approx q$, and with $q = 2p$.

It can be seen that the reduction in fuel cost may be considerable. In a study of new technologies, OECD (1992, Table 21) finds expected fuel costs to be two to three times the capital cost. Thus the firm should be willing to accept a 2–3% increase

---

[1] To simplify notation we assume that $K_g = K_o$. Characterization of the general case can be derived from the results above.

Table 3.1
Reduction in Fuel Cost for Different Parameter Values[a]

ρ	$p \approx q, \delta = 5\%$		$q = 2p, \delta = 5\%$		$p \approx q, \delta = 2\%$	
	$\sigma = 0.1$	$\sigma = 0.2$	$\sigma = 0.1$	$\sigma = 0.2$	$\sigma = 0.1$	$\sigma = 0.2$
0	22%	41%	6%	25%	33%	58%
0.75	11%	22%	1%	6%	17%	33%
0.95	5%	10%	0%	0%	8%	16%

[a] p and q are the gas and oil prices, respectively, δ is the below-equilibrium rate of return shortfall, ρ is the correlation between gas and oil prices, and σ^2 is the variance of the log of gas or oil price 1 year ahead.

in capital cost to achieve a 1% reduction in fuel costs. From this perspective the cost reductions in the case $p \approx q$ are quite substantial. As one would expect, the correlation coefficient is very important here. But even with $\rho = 0.95$, $\delta = 5\%$, and $\sigma = 0.1$, the cost reduction is 5% when the two prices are at about the same level.

3.4.2 Flexibility with Lower Energy Efficiency

In this section we assume that the energy efficiency for the flexible technology is less than for a pure technology. Specifically, to produce the same amount of energy that a pure technology can derive from one unit of fuel, the flexible technology uses $\beta > 1$ units of fuel. This is equivalent to a shift in efficient energy prices, so that p is effectively replaced by βp and q by βq in all results above. The value of a flexible technology is thus

$$
V_f(p, q) = \begin{cases} \frac{A}{r} - \frac{\beta p}{\delta} + \frac{\beta p}{\delta(2\xi+1)} \left(\frac{p}{q}\right)^{\xi} & \text{if } p \leq q \\ \frac{A}{r} - \frac{\beta q}{\delta} + \frac{\beta q}{\delta(2\xi+1)} \left(\frac{q}{p}\right)^{\xi} & \text{if } p \geq q \end{cases}
\tag{3.11}
$$

If the investment cost is equal for all alternatives and the firm invests in state (p, q) the flexible alternative would be chosen if

$$
V_f(p, q) > \max_{i=p,q} V_i(p, q)
$$

For $p \leq q$ the requirement is

$$
-\frac{\beta p}{\delta} + \frac{\beta p}{\delta(2\xi + 1)} \left(\frac{p}{q}\right)^{\xi} > -\frac{p}{\delta}
$$

which can be simplified to

$$
\frac{p}{q} > \left[\frac{(2\xi + 1)(\beta - 1)}{\beta}\right]^{1/\xi}
$$

Using a similar argument for $p > q$ and combining the two requirements we find that the flexible technology is optimal if

$$\left[\frac{(2\xi + 1)(\beta - 1)}{\beta}\right]^{-1/\xi} > \frac{p}{q} > \left[\frac{(2\xi + 1)(\beta - 1)}{\beta}\right]^{1/\xi} \tag{3.12}$$

We refer to the left-hand side expression $[(2\xi + 1)(\beta - 1)/\beta]^{-1/\xi}$ as the reservation level of relative prices. If the relative price exceeds this reservation level and the investment is optimal, then the pure technology with the lowest fuel cost should be chosen. This reservation level is reported below for different parameter values. As above, $\delta = 5$ or 2%. For some parameter values the flexible technology is never optimal, indicated by a — in Table 3.2.

For example, if energy efficiency is 5% more with the pure than with the flexible technology ($\beta = 1.05$), and if $\delta = 5\%$, $\sigma = 0.1$, and $\rho = 0.75$, the flexible technology is the optimal choice if the investment is undertaken when

$$2.24 > \frac{p}{q} > \frac{1}{2.24} = 0.446$$

Note that for parameters in the range studied here, there is only one combination of parameter values in which the flexible technology is never optimal.[2]

3.4.3 Timing of Investment

The regions in which the flexible technology and each of the pure technologies are respectively optimal in the case above are separated by straight lines from the origin, as illustrated in Figure 3.2. Using this observation along with the discussion in Appendix A, we see that in the region in which the flexible technology is chosen its continuation region includes the continuation region for the case in which only the flexible technology is available, and similarly for each of the two other alternatives.

Table 3.2
Reservation Level of Relative Price for Different Parameter Values[a]

ρ	$\beta = 1.05, \delta = 5\%$		$\beta = 1.1, \delta = 5\%$		$\beta = 1.05, \delta = 2\%$	
	$\sigma = 0.1$	$\sigma = 0.2$	$\sigma = 0.1$	$\sigma = 0.2$	$\sigma = 0.1$	$\sigma = 0.2$
0	4.26	7.74	2.22	3.92	4.26	10.77
0.75	2.24	4.26	1.20	2.22	3.44	6.38
0.95	1.05	2.02	—	1.09	1.62	3.10

[a] β is the energy efficiency of flexible technologies relative to pure technologies, δ is the below-equilibrium rate of return shortfall, ρ is the correlation between gas and oil prices, and σ^2 is the variance of the log of gas or oil price 1 year ahead.

[2] The flexible technology is never optimal if $(2\xi + 1)(\beta - 1)/\beta \leq 1$, or $\beta \geq (2\xi + 1)/2\xi$.

Moreover, the function $\max_i V_i(p,q)$ is not smooth around the lines dividing the area. By an argument similar to the one in the proof of Theorem 1, it can be seen that the continuation region must include the lines

$$\frac{p}{q} = \left[\frac{(2\xi + 1)(\beta - 1)}{\beta}\right]^{1/\xi}$$

and

$$\frac{q}{p} = \left[\frac{(2\xi + 1)(\beta - 1)}{\beta}\right]^{1/\xi}$$

Thus, the boundary ∂C_{fpq} of the continuation region must look like the one illustrated in Figure 3.2.

3.5 CONCLUSIONS

In this chapter we have examined how operating flexibility affects the optimal timing of investment. Irreversibility in choices of technology will delay investment. On the other hand, postinvestment operating flexibility reduces the uncertainty of future revenues, making earlier investment optimal.

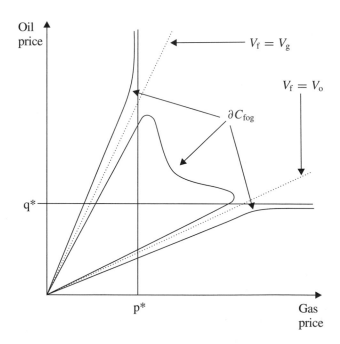

Figure 3.2   The border of the continuation area when all technologies are available. V_f, V_g, and V_o are the present values of the expected cash-flow stream for the flexible and the pure gas and oil technologies, respectively. ∂C_{fgo} is the border of the continuation region when all technologies are available.

We considered the problem facing a firm that has to choose between plants operating with gas and oil fuel. As a benchmark, we used the investment behavior of a firm that ignores the availability of the currently most expensive alternative fuel and behaves as if the cheapest fuel technology is the only one available. We found that when the fuel choice is integrated in the choice of technology and has to be made up front, investment is optimally delayed compared to the benchmark case. Intuitively, more options have to be exercised at the point of initial investment. On the other hand, if the firm can invest in a flexible technology allowing it to switch fuel without cost after the capital equipment is installed, it will invest earlier than in the benchmark case above. This is because the flexibility reduces the uncertainty of future fuel costs.

Flexibility also reduces the level of expected fuel costs. When the initial prices of the two fuel types are about equal, we found that switching flexibility reduced costs significantly (by 5–58%, within a reasonable range of parameter values). This may explain why about 40% of combustible fuel thermal power plants in Europe are multifired (International Energy Agency, 1992).

A caveat is in order here. We have assumed throughout the chapter that the technology that is chosen when the power plant is built can never be changed. A problem for future research is to consider the case in which the chosen technology itself can be changed, at a cost. Similarly, it would be interesting to extend the model to include nonzero costs of switching between oil and gas with a flexible technology.

Appendix A

The Choice of Technology in General

In the models developed in this chapter, the firm has to choose not only when to invest, but also the technology. With more alternative technologies the total value of the option to invest is higher, and the firm is more reluctant to invest early. This result holds in more general models.

To see this, let X_t be an n−dimensional diffusion process, and let $V_i(x)$ be the value function if technology i is chosen. If only technology i is available, the value of the option to invest is

$$V_i^*(x) = \sup_\tau E^x[V_i(X_\tau)e^{-r\tau}] \tag{3.A1}$$

and the corresponding continuation region is

$$C_i = [x : V_i^*(x) > V_i(x)] \tag{3.A2}$$

Similarly, if all technologies are available, the value of the option to invest is

$$V^*(x) = \sup_\tau E^x[\max_i V_i(X_\tau)e^{-r\tau}] \geq \max_i V_i^*(x) \tag{3.A3}$$

with continuation region

$$C = [x : V^*(x) > \max_i V_i(x)]$$

Define

$$M_i = [x : V_i(x) = \max_j V_j(x)] \qquad (3.A4)$$

as the region where i would be the optimal technology if the firm is forced to invest immediately. For any $x \in C_i \cap M_i$, $V^*(x) \geq V_i^*(x) \geq \max_j V_j(x)$, so that

$$C \supseteq \bigcup_i (C_i \cap M_i)$$

In other words, at the point at which i would be the optimal technology if forced to invest ($x \in M_i$), the firm will not invest at that state unless it is optimal even when technology i is the only technology available. However, this is only a necessary condition. There may be points $x \in C \cap M_i$ with $x \notin C_i$. That is, we may be less prone to invest since we not only make an irreversible expansion of production capacity, but the chosen technology is irreversible as well.

Appendix B

An Approximation to the Value of the Flexible Option

We do not have an explicit solution for the value of the option to invest in a flexible technology, but we are able to derive upper and lower bounds on this option value. In this Appendix we discuss the approximation technique used and then apply it to the model in Section 3.3.3 to derive the upper bound.

Let X_t be an Ito diffusion process of the form

$$dX_t = a(X_t)dt + b(X_t)dB_t$$

Consider the optimal stopping problem

$$V^*(x) = \sup_\tau E^x \left[V(X_t)e^{-r\tau} \right] \qquad (3.B1)$$

The central idea of the approximation technique used is the following. Let h be any C^2 function such that $Lh = 0$, where L is the discounted infinitesimal generator for the process X_t. Then for any stopping rule τ, we have by Dynkin's formula (see Øksendal, 1991, Theorem 7.10)

$$E^x[h(X_\tau)e^{-r\tau}] = h(x) + \int_0^\tau e^{-rt} Lh(X_t)dt = h(x) \qquad (3.B2)$$

so that $M_t = h(X_t)e^{-rt}$ is a martingale.

With $\tilde{V}(x) = V(x) - h(x)$, the martingale property of M_t implies that

$$\tilde{V}^*(x) = \sup_\tau E^x \left[\tilde{V}(X_t)e^{-r\tau} \right] = V^*(x) - h(x) \tag{3.B3}$$

Next we need to find h such that $\tilde{V}$ is small, or can be signed. Suppose that we can choose some function h, with $Lh = 0$, and a continuation region $\hat{C}$ such that $[V(p,q) - h(p,q)] > 0$ for all $(p,q) \in \partial \hat{C}$. Then it follows that

$$\sup_\tau E^{*p,q} \left\{ [V(P_\tau, Q_\tau)]e^{-r\tau} \right\} - h(p,q) \geq$$

$$E^{*p,q} \left\{ [V(P_\tau, Q_\tau) - h(P_\tau, Q_\tau)]e^{-r\tau} \right\} \text{ for } \tau = \tau_{\hat{C}} \tag{3.B4}$$

where $\tau_{\hat{C}}$ is the first time the process X_t exits from the set $\hat{C}$. Since the right-hand side is positive, we derive a lower bound on V^*

$$V^*(p,q) \geq h(p,q) \tag{3.B5}$$

Similarly we can construct upper bounds on V^*.

We use this technique to prove Eq. (3.8), in Section 3.3.3, that the present value of future cash flows with a flexible technology is

$$V_f(p,q) = \begin{cases} \frac{A}{r} - \frac{p}{\delta} + \frac{p}{\delta(2\xi+1)} \left(\frac{p}{q}\right)^\xi & \text{for } p \leq q \\ \frac{A}{r} - \frac{q}{\delta} + \frac{q}{\delta(2\xi+1)} \left(\frac{q}{p}\right)^\xi & \text{for } q \leq p \end{cases} \tag{3.B6}$$

$$= \begin{cases} \frac{A}{r} - \frac{p}{\delta} + h_p(p,q) & \text{for } p \leq q \\ \frac{A}{r} - \frac{q}{\delta} + h_q(p,q) & \text{for } q \leq p \end{cases} \tag{3.B7}$$

and that

$$V_f^*(p,q) - h_p(p,q) \leq V_p^*(p,q) \qquad \text{for } (p,q) \in C_p \cap C_f$$

First to see that V_f really is the present value of net future cash flows $A - \min(P_t, Q_t)$, we have to check that

$$LV_f(p,q) = \begin{cases} p - A & \text{for } p \leq q \\ q - A & \text{for } q \leq p \end{cases}$$

where

$$L \equiv -r + (r - \delta)\left(p\frac{\partial}{\partial p} + q\frac{\partial}{\partial q}\right) + $$
$$\frac{1}{2}\sigma^2\left(p^2\frac{\partial^2}{\partial p^2} + 2\rho pq\frac{\partial^2}{\partial q\partial p} + q^2\frac{\partial^2}{\partial q^2}\right) \tag{3.B8}$$

We further require the high contact condition that V_f is continuously differentiable at the line $p = q$. The reader can easily verify that these conditions hold. The claim that

V_f is the expected present value then follows by adopting the verification theorem in Brekke and Øksendal (1994).

Next, to derive the upper bound on V_f^* note that the functions h_p and h_q satisfy $Lh_p = 0$ and $Lh_q = 0$. It follows that

$$V_f^*(p, q) = h_p(p, q) + \sup_\tau E^{p,q} \left[\frac{A}{r} - \frac{P_\tau}{\delta} + R_p(P_\tau, Q_\tau) \right]$$

where the residual function is given by

$$R_p(p, q) = \begin{cases} 0 & \text{for } p \leq q \\ \frac{p-q}{\delta} + h_q(p, q) - h_p(p, q) & \text{for } q \leq p \end{cases} \tag{3.B9}$$

Now $R_p(q, p) \leq 0$ since $R_p(p, q) = 0$ and $\partial R/\partial p = 0$ for $p = q$; moreover, $\partial^2 R_p/\partial p^2 < 0$ for $p > q$. Given the sign of R_p, we have

$$V_f^*(p, q) - h_p(p, q) \leq \sup_\tau E^{p,q} \left(\frac{A}{r} - \frac{P_\tau}{\delta} \right) = V_p^*(p) \tag{3.B10}$$

QED.

Appendix C

Proof of Theorem 1

We first prove that the set $[(p, q) : p > p^*$ and $q > q^*]$ is in the continuation region when the only technologies available are the two pure technologies. Obviously, the option value when both technologies are available must be at least as high as the option value when only one technology is available. Since $V_p^*(p) > [(A/r - p/\delta_p)]$ for $p > p^*$, and similarly for $q > q^*$, it follows that for $p > p^*$ and $q > q^*$,

$$V_{og}^*(p, q) \geq \max[V_o^*(p), V_g^*(q)] > \max(\frac{A}{r} - \frac{p}{\delta_p} - K_g, \frac{A}{r} - \frac{q}{\delta_q} - K_o) \tag{3.C1}$$

Hence (p, q) is in the continuation region.

To see that the line $p/\delta_p - K_g = q/\delta_q - K_o$ is in the continuation area, let $f_n(p, q) = (A/r) - (1/2)[(p/\delta_p) + (q/\delta_q) + K_g + K_o] + n[(p/\delta_p) + K_g - (q/\delta_q)]^2$ for $n = 1, 2, \ldots$. For any point (p, q) with $p/\delta_p + K_g = q/\delta_q + K_o$, we can choose an open neighborhood B_n such that $f_n(p, q) \leq V(p, q)$ for all $(p, q) \in B_n$. For n sufficiently large, $Lf_n > 0$, where

$$L \equiv -r + (r - \delta_p)p\frac{\partial}{\partial p} + (r - \delta_q)q\frac{\partial}{\partial q} \tag{3.C2}$$

$$+ \frac{1}{2}(\sigma_p p)^2 \frac{\partial^2}{\partial p^2} + \rho\sigma_p\sigma_q pq \frac{\partial^2}{\partial q \partial p} + \frac{1}{2}(\sigma_q q)^2 \frac{\partial^2}{\partial q^2}$$

is the present value infinitesimal generator for the (P_t, Q_t) process. Let τ_n denote the first exit time of B_n. Then by Dynkin's formula

$$E^{*p,q}[V_{pq}(P_{\tau_n}, Q_{\tau_n})] \geq E^{*p,q}[f_n(P_{\tau_n}, Q_{\tau_n})] \tag{3.C3}$$

$$= f_n(p, q) + \int_0^{\tau_n} \hat{L} f_n(P_t, Q_t) e^{-rt} dt$$

$$> V_{og}(p, q)$$

Thus stopping at a point where $p/\delta_p + K_g$ equals $q/\delta_q + K_o$ cannot be optimal since this policy can be improved upon. QED.

ACKNOWLEDGMENTS

Thanks to Lenos Trigeorgis, Michael J. Brennan, Bernt Øksendal, Jon Gjerde, and two anonymous referees for helpful comments.

REFERENCES

Abel, A., and J. C. Eberly. (1996). Optimal Investment with Costly Reversibility. *Review of Economic Studies* 63(4), 581–593.

Arntzen, H. (1995). Optimal Choice of Production Capacity in a Random Market. *Stochastics and Stochastic Reports* 45, 87–120.

Brekke, K. A., and B. Øksendal. (1991). The High Contact Principle as a Sufficiency Condition for Optimal Stopping. In D. Lund and B. Øksendal (eds.), *Stochastic Models and Option Values*. Amsterdam: North Holland.

Brekke, K. A., and B. Øksendal. (1994). Optimal Switching in an Economic Activity under Uncertainty. *SIAM Journal of Control and Optimization* 32, 1021–1036.

Brennan, M. J., and E. S. Schwartz. (1985). Evaluating Natural Resource Investments. *Journal of Business* 58(2), 135–157.

Dixit, A. (1989). Entry and Exit Decisions under Uncertainty. *Journal of Political Economy* 97(3), 620–638.

Dixit, A., and R. Pindyck. (1994). *Investment under Uncertainty*. Princeton, NJ: Princeton University Press.

Duffie, D. (1988). *Securities Markets: Stochastic Models*. San Diego, CA: Academic Press.

He, H., and R. Pindyck. (1992). Investment in Flexible Production Capacity. *Journal of Economic Dynamics and Control* 16, 575–599.

International Energy Agency. (1992). Energy Statistics of OECD Countries 1989-90. Luxembourg: IEA.

Kobila, T. Ø. (1993). A Class of Solvable Stochastic Investment Problems Involving Singular Control. *Stochastics and Stochastic Reports* 43, 29–63.

Kulatilaka, N. (1993). The Value of Flexibility: The Case of a Dual-Fuel Industrial Steam Boiler. *Financial Management* 33(2), 271–280.

Kulatilaka, N. (1995). The Value of Flexibility: A General Model of Real Options. In L. Trigeorgis (ed.), *Real Options in Capital Investment: Models, Strategies and Applications*. Westport, CT: Praeger.

McDonald, R., and D. Siegel. (1986). The Value of Waiting to Invest. *Quarterly Journal of Economics* 101(4), 707–728.

OECD (1992). Projected Costs of Generating Electricity, Update 1992. Paris: OECD.

Øksendal, B. (1991). *Stochastic Differential Equations: An Introduction with Applications*, 3rd edition. Heidelberg: Springer-Verlag.

4

Expandability, Reversibility, and Optimal Capacity Choice

AVINASH K. DIXIT

ROBERT S. PINDYCK

We develop continuous-time models of capacity choice when demand fluctuates stochastically, and the firm has limited opportunities to expand or contract. Specifically, we consider costs of investing or disinvesting that vary with time, or with the amount of capacity already installed. The firm's limited opportunities to expand or contract create call and put options on incremental units of capital; we show how the values of these options affect the firm's investment decisions.

4.1 INTRODUCTION

Our recent book and survey articles on the real options approach to investment identify three characteristics of most investment decisions: (1) uncertainty over future profit streams, (2) irreversibility, i.e., the existence of some sunk costs that cannot be recouped if the firm changes its mind later, and (3) the choice of timing, i.e., the opportunity to delay the investment decision.[1] We argued that because of the *interaction* of these three forces, optimal investment decisions have to satisfy more stringent hurdles for their expected rates of return than the naive net present value (NPV) criterion would indicate. The uncertainty implies that there may be future eventualities where the firm would regret having invested. The irreversibility implies that if the firm invests now, it cannot costlessly disinvest should such an eventuality materialize. And the opportunity to wait allows it to learn more about the uncertain future and reduce the likelihood of such regret.

By analogy with financial options, the opportunity to invest is a call option—a right but not an obligation to make the investment. To invest is to exercise the option. Because of the uncertainty, the option has a time premium or holding value: it should

[1] See Dixit (1992), Pindyck (1991), and Dixit and Pindyck (1996).

50

not be exercised as soon as it is "in the money," even though doing so has a positive NPV. The optimal exercise point comes only when the option is sufficiently "deep in the money," i.e., the NPV of exercise is large enough to offset the value of waiting for more information. This conclusion is probably the most widely known "result" of the real options literature.

Of the triad of conditions mentioned above, most of the literature has focused on irreversibility. But most formal models assume simultaneously total irreversibility and a completely costless ability to wait, so they cannot separately identify the contributions of these two conditions. Exceptions to this include the seminal article by Brennan and Schwartz (1985), which examined an investment in a mining project and allowed for both an option to invest and an abandonment option, the models developed by Trigeorgis (1993, 1996) that allow for a variety of different options interacting within a single project, including options to expand and contract, and the work of Kulatilaka (1995) on substitutability and complementarity in real options. Another exception is our recent article co-authored with Abel and Eberly (1996), which developed a two-period model that allowed for arbitrary degrees of irreversibility and future expandability.

Abel, Dixit, Eberly, and Pindyck (henceforth referred to as ADEP) showed that a firm that makes an investment that is partially or totally reversible acquires a put option, namely the ability to pull out should future conditions be sufficiently adverse. This option has value if future uncertainty involves a sufficiently large downside with a positive probability that the firm will want to exercise the option. Recognition of this put option will make the firm *more* willing to invest than it would be under a naive NPV calculation that assumes that the project continues for its physical lifetime and omits the possibility of future disinvestment.[2] Likewise, a firm that can expand capacity by making an investment now or in the future (at a specified cost) is exercising a call option, acting now when it might have waited. This option has value if future uncertainty has a sufficiently large downside that waiting would have been preferable. Recognition of this call option will make the firm *less* willing to invest than it would be under a naive NPV calculation that assumes that the project must be started now or never, ignoring the possibility of a future optimal startup decision.

For many real-world investments, both of these options exist to some degree. Firms typically have at least some ability to expand their capacity at a time of their choosing, and sometimes can partially reverse their decisions by selling off capital to recover part of their investment. The net effect of these two options is in general ambiguous, depending on the degrees of reversibility and expandability, and the extent and nature of the uncertainty.

If the investment is totally irreversible, i.e., there is only a call option and no put option, the investment must necessarily satisfy a stiffer hurdle than a positive NPV (naively calculated). But as ADEP pointed out, it is not the irreversibility that gives rise to the call option; it is the *expandability* that does so. What irreversibility does is to eliminate the put option that acts in the opposite direction.

---

[2] The option to abandon a project midstream is an example of this. Myers and Majd (1984) showed how this option can be valued as an American put option and its implications for the investment decision.

One might argue that in practice irreversibility is often more important than limited expandability, in part because of "lemons effects," but mostly because many unpredictable shocks are industry specific.[3] However, expandability can also be limited, e.g., because of limited land, natural resource reserves, or because of the need for a permit or license, only a limited number of which are being issued. Thus it is important to recognize and clarify the effects of these different underlying economic conditions.

In this chapter, we move beyond the two-period analysis in ADEP to examine a set of continuous-time models that allows for incremental capacity expansion and/or contraction over time, and thereby provides further insight into the effects of irreversibility, expandability, and the ability to wait. In this continuous-time setting, limited reversibility and expandability lead to clearly identifiable (and measurable) put and call options, which have opposite effects on the firm's incentive to invest.

Most of our analysis deals with exogenous and time-dependent limitations on the firm's ability to expand or contract. Specifically, we consider models in which the cost of investing increases over time (limited expandability) and the price that the firm can get by selling previously installed capital declines over time (limited reversibility). Our general framework is described in Section 4.2. In Section 4.3, models with time-varying costs are presented in detail and their implications for investment and capacity choice are examined. Section 4.4 examines the static and dynamic effects of sunk costs. In Section 4.5 we briefly discuss capacity choice decisions when the cost of investing or disinvesting varies with the amount of capacity already installed. In the concluding section, we suggest some extensions of our model for future work.

4.2 CONTINUOUS-TIME MODELS OF CAPACITY CHOICE

The two-period model developed in ADEP showed the effects of the call and put options associated with investment in the simplest possible way. For a more realistic analysis, however, we need a longer horizon, with ongoing uncertainty and repeated opportunities for the firm to expand or contract in response to changing circumstances. In such a setting, partial reversibility and expandability will arise when the costs of capacity contraction or expansion vary in response to changes in one or more exogenous or endogenous variables. In this chapter we consider two such variables.

First, we examine what happens when the cost of investing or disinvesting varies exogenously with time. This would be the case, for example, if the cost of capacity expansion rises over time as the resources needed for expansion (e.g., land or mineral reserves) are used up by other firms or dwindle for physical reasons (such as land erosion or the depletion of a potentially discoverable resource base). Likewise, the resale price of used capital is likely to fall over time, partly as a result of the increasing obsolescence of capital.

---

[3] For example, a steel manufacturer will want to sell a steel plant when the steel market is depressed, but that is precisely the time when no one else will want to pay a price for it anywhere near its replacement cost. Therefore investment in a steel plant is largely irreversible.

Second, we examine investment decisions when the cost of investing varies endogenously with the amount of capacity already installed by the firm. This kind of limited expandability would arise when the firm itself (which presumably has some monopoly power) uses up limited resources as it expands.

In both cases we assume that the firm faces an isoelastic demand curve of the form

$$P = \theta(t) Q^{-1/\eta} \tag{4.1}$$

where P is the price, Q is the quantity demanded, η is the elasticity of demand, and the demand shift variable θ varies stochastically according to the geometric Brownian motion:

$$d\theta = \alpha\theta \, dt + \sigma\theta \, dz \tag{4.2}$$

Although this is not critical, we assume for convenience that the uncertainty over future values of θ is spanned by the capital markets. Hence there is some risk-adjusted rate of return for θ, which we denote by μ, that allows risk-free discounting. We let $\delta = \mu - \alpha$ denote the rate-of-return shortfall.

To simplify matters, we assume that the firm has zero operating costs and hence will always produce at capacity, denoted by K. This eliminates any "operating options" that can affect the value of a unit of installed capital, allowing us to focus exclusively on options associated purely with the investment or disinvestment decision.[4]

As in Pindyck (1988), we examine the firm's incremental investment decisions. Let $\Delta V(K; \theta, t)$ denote the value of the last incremental unit of installed capital, and let $\Delta F(K; \theta, t)$ denote the value of the firm's option to install one incremental unit. In the standard neoclassical model of investment, ΔV would simply be the present value of the expected flow of marginal revenue from the unit in perpetuity, i.e.,

$$\Delta V_0(K; \theta, t) = \omega(K)\theta \tag{4.3}$$

where

$$\omega(K) \equiv \left(\frac{\eta - 1}{\eta\delta}\right) K^{-1/\eta} \tag{4.4}$$

Likewise, ΔF is the greater of zero or the NPV of immediate investment in this incremental unit. If the cost of an incremental unit of capital were fixed at k_0, then ΔF in the neoclassical model would be given by

$$\Delta F_0(K; \theta, t) = \max[0, \ \omega(K)\theta - k_0] \tag{4.5}$$

---

[4] The most important operating option is the ability of the firm to reduce output or to shut down and thereby avoid variable operating costs. As demonstrated by McDonald and Siegel (1985), this operating option raises the value of a unit of capital. For a discussion of this and other operating options, see Chapter 6 of Dixit and Pindyck (1996).

The neoclassical model, however, ignores the value of the firm's options to buy or sell capacity in the future. These option values depend on the firm's ability to make such purchases or sales, and the prices it will pay or receive for capital. In the next section, we allow those prices to vary with time.

4.3 TIME-DEPENDENT COSTS

Suppose that additional capacity can be added at a cost $k(t) = k_0 e^{\rho t}$ per unit, with $\rho \geq 0$. In this setting, if $\rho > 0$ so that the cost of adding capacity is rising over time, there is *limited expandability*; with $\rho = 0$ there is complete expandability; and for $\rho \to \infty$ there is no expandability. In this model, limits to expandability are exogenous to the firm's actions; $k(t)$ might rise, for example, because of continual entry or expansion by other firms that pushes up capital costs. Although we consider only values of $\rho \geq 0$, in practice ρ may in some cases be negative. This could occur, for example, if continual technological improvements or learning by doing cause per unit capital costs to fall over time.

Similarly, we assume that installed capital can be sold, but only for a price $S(t) = k_1 e^{-st}$ per unit, with $s \geq 0$. Hence there is *partial reversibility* that is completely time dependent, reflecting, for example, the increasing obsolescence of capital (as opposed to its physical depreciation). If $k_1 = k_0$, then at $s = 0$ investment is completely reversible. If $k_1 < k_0$, there is some irreversibility (even if $s = 0$); this can arise because of "lemons" effects. In either case, if $s \to \infty$, investment is completely irreversible. We call the effect of an initial gap between the purchase and sale prices of capital the "static" aspect of irreversibility, and the widening of the gap over time because of $\rho > 0$ and $s > 0$ the "dynamic" effect. At first we focus on the dynamic effect by assuming $k_1 = k_0$. In Section 4.4 we bring in the static effect, and compare the two.

At this point it is useful to explain our modeling choices. In making the cost of installing capital purely a function of time, we have in mind that cost increases are largely the result of the activities of other firms. For example, in an extractive industry such as oil or copper, other firms will deplete the potentially discoverable resource base over time; then expansion by a given firm becomes more expensive over time as new deposits are harder to find and costlier to develop. In the residential and commercial construction industries, other firms will buy and develop choice parcels of land over time, making expansion by a given firm more expensive. Ideally, this process should be modeled in an equilibrium setting, so that each firm in the industry (including possible new entrants) makes its decisions consistent with rational expectations of the optimal behavior of all other firms. Although equilibrium models of entry and exit with sunk costs are available in the literature [e.g., see Chapters 8 and 9 of Dixit and Pindyck (1996) for an overview], here we focus on the optimal decisions of the manager of one firm. Most managers base their decisions on expectations of changes in market parameters, including capital purchase and resale prices. Managers may or may not think in terms of an overall industry equilibrium when they form these expectations, but they often tend to treat these price movements as exogenous functions of time, much as we treat them here.

We offer a similar justification for our assumption that capital can be sold for a price that declines with time, irrespective of when the capital was purchased. Again, we have in mind a pattern of obsolescence that is largely caused by other firms that are continually developing superior processes and/or products.[5]

Finally, one might question our assumption that the purchase and sale prices of capital evolve *exponentially* with time, which was chosen for analytical convenience. Although other forms of time dependence might be introduced that may be more realistic for particular industries, this would complicate the algebra that follows.

With these caveats in mind, the basic idea we develop is that limited expandability and reversibility create options that must be taken into account when determining the firm's optimal investment rules. In contrast to the neoclassical model, ΔV actually has two components: the value of the expected profit flow from the use of the incremental unit of capital and the value of the (put) option to sell the unit in exchange for the salvage amount $k_0 e^{-st}$. Likewise, ΔF accounts for the full option value of the investment, i.e., the fact that the option has a time value and need not be exercised immediately.

Using standard methods, it is easy to show that ΔV must satisfy the following differential equation:

$$\tfrac{1}{2}\sigma^2\theta^2 \Delta V_{\theta\theta} + (r-\delta)\theta \Delta V_\theta + \Delta V_t - r\Delta V + \delta\omega(K)\theta = 0 \qquad (4.6)$$

where $\omega(K)$ is given by Eq. (4.4). The solution must also satisfy the following boundary conditions:

$$\lim_{\theta\to\infty}(\Delta V/\theta) = \omega(K) \qquad (4.7)$$

$$\Delta V(K;\theta^{**},t) = \Delta F(K;\theta^{**},t) + k_0 e^{-st} \qquad (4.8)$$

$$\Delta V_\theta(K;\theta^{**},t) = \Delta F_\theta(K;\theta^{**},t) \qquad (4.9)$$

Here $\theta^{**} = \theta^{**}(K,t)$ is the critical value of θ below which it is optimal to exercise the put option and sell the unit of capital. Boundary condition (4.7) simply says that if θ is very large, the firm will never want to sell off the unit of capital, so that its value is just the present value of the expected profit flow that it generates. Conditions (4.8) and (4.9) are the standard value matching and smooth pasting conditions that apply at the critical exercise point θ^{**}.

Likewise, ΔF must satisfy

$$\tfrac{1}{2}\sigma^2\theta^2 \Delta F_{\theta\theta} + (r-\delta)\theta \Delta F_\theta + \Delta F_t - r\Delta F = 0 \qquad (4.10)$$

subject to the boundary conditions:

$$\Delta F(K;0,t) = 0 \qquad (4.11)$$

---

[5] Again, a fuller theory of such a pattern of technological "leapfrogging" might best be described in an equilibrium framework, but that goes beyond what we aim to do here. [Hence we are not considering physical depreciation, as in Chapter 6 of Dixit and Pindyck (1996), where the sale price begins declining only after the capital has been purchased.]

$$\Delta F(K; \theta^*, t) = \Delta V(K; \theta^*, t) - k_0 e^{\rho t} \tag{4.12}$$

$$\Delta \dot{F}_\theta(K; \theta^*, t) = \Delta V_\theta(K; \theta^*, t) \tag{4.13}$$

$$\lim_{t \to \infty} \Delta F(K; \theta, t) = 0 \tag{4.14}$$

Of these, the first three conditions are standard; the last one says that (with $\rho > 0$) the value of the call option to install an incremental unit of capital approaches zero as time passes, because the cost of exercising the option is rising exponentially.

To clarify the nature of the optimal investment decision, it is best to proceed in steps. As we noted in the introduction in Section 4.1, most of the literature assumes that investment is completely irreversible and completely expandable. We will begin by considering the case in which investment is completely irreversible but only partially expandable, so that there is only a single boundary, $\theta^*(K, t)$, which triggers investment. This special case helps to elucidate the nature of the call option and its dependence on the extent of expandability. In Section 4.3.2 we examine the case in which investment is partially reversible but completely nonexpandable, so that investment entails only a put option (the value of which depends on the extent of reversibility), but no call option. In this case there is again only a single boundary, $\theta^{**}(K, t)$, which triggers disinvestment. We return to the general case set forth above in Section 4.3.3.

4.3.1 Complete Irreversibility, Partial Expandability

In this special case $s = \infty$, so the firm cannot disinvest. Then ΔV is simply the present value of the flow of marginal revenue from an incremental unit of capital:

$$\Delta V(K; \theta, t) = \left(\frac{\eta - 1}{\eta \delta}\right) K^{-1/\eta} \theta = \omega(K) \theta \tag{4.15}$$

We can find the solution to Eq. (4.10) for the value of the option to install an additional unit of capital by guessing a functional form and choosing its parameters to satisfy all of the boundary conditions.

We guess (and then verify) that the solution to Eq. (4.10) for ΔF has the form

$$\Delta F = a(K) \theta^{\beta_1} e^{-gt} \tag{4.16}$$

The parameters β_1, g, and $a(K)$, along with the critical value θ^*, are found from the boundary conditions (4.11)–(4.14). By substituting Eq. (4.16) for ΔF into Eq. (4.10), we know that β_1 must be a solution to the fundamental quadratic equation

$$\tfrac{1}{2}\sigma^2 \beta_1(\beta_1 - 1) + (r - \delta)\beta_1 - r - g = 0 \tag{4.17}$$

From condition (4.11), β_1 must be the positive solution to this equation, i.e.,

$$\beta_1 = \tfrac{1}{2} - \frac{(r - \delta)}{\sigma^2} + \sqrt{[(r - \delta)/\sigma^2 - \tfrac{1}{2}]^2 + 2(r + g)/\sigma^2} \; > 1 \tag{4.18}$$

From conditions (4.12) and (4.13), the critical value θ^* is given by

$$\theta^*(K,t) = \left(\frac{\beta_1}{\beta_1 - 1}\right)\left(\frac{\eta\delta}{\eta - 1}\right) K^{1/\eta} k_0 e^{\rho t} \qquad (4.19)$$

Substituting this into boundary condition (4.12) gives the following expression for $a(K)$:

$$a(K) = (\beta_1 - 1)^{\beta_1 - 1}\left(\frac{\eta - 1}{\eta\delta\beta_1}\right)^{\beta_1} K^{-\beta_1/\eta} k_0^{1-\beta_1} e^{[g - \rho(\beta_1 - 1)]t} \qquad (4.20)$$

Since $a(K)$ cannot depend on t, $g = \rho[\beta_1(g) - 1]$. Substituting Eq. (4.18) for $\beta_1(g)$ gives

$$g = \rho\left[-\tfrac{1}{2} - \frac{(r - \delta - \rho)}{\sigma^2} + \right.$$
$$\left. \sqrt{[(r - \delta - \rho)/\sigma^2 + \tfrac{1}{2}]^2 + 2\delta/\sigma^2}\right] > 0 \qquad (4.21)$$

This solution for g and the relationship between g and β_1 can be seen more intuitively by rewriting (4.17) as

$$g = \tfrac{1}{2}\sigma^2\beta(\beta - 1) + (r - \delta)\beta - r$$

and plotting this along with the line $g = \rho[\beta - 1]$, as shown in Figure 4.1. The solution for g and β_1 is found at that intersection of these two curves at which $\beta > 1$.

Here, $\beta_1/(\beta_1 - 1) > 1$ is the standard "wedge" that arises in irreversible investment problems. But as $\rho \to \infty$, $\beta_1 \to \infty$ and $g \to \infty$. This can be seen algebraically from Eqs. (4.17) and (4.21) (or graphically from Figure 4.1) by observing that as ρ increases, the line $g = \rho(\beta - 1)$ twists counterclockwise around the point (1,0). Then $\beta_1/(\beta_1 - 1) \to 1$, so that for $t = 0$, $\theta^* \to k_0/\omega(K)$, i.e., the value it

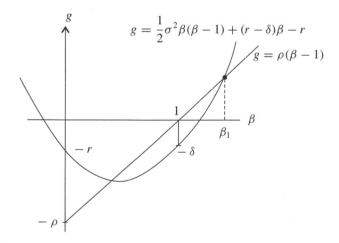

Figure 4.1 Complete irreversibility, partial expandability—graphs of Eq. (4.17) and the line $g = \rho(\beta - 1)$, providing solution for g and β_1.

would have in the absence of uncertainty. One can also see from Figure 4.1 that if $\rho \to \infty$, $\beta_1 \to \infty$ and $g \to \infty$, so that $\Delta F(K; \theta, t) = 0$ for $t > 0$, and

$$\Delta F = \max [0, \, \omega(K)\theta - k_0]$$

for $t = 0$. In this case ΔF is either zero or the net present value of the incremental investment—there is no option to invest after $t = 0$.

Figure 4.2 shows the optimal threshold $\theta^*(K, t)$, plotted as a function of capacity (K) for three values of t. (The parameter values are $r = 0.05$, $\delta = 0.05$, $\sigma = 0.40$, $\eta = 1.20$, $\rho = 0.20$, and $k_0 = 3.0$.) Observe that the threshold boundary moves up over time as the cost of investing increases. Figure 4.3 shows $\theta^*(K, t)$ as a function of K at $t = 3$, for three different values of the volatility σ. As is typical in investment problems of this kind, the value of the call option increases as σ increases, and so does the threshold θ^* that triggers investment.

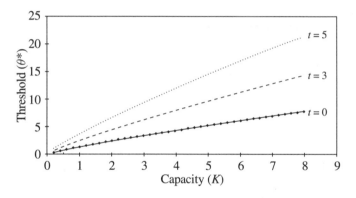

Figure 4.2   Complete irreversibility, partial expandability—demand threshold $\theta^*(K, t)$ as a function of capacity K. Parameter values: $r = 0.05$, $\delta = 0.05$, $\sigma = 0.40$, $\eta = 1.20$, $\rho = 0.20$, and $k_0 = 3.0$.

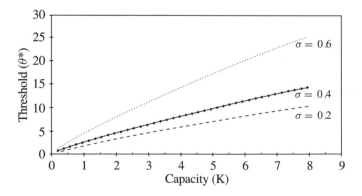

Figure 4.3   Complete irreversibility, partial expandability—dependence of investment threshold $\theta^*(K, t)$ on volatility σ.

Finally, if in addition to $s = \infty$ we let $\rho = 0$, we have the case that has received the most attention in the literature, namely complete irreversibility and complete expandability. In this special case, $g = 0$, β_1 is the solution to the standard quadratic equation, and θ^* becomes independent of time (see Dixit and Pindyck, 1996).

4.3.2 Partial Reversibility, No Expandability

This is the case for which $\rho = \infty$ and $s > 0$, so the firm can disinvest but cannot expand. Now the solution to Eq. (4.6) for ΔV is of the form

$$\Delta V(K; \theta, t) = b(K)\,\theta^{\beta_2} e^{-ht} + \left(\frac{\eta - 1}{\eta\delta}\right) K^{-1/\eta}\theta \qquad (4.22)$$

where the first term on the right-hand side is the value of the put option to sell the unit of capital. This solution can be verified by direct substitution in (4.6), and expressions for β_2, h, $b(K)$, and the critical value θ^{**} can be found using boundary conditions (4.7)–(4.9).

Investment can either occur immediately (at $t = 0$) or never, so ΔF is given by the standard NPV rule:

$$\Delta F(K; 0, t) = \max[0,\ \Delta V(K; \theta, t) - k_0] \qquad (4.23)$$

for $t = 0$, and $\Delta F = 0$ for $t > 0$. In this case the boundary conditions that apply to ΔV are not linked to those for ΔF, so we can determine ΔV independently from ΔF. Since the firm has no call option to invest in the future, it will set its initial capacity K at the point where $\Delta V(K; \theta, 0) = k_0$. Hence the only issue is to determine ΔV.

Substituting Eq. (4.22) into (4.6) and using boundary condition (4.7), we find that β_2 is the negative solution to the quadratic Eq. (4.17), with g replaced by h, i.e.,

$$\beta_2 = \tfrac{1}{2} - \frac{(r - \delta)}{\sigma^2} - \sqrt{[(r - \delta)/\sigma^2 - \tfrac{1}{2}]^2 + 2(r + h)/\sigma^2} < 0 \qquad (4.24)$$

To obtain solutions for h, $b(K)$, and θ^{**}, we proceed as in the previous case, using boundary conditions (4.8) and (4.9) and the fact that $b(K)$ must be independent of t:

$$\theta^{**}(K, t) = \left(\frac{\beta_2}{\beta_2 - 1}\right) \left(\frac{\eta\delta}{\eta - 1}\right) K^{1/\eta} k_0 e^{-st} \qquad (4.25)$$

$$b(K) = -\frac{1}{\beta_2} \left(\frac{\beta_2 - 1}{\beta_2}\right)^{\beta_2 - 1} \left(\frac{\eta - 1}{\eta\delta}\right)^{\beta_2} K^{-\beta_2/\eta} k_0^{1-\beta_2} \qquad (4.26)$$

and

$$h = s\left[\tfrac{1}{2} + \frac{(r - \delta + s)}{\sigma^2} + \sqrt{[(r - \delta + s)\sigma^2 + \tfrac{1}{2}]^2 + 2\delta/\sigma^2}\right] > s \qquad (4.27)$$

Note that $0 < \beta_2/(\beta_2 - 1) < 1$. As σ increases, β_2 increases toward 0, so that this multiple becomes smaller in magnitude. Thus the more uncertainty there is, the lower is the critical value of θ that will trigger disinvestment. This is a standard result [see the model of entry and exit in Dixit (1989) or Chapter 7 of Dixit and Pindyck (1996)], but now this multiple depends on s, the rate at which the resale value of capital is falling. The larger is s, the closer this multiple is to one, and the smaller is $b(K)$ and hence the value of the put option. As $s \to \infty$, $\beta_2 \to -\infty$, and $\beta_2/(\beta_2 - 1) \to 1$; then there is no put option, so that for $t = 0$, $\theta^{**}(K) \to k_0/\omega(K)$, which is the value it would have in the absence of uncertainty.

Figure 4.4 shows the solution for the critical disinvestment threshold $\theta^{**}(K, t)$, again plotted as a function of capacity (K) for three values of t. (As before, the parameter values are $r = 0.05$, $\delta = 0.05$, $\sigma = 0.40$, $\eta = 1.20$, and $k_0 = 3.0$, and now $s = 0.20$.) Observe that the boundary moves down over time as the price that the firm can receive for installed capital decreases. Figure 4.5 shows $\theta^{**}(K, t)$ as a function of K at $t = 3$, for three different values of σ. Since the value of the firm's put option increases as σ increases, the threshold that triggers disinvestment moves down.

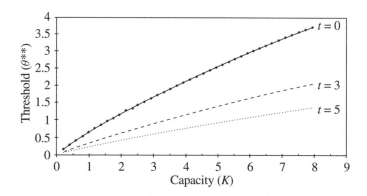

Figure 4.4   Partial reversibility, no expandability—disinvestment threshold $\theta^{**}(K, t)$ as a function of capacity K. Parameter values: $r = 0.05$, $\delta = 0.05$, $\sigma = 0.40$, $\eta = 1.20$, $k_0 = 3.0$, and $s = 0.20$.

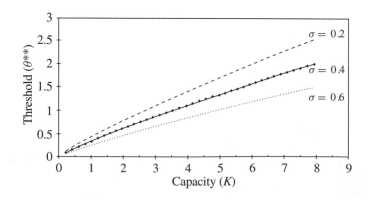

Figure 4.5   Partial reversibility, no expandability—dependence of disinvestment threshold $\theta^{**}(K, t)$ on volatility σ.

4.3.3 The General Case with Expandability and Reversibility

In the general case, both ρ and s are positive and finite. Now ΔV satisfies Eq. (4.6) subject to boundary conditions (4.7)–(4.9), and ΔF satisfies Eq. (4.10), subject to boundary conditions (4.11)–(4.14). However, Eqs. (4.6) and (4.10) cannot be solved analytically in this case. Furthermore, it is difficult even to obtain numerical solutions; although these are parabolic partial differential equations, they are linked to each other through the two sets of boundary conditions. Fortunately, however, we can obtain approximate solutions as long as gt and ht are not too small.

If gt and ht are large, the investment and disinvestment boundaries will be far apart, and thus the two sets of boundary conditions will be relatively independent of each other. (Intuitively, if the investment boundary is hit, it is likely to take a long time before the disinvestment boundary is also hit, and vice versa.) In that case, the solutions to (4.6) and (4.10) will be of the time-separable form:

$$\Delta F = A(K)\,\theta^{\beta_1} e^{-gt} \tag{4.28}$$

and

$$\Delta V(K; \theta, t) = B(K)\,\theta^{\beta_2} e^{-ht} + \left(\frac{\eta - 1}{\eta \delta}\right) K^{-1/\eta}\theta \tag{4.29}$$

with β_1, β_2, g, and h as given by Eqs. (4.18), (4.24), (4.21), and (4.27). The functions $A(K)$ and $B(K)$ and the critical values $\theta^*(K, t)$ and $\theta^{**}(K, t)$ can then be found from boundary conditions (4.8), (4.9), (4.12), and (4.13). Making these substitutions, the conditions become

$$B(K)(\theta^{**})^{\beta_2} e^{-ht} + \omega(K)\theta^{**} = A(K)(\theta^{**})^{\beta_1} e^{-gt} + k_0 e^{-st} \tag{4.30}$$

$$\beta_2 B(K)(\theta^{**})^{\beta_2-1} e^{-ht} + \omega(K) = \beta_1 A(K)(\theta^{**})^{\beta_1-1} e^{-gt} \tag{4.31}$$

$$A(K)(\theta^*)^{\beta_1} e^{-gt} = B(K)(\theta^*)^{\beta_2} e^{-ht} + \omega(K)\theta^* - k_0 e^{\rho t} \tag{4.32}$$

$$\beta_1 A(K)(\theta^*)^{\beta_1-1} e^{-gt} = \beta_2 B(K)(\theta^*)^{\beta_2-1} e^{-ht} + \omega(K) \tag{4.33}$$

For values of K and t, these four equations can be solved numerically for $A(K)$, $B(K)$, $\theta^*(K, t)$, and $\theta^{**}(K, t)$. We can also check the accuracy of these approximate solutions by determining whether $A(K)$ and $B(K)$ remain constant as t varies.

This is illustrated in Figure 4.6, which shows numerical solutions of Eqs. (4.30)–(4.33) for $A(K)$ and $B(K)$ for $K = 3$, as t varies from 0 to 9. (The parameter values are $r = \delta = 0.05$, $\sigma = 0.40$, $\eta = 1.20$, $k_0 = 3.0$, and $\rho = s = 0.20$.) Observe that $A(K)$ and $B(K)$ become roughly constant once t is greater than about 2.

Figure 4.7 shows solutions for the investment and disinvestment thresholds, $\theta^*(K)$ and $\theta^{**}(K)$, as functions of K for $t = 2$ and 5. There are now three regions: If $\theta > \theta^*(K)$, the firm should invest immediately, increasing K (and thus increasing θ^*) until $\theta = \theta^*$. If $\theta < \theta^{**}(K)$, the firm should disinvest until $\theta = \theta^{**}(K)$. If $\theta^{**} \le \theta \le \theta^*$, the firm should take no action. Note that the thresholds $\theta^*(K)$ and $\theta^{**}(K)$ move apart over time, increasing the zone of inaction. This is illustrated in Figure 4.8, which shows θ^* and θ^{**} as functions of time for $K = 3$.

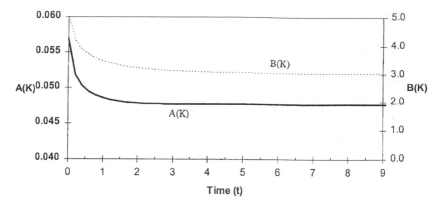

Figure 4.6 General case—numerical solutions for $A(K)$ and $B(K)$. Parameter values: $r = \delta = 0.05$, $\sigma = 0.40$, $\eta = 1.20$, $k_0 = 3.0$, and $\rho = s = 0.20$.

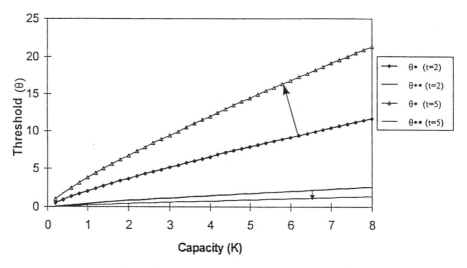

Figure 4.7 General case—investment and disinvestment thresholds, θ^* and θ^{**}, as functions of capacity K, for $t = 2$ and $t = 5$.

Figure 4.9 shows sample paths for the demand shift variable $\theta(t)$ and for capacity $K(t)$. Starting with no capital, the firm immediately invests at time t_0, bringing its capacity to K_0, such that $\theta_0 = \theta^*(K_0, t_0)$. From t_0 until t_1, $\theta^{**}(K_0, t) < \theta(t) < \theta^*(K_0, t)$, so the firm neither invests nor disinvests. Over this interval of time, the investment threshold θ^* increases gradually as the cost of adding capacity increases, while the threshold θ^{**} decreases gradually as the selling price of used capacity decreases. At time t_1, $\theta(t)$ hits the upper threshold θ^*, so the firm adds extra capacity. Over the interval t_1 to t_2, $\theta(t)$ is increasing, and capacity is increased from K_0 to K_1, so that $\theta^*(K, t) = \theta(t)$.[6] From t_2 to t_3, $\theta^{**}(K_1, t) < \theta(t) < \theta^*(K_1, t)$, so the firm is

---

[6] Note that the lower threshold $\theta^{**}(K, t)$ also increases as K increases.

again inactive. At time t_3, $\theta(t)$ hits the lower threshold θ^{**} and the firm disinvests. From t_3 to t_4, $\theta(t)$ continues to fall and the firm's capacity is gradually reduced from K_1 to K_2. After t_4 the firm is again inactive. Observe that as time goes on, $\theta^*(K_2, t)$ gradually increases and $\theta^{**}(K_2, t)$ decreases, so that the periods of investment or disinvestment become less and less frequent.

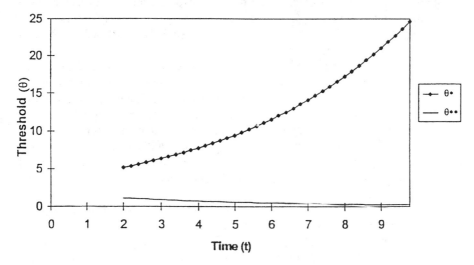

Figure 4.8 General case—movement of investment and disinvestment thresholds over time, for a given capacity $K = 3$.

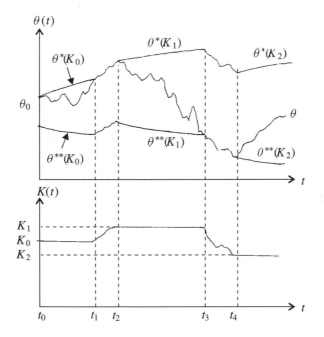

Figure 4.9 Optimal investment and disinvestment—sample paths of $\theta(t)$ and capacity $K(t)$.

4.4 STATIC VERSUS DYNAMIC EFFECTS OF SUNK COSTS

A significant difference between the *current* prices at which capital can be bought or sold will by itself create a zone of inaction in which the firm neither increases nor decreases capacity. This "static effect" of sunk costs of entry and exit is a standard result (e.g., see Chapter 7 of Dixit and Pindyck, 1996). Further, the expectation that the purchase and sales prices will diverge further *in the future* also affects the *current* investment thresholds. It is useful to separate these "static" and "dynamic" effects of limited expandability and reversibility.

Let us begin at some time t_1 when the purchase price of a unit of capital, k_p, exceeds the resale price, k_r. To determine the static effect of this differential, we calculate the investment and disinvestment thresholds, $\theta^*(K)$ and $\theta^{**}(K)$, under the assumption that these prices will remain fixed over time from t_1 onward.[7] Next, we calculate $\theta^*(K, t)$ and $\theta^{**}(K, t)$ under the assumption that at any future time $t > t_1$, the purchase price will be $k_p e^{\rho(t-t_1)}$ and the resale price will be $k_r e^{-s(t-t_1)}$. Although this "dynamic" $\theta^*(K, t)$ will rise over time and the "dynamic" $\theta^{**}(K, t)$ will fall over time, it is of interest to compare the static and dynamic thresholds at the initial time, t_1.

This is illustrated in Figure 4.10, starting out at $t = 5$ with $k_p = k_0 e$ and $k_r = k_0 e^{-1}$. (The other parameter values are $r = \delta = 0.05$, $\sigma = 0.40$, $\eta = 1.20$, $k_0 = 3.0$, and $K = 3$.) Static thresholds are calculated assuming k_p and k_r remain fixed at these levels, while dynamic thresholds are calculated assuming that $k_p(t) = k_0 e^{\rho t}$ and $k_r(t) = k_0 e^{-st}$. Initially the zone of inaction is smaller in the dynamic case than in the static one. However, this zone of inaction grows in the dynamic case as θ^* rises and θ^{**} falls, and it eventually exceeds the zone in the static case.

Why is $\theta^*(K)$ initially lower in the dynamic case? There are two forces at work, with opposite effects. First, the fact that the purchase price of capital is expected to rise in the future reduces the value of the firm's call option on an incremental unit of capital, which reduces the value of waiting and so reduces $\theta^*(K)$. Second, the fact that the resale price of capital is expected to fall in the future reduces the value of the firm's put option to abandon installed capital, and so pushes $\theta^*(K)$ up. In the example shown in Figure 4.10 the first effect outweighs the second, so $\theta^*(K)$ falls.

The situation is similar with respect to $\theta^{**}(K)$. Again, the fact that the resale price k_r is expected to fall reduces the value of the firm's put option on an incremental unit of capital, which reduces the value of waiting to disinvest, and pushes $\theta^{**}(K)$ up. And the fact that the purchase price k_p is expected to rise reduces the value of the call option, which raises the cost of disinvesting now, and pushes $\theta^{**}(K)$ down. Once again, in this example the first effect outweighs the second, so $\theta^{**}(K)$ rises.

Of course, the magnitudes of these effects depend on various parameter values, besides those of ρ and s. For example, Figures 4.11 and 4.12 show the static and dynamic thresholds, and their movements over time, for two different values of the volatility of demand fluctuations, σ; when σ is larger, both the static and dynamic investment thresholds are higher, and the static and dynamic disinvestment thresholds are lower.

---

[7] The thresholds will, of course, also be fixed through time.

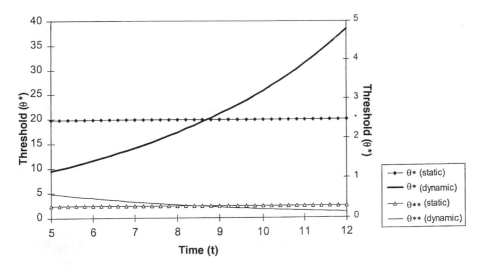

Figure 4.10 Investment and disinvestment thresholds for static versus dynamic capital costs. Starting at $t = 5$, purchase price is $k_p = k_0 e$ and resale price is $k_r = k_0 e^{-1}$. Other parameters: $r = \delta = 0.05$, $\sigma = 0.40$, $\eta = 1.20$, $k_0 = 3.0$, $K = 3$, and $s = \rho = 0.2$.

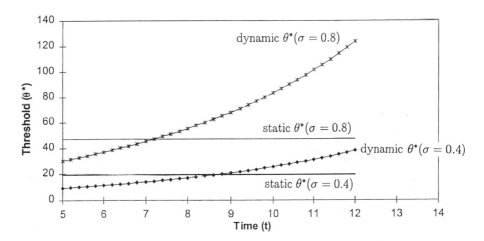

Figure 4.11 Static and dynamic investment thresholds for different levels of volatility ($\sigma = 0.4$ and 0.8).

Now that we have a better understanding of the source and nature of the dynamic effects, we can show their dependence on the rates of change of the purchase and resale prices of capital, ρ and s, respectively. We do this for a representative case in Table 4.1. The initial investment cost is 3 and the initial resale value is 1. This gap and the uncertainty ($\sigma = 0.4$) are so large that under static conditions ($\rho = s = 0$ from here on) the initial investment threshold is more than 6.5, and

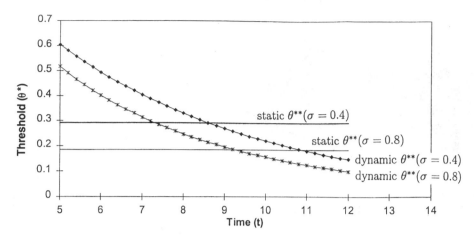

Figure 4.12   Static and dynamic disinvestment thresholds for different levels of volatility ($\sigma = 0.4$ and 0.8).

the initial disinvestment threshold less than 0.1. Table 4.1 shows what happens to the corresponding initial values of the dynamic thresholds as we vary ρ and s. Panel A shows that the dynamic investment threshold θ^* decreases as ρ increases, since the call option becomes less valuable. In fact, for very large values of ρ, it may become optimal to invest even though θ is less than the purchase price of capital; the latter is expected to grow so fast that it pays the firm to acquire the capital right away while it is cheap. Also, θ^* increases as s increases, because the put option of disinvesting is less valuable. These results confirm the intuition we gave above. But the numerical calculations reveal an interesting insensitivity: the effect of s on θ^* is very small. The gap between the two thresholds is sufficiently large that when θ is at the upper threshold, it is unlikely to fall to the lower threshold in the reasonable future. Therefore options that get exercised in that unlikely and remote eventuality do not have a significant effect on today's decision. The investment and disinvestment thresholds effectively become separated, as in the case discussed earlier in Sections 4.3.1 and 4.3.2. Given our assumption of a widening gap between purchase and resale prices, this seems to be a robust feature of our numerical calculations, and it may provide a useful simplification for the solution of combined investment and disinvestment problems when one or both of the degrees of irreversibility and uncertainty are large.[8]

Panel B of Table 4.1 shows the dynamic disinvestment threshold θ^{**} as we vary ρ and s. The results confirm the intuition stated above: the threshold rises as s increases because the put option exercised by disinvesting is less valuable, and it falls as ρ increases because the call option that would be acquired upon investment is less valuable. Again we find an effective separation of the two decisions: θ^{**} is relatively insensitive to changes in ρ, particularly for higher values.

---

[8] Bonomo (1994) discusses a similar issue in the context of models of impulse control, namely when a one-sided s–S rule is a sufficiently good approximation to a two-sided s–S policy.

Table 4.1
Effects of ρ and s on the Investment and Disinvestment Thresholds[a]

		s		
ρ	0.0	0.2	0.4	0.6
	A. *Initial dynamic investment threshold* $\theta^*(t_1)$			
0.0	6.586	6.716	6.716	6.716
0.2	3.073	3.144	3.144	3.144
0.4	2.469	2.528	2.528	2.528
	B. *Initial dynamic disinvestment threshold* $\theta^{**}(t_1)$			
0.0	0.098	0.246	0.283	0.300
0.2	0.084	0.201	0.231	0.244
0.4	0.084	0.200	0.230	0.244

[a] Parameters: $r = 0.05$, $\delta = 0.05$, $\sigma = 0.4$, $\eta = 1.2$, $k_p = 3$, $k_r = 1$. Static thresholds: $\theta^* = 6.58$, $\theta^{**} = 0.098$.

4.5 CAPACITY-DEPENDENT COSTS

In this section we examine endogenous variations in the costs of investing and disinvesting. We briefly consider situations in which the ability of the firm to add or reduce capacity in the future is dependent on its own past actions, in particular on the amount of capacity that it already has in place, rather than the amount of time that has elapsed.

Specifically, we assume that the firm can add capacity at any time in the future at a cost $k_0 + \rho(K)$ per unit of capital, with $d\rho/dK > 0$. In effect, it becomes more expensive to add capacity the more capacity the firm already has. Such limits to expandability may be driven by market parameters, such as population and available land, but depend on the firm's own actions rather than the actions of its competitors. In the simplest case, the incremental cost of capacity expansion may be linear, i.e., $\rho(K) = \rho K$. Then, if $\rho = \infty$ there is no expandability (even from zero), while if $\rho = 0$ there is complete expandability.

Likewise, we assume that the firm can sell off capacity at any time in the future such that if its current capacity is K, it will receive $s_0 k_0 + s_1 \rho(K)$ for an incremental unit, with $0 \le s_0 \le 1$ and $s_1 < 1$. In the simplest linear case, the firm receives $s_0 k_0 + s_1 \rho K$. Thus the degree of irreversibility is different for each marginal unit. We would expect that irreversibility would be greater the greater is K, since the demand for used industry-specific capital is likely to be smaller the greater is the amount of installed capacity already in place. In this case, $s_1 < s_0$. Also, it might be the case that $s_1 < 0$, so that if K is large enough the firm receives a negative amount on its sale of an incremental unit. This could occur, for example, if the firm faces land reclamation costs. Finally, if $s_0 = s_1 = 0$ there is complete irreversibility, and if $s_0 = s_1 = 1$ there is complete reversibility.

Equations (4.6) and (4.10) will again apply for ΔV and ΔF, but now without the ΔV_t and ΔF_t terms. Hence the investment problem is now much simpler: θ^{**} and θ^* each depends only on K, and not on t. In the general case, the boundary conditions again result in four nonlinear equations for $A(K)$, $B(K)$, $\theta^{**}(K)$, and $\theta^*(K)$, which can easily be solved numerically for each value of K.

We do not present numerical solutions here because the basic effects are similar to those in the entry/exit models discussed in Dixit and Pindyck (1996). What is different here is that the investment and disinvestment thresholds, $\theta^*(K)$ and $\theta^{**}(K)$, depend on K. As K increases, the direct value (i.e., the present value of the marginal revenue stream) of an incremental unit of capital falls, as does the value of the call option on the unit. The drop in the direct value raises the investment threshold $\theta^*(K)$, while the drop in the option value reduces the threshold. The first effect dominates, however, so that $\theta^*(K)$ increases with K. The opposite may be true for the disinvestment threshold, $\theta^{**}(K)$. As K increases, the direct value of the incremental unit of capital falls, but the value of the put option on the unit increases. The degree of reversibility (i.e., the resale value of capital) determines whether the value of the put option exceeds the direct value of the incremental unit. If it does, $\theta^{**}(K)$ will also increase with K.

4.6 CONCLUDING REMARKS

We have analyzed how the call and put options associated with limited expandability and reversibility interact to affect a firm's optimal capacity decisions and the evolution of capacity over time. Expandability and reversibility can take a variety of forms. For example, a firm might be able to expand only at specific points in time (e.g., a forest products or extractive resource firm might have to wait for the government to auction off land or resource reserves), in which case its ability to sell existing capital might occur unpredictably as a Poisson arrival (e.g., when there are very few potential buyers who might become interested in a specialized piece of capital). We have examined here only a very special form of expandability and reversibility—namely, one in which capital purchase and sales prices evolve exogenously with time, or endogenously with the level of installed capacity. Nonetheless, we believe this analysis helps to elucidate the basic effects. Most importantly, we can see how the future rates of growth of the investment cost and the resale price of capital affect the values of the call and put options associated with expansion and disinvestment. Our numerical results reveal that the investment and disinvestment decisions become separated when the initial gap between the purchase and resale prices of capital is substantial, or the rate at which this gap grows is rapid. This condition simplifies both the analytical and numerical solution of these problems.

This analysis can be extended or generalized in several ways. (1) Various aspects of increased realism can be added to the model, albeit at the cost of increased complexity. For example, we took variable costs to be zero, so that we could ignore the firm's operating options. It would be messy but not overly difficult to extend our model by including a positive variable cost and allowing the firm to vary its capacity utilization. Similarly, other operating options can be added. (2) We considered a firm's decision problem in isolation, treating as exogenous the rates of variation of the purchase and resale prices, whether as functions of time or as functions of existing capacity. These can be endogenized in a more complete general equilibrium analysis. (3) We confined ourselves to a setting in which the maximization problem is well behaved. An aspect of this was our assumption in the previous section that the purchase price of capital increases with capacity. If instead we allowed the purchase price to decrease with capacity, the firm would enjoy increasing returns to capacity expansion and its optimal policy could consist of infrequent large jumps in its capital stock. Dixit (1995) shows how to find the optimal timing and size of such jumps, but numerical work for more specific parameterized models can provide further useful insights. (4) The physical depreciation of capital can be modeled more realistically. The resale price of a newly installed machine would equal its purchase price, but would fall with the *age* of the machine, not with *calendar time* as in our present model. This, however, would require keeping track of the installation dates or age profiles of the entire stock of machines, making the state variable infinite dimensional, and presenting daunting modeling and numerical solution challenges.

ACKNOWLEDGMENTS

The research leading to this chapter was supported by the National Science Foundation through grants to both authors, and by M.I.T.'s Center for Energy and Environmental Policy Research. Our thanks to Tomomi Kumagai for superb research assistance and for pointing out errors in earlier drafts, and to Michael Brennan, Lenos Trigeorgis, and two anonymous referees for their helpful comments and suggestions.

REFERENCES

Abel, A. B., A. K. Dixit, J. C. Eberly, and R. S. Pindyck. (1996). Options, the Value of Capital, and Investment. *Quarterly Journal of Economics* 111(446), 753–777.

Bonomo, M. (1994). Optimal Two-Sided and Suboptimal One-Sided Pricing Rules. Working Paper No. 313, Pontificia Universidade Catolica, Rio de Janeiro.

Brennan, M. J., and E. S. Schwartz. (1985). Evaluating Natural Resource Investments. *Journal of Business* 58, 135–157.

Dixit, A. K. (1989). Entry and Exit Decisions Under Uncertainty. *Journal of Political Economy* 97(3), 620–638.

Dixit, A. K. (1992). Investment and Hysteresis. *Journal of Economic Perspectives* 6(1), 107–132.

Dixit, A. K. (1995). Irreversible Investment with Uncertainty and Scale Economies. *Journal of Economic Dynamics and Control* 19(1), 327–350.

Dixit, A. K., and R. S. Pindyck. (1996). *Investment Under Uncertainty*. Princeton, NJ: Princeton University Press (second printing).

Kulatilaka, N. (1995). Operating Flexibilities in Capital Budgeting: Substitutability and Complementarity in Real Options. In L. Trigeorgis (ed.), *Real Options in Capital Investment*. New York: Praeger.

McDonald, R., and D. R. Siegel. (1985). Investment and the Valuation of Firms When There Is an Option to Shut Down. *International Economic Review* 26, 331–349.

Myers, S. C., and S. Majd. (1984). Calculating Abandonment Value Using Option Pricing Theory. Working Paper No. 1462-83, MIT Sloan School of Management.

Pindyck, R. S. (1988). Irreversible Investment, Capacity Choice, and the Value of the Firm. *American Economic Review* 79(5), 969–985.

Pindyck, R. S. (1991). Irreversibility, Uncertainty, and Investment. *Journal of Economic Literature* 29(3), 1110–1152.

Trigeorgis, L. (1993). The Nature of Option Interactions and the Valuation of Investments with Multiple Real Options. *Journal of Financial and Quantitative Analysis* 28(1), 1–20.

Trigeorgis, L. (1996). *Real Options*. Cambridge, MA: MIT Press.

5

Entry and Exit Strategies under Non-Gaussian Distributions

SVETLANA I. BOYARCHENKO

SERGEI Z. LEVENDORSKIĬ

This chapter develops a discrete-time model of entry and exit strategies under uncertainty, extending the standard model of investment based on the Brownian motion to the case of non-Gaussian stochastic processes. It is shown that the values of the entry and exit thresholds change significantly as the Gaussian distribution is replaced by a non-Gaussian one with the same variance. The upper (entry) threshold becomes higher, implying it is optimal to wait more, while the lower (exit) one does not decrease as much. The discrepancy between the thresholds may grow as volatility rises.

5.1 INTRODUCTION

To better understand the investment behavior of competitive firms or industries, managers and policy makers should view the evolution of the firm as a dynamic process. In the course of this dynamic process, the firm is periodically hit by various shocks, some of which affect the firm favorably and induce new capital investment, while others bring forth disinvestment or exit. Since reversal of decisions may be costly and take time, preventing instantaneous adjustment of the capital stock, anticipation about the future economic environment and choices affects current investment decisions. To assess a new investment project or design an optimal investment strategy for the firm, one needs models that take into account as many of these essential elements as possible, but yet are tractable and preferably admit closed-form solutions or a reduction to simpler problems.

The investment literature of the last two decades has recognized the importance of the interaction between (partial) irreversibility of investment or disinvestment, uncertainty in the future economic environment, and the choice of the timing and/or scale of new investment or disinvestment.[1] For any of these models of firm investment behavior in a stochastic economic environment, assumptions about the nature of stochastic processes are crucial. In the majority of papers, the continuous-time stochastic processes are used to model returns or prices. Usually, geometric Brownian motion is assumed for the movement of underlying variables such as the general price level or prices of financial instruments (e.g., Fisher, 1975; Black and Scholes, 1973); in some cases, the (geometric) mean-reverting process is used (e.g., Dixit and Pindyck, 1994; Metcalf and Hassett, 1995).

In the cases mentioned above, a stochastic shift variable X is characterized by a stochastic differential equation of the form

$$dX = \alpha(X, t) \, dt + \sigma(X, t) \, dz \tag{5.1}$$

where dz is the increment of a standard Wiener process (having zero mean and unit variance). Model (5.1) is very convenient since it leads to tractable economic models and often allows obtaining closed-form solutions.

At the same time, however, there is some empirical evidence against the modeling of observables as normal random variables. For instance, Mantegna and Stanley (1995) find that the probability distribution of the Standard & Poor's 500 index can be described by a non-Gaussian process with dynamics that, for the central part of the distribution, correspond to the dynamics predicted for a Lévy stable process. The shorter the observation interval, the more do financial–returns data tend to deviate from the benchmark normal distribution, exhibiting leptokurtosis (fat tails). More specifically, in the central part of the distribution, the falloff is governed by a power law [a normal distribution decays much faster, as $\exp(-\alpha x^2)$]. Eventually, in the tails of the distribution, the falloff deviates from that for a Lévy stable process: it is approximately exponential, ensuring that (as one would expect for a price difference distribution) the variance of the distribution is finite. Recently, Cont et al. (1997) give a formula for the probability distribution of the Standard & Poor's 500 index futures, which explicitly describes the exponential falloff and fits the data.

An explanation of fat tails can be provided by the theory of "self–organized criticality"—see Bak (1996) and the bibliography therein—which deals with situations when power–law distributions appear. This happens in time series when very large fluctuations cannot, in general, be ignored in favor of the cumulative effect of small ones. The emergence of power laws in economics can be explained within the framework of different economic models (e.g., see De Long et al., 1990; Romer, 1993). Romer suggests that in complex systems, catastrophes—that is, very large fluctuations—occur more frequently than implied by the Gaussian distribution.

However, one should expect truncated fat tails in economic processes because of the influence of barriers of a different sort: extreme fluctuations are less probable than in physical systems since new agents (e.g., firms) appear or some of the old ones disappear (exit) from the market, causing damping of the fluctuations.

---

[1] See Merton (1971), Pindyck (1982, 1988), Abel (1983), Bertola (1990), Dixit (1993), Dixit and Pindyck (1994), Abel and Eberly (1994), Bertola and Caballero (1994), Metcalf and Hassett (1995), Abel et al. (1996), Caballero and Pindyck (1996); see also the bibliography in Dixit and Pindyck (1994).

This paper is a sequel to Boyarchenko and Levendorskiĭ (1997). In that paper, we suggested a discrete–time model that

1. was almost as tractable as the most popular continuous–time models based on the Brownian motion;
2. used only observed quantities and did not make specific assumptions regarding the probability distribution.

In particular, we did not assume that it is possible to pass to the limit ($\Delta t \to 0$) and describe the process by a continuous–time model. We believe that this model is especially useful in cases in which the time interval between observations is not very small, as it may be the case with real options. The only essential requirement was that the probability distribution is integrable with an exponential weight $\exp(\lambda|x|)$, $\lambda > 1$. For simplicity, we considered only symmetric distributions, though the method is applicable to more general distributions as well. We applied our method to the simplest variant of the planner's problem, following the treatment in Dixit (1993, Section 2). The uncertainty was on the demand side; it was assumed that there was no variable cost and the investment was completely irreversible.

In this chapter, we consider the more realistic situations in which

1. a variable cost is present, and
2. the investment is partially reversible in the form of firm exit as well as entry timing options. That is, we examine not only the upper boundary (for the price of the output), which triggers new investment, but also the lower boundary, which forces disinvestment or exit.

For the case of Gaussian processes, this problem was considered by Dixit (1993) and Dixit and Pindyck (1994, see also the bibliography therein); we modify the treatment of Dixit (1993) and derive a system of two nonlinear equations for the upper (entry) and lower (exit) thresholds.

In the simple case treated in Section 2 of Dixit (1993) and in Boyarchenko and Levendorskiĭ (1997), where there was no exit option (and hence no lower threshold) at all, closed–form solutions could be obtained and so it was relatively simple to compare results with the standard model. Under certain additional natural assumptions about the fat-tailed distribution, our model gave larger values for the investment threshold—to be more specific, for the factor $\beta/(\beta - 1)$, which Dixit (1993) and Dixit and Pindyck (1994) introduce into the Marshallian law.[2] (In our notation below, β_+ is analogous to β.)

In addition, we showed that our assumptions were satisfied by symmetric distributions from a three-parameter family that includes Gaussian and truncated Lévy distributions[3] and proved that the investment threshold grows, and hence investment

---

[2] The larger the factor $\beta/(\beta - 1)$, the higher the threshold and the larger the discrepancy with the Marshallian law.

[3] In the form suggested by Koponen (1995). A first variant of truncated Lévy distributions was introduced by Mantegna and Stanley—see bibliography in Mantegna and Stanley (1995); Koponen's variant allows for an analytic description in terms of the Fourier transform.

should be delayed, if we replace a Gaussian distribution with a non-Gaussian one with the same variance.[4]

In the present chapter, due to the high nonlinearity of the system when the higher and lower thresholds are unknowns, it is impossible to find an analytical solution so in applications it has to be solved numerically. This applies to both the standard model of Dixit (1993) and Dixit and Pindyck (1994) and to our model. We produce numerical examples that show the following:

1. The value of the upper (entry) threshold can increase significantly if we replace a Gaussian distribution with a non-Gaussian one with the same variance, hence optimal investment would be delayed, other things equal.

2. When investment is partially reversible with nonzero operating costs, the investment (entry) threshold always increases whereas the lower (exit) one may either increase or decrease, i.e., exit may either be enhanced or delayed depending on the properties of the distribution.

3. Whereas both the upper and lower Marshallian thresholds go to 0 as the volatility grows (implying that the region where exit is optimal shrinks along with the inaction region, while entry becomes optimal for almost all parameter values), our model gives relatively stable thresholds. When the volatility becomes quite high, even the disinvestment threshold increases and exit occurs sooner. At high levels of volatility, the incentives to invest, and especially to disinvest, become almost insensitive to further increases in volatility.

4. For the special case of completely irreversible investment with zero operating cost, we prove that in the high volatility limit (which corresponds to the condition $\beta \rightarrow 1$), the investment threshold stabilizes to a finite value, and derive an approximate Tobin-type q formula for the upper threshold. The existence of the limit is not evident since q is the product of two factors, one of which [namely, $\beta/(\beta - 1)$] goes to infinity while the other goes to zero. The latter factor enters into the Marshallian law suggesting that the investment threshold goes to zero in the high volatility limit.

5.2 THE PLANNER'S PROBLEM

Consider a planner who is contemplating investment (or disinvestment) of a unit of capital. Each unit of capital costs K to install, and the cost of abandoning a unit of capacity is J. If the investment is partially reversible, J can be negative as there can be positive salvage value (usually, $-J < K$).

The present value of the cash flow when Q units of capital are installed is given by $XC(Q)$, where X is the stochastic shift variable. The interest rate r is assumed to be constant. The variable cost per unit, v, is positive, so that the installed capital may be reduced should X fall to very low levels.

---

[4] Cont et al. (1997) found that a distribution of this family could be used to describe the Standard & Poor's 500 index futures.

The planner's objective is to maximize the present value of expected cash flows net of capital installation (or abandonment) costs, where valuation is by expected value under the equivalent martingale measure. When X rises, the planner must decide whether to install a unit of capital or not. In other words, the planner has to determine an upper threshold for X, $H(Q)$, that triggers new investment. Similarly, disinvestment will be triggered if a lower threshold, $L(Q)$, is hit.

We assume that X is observed at equally spaced discrete time intervals t_j, with $t_j - t_{j-1} \equiv \Delta t$ being fixed (and small). We assume that $X_j \equiv X(t_j)$ satisfy

$$\ln X_j - \ln X_{j-1} = \alpha \Delta t + Y_j \tag{5.2}$$

where Y_j are independently identically distributed (i.i.d.) random variables with zero mean and a probability density function $p(x)$ that admits a bound

$$p(x) \le D \exp(-\lambda |x|) \tag{5.3}$$

where D and $\lambda > 1$ are independent of x.[5] Note that α, p, D, and λ depend on Δt, and that for Gaussian distributions (5.3) holds with any λ.

Let $W(Q, X)$ denote the value of the project when the initial state has a demand shock at X and an amount Q of capacity is installed. Decomposing W into the cash flow over the next time interval, Δt, and the project continuation value, assuming that the cost is incurred at the beginning of each period, we have

$$W(Q, X_{j-1}) = \left[X_{j-1} C(Q) - vQ \right] \Delta t + E \left[W(Q, X_j) \exp(-r \Delta t) \right]$$

or

$$W(Q, X_{j-1}) = \left[X_{j-1} C(Q) - vQ \right] \Delta t + E \left\{ W \left[Q, X_{j-1} \exp(\alpha \Delta t + Y_j) \right] \right\} \exp(-r \Delta t)$$

Here X_j is demand at time t_j, $C(Q)$ is the present value of cash flow with Q units of capacity, and E is the (risk-neutral) expectation operator under the equivalent martingale measure.

If we fix j and denote $x \equiv \ln X_{j-1}$, we have

$$W \left[Q, \exp(x) \right] = \left[\exp(x) \, C(Q) - vQ \right] \Delta t + \exp(-r \Delta t)$$
$$\int_{-\infty}^{+\infty} p(y) \, W \left[Q, \exp(x + \alpha \Delta t + y) \right] dy \tag{5.4}$$

For given Q, (5.4) is a linear equation with respect to the unknown function $w(x) \equiv W[Q, \exp(x)]$:

$$w(x) = \exp(-r \Delta t)(Pw)(x + \alpha \Delta t) + f(x) \tag{5.5}$$

where $f(x) \equiv [\exp(x)C(Q) - vQ]\Delta t$, and the linear operator $P \equiv P_{\Delta t}$ acts as follows:

[5] This condition is needed to ensure that the expectation values of X_{j+1} and $X_{j+1}^{\beta_\pm}$ below are finite.

$$(Pw)(x) \equiv \int_{-\infty}^{+\infty} p(y) \, w(x+y) \, dy$$

The usual way to treat equations like (5.5) is to expand the right-hand side (RHS) of (5.5) in the Taylor series with respect to Δt, cancel zero-order terms, divide by Δt, and pass to the limit as $\Delta t \to +0$ (e.g., see Dixit and Pindyck, 1994). As a result, one obtains a second-order differential equation in w.

To implement this scheme, one has to impose certain (rather serious) conditions on the operator $P = P_{\Delta t}$ in (5.5), which may not hold for the real processes described in the introduction. In addition, the very procedure of passing to the limit as $\Delta t \to 0$ is a little dubious since it presupposes that the processes evolve in continuous time and therefore can be observed at each moment; in reality, only observations made at fixed moments of time are available, and Δt cannot be made arbitrarily small.

Our approach is to solve Eq. (5.5), without using limiting arguments. Since (5.5) is a linear inhomogeneous equation, any solution is of the form

$$w = w_1 + w_0$$

where w_1 is a particular solution to (5.5) (the same for all w) and w_0 is a solution to the corresponding homogeneous equation:

$$w(x) = \exp(-r\Delta t)(Pw)(x + \alpha \Delta t) \tag{5.6}$$

Due to the special form of $f(x) = [\exp(x)C(Q) - vQ]\Delta t$, it is natural to look for a particular solution w_1 of the form

$$w_1(x) = A \exp(x) + B \tag{5.7}$$

where A and B are constants. Denote by $M(\mu)$ the moment generating function

$$M(\mu) = \int_{-\infty}^{+\infty} p(y) \exp(\mu y) \, dy$$

and set $m(\mu) = \ln M(\mu)/\Delta t$.[6]

By substituting (5.7) into (5.5) and using the equality

$$\int_{-\infty}^{+\infty} p(y) \exp\left[\mu(x+y)\right] dy = \exp\left[\mu x + m(\mu)\Delta t\right] \tag{5.8}$$

we obtain an expression for A:

$$A\{1 - \exp\left[\left[\alpha - r + m(1)\right]\Delta t\right]\}\exp(x) = \exp(x)C(Q)\Delta t$$

giving $A = C(Q)/c(r, \alpha, \Delta t, p, 1)$, where

$$c(r, \alpha, \Delta t, p, \mu) \equiv \{1 - \exp\left[\left[\alpha \mu - r + m(\mu)\right]\Delta t\right]\}/\Delta t$$

---

[6] For a Gaussian process, $m(\mu) = \frac{1}{2}\sigma^2\mu^2$.

Similarly, we find $B = -vQ/c(r, \alpha, \Delta t, p, 0)$. The particular solution is given by

$$w_1(x) = \frac{\exp(x)C(Q)}{c(r, \alpha, \Delta t, p, 1)} - \frac{vQ}{c(r, \alpha, \Delta t, p, 0)} \tag{5.9}$$

[Note that due to Eq. (5.3), $m(1) < +\infty$.] This is the net present value of the project if no further investment or disinvestment is ever undertaken. For Q constant, the expected cash flow grows each period Δt by a factor $\exp\{[\alpha + m(1)]\Delta t\}$ and is discounted back at the rate $\exp(-r\Delta t)$, satisfying the equation

$$w(x) = \exp(x)C(Q)\Delta t + \exp\{[\alpha - r + m(1)]\Delta t\} w(x)$$

The solution is the first term in the RHS of (5.9), while the second term is the discounted life-time cost. For the RHS in (5.9) to be positive and finite, we require

$$r - \alpha - m(1) > 0 \tag{5.10}$$

In realistic economic situations, $[r - \alpha - m(1)]\Delta t$ and $r\Delta t$ are small, and therefore, approximately,

$$c(r, \alpha, \Delta t, p, 0) = r, \quad c(r, \alpha, \Delta t, p, 0) = r - \alpha - m(1)$$

up to relatively small errors. If a process is Gaussian, $m(1) = \sigma^2/2$, and $r - \alpha - m(1) = r - \alpha - \sigma^2/2$ coincides with the denominator in the corresponding formula in Dixit (1993) and Dixit and Pindyck (1994).

Consider now the homogeneous linear equation (5.6), seeking for solutions of the form $w(x) = \exp(\mu x)$. By substituting $w(x) = \exp(\mu x)$ into (5.6) and using (5.8), we see that this function is a solution to Eq. (5.6) if and only if μ is a root of the characteristic equation

$$1 - \exp\{[\alpha\mu - r + m(\mu)]\Delta t\} = 0 \tag{5.11}$$

The following theorem describes the set of real roots of Eq. (5.11).[7]

Theorem 1. *(a) Equation (5.11) has at most one positive root, β_+, and one negative root, β_-, which coincide with the real roots of the equation*

$$m(\mu) + \alpha\mu - r = 0 \tag{5.12}$$

(b) Equation (5.11) has a root on $(-\lambda, 0)[$on $(0, \lambda)]$ if and only if

$$\lim_{\mu \to -\lambda} [m(\mu) + \alpha\mu - r] > 0 \quad (\text{respectively,} \lim_{\mu \to \lambda} [m(\mu) + \alpha\mu - r] > 0) \tag{5.13}$$

Equation (5.12) plays the part of the characteristic equation in the theory of ordinary differential equations; in Dixit and Pindyck (1994) this equation is called the fundamental quadratic, since its order is two in cases arising there.

---

[7] See Theorem 2.1 in Boyarchenko and Levendorskiĭ (1997).

In Boyarchenko and Levendorskiĭ (1997) we argued that in realistic situations the nonreal roots of Eq. (5.11) have large imaginary parts. Such roots give rise to wildly oscillating solutions to the homogeneous equation. Disregarding these solutions as having little economic sense and assuming that (5.13) holds, we arrive at the following general solution of Eq. (5.5):

$$w(x) = w_1(x) + A \exp(\beta_- x) + B \exp(\beta_+ x) \tag{5.14}$$

where w_1 is given by (5.9), and $\beta_\pm$ are the real solutions to Eq. (5.12). Recall that (5.14) is valid under condition (5.10), and that w_1 and A, B depend on Q.

Having found the general solution (5.14) to Eq. (5.5), we can next proceed similarly to Dixit (1993) and Dixit and Pindyck (1994). Returning to the initial variables $X = \exp(x)$ and $W = W(Q, X)$, we can rewrite (5.14) as

$$W(Q, X) = \frac{XC(Q)}{c(1)} - \frac{vQ}{c(0)} + A(Q)X^{\beta_-} + B(Q)X^{\beta_+} \tag{5.15}$$

where $A(Q)$ and $B(Q)$ are arbitrary constants, and $c(s) \equiv c(r, \alpha, \Delta t, p, s)$.

Equation (5.15) for the value of capacity Q was derived assuming no local change in Q, therefore it is valid only in the region between the disinvestment and investment thresholds $[L(Q) < X < H(Q)]$. By using the envelope condition for the Bellman equation at the upper and lower boundaries of the inaction region $L(Q) < X < H(Q)$, we derive the following conditions:

$$W_Q(X, Q) = K + XC'(Q)\Delta t, \quad W_{QX}(X, Q) = C'(Q)\Delta t, \quad \text{at } X = H(Q) \tag{5.16}$$

$$W_Q(X, Q) = -J + XC'(Q)\Delta t, \quad W_{QX}(X, Q) = C'(Q)\Delta t, \quad \text{at } X = L(Q) \tag{5.17}$$

As $\Delta t \to 0$, (5.16) and (5.17) become the usual conditions in the continuous-time model in Dixit (1993) and Dixit and Pindyck (1994), i.e., at the upper threshold $X = H(Q)$: $W_Q = K$ and $W_{QX} = 0$, and at the lower threshold $X = L(Q)$: $W_Q = -J$ and $W_{QX} = 0$.

The four equations in (5.16) and (5.17) determine the functions $A(Q)$, $B(Q)$, and the thresholds $H(Q)$, $L(Q)$. By using (5.15), we can write these equations explicitly:

$$\frac{H(Q)C'(Q)(1 - c(1)\Delta t)}{c(1)} - \frac{v}{c(0)} + A'(Q)H(Q)^{\beta_-} + B'(Q)H(Q)^{\beta_+} = K \tag{5.18}$$

$$\frac{C'(Q)(1 - c(1)\Delta t)}{c(1)} + \beta_- A'(Q)H(Q)^{\beta_- - 1} + \beta_+ B'(Q)H(Q)^{\beta_+ - 1} = 0 \tag{5.19}$$

$$\frac{L(Q)C'(Q)(1 - c(1)\Delta t)}{c(1)} - \frac{v}{c(0)} + A'(Q)L(Q)^{\beta_-} + B'(Q)L(Q)^{\beta_+} = -J \tag{5.20}$$

$$\frac{C'(Q)(1 - c(1)\Delta t)}{c(1)} + \beta_- A'(Q)L(Q)^{\beta_- - 1} + \beta_+ B'(Q)L(Q)^{\beta_+ - 1} = 0 \tag{5.21}$$

These equations are very similar to Eqs. (3.28)–(3.31) in Dixit (1993): only the constant factors are different, and the part of α, β in Dixit (1993) is played here by β_-, β_+, respectively.

If we set $K^* = K + v/c(0)$, $K_* = -J + v/c(0)$ and use Kramer's rule, we can solve the system of Eqs. (5.18)–(5.21) with $A'(Q)L(Q)^{\beta_-}$, $A'(Q)H(Q)^{\beta_-}$, $B'(Q)L(Q)^{\beta_+}$, $B'(Q)H(Q)^{\beta_+}$ as the unknowns, obtaining

$$A'(Q)L(Q)^{\beta_-} = \frac{K_* \beta_+ + (1 - \beta_+)L(Q)C'(Q)(1 - c(1)\Delta t)/c(1)}{\beta_+ - \beta_-}$$

$$A'(Q)H(Q)^{\beta_-} = \frac{K^* \beta_+ + (1 - \beta_+)H(Q)C'(Q)(1 - c(1)\Delta t)/c(1)}{\beta_+ - \beta_-}$$

$$B'(Q)L(Q)^{\beta_+} = -\frac{K_* \beta_- + (1 - \beta_-)L(Q)C'(Q)(1 - c(1)\Delta t)/c(1)}{\beta_+ - \beta_-}$$

$$B'(Q)H(Q)^{\beta_+} = -\frac{K^* \beta_- + (1 - \beta_-)H(Q)C'(Q)(1 - c(1)\Delta t)/c(1)}{\beta_+ - \beta_-}$$

Next we can eliminate $A'(Q)$ and $B'(Q)$:

$$\left(\frac{H(Q)}{L(Q)}\right)^{\beta_-} = \frac{K^* \beta_+ + (1 - \beta_+)H(Q)C'(Q)\left[1 - c(1)\Delta t\right]/c(1)}{K_* \beta_+ + (1 - \beta_+)L(Q)C'(Q)\left[1 - c(1)\Delta t\right]/c(1)} \quad (5.22)$$

$$\left(\frac{H(Q)}{L(Q)}\right)^{\beta_+} = \frac{K^* \beta_- + (1 - \beta_-)H(Q)C'(Q)\left[1 - c(1)\Delta t\right]/c(1)}{K_* \beta_- + (1 - \beta_-)L(Q)C'(Q)\left[1 - c(1)\Delta t\right]/c(1)} \quad (5.23)$$

If we set $\omega_\pm = (\beta_\pm - 1)[1 - c(1)\Delta t]/[\beta_\pm c(1)]$ and divide the numenator and the denominator in the RHS of Eq. (5.22) [respectively, Eq. (5.23)] by β_+ (respectively, by β_-), we obtain

$$\left[\frac{H(Q)}{L(Q)}\right]^{\beta_-} = \frac{K^* - \omega_+ H(Q)C'(Q)}{K_* - \omega_+ L(Q)C'(Q)} \quad (5.24)$$

$$\left[\frac{H(Q)}{L(Q)}\right]^{\beta_+} = \frac{K^* - \omega_- H(Q)C'(Q)}{K_* - \omega_- L(Q)C'(Q)} \quad (5.25)$$

The system (5.24)–(5.25) is highly nonlinear and an analytical solution is impossible, so one has to resort to numerical simulations. The only exception is the special case of irreversible investment with zero operating cost, when there is no lower (exit) threshold and it is possible to write down an analytic expression for the upper (entry) threshold:

$$H(Q)C'(Q) = \frac{c(1)\beta_+}{\beta_+ - 1} K \quad (5.26)$$

We consider this special case in more detail in the next section, before we present general numerical simulation results in Section 5.4.

5.3 A TOBIN-TYPE FORMULA FOR THE INVESTMENT THRESHOLD

Let parameters of the model vary in such a way that $\beta_+ \to 1$. Then, using an approximate formula $c(1) \sim r - \alpha - m(1)$, and applying the Lagrange formula to $m(\beta_+) + \alpha\beta_+ - r \ (= 0)$, we obtain the approximate equality:

$$m'(1)(\beta_+ - 1) + \alpha(\beta_+ - 1) - c(1) = 0$$

Hence,

$$c(1)\beta_+/(\beta_+ - 1) = m'(1) + \alpha$$

and expression (5.26) for the investment threshold in the case of irreversible investment can be written as

$$H(Q) = qK/C'(Q)$$

where $q = m'(1) + \alpha$.

Recall that $m(\mu) = \ln M(\mu)/\Delta t$, so that

$$m'(1) = M'(1)/M(1)\Delta t \qquad (5.27)$$

and

$$M_{\Delta t}(1) = 1 + \sigma_{\Delta t}^2/2 + \text{kurtosis}/24 + \cdots \qquad (5.28)$$

$$M'_{\Delta t}(1) = \sigma_{\Delta t}^2 + \text{kurtosis}/6 + \cdots \qquad (5.29)$$

Typically, for small Δt one expects for the $\sigma_{\Delta t}^2$ to be small and for the tails in (5.28) and (5.29) to be small with respect to $\sigma_{\Delta t}^2$. If this is the case, we can simplify (5.27) and write

$$q \approx \alpha + \sigma_{\Delta t}^2/\Delta t + \text{kurtosis}/(6\Delta t) \qquad (5.30)$$

If the process is close to a Gaussian one in the sense that the kurtosis is small relative to the variance, we can simplify (5.30) further and write

$$q \approx \alpha + \sigma_{\Delta t}^2/\Delta t \qquad (5.31)$$

Note that for a Gaussian process with constant parameters α and σ, the condition $\beta_+ \to 1$ is equivalent to $\sigma^2/2 \to r - \alpha$, so that (5.31) can be written in either of the following two forms:

$$q \approx \alpha + \sigma^2 \quad \text{or} \quad q \approx r + \sigma^2/2$$

If the tails of the distribution are fat and the kurtosis is relatively large, its contribution to Eq. (5.30) cannot be neglected. That is, for fat-tailed distributions (5.30) should fit better than (5.31).

5.4 A NUMERICAL ILLUSTRATION

We will illustrate our valuation using Koponen's (1995) family of truncated Lévy distributions. For simplicity, we consider only symmetric distributions of this family given by

$$\hat{p}_\nu(k) = \exp\left\{c_1\left[\lambda^\nu - (k^2 + \lambda^2)^{\nu/2}\cos\left[\nu\arctan(k/\lambda)\right]\right]/\nu(\nu - 1)\right\} \quad (5.32)$$

where $\hat{p}_\nu(k)$ is the Fourier transform of $p_\nu(y)$, and $c_1 < 0$, $\lambda > 0$ and $\nu \in (0, 2]$, $\nu \neq 1$. We suppress the indices c_1 and λ to avoid cumbersome notation but keep ν since it is the most important parameter: ν governs the rate of decay in the central part of the distribution, while λ the rate of exponential decay in the far parts of the tails. For $\nu = 2$, we obtain $\hat{p}_2(k) = \exp(c_1 k^2/2)$ so that p_2 is the Gaussian distribution (and the parameter λ is redundant). As ν moves from 2 downward, p_ν deviates from a Gaussian distribution and for fixed $\nu \in (0, 2)$, $\nu \neq 1$, in the limit as $\lambda \to +0$, p_ν becomes a Lévy distribution with $\hat{p}_\nu(k) = \exp[-c_1|k|^\nu \cos(\nu\pi/2)/\nu(\nu - 1)]$.

In Boyarchenko and Levendorskiĭ (1997) we showed that with the choice

$$c_1 = -\sigma^2 \Delta t\, \lambda^{2-\nu}$$

the variance is independent of ν, and

$$m_\nu(\mu) = \frac{\sigma^2 \lambda^2}{2\nu(\nu - 1)}[(1 + \mu/\lambda)^\nu + (1 - \mu/\lambda)^\nu - 2]$$

We also added two (families of) distributions, p_0 and p_1; in terms of $m_\nu(\mu) = \ln M_\nu(\mu)/dt$, where $M_\nu(\mu)$ is the moment-generating function, they are given by

$$m_0(\mu) = -\frac{\sigma^2 \lambda^2}{2}\ln(1 - \mu^2/\lambda^2)$$

$$m_1(\mu) = \frac{\sigma^2 \lambda^2}{2}[(1 + \mu/\lambda)\ln(1 + \mu/\lambda) + (1 - \mu/\lambda)\ln(1 - \mu/\lambda)]$$

These distributions also have constant variance, σ^2.

We showed that for all ν, nonreal roots of the characteristic Eq. (5.11) either do not exist or have large imaginary parts, and that β_+ exist if and only if either $\nu = 0$ or $\nu = 1$ and $2\ln 2 \pm \alpha - r > 0$ or $\nu \in (0, 2]$, $\nu \neq 1$ and $m_\nu(\lambda) \pm \alpha\lambda - r > 0$.

We also proved the following theorem that characterizes the dependence of roots $\mu_\pm = \mu_{\sigma,\lambda,\nu,\pm}$ and factors $\kappa \equiv \beta_+/(\beta_+ - 1)$ on σ, λ, ν, with the other parameters being fixed.

Theorem 2. *If $\nu_1 \leq \nu_2$, $\lambda_1 \leq \lambda_2$, $\sigma_1 \geq \sigma_2$, and one of the inequalities is strict, then*

$$\mu_{\sigma_2,\lambda_2,\nu_2,-} < \mu_{\sigma_1,\lambda_1,\nu_1,-} < 0 < \mu_{\sigma_1,\lambda_1,\nu_1,+} < \mu_{\sigma_2,\lambda_2,\nu_2,+}$$

If, in addition, $\mu_{\sigma_1,\nu_1,\lambda_1,+} > 1$, then

$$\kappa_{\sigma_1,\lambda_1,\nu_1} > \kappa_{\sigma_2,\lambda_2,\nu_2} > 1 \quad (5.33)$$

Equation (5.33) says that if one applies the standard model of irreversible investment of Dixit and Pindyck (1994) when the underlying stochastic process actually obeys the non-Gaussian process (5.32) with $\nu < 2$, one obtains a lower investment threshold than the one predicted by our model. That is, if the distribution is non-Gaussian, the firm should wait more before it invests. The smaller v and λ, i.e., the greater the deviation from normality, the larger the discrepancy.

Below we present values for the higher (upper) and lower thresholds for the non-Gaussian process, $H = H_v$ and $L = L_v$, and for the Marshallian thresholds,

$$HM = HM_v = \frac{K^*c(1)}{C'(Q)[1 - c(1)\Delta t]}, \qquad LM = LM_v = \frac{K_*c(1)}{C'(Q)[1 - c(1)\Delta t]}$$

as v goes from 2 down to 0 (i.e., as the deviation from normality increases). We use values for r, α, and σ that are typical for the examples in Dixit and Pindyck (1994).

From Table 5.1.A we see that H and L increase, whereas the Marshallian equivalents HM and LM decrease, as v declines. The lower threshold (L) does not change significantly with v, whereas the upper one (H) can increase by up to 33% as v varies from 2.0 to 0.0.

More interesting still is the relation of the non-Gaussian thresholds to the Marshallian thresholds: H is higher than the upper Marshallian threshold HM, suggesting that investment should be further delayed, while L is (usually) lower than the Marshallian threshold LM (implying that disinvestment should be postponed as well). Overall, the range of inaction may increase with deviation from normality and with volatility. The higher the volatility (see Table 5.1.B when σ increases from 0.3 to 0.4), the larger the discrepancy between the upper thresholds will get (whereas the discrepancy between lower thresholds may shrink).

5.5 CONCLUSIONS

In the real-life dynamic stochastic environment, random variables of complex systems are frequently characterized by power law distributions involving fat tails. Usually,

Table 5.1
Upper (Entry) and Lower (Exit) Investment Thresholds under a Non-Gaussian Distribution, H and L, versus the Marshallian Thresholds, HM and LM, for Different Values of v.[a]

					(A) $\sigma = 0.3$						
v	2.0	1.8	1.6	1.4	1.2	1.0	0.8	0.6	0.4	0.2	0.0
H	5.93	6.02	6.13	6.28	6.45	6.64	6.80	7.08	7.35	7.62	7.92
HM	2.67	2.66	2.65	2.63	2.60	2.58	2.54	2.50	2.46	2.41	2.35
L	0.41	0.41	0.41	0.42	0.42	0.42	0.43	0.43	0.43	0.44	0.44
LM	0.93	0.93	0.92	0.91	0.90	0.89	0.88	0.86	0.84	0.82	0.80
					(B) $\sigma = 0.4$						
v	2.0	1.8	1.6	1.4	1.2	1.0	0.8	0.6	0.4	0.2	0.0
H	6.68	6.75	6.84	6.95	7.09	7.26	7.45	7.66	7.90	8.17	8.46
HM	1.01	0.97	0.94	0.90	0.86	0.81	0.75	0.67	0.59	0.50	0.40
L	0.28	0.28	0.28	0.28	0.29	0.29	0.29	0.29	0.30	0.30	0.31
LM	0.35	0.34	0.33	0.32	0.30	0.28	0.26	0.24	0.21	0.17	0.14

[a] $r = 0.05, \alpha = -0.05, \lambda = 2, K^* = 100, K_* = 35, C'(Q) = 2$.

such fat tails are caused by (and serve as indicators of) processes of self-organization; in economics, such processes appear when agents (e.g., firms) in the market are too sensitive to the behavior of other firms in their reference groups. The existence of fat-tailed distributions in economics is well documented for interest rates and stock indices. At the same time, such fat tails are often truncated (eventually exhibiting exponential falloff) due to the existence of entry and exit thresholds as a result of equilibrating mechanisms in the market place.

In this chapter, we developed a discrete-time model of investment behavior under uncertainty which is applicable to the more general case of non-Gaussian distributions. This model is analogous to, and almost as tractable as, the standard continuous-time model based on the geometric Brownian motion [used by Dixit and Pindyck (1994) and other authors]. Our model allows one to treat more complex and general processes and does not rely on the passing to the continuous-time limit. Thus, in cases when the underlying stochastic process is a mixture of continuous and jump processes, our model does not require the separation of the mixture, as standard models do.

We showed that a certain three-parameter family of non-Gaussian distributions can be used in essentially the same manner as Gaussian distributions. In standard models of irreversible investment under uncertainty, only information about the mean and variance is used. In our model, moments of higher order, such as kurtosis, may be relevant as well in determining option value and the investment thresholds.

According to standard models, volatility is the primary determinant of option value and significantly influences the investment thresholds: the higher the volatility the higher the threshold price needed to trigger new investment, and the lower the threshold price needed for disinvestment or exit.

Our model shows that in the case of fat-tailed distributions, the upper threshold can be even higher since it can grow with the kurtosis even if the volatility remains the same. On the contrary, the lower threshold may grow somewhat as the kurtosis gets very high, and can potentially become higher than the Marshallian exit threshold with extreme kurtosis.

In the special case of irreversible investment (i.e., with no option to exit) with zero operational cost, we derived a Tobin-type formula for the upper investment threshold and for q. Under additional assumptions, we provided fairly simple approximate formulas for q and showed that for fat-tailed distributions the q depends not only on the variance but on kurtosis as well.

ACKNOWLEDGMENTS

This research is partially supported by RGNF, Grant 96-02-02231, and the Russia Program of Economics Education Research Consortium (EERC). Programs of the Consortium are managed by the Eurasia Foundation. The aim of the EERC is the development of research potential in the field of economics by means of sponsoring economics research conforming to international standards and creating a scientific center of economic research for the whole Russia. EERC is supported by the Eurasia Foundation via a major grant from the U.S. Agency for International Development (AID), the Ford Foundation, Open Society Institute, the Soros Foundation, and the

World Bank. The authors are grateful to two anonymous referees and the editors, Michael Brennan and Lenos Trigeorgis, for many useful remarks; all remaining errors are ours.

REFERENCES

Abel, A. (1983). Optimal Investment Under Uncertainty. *American Economic Review* 73, 228–233.

Abel, A. B., A. K. Dixit, J. C. Eberly, and R. S. Pindyck. (1996). Options, the Value of Capital, and Investment. *Quarterly Journal of Economics* 111(3), 753–777.

Abel, A., and J. C. Eberly. (1994). A Unified Model of Investment Under Uncertainty. *American Economic Review* 84, 1369–1384.

Bak, P. (1996). *How Nature Works: The Science of Self-Organized Criticality.* Berlin: Copernicus/Springer.

Black, F., and M. Scholes. (1973). The Pricing of Options and Corporate Liabilities. *Journal of Political Economy* 3, 637–659.

Bertola, G. (1990). Irreversible Investment. Working Paper, Princeton University.

Bertola, G., and R. J. Caballero. (1994). Irreversibility and Aggregate Investment. *Review of Economic Studies* 61, 223–246.

Boyarchenko, S. I., and S. Z. Levendorskiĭ. (1997). A Model of Investment Under Uncertainty: The Case of Non-Gaussian Distributions. *Econometrica*, under revision.

Caballero, R. J., and R. S. Pindyck. (1996). Uncertainty, Investment, and Industry Evolution. *International Economic Review* 37(3), 641–662.

Cont, R., M. Rotters, and J.-P. Bouchaud. (1997). Scaling in Stock Market Data: Stable Laws and Beyond. *cond-mat/970587.*

De Long, J. B., A. Shleifer, L. H. Summers, and R. J. Waldman. (1990). Noise Trader Risk in Financial Markets. *Journal of Political Economy* 98, 703–738.

Dixit, A. K. (1993). Irreversible Investment and Competition Under Uncertainty. In K. Basu, M. Majumdar, and T. Mitra (eds.), *Capital, Investment and Development.* Cambridge, MA: Basil Blackwell.

Dixit, A. K., and R. S. Pindyck. (1994). *Investment under Uncertainty.* Princeton, NJ: Princeton University Press.

Fischer, S. (1975). The Demand for Index Bonds. *Journal of Political Economy* 83, 509–534.

Koponen, I. (1995). Analytic Approach to the Problem of Convergence of Truncated Lévy Flights towards the Gaussian Stochastic Process. *Physical Review E* 52(1), 1197–1199.

Mantegna, R. N., and H. E. Stanley. (1995). Scaling Behavior in the Dynamics of an Economic Index. *Nature* 376, 46–49.

Merton, R. C. (1973). The Theory of Rational Option Pricing. *Bell Journal of Economics* 4, 141–183.

Metcalf, G. E., and K. A. Hassett. (1995). Investment Under Alternative Return Assumptions: Comparing Random Walks and Mean Reversion. *Journal of Economic Dynamics and Control* 19, 1471–1488.

Pindyck, R. S. (1982). Adjustment Costs, Uncertainty, and the Behavior of the Firm. *American Economic Review* 72, 415–427.

Pindyck, R. S. (1988). Irreversible Investment, Capacity Choice, and the Value of the Firm. *American Economic Review* 78, 969–985

Romer, D. (1993). Rational Asset-Price Movements Without News. *American Economic Review* 83, 1112–1130.

6

Evaluating Research and
Development Investments

EDUARDO S. SCHWARTZ
MARK MOON

In this chapter investments in research and development (R&D), in particular to develop a new drug, are analyzed using the real options approach. The uncertainties of an R&D project are summarized into three stochastic processes relating to (1) uncertainties about the required investment cost, (2) uncertainties about the future payoffs from the investment, and (3) the possibility that a catastrophic event may put an end to the project. The value of the investment opportunity in R&D is modeled as a contingent claim that has as its underlying state variables the value of the asset obtained at completion of the project and the expected cost to completion. The solution of the resulting partial differential equation provides not only the value of the project but also the investment policy, that is, the values of the state variables at which it is optimal to proceed with the investment.

6.1 INTRODUCTION

The analysis of investments in research and development (R&D) is surely one of the most difficult problems of investment under uncertainty. In R&D projects, which are usually irreversible, there is uncertainty about the investment cost, the future payoffs from the investment, and the possibility of unforeseen catastrophic events that may terminate the whole effort. The problem might seem to be of such complexity as to preclude the possibility of systematic ways to deal with it. The analysis of investment projects as complex options has been a subject of much research in the past 10 years. It has been applied to value mines (Brennan and Schwartz, 1985), oil leases (Paddock, et al., 1988), and projects with uncertain cost (Pindyck, 1993), among many others.[1]

---

[1] For an excellent review on the subject see the books by Dixit and Pindyck (1994) and Trigeorgis (1996).

In this chapter investments in R&D are analyzed using the real options approach. In particular, the framework is applied to evaluate the development of a new drug, a sequential investment process that can easily last for more than 10 years.

In the approach taken here the uncertainties of an R&D project are summarized into three stochastic processes. The first process relates to the uncertainties about the investment cost required for the completion of the project. These uncertainties may be important in investments that take a long time to complete. Following Pindyck (1993), changes in the expected cost to completion of the project are assumed to follow a diffusion process with variance proportional to the level of investment. This implies that learning about the total expected cost to completion of the project can occur only with investment. The mean and the variance of investment cost are the only moments needed to estimate the parameters of the expected cost process.

The second stochastic process relates to the uncertainties about the future payoffs from the investment. These are summarized into the value of the asset obtained at the completion of the investment in R&D if the project is successful. This asset value represents the present value of the expected net cash flows from the project at the time the project is completed. The change in this value is assumed to follow a geometric Brownian motion.

Finally, the third stochastic process relates to the possibility that a catastrophic event may put an end to the project. This uncertainty is modeled as a Poisson process such that there is some probability per unit of time that the value of the project will jump to zero.

The value of the investment opportunity in R&D is then modeled as a contingent claim that has as its underlying state variables the value of the asset obtained at the completion of the project and the expected cost to completion. The solution of the partial differential equation obtained from this analysis provides not only the value of the project, but also the investment policy, that is, the values for the state variables at which it is optimal to proceed with the investment. The intuitive reason why valuation and investment policy are jointly determined is that the value of the project depends on the investment criteria and, at the same time, the investment criteria are chosen to maximize the value of the project.

This basic model is extended to deal with situations in which an R&D project has many stages, each with different characteristics (i.e., probability of failure, maximum level of possible investment, etc.). The approach is then applied to the development of a new drug using data that are representative of real-world situations.

The rest of the chapter is organized as follows. The next section provides a discussion of a complex R&D project: the development of a new drug. This provides a concrete example of the main issues related to an R&D investment opportunity as well as the institutional background for the illustration given in Section 6.5. Section 6.3 presents the basic valuation model. Section 6.4 provides some comparative static results, in particular with respect to the effect that different types of uncertainty have on the value of the project and on the optimal investment rule. Section 6.5 extends the basic model to allow for different investment phases and applies it to the development of a new drug. Section 6.6 concludes.

6.2 DRUG DEVELOPMENT PROCESS

The process of drug development is lengthy, complex, and risky. Before a new drug can be marketed in the United States, it must be approved by the Food and Drug Administration (FDA). Approval gives the maker the ability to market the drug in the United States to be used for a designated indication. Because of this regulation, the process for drug development is somewhat standardized in the sense that it is composed of several discrete stages that are reasonably easy to identify. The phases include preclinical testing, phase I, phase II, phase III, submission of a New Drug Application (in the case of a pharmaceutical drug or a Product License Application in the case of a biotechnology drug) to the FDA, and the FDA review.

There are several goals of the development process. These include establishing safety and efficacy, dosing, and demonstrating statistically significant benefits of the new drug. The process is quite risky since the drug can be knocked out in any one of the stages, due to toxicity, lack of efficacy, lack of proprietary position, disappearance of the target population, or the development of substitute drugs. Because of these risks only 20% of pharmaceutical drugs passing into phase I clinical trials are ultimately approved by the FDA. The entire process takes from 10 to 12 years for a single successful drug.

6.2.1 Preclinical Testing

Before a drug may enter phase I clinical trials, it exists in what is known as preclinical testing. At this early stage of the process, a new molecule has been discovered and is being investigated in both laboratory experiments and animal models. The work with the potential drug is being done exclusively by researchers, as opposed to clinical development people. In this stage nonhuman experimenting has led scientists to believe that the substance may be useful for a specific application in humans. The drug is believed to cause a potentially useful biological effect. Potential safety and biological activity of the drug are assessed in this stage. Also, patents are filed and investigated in order to make sure that some sort of proprietary position in the drug might be gained. The length of this stage is about 2 years. One percent of the molecules pass from preclinical testing into phase I clinical trials.

6.2.2 Phase I Clinical Trials

Before human testing may be done, an Investigational New Drug form must be submitted to the FDA. If the FDA does not respond within 30 days, phase I testing may begin. The primary goal of this stage is to assess the toxicity and dosing of the drug in humans. The subjects consist of 20 to 80 usually healthy volunteers. These trials last about 2 years. During this stage, it can become clear that the drug has serious enough toxicity effects in humans such that development should not proceed. Approximately 70% of drugs entering this stage make it to the next phase of development, phase II.

6.2.3 Phase II Clinical Trials

There are several goals of phase II clinical trials, which include verifying the biological effectiveness of the drug, profiling the side effects, and obtaining dosing information. These trials are far bigger in scale than phase I trials, consisting of 100 to 300 sick subjects. These trials also last about 2 years. On average, 47% of drugs pass from phase II into phase III trials.

6.2.4 Phase III Clinical Trials

The main goal of this phase is to demonstrate statistical significance of the drug. Trials are typically double blind and employ randomization and test versus control groups. Phase III studies are carefully designed to build a case for FDA approval of the drug. Studies are designed in order for significance to be shown as clearly as possible. Often this means focusing on specific conditions that may not comprise a lucrative market for the approved product, but do work well for showing efficacy of the drug. This is possible because although the FDA approves drugs to be marketed for a particular indication, doctors can use FDA approved products for any use that they believe is appropriate.

Consisting of from 1000 to 3000 sick people, phase III trials are of an order of magnitude larger that phase II trials. A large expense that also occurs during this trial is the construction of a plant to manufacture the drug commercially. This expense can range from 50 to 80 million dollars. These trials last about 3 years. Approximately 82% of drugs in phase III pass to the next phase.

6.2.5 Submission to the FDA

After statistical significance is demonstrated in phase III clinical trials, a large package of information detailing the clinical studies is assembled and submitted to the FDA. This package is known as a Product License Application in the case of a biopharmaceutical, or New Drug Application in the case of a traditional pharmaceutical. The FDA takes about 2.5 years to review these applications. Preference may be given to drugs with greater perceived benefits. The FDA can ask for additional information or studies, approve the drug for a particular indication, or not approve the drug. About 74% of drugs in this stage are approved by the FDA. On approval, selling of the drug typically begins immediately, as the manufacturer usually has set everything in place to begin selling as soon as approval is granted.

The process of drug development described above is linear in the sense that one stage has to be finished before the next can start. In practice there are some nonlinearities in the process. These include things such as multiple phase II/III trials being conducted simultaneously, and the drug being knocked out of one phase and placed back into a previous phase. In addition, the stages often have ragged beginnings and endings, and can even overlap, as the actual process consists of signing up individual doctors and patients to participate in the trials. There is no reason for synchronizing the starting or ending of all the trials. Also, for drugs with very powerful and clear effects, phase II and phase III have at times been combined.

The degree of difficulty of development varies according to the particular compound and the related biological activity. Much can depend on what is being measured in the clinical trials. Very specific biological effects can be subject to far less measurement error than changes in more general conditions. For example, contrast studying the increase of a particular, easy to measure, red blood cell count with a change in a condition where the variable being measured is chronic pain. In the latter case, the noise in measurement is substantial, as pain is difficult to measure objectively. Thus showing statistical significance can be very difficult.

For pharmaceutical drugs, 1 in 4000 compounds discovered eventually results in an FDA approved drug, and 1 in 5 drugs to enter phase I clinical trials results in an FDA approved drug. Development costs per drug can range from 100 to 200 million dollars. There is some evidence that the probabilities of success are higher for biopharmaceutical drugs. At the present time, however, there is not much data relating to biopharmaceutical drug development due to the relatively young age of the industry.

6.3 THE VALUATION MODEL

The approach used in this chapter is based on the model developed by Pindyck (1993). Consider an investment in an R&D project that takes time to complete (sometimes over 10 years). Assume that the maximum rate at which the firm can invest is I_m and that the total cost to completion is a random variable $\tilde{K}$ with expected cost $K = E(\tilde{K})$. When the project is successfully completed, the firm receives an asset (e.g., a new drug) whose value, V, is determined as the present value of expected future net cash flows from the completed project. Finally, during the long period of investment there is some probability per unit of time, λ, that the project's value will jump to zero. That is, the investment opportunity can disappear, for example, because another firm wins the race to obtain a patent on the product, the drug turns out to have some terrible side effects, or some other catastrophic event occurs that puts an end to the project.

6.3.1 Cost Uncertainty

The expected cost to completion, K, is assumed to follow the controlled diffusion process:

$$dK = -I\,dt + \beta(IK)^{1/2}\,dz \tag{6.1}$$

where I is the rate of investment (the control) and dz is an increment to a Gauss–Wiener process that is assumed to be uncorrelated with the market portfolio (and with aggregate wealth). This is the type of uncertainty that Pindyck (1993) calls technical uncertainty since it can be resolved only by investing.[2] Equation (6.1) shows that the

---

[2] Pindyck (1993) also considers input cost uncertainty that may be correlated with the market.

expected cost declines with investment, but it is also affected by a stochastic term with mean zero and a variance linear in both the level of investment I and the expected cost K. Uncertainty decreases with expected cost to completion and "learning" occurs only when there is investment. That is, when there is no investment ($I = 0$), expected cost to completion does not change ($dK = 0$). The total cost (a random variable) is the summation (or integral) of actual investments along a path.

Stochastic process (6.1) is a reasonable representation of uncertainty about expected cost in an R&D investment project. In addition, it has some attractive computational advantages. First, as will be shown later, this process gives rise to a bang–bang solution for the optimal control. That is, the optimal investment strategy takes only two possible extreme values: to invest zero or to invest at the maximum possible rate.[3] Second, the variance of the cost to completion has a simple analytical expression:[4]

$$\text{Var}(\tilde{K}) = \left(\frac{\beta^2}{2 - \beta^2} \right) K^2 \tag{6.2}$$

This expression relates the parameter β to the variance of the project's total cost and will be used in the implementation of the approach to obtain reasonable values for this parameter. Finally, the probability distribution of cost to completion or, equivalently, the first passage time of process (6.1) to zero can be obtained analytically.[5]

6.3.2 Asset Value Uncertainty

The estimated value of the asset received on successful completion of the project, V, is assumed to follow the stochastic process:

$$dV = \mu V \, dt + \sigma V \, dw \tag{6.3}$$

where σ is the instantaneous standard deviation of the proportional changes in the value received at completion and dw is an increment to a Gauss–Wiener process that is assumed to be uncorrelated with the uncertainty in expected costs (i.e., with dz), but may be correlated with the market portfolio (or aggregate wealth). The drift component, μ, reflects the characteristics of a particular R&D program. There are examples of R&D programs in which the value of the asset would have a positive drift (e.g., pharmaceutical products tied to other medical products that are growing in use), as well as R&D programs in which the value of the asset has a negative drift (e.g., where there is a growing foreign competition and hence a shrinking market for the product). The drift term, if negative, could also represent the opportunity cost of delaying the investment.[6]

---

[3] This occurs because the variance of the process is linear in investment.

[4] For a derivation see Karlin and Taylor (1981, p. 203) or the appendix in Pindyck (1993). They also show that the mean cost to completion implied by this stochastic process is indeed the expected cost.

[5] See Appendix A.

[6] We thank the referee for suggesting these points.

The estimated asset value can be interpreted as the present value of the expected net cash flows to the project once the investment is completed, discounted at a risk-adjusted discount rate. Since at this later stage many of the option characteristics of the investment have disappeared, traditional methods can be used to discount future expected cash flows. As time and investment progress, new information about the payoffs from the project becomes available, changing the assessment of the value of the asset obtained at completion as described in (6.3).[7]

6.3.3 Catastrophic Events

The third source of uncertainty considered in the model is an independent Poisson process indicating the occurrence of a catastrophic event that suddenly drives the value of the project to zero. If λ is the probability per unit of time that the project's value will jump to zero, then $\lambda\, dt$ is the probability that the catastrophic event occurs once in the time interval dt and $1 - \lambda\, dt$ is the probability that the event does not occur in this time interval.[8]

6.3.4 Value of the Investment Opportunity

Let $F(V, K)$ be the value of the investment opportunity. Note that the two state variables in this model, V and K, are not traded assets. K is the expected value of the random costs to completion and V is the estimated value of an asset to be obtained sometime in the future. Given that the sources of uncertainty described above cannot be hedged, the derivation of the Bellman equation for the stochastic optimal investment problem requires the use of an equilibrium model. The stochastic process for the expected cost to completion and the Poisson process for the occurrence of a catastrophic event are uncorrelated with the market so there is no risk premium associated with these sources of uncertainty. The stochastic process for the value of the asset obtained at completion of the investment, however, is correlated with the market. Its risk-adjusted drift is then the original drift minus an adjustment for risk that comes from the equilibrium model. In the framework of the intertemporal capital asset pricing model (see Merton, 1973) the adjustment for risk would be the beta of the asset times the market risk premium. Following arguments now standard in the literature (see Merton, 1976; Brennan and Schwartz, 1985; or Dixit and Pindyck, 1994) it can be shown that $F(V, K)$ must satisfy the following partial differential equation:

[7] As pointed out by Donaldson and Kamstra (1996), the standard deviation σ in (6.3) should be a cross-sectional standard deviation. Most applications, however, use the standard deviation from the time series of returns.

[8] It should be pointed out that there is an alternative and equivalent way of modeling the catastrophic events. As in Merton (1976), the Poisson process that can suddenly drive the value of the project to zero could be appended to Eq. (6.3). This alternative way of thinking about the catastrophic events would not change any of the results of our analysis.

$$\text{Max}_I \left[\tfrac{1}{2}\sigma^2 V^2 F_{VV} + \tfrac{1}{2}\beta^2 IK F_{KK} + \right.$$
$$\left. (\mu - \eta)V F_V - I F_K - (r + \lambda)F - I \right] = 0 \qquad (6.4)$$

where $(\mu - \eta)$ is the risk-adjusted drift for the value of the asset, and r is the risk-free rate of interest. Asset value uncertainty represented by the standard deviation σ enters the first term of Eq. (6.4), cost uncertainty represented by the parameter β enters the second term, and the possibility of catastrophic events represented by the Poisson probability λ simply increases the interest rate.

Since Eq. (6.4) is linear in I, the rate of investment that maximizes the value of the project must always be equal to either the maximum rate I_m or zero:

$$I = \begin{cases} I_m & \text{for } \tfrac{1}{2}\beta^2 K F_{KK} - F_K - 1 \geq 0 \\ 0 & \text{otherwise} \end{cases} \qquad (6.5)$$

Then, Eq. (6.4) is an elliptic partial differential equation with a free boundary along the line $V^*(K)$ such that $I = I_m$ when $V > V^*(K)$ and $I = 0$ otherwise. The set of critical asset values, $V^*(K)$, must be found as part of the solution for $F(V, K)$ and satisfy

$$\tfrac{1}{2}\beta^2 K F_{KK}(V^*, K) - F_K(V^*, K) - 1 = 0 \qquad (6.6)$$

Therefore, when $V > V^*(K)$ the value of the investment opportunity must satisfy

$$\tfrac{1}{2}\sigma^2 V^2 F_{VV} + \tfrac{1}{2}\beta^2 I_m K F_{KK} + (\mu - \eta)V F_V - I_m F_K - (r + \lambda)F - I_m = 0 \quad (6.7)$$

and otherwise it must satisfy

$$\tfrac{1}{2}\sigma^2 V^2 F_{VV} + (\mu - \eta)V F_V - (r + \lambda)F = 0 \qquad (6.8)$$

The solution must also satisfy the following boundary conditions:

$$F(V, 0) = V \qquad (6.9)$$

$$F(0, K) = 0 \qquad (6.10)$$

$$\lim_{K \to \infty} F(V, K) = 0 \qquad (6.11)$$

and $F(V, K)$ must be continuous at $V^*(K)$. Boundary condition (6.9) implies that at completion of the investment opportunity the asset value is realized, and condition (6.10) reflects the fact that zero is an absorbing boundary for the stochastic process for V. Finally, condition (6.11) says that when expected costs are very large there is a very small probability that the project will ever be undertaken.

6.3.5 Traditional Valuation (NPV)

Consider now a traditional net present value (NPV) valuation in which risky cash flows are discounted at a risk-adjusted discount rate. We can interpret the probability of a catastrophic event as an annual "tax rate" λ on the value of the project (since on average a fraction λ of the project would be lost every year).[9] In this framework the time to completion would be $T = K/I_m$, the appropriate discount rate for the asset value would be $r + \lambda - \mu + \eta$, and the appropriate discount rate for the expected cost to completion would be $r + \lambda$. The present value of the cost to completion would then be

$$K_{PV} = \int_0^T I_m e^{-(r+\lambda)t}\, dt = \frac{I_m}{r+\lambda}\left[1 - e^{-(r+\lambda)T}\right] \tag{6.12}$$

and the present value of the asset

$$V_{PV} = V e^{-(r+\lambda-\mu+\eta)T} \tag{6.13}$$

The NPV of the project would thus be

$$\text{NPV} = V_{PV} - K_{PV} = V e^{-(r+\lambda-\mu+\eta)(K/I_m)} - \frac{I_m}{r+\lambda}\left[1 - e^{-(r+\lambda)(K/I_m)}\right] \tag{6.14}$$

The optimal investment rule would be to proceed with the investment if and only if the NPV is positive. Not surprisingly, (6.14) satisfies partial differential Eq. (6.7) with $\sigma = \beta = 0$. The NPV solution in (6.14) not only provides a benchmark with which to compare the value of the project and the optimal investment strategy under uncertainty, but also serves as a starting solution for the numerical procedure used to solve the system of elliptic partial differential Eqs. (6.7) and (6.8) subject to the appropriate boundary conditions.

6.3.6 Volatility and Beta of the Investment Opportunity

By a direct application of Ito's Lemma and using stochastic processes (6.1) and (6.3) it is possible to derive the process for the rate of return on the project while alive as

$$\frac{dF}{F} = (\cdot)\, dt + \frac{\sigma V F_V}{F}\, dw + \frac{\beta (IK)^{1/2} F_K}{F}\, dz \tag{6.15}$$

where $(\cdot)$ represents the expected return on the project. The expression for the variance of the rate of return on the project can be obtained directly from (6.15), recalling that the two stochastic processes are assumed to be uncorrelated:

$$\sigma_F^2 = \left(\frac{\sigma V F_V}{F}\right)^2 + IK\left(\frac{\beta F_K}{F}\right)^2 \tag{6.16}$$

with $I = 0$ when there is no investment and $I = I_m$ when investment is undertaken at the maximum possible rate.

Similarly, using Merton's (1973) intertemporal capital asset pricing model, it is straightforward to derive the beta of the investment opportunity as a function of

---

[9] For this interpretation see Brennan and Schwartz (1985).

the beta of the asset value obtained at the completion of the project (see Black and Scholes, 1973):

$$\beta_F = \beta_V \left(\frac{V F_V}{F} \right) \tag{6.17}$$

6.4 COMPARATIVE STATICS AND RESULTS

In the previous section we presented a general framework for valuing projects that is especially suited for evaluating investments in research and development. It took into account three types of uncertainty: investment cost uncertainty, uncertainty about the value of the asset obtained at completion of the project, and uncertainty about the occurrence of a catastrophic event that causes the "sudden death" of the project. The framework not only gives the value of the project, but also the optimal investment strategy: for every level of expected cost to completion it provides a critical value of the asset above which it is optimal to invest at the maximum possible rate.

The value of the investment opportunity must satisfy Eq. (6.7) when investment takes place, and Eq. (6.8) when there is no investment; in the free boundary between them it must satisfy condition (6.6). This system of equations does not have a known closed-form solution. Thus, it must be solved by numerical procedures. The method used in this chapter is successive over-relaxation iterated so that condition (6.6) holds at the free boundary.[10]

This section provides some comparative statics results on the value of a simple investment opportunity and the critical points at which investment is optimally triggered. Table 6.1 shows the data for the basic example used to illustrate the effect of changes in uncertainty on the project's value and the optimal investment. Figure 6.1 shows the value of the project for the parameters of Table 6.1 as a function of the two state variables: asset value and expected cost to completion. The value of the project is equal to the asset at completion ($K = 0$) and it is zero when the asset is worthless ($V = 0$). The value of the investment opportunity is increasing in the asset

Table 6.1

Parameters for Basic Example

Asset value uncertainty (σ)	0.35
Drift of asset value process (μ)	0.0
Cost uncertainty (β)	0.50
Probability of failure (λ)	0.10
Risk-free interest rate (r)	0.05
Risk premium on asset return (η)	0.08
Maximum investment per year (I_m)	20
Range of asset values	0 to 300
Range of expected costs	0 to 100

[10] A brief description of the numerical procedure is given in Appendix B.

value and decreasing in the expected cost. It is easier to appreciate these relations in a two-dimensional graph. Figure 6.2 gives three sections of Figure 6.1 for an expected completion cost equal to 20, 50, and 80. Since the solution is continuous and smooth at the free boundary (6.6), it is not possible to see in Figures 6.1 and 6.2 the critical asset value above which it is optimal to invest at the maximum possible rate.

Critical asset values for different levels of expected cost are shown in Figure 6.3. The middle line gives the value of the asset for which the NPV of the project, computed using Eq. (6.14), is equal to zero, and is used as a benchmark with which to compare optimal investment under uncertainty. The upper line shows the critical asset values using the parameters of the basic example, except that the cost uncertainty parameter has been reduced to zero; that is, this line shows the effect of asset value uncertainty on the critical, or threshold, investment values. Increases in the volatility of the asset value process have the effect of increasing the critical value of the option to invest. The lower line in Figure 6.3 is computed with the same parameters as in the basic example, except that this time the asset value uncertainty parameter has been reduced to zero. Uncertainty in expected cost has the opposite effect on critical asset values than uncertainty in asset values, i.e., increases in the uncertainty parameter of expected cost decrease the critical value of the option to invest. The reason for this effect, as pointed out by Pindyck (1993), is that investing reveals information about the

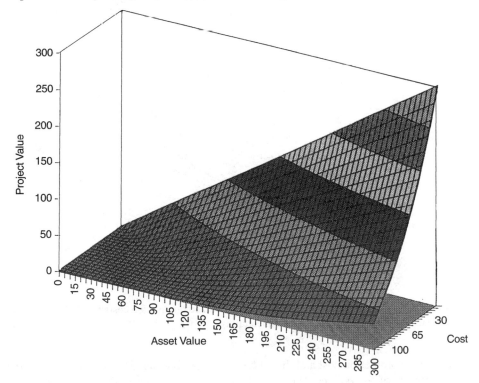

Figure 6.1 Project value as function of asset value and expected completion cost.

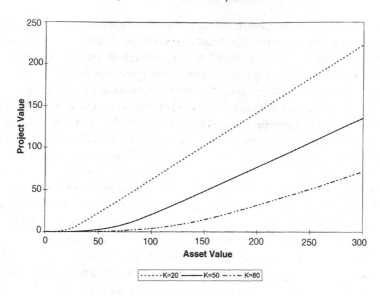

Figure 6.2   Project value as function of asset value for various expected completion costs ($K = 20, 50, 80$).

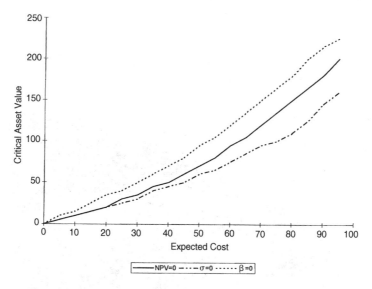

Figure 6.3   Critical asset values for different expected completion costs (for NPV $= 0$, asset value uncertainty $\sigma = 0$, and for cost uncertainty $\beta = 0$).

expected completion cost and thus it has value beyond its direct contribution to the completion of the project. The critical asset values for the basic example together with the zero-NPV values are presented in Figure 6.4. In this case the two lines cross, i.e., for expected cost below 70 asset value uncertainty dominates, but for

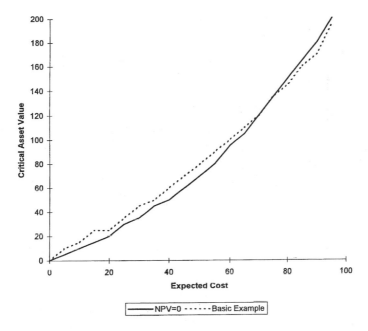

Figure 6.4 Critical asset values at different expected completion costs for basic example and for NPV = 0.

expected cost above 75 it is cost uncertainty that dominates so that investment should optimally proceed at asset values below those indicated by the NPV criterion. Note that the lack of smoothness in these figures is due to the discreetness of the numerical solution.[11]

Figure 6.5 shows the option value of the project as a function of the asset value when the expected cost to completion is 80. Option value is defined as the difference between the value of the project when cost and/or asset value uncertainty are considered and the traditional NPV of the project is computed using (6.14). The upper line represents the option value for the basic example where both cost and asset value uncertaint are included. The highest value of the curve at $V = 150$ corresponds to the point where the traditional NPV of the project is zero. The other two curves in Figure 6.5 show the option value when only cost uncertainty ($\sigma = 0$) or asset value uncertainty ($\beta = 0$) are considered in the basic example.

Cost uncertainty has two distinct effects on the value of the project, both of which are positive. The first effect comes from the option to abandon the project midstream when the expected cost to completion becomes too large. The second effect, unrelated to the option to abandon the project, comes from Jensen's inequality and the convexity of the NPV of the project [Eq. (6.14)] with respect to the expected cost to completion K.[12] A project is more valuable if the cost to completion is uncertain, even if the

[11] The step size in the numerical solution is 5, so critical values can change only by that amount.
[12] This effect is similar to the one induced by interest rate uncertainty, as shown in Ingersoll and Ross (1992).

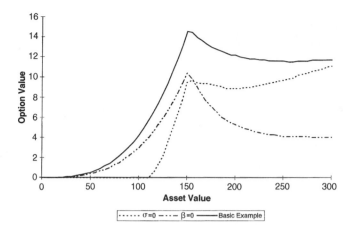

Figure 6.5 Option value of the project as function of asset value for expected completion cost of $K = 80$.

probability of abandoning the project is zero. For example, assume that $V = 150$ and that the cost to completion can take one of two values with equal probability, 80 and 20; the NPVs for these two cases would be 0 and 100.6 with an expected value of 50.3. If the cost to completion is known to be 50, the NPV of the project would be only 42.7. In Figure 6.5 it can be seen that for larger values of V the second effect dominates, since the value of the abandonment option decreases with V. Asset value uncertainty increases the value of the project only through the option to temporarily (or permanently) stop investing until prospects improve (if ever). The Jensen's inequality effect does not exist because the NPV in (6.14) is linear in V. This can be seen in Figure 6.5 where the option value decreases when the option is "in the money" (for large values of V). When both types of uncertainty are present, the different effects combine in a complex manner as shown in the top curve in Figure 6.5.

To summarize the findings of this section, consider an investment opportunity with expected cost to completion of 80 and with a current value of the asset at completion of 150. Since the maximum investment per year is 20, it would take 4 years to completion at full speed. The NPV of this project, computed using Eq. (6.14), is zero and the critical asset value above which investment is optimal is $V^* = 150$, so the project seems to be marginal. Taking into account only asset value uncertainty causes the value of the project to increase to 10.4 and the critical asset value to increase to $V^* = 180$. Even though there is a substantial increase in the value of the project, it is not optimal to invest at $V = 150$. If only cost uncertainty is considered, the value of the project is 9.5 and the critical asset value decreases to only 110. Finally, if both cost and asset value uncertainties are considered the value of the project increases to 14.6 and the critical asset value becomes 145. These results are shown in Table 6.2. As can be seen from Table 6.2, uncertainty always increases the value of the project. The effect on the critical asset value, however, is opposite for these two types of uncertainty. Increases in asset value uncertainty increase critical asset values (wait longer to invest), whereas increases in cost uncertainty decrease critical asset values (invest sooner).

Table 6.2
Project Value and Critical Asset Value

Investment criteria	Parameter values	*Project value for* $V = 150$ *and* $K = 80$	*Critical asset value* V^* *for* $K = 80$	*Project value at* V^* *for* $K = 80$	*Optimal action for* $V = 150$, $K = 80$
NPV criterion	$\sigma = 0, \beta = 0$	0	150	0	Indifferent
Asset value uncertainty only	$\sigma = 0.35, \beta = 0$	10.4	180	18.2	Don't invest
Cost uncertainty only	$\sigma = 0, \beta = 0.5$	9.5	110	0	Invest
Cost and asset value uncertainties	$\sigma = 0.35, \beta = 0.5$	14.6	145	13.1	Invest

6.5 EXTENSION OF THE VALUATION MODEL TO MULTIPLE PHASES

The model developed in Section 6.3 has many of the features of an investment in research and development, such as the development of a new drug. This basic model, however, lacks some important aspects of a real-world problem. As explained in Section 6.2, after the preclinical testing the drug development process consists of three distinct phases plus the FDA review, which can be considered as a fourth phase in the cycle. Each one of these phases has very different characteristics from the point of view of the amount of investment it may require, the maximum rate at which investment can proceed, and the probability of failure or of a catastrophic event occurring during the phase. In addition, there may be differences in the uncertainty related to the cost to completion and to the asset value obtained at completion.

In this section the basic model is extended to allow for an arbitrary number of phases, each with different characteristics. The approach taken here is that of compound real options. Completion of investment in the first phase (e.g., drug development) gives the owner the option to start the second phase, and so on. Technically, the boundary condition of each phase of the investment is the beginning value for the next phase. The problem is solved recursively starting from the last phase, which has as its terminal boundary condition the asset value at completion as developed in Section 6.3. The penultimate phase has as its terminal boundary condition the value of the project before the last investment phase is done, and so on.[13]

The approach described above (which is used in the example that follows) implicitly assumes that, while expected cost to completion of a particular phase

---

[13] We should point out that if the investment in each of the phases is known with certainty, or once committed cannot be stopped, the problem can be solved in a simpler setup as a multistage investment problem with only a few (three of four) stages of investment. Our setup becomes interesting when the investment cost is uncertain *and* there is the possibility to stop investing at any time, as is usually the case in pharmaceutical R&D programs.

changes stochastically as investment progresses in that phase, the expected cost to completion in subsequent phases can change only once investment in those phases begins. That is, "learning" about cost to completion occurs only for the phase in which investment is being made. This might be a good approximation for some research and development investments where the process of investment is sequential, such as in the development of a new drug. The framework could also be extended to deal with situations in which investment in one phase can affect expected cost in subsequent phases. In this case, however, the particular characteristics of investment in each phase, such as the maximum rate of investment and the probability of failure, must be expressed as functions of the total cost to completion rather than the cost to completion of each particular phase.

To illustrate the approach, in Section 6.2 consider again the development of a new drug that has three phases of development plus the FDA review (phase IV). Assume a representative drug development program with a total initial expected cost of 84 million dollars and an expected time to completion of 9.5 years. Also assume that the relative expected costs and the probabilities of catastrophic events in each phase are of the same order of magnitude discussed in Section 6.2. Phase I, where only a small number of healthy volunteers are included, has expected cost to completion of 4 million dollars with a maximum rate of investment of 2 million per year, resulting in an expected time to completion of 2 years. The failure probability in this phase is 0.15 per year. Phase II, which consists of trials on around 200 sick subjects, has expected cost of 10 million and a maximum investment rate of 5 million, also giving an expected time to completion of 2 years. The probability of failure per year increases to 0.25. In phase III the major investment in the project is typically made since, in addition to tests on thousands of sick people, it involves the construction of the plant to produce the drug. Expected cost in this phase is 60 million and the maximum rate of investment per year is 20 million; expected time to completion is therefore 3 years. The probability of failure in this phase is 0.06. Finally, during the FDA review expected costs are 10 million with a maximum annual investment rate of 4 million, resulting in an expected time for the review of 2.5 years. The probability of failure in this final phase is 0.10 per year. The above information is summarized in Table 6.3.

Table 6.3 also contains the values of volatility parameters for the two stochastic processes, the drift of the asset value process, the interest rate, and the risk premium on the asset return, all of which are assumed to be the same for all phases of the project. The value of 0.50 for the volatility parameter of the expected cost process implies from Eq. (6.2) that the ratio of the standard deviation to the expected cost is equal to 0.38. That is, if expected cost is 100 one standard deviation is 38. The density function of cost to completion can be computed from (6.A1) in Appendix A and is shown, for the case of an expected cost of 100, in Figure 6.6. The value of 0.35 for the volatility of the asset value process corresponds approximately to the volatility of an operating biotechnology firm. In addition, the beta of the asset obtained at completion of the project is assumed to be equal to one, which is typical of an operating biotechnology firm. Finally, the drift of the asset value process is assumed to be equal to zero.

Table 6.4 and Figures 6.7 and 6.8 present the results of the new drug development project. The first row of Table 6.4 gives the critical asset values for the different phases

Table 6.3
Data for New Drug Development

	Phase I	*Phase II*	*Phase III*	*FDA review*
Expected cost (million)	4	10	60	10
Maximum rate of investment per year (million)	2	5	20	4
Probability of failure (λ)	0.15	0.25	0.06	0.10
Asset return volatility (σ)	0.35	0.35	0.35	0.35
Drift of asset value process (μ)	0.0	0.0	0.0	0.0
Volatility of cost (β)	0.50	0.50	0.50	0.50
Interest rate (r)	0.05	0.05	0.05	0.05
Risk premium (η)	0.08	0.08	0.08	0.08

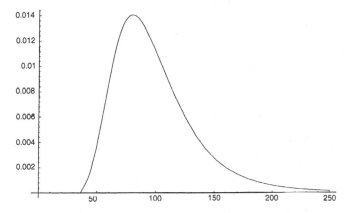

Figure 6.6 Cost to completion density function with expected cost to completion $K - 100$ and $\beta - 0.5$.

Table 6.4
Evaluation of New Drug Development[a]

	For asset value V	*Phase I*	*Phase II*	*Phase III*	*FDA review*
Critical asset value (V^*)		250	215	180	15
Project value	300	5.7	13.9	45.2	164.7
Project volatility	300	1.15	1.15	0.98	0.43
Project beta	300	3.06	2.82	2.13	1.05
Project value	500	20.2	43.3	110.9	280.0
Project volatility	500	0.78	0.76	0.64	0.42
Project beta	500	2.00	1.80	1.50	1.03

[a] All values in millions of dollars.

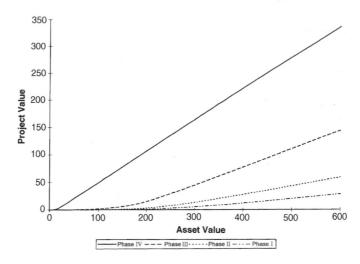

Figure 6.7   Project value at each of the four phases of new drug development.

of the project. It is optimal to start investing in Phase I of the project when the value of the underlying asset is larger than 250 million. The reason for this high value is that it is realized only in approximately 10 years after investment starts. In the event that Phase I is successful, the critical asset value in Phase II decreases to 215 million. In Phase III, when the most substantial part of the investment is about to begin, it decreases again to 180 million. Finally, the critical asset value drops to 15 million at the start of the FDA Review since only 10 million remains to be invested.

Figure 6.7 shows the value of the investment opportunity at the beginning of each of the four phases of the new drug development process for asset values ranging from 0 to 600 million. In Figure 6.8A–D the corresponding volatilities of the project are presented as a function of the asset value, starting in each phase at the critical asset value. Increases in asset value always increase the value of the project and decrease its volatility. The last six rows of Table 6.4 report the value of the project, the volatility of its rate of return, and the beta of the project for asset values of 300 and 500 million. At these levels of asset value it is optimal to keep investing in all phases. Notice that the volatility of the project and its beta are substantially higher than the volatility and beta of the asset obtained at completion (the elasticity is greater than one).

In the example presented above, the different phases of the project have different expected costs, maximum rates of investment, and probabilities of failure. The other parameters of the model could also be different across phases without additional complications.

6.6 CONCLUSIONS

More than any other type of investment opportunity, research and development projects have the characteristics of compound real options. The successful completion of one stage of development gives the owner the option to continue into the next stage. Moreover, few projects involve so much risk, especially at the earlier stages. The

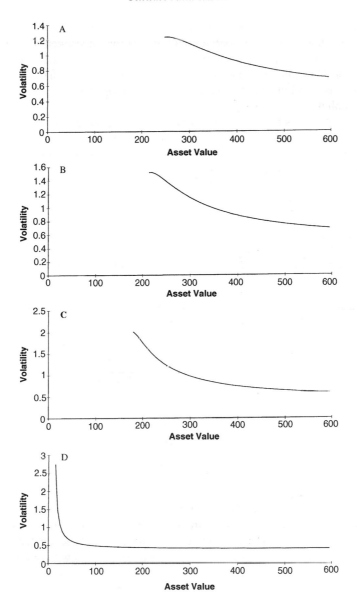

Figure 6.8 Volatility of project (as a function of the asset value) in phase (A) I, (B) II, (C) III, and (D) IV.

uncertainties involved in this type of investment are so diverse that it is practically impossible, without a formal model, to assess the impact that they may have on the value of the project and the optimal investment rule.

The real options model developed to evaluate investments in research and development considers three types of uncertainty: uncertainty about the cost to completion, about the payoffs from the project, and about the possibility of a catastrophic event ending the investment opportunity.

The approach is applied to evaluate the development of a new drug, a problem that has eluded satisfactory methods of analysis. This study provides important insights into the valuation of drug development and the optimal investment rule in terms of the expected cost to completion and the value of the project obtained if development is successful. This framework also allows systematic investigation of the impact that the different types of uncertainty have on investment opportunity value and optimal operating policy.

There is still work to be done in order to incorporate more of the features existing in the real world. It is the authors' belief, however, that the framework developed herein can be usefully implemented in practice as a first step in the analysis of investments in research and development.

Appendix A

Probability Distribution of Cost to Completion

For stochastic process (6.1), the probability that the total cost to completion of the project is less than k, conditional on an initial expected cost to completion K, is given by

$$H(k) = 1 - \sum_{n=0}^{\infty} \frac{e^{-y} y^{n+1-x}}{\Gamma(n+2+x)}$$

where

$$y = \frac{2K}{k\beta^2} \tag{6.A1}$$

$$x = \frac{2}{\beta^2}$$

With Γ being the cumulative gamma distruction.

This expression can be obtained directly from Eq. (6.41) in Cox and Ross (1976, p. 164) by making appropriate substitutions. The density function for the cost to completion can be obtained by taking the derivative of (6.A1) with respect to k.

Appendix B

Numerical Procedure for Solving System of Equations

Equation (6.7) is an elliptic partial differential equation that can be solved numerically using the successive over-relaxation method described in Press et al. (1992, p. 860). When there is no investment, Eq. (6.8) holds, which is identical to Eq. (6.7), except that $I_m = 0$. So, the grid has two areas: one in which there is investment and the coefficients come from Eq. (6.7), and one in which there is no investment and the coefficients come from Eq. (6.8). In the boundary between the two areas, condition (6.6) must hold.

The iterative procedure starts from the NPV solution given in Eq. (6.14). It is assumed that in the area in which the NPV is positive Eq. (6.7) holds, and in the area in which the NPV is negative Eq. (6.8) holds. After the first iteration condition (6.6) is computed for each point of the grid: if it is positive Eq. (6.7) is assumed to hold, otherwise (6.8) is assumed to hold. This procedure is repeated until convergence is obtained.

ACKNOWLEDGMENTS

This chapter was written while the first author was a visiting scholar at the University of British Columbia in Vancouver during the summer of 1994. We thank Michael Brennan, Rajna Gibson, Lenos Trigeorgis, an anonymous referee, and seminar participants at UBC, Siena, Geneva, and Universidad Catolica de Chile for many helpful comments.

REFERENCES

Black, F., and M. Scholes. (1973). The Pricing of Options and Corporate Liabilities. *Journal of Political Economy* 81, 637–654.

Brennan, M. J., and E. S. Schwartz. (1985). Evaluating Natural Resource Investments. *Journal of Business* 58, 135–157.

Cox, J. C., and S. A. Ross. (1976). The Valuation of Options for Alternative Stochastic Processes. *Journal of Financial Economics* 7, 229–263.

Dixit, A. K., and R. S. Pindyck. (1994). *Investment under Uncertainty.* Princeton, NJ: Princeton University Press.

Donaldson, R. G., and M. Kamstra. (1996). A New Dividend Forecasting Procedure That Rejects Bubbles in Asset Prices: The Case of 1929's Stock Crash. *Review of Financial Studies* 9(2), 333–383.

Ingersoll, J. E., Jr., and S. A. Ross. (1992). Waiting to Invest: Investment and Uncertainty. *Journal of Business* 65, 1–29.

Karlin, S., and H. M. Taylor. (1981). *A Second Course in Stochastic Processes.* New York: Academic Press.

Merton, R. C. (1973). An Intertemporal Capital Asset Pricing Model. *Econometrica* 41, 867–887.

Merton, R. C. (1976). Option Pricing When Underlying Stock Returns Are Discontinuous. *Journal of Financial Economics* 3, 125–144.

Paddock, J. L., D. R. Siegel, and J. L. Smith. (1988). Option Valuation of Claims on Real Assets: The Case of Offshore Petroleum Leases. *Quarterly Journal of Economics* 103, 479–508.

Pindyck, R. S. (1993). Investments of Uncertain Cost. *Journal of Financial Economics* 34, 53–76.

Press, W. H., S. A. Teukolsky, W. T. Vetterling, and B. P. Flannery. (1992). *Numerical Recipes in Fortran: The Art of Scientific Computing*, 2nd edition. Cambridge: Cambridge University Press.

Trigeorgis, L. (1996). *Real Options: Managerial Flexibility and Strategy in Resource Allocation*. Cambridge, MA: MIT Press.

Part II

Agency, Contracts, and Incentives

7

A Self-Enforced Dynamic Contract for Processing of Natural Resources

PETTER BJERKSUND

GUNNAR STENSLAND

This chapter analyzes an optimal contracting principal-agent problem in a dynamic context. The principal who is the owner of a resource (a natural gas field) must get it to the market (through a pipeline) that is owned and operated by a second party (the agent). It is costly to operate the pipeline, but the cost is private information to the agent. The market price of the resource is stochastic. We devise a contract where the principal compensates the agent according to an output price-dependent payment flow schedule, such that the processing decision can be delegated to the agent. The contract ensures that the net cash-flow stream to each party is nonnegative at each future date. Consequently, as compared to compensating the agent up front, the incentives for opportunistic behavior are eliminated.

7.1 INTRODUCTION

The North Sea transportation system (pipelines) links the Norwegian offshore petroleum resources to onshore processing facilities and to major energy markets in the European Union (E.U.). Ownership, exploration, and extraction of petroleum are typically undertaken by parties different from those handling transportation and processing. The Norwegian government controls at least a 50% share of each business entity, which is granted licence. The pipelines and processing facilities are owned by a mixture of private and government-controlled companies. Further complicating the picture is the Norwegian tax code, whereby the offshore petroleum income is subject to a 78% tax rate, rather than the regular 28% corporate income tax rate.

Consider a natural gas owner who must decide on how best to utilize the future production flow from a natural gas field in the North Sea. One alternative is to engage the owner of the existing pipeline system to process and transport the gas to the E.U. in order to sell it in the market. The spot price of gas P_t in this market is uncertain.

It is also costly to operate the pipeline system. This cost is private information to the pipeline owner, and consequently there is a potential rent to be gained from this private information. If E.U. gas exports were the only available alternative, the pipeline owner would be holding the upper hand when settling the terms of the contract. However, the gas is taken onshore Norway before exported across the North Sea to the E.U. Thus, a relevant alternative to E.U. export is for the natural resource owner to transform the gas onshore Norway into other products, such as electricity or methanol.

The aim of the chapter is to devise an optimal contract between the two parties. The analysis is undertaken within a dynamic principal–agent framework, with the natural resource owner (e.g., the government) being the principal and the pipeline owner being the agent. We assume that the natural resource owner can switch costlessly between two alternative uses of the resource flow. The first alternative is to let the agent process and transport the resource (through the pipeline) in order to sell it in the (E.U. gas) market. In this case, the processing-dependent cost n (which is private information) incurs at the agent, while the principal receives the market spot price P_t (uncertain). The other alternative is for the principal to transform the resource into another product (e.g., electricity or methanol). In this case, the principal receives the opportunity value p (constant), whereas the agent gets zero.

The contracting mechanism is as follows: The principal designs the contract, with terms dependent on the processing cost (signal) reported by the agent. The contract consists of (1) a processing strategy, which defines the set of output prices P_t for which the resource will be processed, transported, and sold; and (2) a transfer from the principal to the agent, reflecting the future costs and the rent from private information.

The traditional principal–agent literature typically focuses on the optimal contract between two parties given individual risk preferences (utility functions) (see, e.g., Grossman and Hart, 1983). Hampson et al. (1991) consider a production sharing rule for a particular petroleum exploration venture. They model the behavior of the company (agent) by a specific utility function, and apply a specific geological model. They find that the contract implemented by U.S. authorities is inefficient, and suggest a different sharing rule. However, the optimal contract depends rather heavily on parameters in the utility function.

A basic premise of this chapter is that both parties maximize *market values*. The business entities that typically are involved with natural resources are controlled by governments or by large multinational companies, which are well diversified. Within this capital market framework, the design of the optimal contract is *separated* from the individual risk-taking decisions. The idea is that once the optimal contract (with respect to market values) is settled, each party can use the capital market to optimize individual risk exposure, taking into account own risk preferences and market views.

Our results on optimal contract design are thus based on applying *value additivity*, which is a basic property of capital-market valuation models. Examples include partial valuation models based on the no-arbitrage argument, such as the Black–Scholes option pricing model (OPM), as well as equilibrium models, such as the capital asset pricing model (CAPM).[1]

---

[1] The structure underlying these models is that the relevant Arrow–Debreu state-contingent prices exist and are unique.

In a first-best situation with symmetric information, the optimal processing strategy for the principal is to process the resource whenever the output price P_t exceeds the sum of the opportunity value and the processing cost, $p + n$. The up front compensation corresponds to the market-value equivalent of the future processing costs incurred by implementing this strategy.

In the case of asymmetric information we implement the revelation principle.[2] This principle states that, with no loss of generality, we can restrict our attention to contracts for which it is optimal for the agent to report the cost (n) truthfully. The processing strategies considered are to process whenever the output price P_t exceeds the sum of the opportunity value plus a margin, $p + z$, and derive the optimal margin, z. We find that the principal can replace the up front compensation to the agent by an equivalent output price-dependent *flow* schedule.

The concept of self-enforced contracts is discussed and implemented in several articles.[3] According to Telser (1980), "in a self-enforcing agreement each party decides unilaterally whether he is better off continuing or stopping his relation with the other parties. He stops if and only if the current gain from stopping exceeds the expected present value of his gains continuing." Self-enforcement does not, however, preclude opportunistic behavior (see Williamson, 1975).

Note that the above definition includes contracts where the agent or the principal suffers a temporary loss. We find it useful to introduce the following concept: "A contract is said to be *strongly self-enforced* if the net instantaneous cash-flow stream to each party from participating is nonnegative in all possible future states." Clearly, a strongly self-enforced contract eliminates the probability of bankruptcy. We show that the optimal contract, when implemented in terms of the equivalent output price-dependent compensation flow, is strongly self-enforced, such that the processing decision can be delegated to the agent.

The chapter is organized as follows: Section 7.2 discusses market valuation and assesses the cost and revenue flows to the agent and the principal. Section 7.3 presents the agent's and the principal's decision problems, the revelation principle, and the optimal contract with symmetric information. Section 7.4 considers asymmetric information and derives the optimal processing strategy and the optimal transfer. Section 7.5 considers the case of a perpetual resource flow as an illustration. By invoking additional standard assumptions on the output price dynamics and the market, we obtain familiar valuation results on future cost, revenue, and the up front transfer. Section 7.6 concludes.

7.2 VALUE OF COST AND REVENUE

7.2.1 Market Valuation

We are focusing on the market value of future output price-dependent cash flows. A basic property underlying the standard assumptions of option pricing theory is that the

---

[2] See, e.g., Myerson (1979), Baron and Myerson (1982), and Laffont and Tirole (1993).

[3] See, e.g., Baldwin (1983), Telser (1980), Becker and Stigler (1974), Klein et al. (1978), and Klein and Leffler (1981).

capital market is *dynamically complete*. This means that the output price uncertainty is spanned in the capital markets. The basic idea is that a future cash flow, which is dependent on the stochastic output price P_t, in principle can be replicated in the capital market by an appropriate choice of financial instruments or a self-financing strategy. To preclude arbitrage opportunities, the current value of the claim must equal the current value of the replicating portfolio.

Consider a contingent claim that at future date t provides a payoff $h(t, P_t)$. From contingent claims valuation, the value of a contingent claim in a complete market can be represented by the expectation

$$V_0 [h(t, P_t)] = E_0^* \left[e^{-rt} h(t, P_t) \right] \tag{7.1}$$

where r is the risk-free interest rate (e.g., see Harrison and Pliska, 1979; Harrison and Kreps, 1981). The expectation $E_0^*[\cdot]$ is taken with respect to a unique risk-adjusted probability measure. Existence of such equivalent martingale measure implies no arbitrage opportunities in the economy.

With these assumptions, market values obey value additivity. Consequently, the value of a future contingent cash-flow stream paying $h(t, P_t) \, dt$ from date 0 to T can be represented by the expectation

$$V_0 \left[\int_0^T h(t, P_t) \, dt \right] = E_0^* \left[\int_0^T e^{-rt} h(t, P_t) \, dt \right] \tag{7.2}$$

The above equations are consistent with valuation results from appropriately specified equilibrium models.[4] We also assume that the output price process P_t satisfies the following regularity condition

$$E_0 \left[\int_0^T \delta_{p+z}(P_t) \, dt \right] > 0 \ \forall z \in [0, \infty) \tag{7.3}$$

where $p > 0$ is the opportunity value of the resource, and $\delta_{p+z}(P_t)$ is the Dirac delta function. $\delta_{p+z}(P_t)$ may be interpreted as a function that assumes a value of ∞ if $P_t = p + z$, and zero otherwise, such that its integral is 1. The left-hand side above represents a local time expectation and is often interpreted as the expected time the process will spend at a given level (e.g., see Karlin and Taylor, 1981; Chung and Williams, 1983). A large class of diffusion processes (including the geometric Brownian motion) and mixed jump-diffusion processes satisfy the above condition. All deterministic price processes are excluded, however.

7.2.2 Incurred Cost and Revenue

We consider a dynamic environment in which an owner of a natural resource (the principal) must engage a second party (the agent) to undertake processing and transportation (through a pipeline) in order to sell the resource flow in the market. The market output price P_t is stochastic and the opportunity value p is constant.

---

[4] See, e.g., Constantinides (1989).

We further assume that processing may be switched on and off at no cost any time. With an uncertain output price, P_t, the optimal processing strategy will typically be represented by an output price-dependent switching rule. We model this strategy as follows: Processing takes place at date t if and only if the output price P_t exceeds the opportunity value of the resource p (assumed constant) by a margin z. The optimal margin z is determined below as part of the optimal contract. We assume that the margin z is independent of calendar time t and output price P_t.

Consider next the incurred cost and revenue following from a given processing strategy (i.e., margin parameter z). The processing cost (n) is incurred only when processing takes place. Consequently, the agent's cash-flow stream per unit time, $c(P_t; z, n)$, is given by

$$c(P_t; z, n) = -n\, I(P_t \geq p + z) \tag{7.4}$$

where $I(P_t \geq p + z)$ represents the indicator function, assuming unity whenever $P_t \geq p + z$, and zero otherwise. When processing takes place, the principal receives the market output price, P_t, and the opportunity value, p, otherwise. Hence, the principal's cash-flow stream per unit time, $s(P_t; z)$, is

$$s(P_t; z) = (P_t - p)\, I(P_t \geq p + z) + p \tag{7.5}$$

In a dynamically complete market, we may use valuation result (7.2) to represent the market value of the agent's future cash-flow stream, $C(z, n)$, by

$$C(z, n) \equiv V_0 \left[\int_0^T c(P_t; z, n)\, dt \right]$$

$$= E_0^* \left[\int_0^T e^{-rt}(-n)\, I(P_t \geq p + z)\, dt \right] \tag{7.6}$$

where T is the horizon date. Similarly, we represent the market value of the principal's future cash-flow stream by[5]

$$S(z) \equiv V_0 \left[\int_0^T s(P_t; z)\, dt \right]$$

$$= E_0^* \left[\int_0^T e^{-rt}\, [(P_t - p)\, I(P_t \geq p + z) + p]\, dt \right] \tag{7.7}$$

7.3 THE CONTRACT

Processing itself is costly, and the agent has private information on the processing cost n. It is common knowledge, however, that the agent's processing cost is uni-

---

[5] It is assumed that both $C(z, n)$ and $S(z)$ are continuous with respect to their arguments, and that the partials are well-defined and continuous.

formly distributed over the interval $[\underline{n}, \overline{n}]$. We denote the probability density and the cumulative probability distribution by $f(n)$ and $F(n)$, respectively.[6]

The following contracting mechanism is assumed between the two parties: The principal designs the contract, where the terms are made conditional on a signal y reported by the agent. The contract consists of an up front transfer $W(y)$ from the principal to the agent, and a margin $z(y)$ that defines the output price-dependent processing strategy. Taking the signal-dependent contract as given, the agent reports his signal y and decides thereafter on whether to accept or reject the contract. The contract is assumed enforcable and binding (if accepted).

7.3.1 The Agent's Problem

The agent faces the signal-dependent processing strategy $z(y)$ and up front transfer $W(y)$. The agent chooses the signal y in order to maximize the sum of the market value of his future cash-flow stream $C[z(y), n]$ and the up front transfer $W(y)$, i.e.,

$$C\,[z(y), n] + W(y) \tag{7.8}$$

The optimal signal $y = \rho(n)$, which depends on the true cost n, is given by the first-order incentive compatibility condition

$$C_z\,[z(y), n]\,z'(y) + W_y(y) = 0 \tag{7.9}$$

We assume that the alternative to cooperation is to keep the processing facility idle, yielding a zero net cash-flow stream. To induce the agent to participate (even in the case of $n = \overline{n}$) we impose the constraint

$$C\,\{z\,[\rho(\overline{n})]\,, \overline{n}\} + W\,[\rho(\overline{n})] \geq 0 \tag{7.10}$$

where the right-hand side reflects the agent's reservation value.

7.3.2 The Revelation Principle

To obtain the principal's optimal processing strategy $z[\rho(n)]$ and transfer function $W[\rho(n)]$ we rely on the revelation principle. This principle exploits the fact that there is one degree of freedom in the information exchange between the two parties, which allows principals with no loss of generality to restrict their attention to contracts where truth telling is optimal for the agent, i.e., $y = \rho(n) = n$. By substituting $y = n$ into conditions (7.9)–(7.10), the incentive compatibility and the participation constraints become

$$C_z[z(n), n]\,z'(n) + W_y(n) = 0 \tag{7.11}$$

$$C[z(\overline{n}), \overline{n}] + W(\overline{n}) \geq 0 \tag{7.12}$$

---

[6] The probability functions are $f(n) = 1/(\overline{n} - \underline{n})$ and $F(n) = (n - \underline{n})/(\overline{n} - \underline{n})$.

The optimal transfer function is characterized as follows. Consider the agent's maximum value function

$$\Gamma(n) = C\,[z(n), n] + W(n) \tag{7.13}$$

If we differentiate the above equation with respect to n, and substitute the incentive compatibility constraint (7.11), we obtain

$$\Gamma_n(n) = C_n\,[z(n), n] \tag{7.14}$$

Expressing the maximum value function as

$$\Gamma(n) = \Gamma(\bar{n}) - \int_n^{\bar{n}} \Gamma_n(u)\,du \tag{7.15}$$

it follows from the participation constraint (7.12)—which at the optimum holds with equality—that the first term on the right-hand side is zero. Substituting the definition of $\Gamma(n)$ and Eq. (7.14) into Eq. (7.15), we can express the optimal transfer function as

$$W(n) = -C\,[z(n), n] - \int_n^{\bar{n}} C_n\,[z(u), u]\,du \tag{7.16}$$

Note that the first term on the right-hand side compensates the agent for the future processing costs. The second term may be interpreted as the agent's rent from private information.

7.3.3 The Principal's Problem

The principal's problem is to choose the "best" processing strategy $z(n)$ and transfer function $W(n)$, taking into account the agent's behavior. For a given choice, the total value to the principal is the difference between the market value of future revenue $S[z(n)]$ and the up front compensation $W(n)$, i.e.,

$$S\,[z(n)] - W(n) \tag{7.17}$$

This is conditional on the true processing cost n. The principal considers the true cost n as being stochastic. This uncertainty is assumed independent of the price processes in the capital market. Moreover, it is "washed out" in a well-diversified portfolio. Consequently, the risk-adjusted probability measure of n equals its true probability measure, and is independent of the output-price process.

In some situations, the principal may benefit indirectly from the agent's market value. This is the case if the principal holds a minority interest in the company that is acting as the agent. With the government being the principal, the benefits can be explained by future tax revenue claims on the agent and increased economic activity. Hence, we can assume that the principal maximizes the following weighted sum of market values to each party

$$\Pi = E\big[\,\{S[z(n)] - W(n)\} + a\,\{C[z(n), n] + W(n)\}\,\big]$$

where the constant $0 \le a < 1$ reflects the principal's benefit (if any) from the agent's market value. Observe that $a = 0$ corresponds to the case where principals maximize their own market value.

Hence, the principal maximizes the welfare function

$$\Pi = \int_{\underline{n}}^{\overline{n}} [\{S[z(n)] - W(n)\} + a\{C[z(n), n] + W(n)\}] \, f(n) \, dn$$

$$= \int_{\underline{n}}^{\overline{n}} \{S[z(n)] - (1 - a)W(n) + a\, C[z(n), n]\} \, f(n) \, dn \qquad (7.18)$$

with respect to the processing stategy $z(n)$ and the compensation schedule $W(n)$, subject to the agent's behavior

$$C_z\,[z(n), n]\, z'(n) + W_y(n) = 0 \qquad (7.19)$$

$$C\,[z(\overline{n}), \overline{n}] + W(\overline{n}) \ge 0 \qquad (7.20)$$

We recognize the two constraints above as the incentive compatibility and the participation conditions from the agent's maximization problem, respectively. Equation (7.20) means that the principal—given the common knowledge on n—designs the contract such that the agent will participate with probability 1. In Appendix A, we show that this condition is in fact optimal for the principal.

7.3.4 Symmetric Information Case

Consider first the case of symmetric information, where the processing cost n is common knowledge. The principal's objective function then reduces to

$$\Pi = S[z(n)] - (1 - a)\,W(n) + a\,C[z(n), n] \qquad (7.21)$$

This is maximized with respect to $z(n)$ and $W(n)$, subject to the participation constraint

$$C[z(n), n] + W(n) \ge 0 \qquad (7.22)$$

Under symmetric information (and $a < 1$), the transfer function is determined such that the constraint above holds with equality. It follows that

$$W(n) = -C[z(n), n] \qquad (7.23)$$

i.e., the up front transfer compensates the agent for the future incurred cost from following the optimal processing strategy. Under symmetric information, there is (by definition) no private information, and consequently the agent receives no information rent.

If we substitute the transfer function (7.23) into the welfare function (7.21), we can use (7.6) and (7.7) to express the welfare function in terms of the expectation

$$\Pi = E_0^* \left[\int_0^T e^{-rt} [P_t - (p + n)] \, I\,[P_t \ge p + z(n)] \, dt \right] + \int_0^T e^{-rt} p \, dt \qquad (7.24)$$

The principal's objective function Π is maximized with respect to $z(n)$. It can be seen from (7.24) that the optimal processing strategy in this case is to choose the margin $z(n) = n$. Consequently, processing occurs whenever the output price P_t exceeds the sum of opportunity value and true processing cost, $p+n$. Hence, there is no efficiency loss under symmetric information.

However, compensating future costs by an up front payment is not realistic in practice. One obvious problem is the agent's incentive for future opportunistic behavior (e.g., to take the money and run). Under symmetric information, the up front transfer $W(n)$ represents the market value equivalent from compensating the future incurred cost, i.e.,

$$W(n) = E_0^* \left[\int_0^T e^{-rt} n\, I(P_t \geq p + z)\, dt \right] \qquad (7.25)$$

Consequently, the principal may implement the optimal contract by replacing the up front payment $W(n)$ by the following equivalent output price-dependent flow scheme:

$$w\,[P_t; z(n) = n, n] = n\, I(P_t \geq p + n) \qquad (7.26)$$

Observe that with this arrangement, the net cash-flow stream to the agent is[7]

$$c\,[P_t; z(n) = n, n] + w\,[P_t, z(n) = n, n] \geq 0 \text{ for all } P_t$$

whereas the net cash-flow stream of keeping the processing facility idle is zero. Consequently, the incentives for opportunistic behavior induced by paying the agent up front are eliminated when replacing the payment with the equivalent output price-dependent flow scheme.

7.4 ASYMMETRIC INFORMATION CASE

7.4.1 Optimal Processing Strategy

We now consider the case of asymmetric information. To derive the optimal processing strategy, we substitute Eq. (7.16) into the welfare function (7.18) to obtain

$$\Pi = \int_{\underline{n}}^{\bar{n}} \left\{ S\,[z(n)] + C[z(n), n] + (1 - a) \int_n^{\bar{n}} C_n[z(u), u]\, du \right\} f(n)\, dn \qquad (7.27)$$

It can be shown that[8]

---

[7] In fact, the condition holds with equality.

[8] Integration by parts yields

$$\int_{\underline{n}}^{\bar{n}} \left\{ \int_n^{\bar{n}} C_n[z(u), u]\, du \right\} f(n)\, dn = \left\{ \int_n^{\bar{n}} C_n[z(u), u]\, du\, F(n) \right\}_{\underline{n}}^{\bar{n}} + \int_{\underline{n}}^{\bar{n}} C_n[z(n), n]\, F(n)\, dn$$

The first term on the right-hand side is zero, which leads to Eq. (7.28).

$$\int_{\underline{n}}^{\overline{n}} \left\{ \int_n^{\overline{n}} C_n[z(u), u] \, du \right\} f(n) \, dn = \int_{\underline{n}}^{\overline{n}} C_n[z(n), n] \, F(n) \, dn \qquad (7.28)$$

We can then use the above equation to rewrite the welfare function as

$$\Pi = \int_{\underline{n}}^{\overline{n}} \left\{ S[z(n)] + C[z(n), n] + (1 - a) C_n[z(n), n] \frac{F(n)}{f(n)} \right\} f(n) \, dn \quad (7.29)$$

which is maximized with respect to $z(n)$. Point-wise maximization then yields the condition

$$S_z[z(n)] + C_z[z(n), n] + (1 - a) \, C_{zn}[z(n), n] \frac{F(n)}{f(n)} = 0 \qquad (7.30)$$

from which the optimal processing strategy $z(n)$ is determined.

It follows from Eqs. (7.6)–(7.7) that[9]

$$S_z(z) = E_0^* \left[\int_0^T e^{-rt} (-1)(P_t - p) \delta_{p+z}(P_t) \, dt \right] \qquad (7.31)$$

$$C_z(z, n) = E_0^* \left[\int_0^T e^{-rt} n \delta_{p+z}(P_t) \, dt \right] \qquad (7.32)$$

$$C_{zn}(z, n) = E_0^* \left[\int_0^T e^{-rt} \delta_{p+z}(P_t) \, dt \right] \qquad (7.33)$$

where $\delta_{p+z}(P_t)$ is the Dirac delta function. By substituting Eqs. (7.31)–(7.33) and the probability functions into Eq. (7.30) and rearranging, we obtain the condition

$$E_0^* \left\{ \int_0^T e^{-rt} \left[P_t - p - n - (1 - a)(n - \underline{n}) \right] \delta_{p+z(n)}(P_t) \, dt \right\} = 0 \quad (7.34)$$

Recalling that $\delta_{p+z(n)}(P_t) = 0$ for $P_t \neq p + z(n)$ it can be seen that the optimal processing strategy is

$$z(n) = n + (1 - a)(n - \underline{n}) \qquad (7.35)$$

Note that the processing strategy is linear in n. In the limiting case of $a = 1$ where the principal maximizes the total market value to both parties, we obtain $z(n) = n$, which coincides with the case of symmetric information. With $a < 1$ and $n > \underline{n}$, we have $z(n) > n$, introducing loss in efficiency.

In our analysis above, we have implicitly assumed that the processing strategy (i.e., the margin z) is independent of calendar time t. To justify this, observe that with solution (7.35) the product of the Dirac delta function and the expression inside the squarebrackets in Eq. (7.34) is zero for all t.

---

[9] Condition (7.3) and the existence of a unique equivalent risk-adjusted probability measure ensure that Eqs. (7.31)–(7.33) are well defined.

7.4.2 Optimal Transfer and Implementation

The optimal transfer function $W(n)$ can be determined from condition (7.16) above. We show in Appendix B that the optimal transfer function can be expressed as the market value of a future ouput price-dependent cash-flow stream, namely

$$W(n) = E_0^* \left[\int_0^T e^{-rt} w\,[P_t; z(n), n]\, dt \right] \tag{7.36}$$

where the output price-dependent flow scheme $w[P_t; z(n), n]$ is

$$w\,[P_t; z(n), n] = \begin{cases} 0 & \text{when } P_t < p + (2-a)n - (1-a)\underline{n} \\ \frac{1}{2-a}(P_t - p) + \left(\frac{1-a}{2-a}\right)\underline{n} & \text{when } p + (2-a)n - (1-a)\underline{n} \leq P_t \\ & \text{and } P_t < p + (2-a)\overline{n} - (1-a)\underline{n} \\ \overline{n} & \text{when } p + (2-a)\overline{n} - (1-a)\underline{n} \leq P_t \end{cases} \tag{7.37}$$

Compensating the agent with $W(n)$ up front, however, is not realistic in practice. One reason is that once it receives the up-front compensation, there are clear incentives for the agent to behave in an opportunistic manner. Suppose that both parties commit to the optimal processing strategy $z(n)$, and that the principal chooses to compensate the agent in terms of the equivalent output price-dependent cash-flow stream $w[P_t; z(n), n]$. It is easy to verify that

$$w[P_t; z(n), n] + c[P_t; z(n), n] \geq 0 \text{ for all } P_t$$

which implies that the agent's future net cash flow from cooperating is nonnegative in all possible states. Consequently, the obvious incentives for opportunistic behavior, which would be induced by paying the agent $W(n)$ up front, are eliminated by using the output price-dependent cash-flow stream.

In fact, the principal may implement the contract such that the processing decision can be delegated to the agent. Consider the following arrangement: Whenever the agent chooses to process the resource, the principal compensates the agent according to the output price-dependent schedule:

$$\tau(P_t) = \begin{cases} \frac{1}{2-a}(P_t - p) + \left(\frac{1-a}{2-a}\right)\underline{n} & \text{when } P_t < p + (2-a)\overline{n} - (1-a)\underline{n} \\ \overline{n} & \text{when } p + (2-a)\overline{n} - (1-a)\underline{n} \leq P_t \end{cases} \tag{7.38}$$

Clearly, it will be optimal for the agent to process whenever the compensation exceeds the true incurred cost, i.e., $\tau(P_t) > n$. It is easy to verify that this strategy is equivalent to the optimal processing strategy obtained in Section 7.4.1 above.

7.5 AN ILLUSTRATION WITH PERPETUAL RESOURCE FLOW

The analysis above is quite general. As an illustration, in this section we consider the case of a perpetual resource flow. To obtain the value of cost, revenue, and transfer, we adopt additional standard assumptions from the real options literature on the output price process (geometric Brownian motion) and the valuation framework (Black–Scholes economy).

7.5.1 Assumptions

Firstly, we assume the existence of a default-free zero-coupon bond with price dynamics

$$B_t = B e^{rt} \tag{7.39}$$

where $r > 0$ is the constant risk-free interest rate. Second, we assume a nondividend paying financial risky asset, with price dynamics

$$X_t = X \exp\left[(\mu - \tfrac{1}{2}\sigma^2)t + \sigma Z_t\right] \tag{7.40}$$

Z_t is a standard Brownian motion with expectation $E_0[Z_t] = 0$ and variance $\mathrm{Var}_0[Z_t] = t$. This implies that the future asset price is log normal.[10] Third, we invoke the "perfect frictionless market" assumption.

Assume that the processed resource (output) may be sold in a competitive market with spot price dynamics

$$P_t = P \exp\left[(\mu - \delta - \tfrac{1}{2}\sigma^2)t + \sigma Z_t\right] \tag{7.41}$$

where Z_t is identical to the standard Brownian motion generating the risky financial asset price,[11] and $\delta \geq 0$ can be interpreted as the net convenience yield (see Brennan and Schwartz, 1985; Brennan, 1991). For notational convenience, we define $b \equiv r - \delta$, corresponding to the (net) "cost of carry."

7.5.2 Valuation

The contingent claim value can then be obtained by first replacing the "fair rate of return" μ for the riskless interest rate r in (7.41), inserting this modified output price process into (7.1) or (7.2) above, and calculating the relevant expectation. For our purposes, we use the following valuation results:

$$E_0^*\left[\int_0^\infty e^{-rt}\, dt\right] = 1/r \tag{7.42}$$

$$E_0^*\left[\int_0^\infty e^{-rt} P_t\, dt\right] = P/\delta \tag{7.43}$$

$$E_0^*\left[\int_0^\infty e^{-rt} I(P_t \geq \hat{P})\, dt\right] = \begin{cases} \beta_1 \hat{P}^{-\varepsilon_1} P^{\varepsilon_1} & \text{when } P < \hat{P} \\ \beta_2 \hat{P}^{-\varepsilon_2} P^{\varepsilon_2} + 1/r & \text{when } \hat{P} \leq P \end{cases} \tag{7.44}$$

---

[10] Equations (7.39) and (7.40) correspond to the instantaneous returns being $dB_t/B_t = r\, dt$ and $dX_t/X_t = \mu\, dt + \sigma\, dZ_t$.

[11] It follows that the instantaneous dynamics is $dP_t/P_t = (\mu - \delta)\, dt + \sigma\, dZ_t$.

$$E_0^* \left[\int_0^\infty e^{-rt} P_t \, I(P_t \geq \hat{P}) \, dt \right] = \begin{cases} \beta_3 \hat{P}^{1-\varepsilon_1} P^{\varepsilon_1} & \text{when } P < \hat{P} \\ \beta_4 \hat{P}^{1-\varepsilon_2} P^{\varepsilon_2} + P/\delta & \text{when } \hat{P} \leq P \end{cases} \quad (7.45)$$

where

$$\varepsilon_1 \equiv \left(\frac{1}{2} - \frac{b}{\sigma^2} \right) + \sqrt{\left(\frac{b}{\sigma^2} - \frac{1}{2} \right)^2 + \frac{2r}{\sigma^2}} \; (> 1) \quad (7.46)$$

$$\varepsilon_2 \equiv \left(\frac{1}{2} - \frac{b}{\sigma^2} \right) - \sqrt{\left(\frac{b}{\sigma^2} - \frac{1}{2} \right)^2 + \frac{2r}{\sigma^2}} \; (< 0) \quad (7.47)$$

and

$$\beta_1 \equiv \frac{-\varepsilon_2}{r(\varepsilon_1 - \varepsilon_2)} \; (> 0) \quad (7.48)$$

$$\beta_2 \equiv \frac{-\varepsilon_1}{r(\varepsilon_1 - \varepsilon_2)} \; (< 0) \quad (7.49)$$

$$\beta_3 \equiv \frac{1 - \varepsilon_2}{\delta(\varepsilon_1 - \varepsilon_2)} \; (> 0) \quad (7.50)$$

$$\beta_4 \equiv \frac{1 - \varepsilon_1}{\delta(\varepsilon_1 - \varepsilon_2)} \; (< 0) \quad (7.51)$$

obtained by satisfying the "value matching" and "high contact" conditions.

7.5.3 Market Value of Cost and Revenue

Using the market value of future cost and revenue from (7.6) and (7.7), and the up front compensation from (7.36)–(7.37) above, it follows from value additivity that we can express $C(z, n)$, $S(z)$, and $W(n)$ as

$$C(z, n) = -n E_0^* \left[\int_0^\infty e^{-rt} I(P_t \geq p + z) \, dt \right]$$

$$S(z) = E_0^* \left[\int_0^\infty e^{-rt} P_t \, I(P_t \geq p + z) \, dt \right]$$

$$\quad - p E_0^* \left[\int_0^\infty e^{-rt} I(P_t \geq p + z) \, dt \right]$$

$$\quad + p E_0^* \left[\int_0^\infty e^{-rt} \, dt \right]$$

$$W(n) = (2 - a)^{-1} E_0^* \left[\int_0^\infty e^{-rt} P_t \, I(P_t \geq p + z) \, dt \right]$$

$$\quad - (2 - a)^{-1} \left[p - (1 - a)\underline{n} \right] E_0^* \left[\int_0^\infty e^{-rt} I(P_t \geq p + z) \, dt \right]$$

$$\quad - (2 - a)^{-1} E_0^* \left[\int_0^\infty e^{-rt} P_t \, I(P_t \geq p + \overline{z}) \, dt \right]$$

$$+ (2-a)^{-1}\left[p - (1-a)\underline{n}\right] E_0^* \left[\int_0^\infty e^{-rt} I(P_t \geq p + \bar{z})\, dt\right]$$

$$+ \bar{n}\, E_0^* \left[\int_0^\infty e^{-rt} I(P_t \geq p + \bar{z})\, dt\right]$$

where we use the notation $z \equiv z(n)$ and $\bar{z} \equiv z(\bar{n})$.

Observe that $C(z, n)$, $S(z)$, and $W(n)$ can be interpreted as portfolios of future output price-dependent flows (evaluated in the subsection just above). It follows that

$$C(z, n) = \begin{cases} -n\beta_1(p + z)^{-\varepsilon_1} P^{\varepsilon_1} & \text{when } P < p + z \\ -n\left[\beta_2(p + z)^{-\varepsilon_2} P^{\varepsilon_2} + 1/r\right] & \text{when } p + z \leq P \end{cases}$$

$$S(z) = \begin{cases} \beta_3(p + z)^{1-\varepsilon_1} P^{\varepsilon_1} - p\left[\beta_1(p + z)^{-\varepsilon_1} P^{\varepsilon_1} - 1/r\right] & \text{when } P < p + z \\ \beta_4(p + z)^{1-\varepsilon_2} P^{\varepsilon_2} + P/\delta - p\beta_2(p + z)^{-\varepsilon_2} P^{\varepsilon_2} & \text{when } p + z \leq P \end{cases}$$

$$W(n) = \begin{cases}
\begin{aligned}
& (2-a)^{-1}\beta_3(p + z)^{1-\varepsilon_1} P^{\varepsilon_1} \\
& - (2-a)^{-1}\left[p - (1-a)\underline{n}\right]\beta_1(p + z)^{-\varepsilon_1} P^{\varepsilon_1} \\
& - (2-a)^{-1}\beta_3(p + \bar{z})^{1-\varepsilon_1} P^{\varepsilon_1} \\
& + (2-a)^{-1}\left[p - (1-a)\underline{n}\right]\beta_1(p + \bar{z})^{-\varepsilon_1} P^{\varepsilon_1} \\
& + \bar{n}\beta_1(p + \bar{z})^{-\varepsilon_1} P^{\varepsilon_1} \qquad\qquad\qquad \text{when } P < p + z
\end{aligned} \\[2em]
\begin{aligned}
& (2-a)^{-1}\left[\beta_4(p + z)^{1-\varepsilon_2} P^{\varepsilon_2} + P/\delta\right] \\
& - (2-a)^{-1}\left[p - (1-a)\underline{n}\right]\left[\beta_2(p + z)^{-\varepsilon_2} P^{\varepsilon_2} + 1/r\right] \\
& - (2-a)^{-1}\beta_3\left[(p + \bar{z})^{1-\varepsilon_1} P^{\varepsilon_1}\right] \\
& + (2-a)^{-1}\left[p - (1-a)\underline{n}\right]\beta_1(p + \bar{z})^{-\varepsilon_1} P^{\varepsilon_1} \\
& + \bar{n}\beta_1(p + \bar{z})^{-\varepsilon_1} P^{\varepsilon_1} \qquad\qquad\qquad \text{when } p + z \leq P \\
& \qquad\qquad\qquad\qquad\qquad\qquad\qquad\quad \text{and } P < p + \bar{z}
\end{aligned} \\[2em]
\begin{aligned}
& (2-a)^{-1}\left[\beta_4(p + z)^{1-\varepsilon_2} P^{\varepsilon_2} + P/\delta\right] \\
& - (2-a)^{-1}\left[p - (1-a)\underline{n}\right]\left[\beta_2(p + z)^{-\varepsilon_2} P^{\varepsilon_2} + 1/r\right] \\
& - (2-a)^{-1}\left[\beta_4(p + \bar{z})^{1-\varepsilon_2} P^{\varepsilon_2} + P/\delta\right] \\
& + (2-a)^{-1}\left[p - (1-a)\underline{n}\right]\left[\beta_2(p + \bar{z})^{-\varepsilon_2} P^{\varepsilon_2} + 1/r\right] \\
& + \bar{n}\left[\beta_2(p + \bar{z})^{-\varepsilon_2} P^{\varepsilon_2} + 1/r\right] \qquad\quad \text{when } p + \bar{z} \leq P
\end{aligned}
\end{cases}$$

respectively.

7.6 CONCLUSION

This chapter considers a dynamic situation where a natural resource owner can costlessly switch between two alternative uses of a resource flow: (1) let the agent undertake processing and transportation and sell it in the market; or (2) transform the resource into another product, yielding a constant opportunity value. The agent has private information on his own cost, it is common knowledge that the cost is uniformly distributed, and the spot market price is uncertain.

The two parties focus on market values, and derive the optimal contract between them using a principal–agent framework and the revelation principle. We show that the principal can implement the optimal contract by offering the agent an output price-dependent flow schedule and delegating the processing decision to the agent, such that the arrangement is strongly self-enforced.

ACKNOWLEDGMENTS

We thank P. O. Christensen, A. Eilifsen, S. Ekern, Ø. Gjerde, H. E. Leland, T. E. Olsen, P. Osmundsen, L. Rud, C. W. Smith, Jr., participants of the Second Nordic Symposium on Contingent Claims Analysis in Finance, anonymous referees, and the editors M. J. Brennan and L. Trigeorgis. Financial support from The Research Council of Norway is gratefully acknowledged.

Appendix A

The Participation Constraint

In this Appendix, we establish that the participation condition, as stated in Eq. (7.12), is optimal. Suppose that the principal designs the contract such that the agent is induced to reject it if his true cost n exceeds n^*, where we may interpret the decision variable n^* as the true cost of the marginal agent. This modification of the problem does not affect the optimal processing strategy $z(n)$, whereas the participation constraint becomes

$$C[z(n^*), n^*] + W(n^*) = 0 \tag{7.A1}$$

with $\underline{n} < n^* < \bar{n}$. The optimal transfer function is characterized by

$$W(n) = \begin{cases} -C[z(n), n] - \int_n^{n^*} C_n[z(u), u]\, du & \text{when } n \leq n^* \\ -C[z(n), n^*] & \text{when } n^* < n \end{cases} \tag{7.A2}$$

which induces the agent to reject the contract if $n^* < n$. The maximum value function to the agent is

$$\Gamma(n) = \begin{cases} -\int_n^{n^*} C_n[z(u), u]\, du & \text{when } n \leq n^* \\ C[z(n), n] - C(z(n), n^*) & \text{when } n^* < n \end{cases} \tag{7.A3}$$

In the case where $n^* < n$, the incurred cost exceeds the compensation offered by the principal, hence inducing the agent to reject the contract.

The principal's objective function then becomes

$$\Pi(n^*) = \int_{\underline{n}}^{n^*} \left\{ S\left[z(n)\right] + C\left[z(n), n\right] + (1-a)C_n[z(n), n]\frac{F(n)}{f(n)} \right\} f(n)\, dn$$

$$+ \int_{n^*}^{\bar{n}} \left\{ \int_0^T e^{-rt} p\, dt \right\} f(n)\, dn \qquad (7.A4)$$

The first term on the right-hand side corresponds to the situation where the contract is accepted by the agent, i.e., $n < n^*$, whereas the latter term corresponds to the situation where the agent rejects the contract, i.e., $n^* < n$.

The first-order condition is

$$\Pi'(n^*) = \left\{ S[z(n^*)] + C[z(n^*), n^*] \right.$$

$$\left. + (1-a)C_n[z(n^*), n^*]\frac{F(n^*)}{f(n^*)} - \int_0^T e^{-rt} p\, dt \right\} f(n^*) \qquad (7.A5)$$

Substituting

$$C_n(z, n) = \frac{\partial}{\partial n} E_0^* \left[\int_0^T e^{-rt}(-n)\, I\,(P_t \geq p + z)\, dt \right]$$

$$= E_0^* \left[\int_0^T e^{-rt}(-1)\, I\,(P_t \geq p + z)\, dt \right] \qquad (7.A6)$$

into the first-order condition (7.A5), inserting the probability functions, and simplifying gives

$$\Pi'(n^*) = (\bar{n} - \underline{n})^{-1} \int_0^T e^{-rt} \left[P_t - p - z(n^*) \right]\, I\,(P_t \geq p + z(n^*))\, dt \qquad (7.A7)$$

which is positive for all n^*. Consequently, the optimal choice for the principal is to choose $n^* = \bar{n}$. This means that it is optimal for the principal to design the contract such that the agent will cooperate with probability 1.

Appendix B

Optimal Compensation

Recall from Eq. (7.16) that the optimal transfer is

$$W(n) = -C[n, z(n)] - \int_{\underline{n}}^{\bar{n}} C_n[u, z(u)]\, du \qquad (7.B1)$$

where

$$C(n, z) = E_0^* \left[\int_0^T e^{-rt}(-n)\, I\,(P_t \geq p + z)\, dt \right] \qquad (7.B2)$$

$$C_n(n, z) = \frac{\partial}{\partial n} \left\{ E_0^* \left[\int_0^T e^{-rt} (-n) I(P_t \geq p + z) \, dt \right] \right\}$$

$$= (-1) E_0^* \left[\int_0^T e^{-rt} I(P_t \geq p + z) \, dt \right] \quad (7.B3)$$

Consequently,

$$W(n) = E_0^* \left[\int_0^T e^{-rt} n \, I[P_t \geq p + z(n)] \, dt \right]$$

$$+ \int_n^{\bar{n}} \left\{ E_0^* \left[\int_0^T e^{-rt} I[P_t \geq p + z(u)] \, dt \right] \right\} du$$

$$= E_0^* \left[\int_0^T e^{-rt} n \, I[P_t \geq p + z(n)] \, dt \right]$$

$$+ E_0^* \left[\int_0^T e^{-rt} \left\{ \int_n^{\bar{n}} I[P_t \geq p + z(u)] \, du \right\} dt \right] \quad (7.B4)$$

Applying integration by parts to the expression inside the curly brackets, we obtain

$$\int_n^{\bar{n}} I[P_t > p + z(u)] \, du = [u \, I(P_t \geq p + z)]_n^{\bar{n}}$$

$$+ \int_n^{\bar{n}} u \delta_{p+z}(P_t) z'(u) \, du \quad (7.B5)$$

Defining the new integration variable

$$P_t = p + z(u)$$

$$= p + (2 - a)u - (1 - a)\underline{n} \quad (7.B6)$$

it follows that

$$d P_t = z'(u) \, du \quad (7.B7)$$

$$u = (2 - a)^{-1} \left[P_t - p + (1 - a)\underline{n} \right] \quad (7.B8)$$

Substituting Eqs. (7.B7)–(7.B8) into Eq. (7.B5), we obtain

$$\int_n^{\bar{n}} I[P_t \geq p + z(u)] \, du$$

$$= [u \, I(P_t \geq p + z)]_n^{\bar{n}}$$

$$+ \int_{p+z(n)}^{p+z(\bar{n})} (2 - a)^{-1} \left[P_t - p + (1 - a)\underline{n} \right] \delta_{p+z(u)}(P_t) \, d P_t$$

$$= \bar{n} I [P_t \geq p + z(\bar{n})] - n I [P_t \geq p + z(n)]$$

$$+ (2 - a)^{-1} \left[P_t - p + (1 - a)\underline{n} \right] I [P_t \geq p + z(n)]$$

$$- (2 - a)^{-1} \left[P_t - p + (1 - a)\underline{n} \right] I [P_t \geq p + z(\bar{n})] \quad (7.B9)$$

Substituting back into $W(n)$ and simplifying, we obtain:

$$W(n) = E_0^* \left[\int_0^T e^{-rt} w\left[P_t; z(n), n\right] dt \right] \tag{7.B10}$$

where

$$w[P_t; z(n), n] = (2-a)^{-1} \left[P_t - p + (1-a)\underline{n}\right] I \left[P_t \geq p + z(n)\right] +$$

$$\left\{\overline{n} - (2-a)^{-1} \left[P_t - p + (1-a)\underline{n}\right]\right\} I \left[P_t \geq p + z(\overline{n})\right] \tag{7.B11}$$

This is equivalent to the result stated as Eqs. (7.36) - (7.37) above.

REFERENCES

Baldwin, C. Y. (1983). Productivity and Labor Unions: An Application of the Theory of Self-enforcing Contracts. *Journal of Business* 56(2), 155–185.

Baron, D. P., and R. B. Myerson. (1982). Regulating a Monopolist with Unknown Costs. *Econometrica* 50, 911–930.

Becker, G. S., and G. J. Stiegler. (1974). Law Enforcement, Malfeasance and Compensation of Enforcers. *Journal of Legal Studies* 3, (January), 1–18.

Brennan, M. J. (1991). The Price of Convenience and the Valuation of Commodity Contingent Claims. In D. Lund and B. Øksendal (eds.), *Stochastic Models and Option Values.* Amsterdam: North-Holland.

Brennan, M. J., and E. S. Schwartz. (1985). Evaluating Natural Resource Investments. *Journal of Business* 58, 135–157.

Chung, K. L., and R. J. Williams. (1983). *Introduction to Stochastic Integration.* Boston, MA: Birchäuser.

Constantinides, G. M. (1989). Theory and Valuation: Overview and Recent Developments. In S. Bhattacharya and G. M. Constantinides (eds.), *Theory of Valuation.* Totowa, NJ: Rowman & Littlefield.

Grossman, S. J., and O. D. Hart. (1983). An Analysis of the Principal-Agent Problem. *Econometrica* 51, 7–45.

Hampson, P., J. Parsons, and C. Blitzer. (1991). A Case Study in the Design of an Optimal Production Sharing Rule for a Petroleum Exploration Venture. *Journal of Financial Economics* 30, 45–67.

Harrison, J. M., and D. Kreps. (1979). Martingales and Arbitrage in Multiperiod Security Markets. *Journal of Economic Theory* 20 (July), 381–408.

Harrison, J. M., and S. Pliska. (1981). Martingales and Stochastic Integrals in the Theory of Continuous Trading. *Stochastic Processes and Their Applications* 11, 215–260.

Karlin, S., and H. M. Taylor. (1981). *A Second Course in Stochastic Processes.* San Diego, CA: Academic Press.

Klein, B., R. G. Crawford, and A. A. Alchian. (1978). Vertical Integration, Appropriable Rents, and the Competitive Contracting Process. *Journal of Law and Economics* 21 (October), 297–326.

Klein, B., and K. B. Leffler. (1981). The Role of Market Forces in Assuring Contractual Performance. *Journal of Political Economy* 89 (August), 615–641.

Laffont, J., and J. Tirole. (1993). *A Theory of Incentives in Procurement and Regulation.* Cambridge, MA: MIT Press.

Myerson, R. B. (1979). Incentive Compatibility and the Bargaining Problem. *Econometrica* 47, 61–74.

Telser, L. G. (1980). A Theory of Self-enforcing Agreements. *Journal of Business* 53(1), 27–44.

Williamson, O. E. (1975). *Markets and Hierarchies: Analysis and Antitrust Implications*. New York: Free Press.

8

Bidding for the Antamina Mine

Valuation and Incentives in a Real Options Context

ALBERTO MOEL

PETER TUFANO

This chapter studies the bidding for a copper mine that was offered for sale by the Peruvian government as part of the country's privatization program. The mine itself had a valuable real option component, in the form of the right to develop the mine after completing exploration, which we analyze using Monte Carlo simulation methods. A novel aspect of the transaction was the type of bid requested by the Peruvian government, essentially asking bidders to state both the *premium* that they would pay and the *exercise price* (pledged development expenditure) they would set for this real option. This structure gave rise to incentives that affected the amount that firms would offer, their preferences between bidding premium and exercise price, the identity of bidders, the likelihood of ultimate development, and the likelihood of ex post renegotiation of the contract.

8.1 INTRODUCTION

Since the publication of the seminal work on real options, it has been recognized that real option analysis is a valuable analytical tool that allows managers to quantify the value of flexibility. While the rate of adoption of real option analysis has been uneven across industries, it has been embraced most enthusiastically in the natural resources industry, where academic research first proposed the application of these techniques. This chapter details the bidding for a classic real option in a natural resource industry: the right to develop a copper deposit.

In 1996, the Peruvian government privatized a number of state-owned assets. One of the first to be privatized was Antamina, a polymetallic ore deposit about 500 km north of Lima, Peru. The winning bidder would have 2 years to explore the property before deciding whether or not to develop the site. This ability to wait and see gave rise to a classic development option, which bidders would need to incorporate into their valuation. The first section of the chapter discusses the practical issues involved in carrying out a real options analysis, in the tradition of the work of Paddock et al. (1988) and others.

What is unique about bidding for Antamina, however, is not the valuation of the project per se, but rather the real option *embedded in the bidding rules* set up by the Peruvian government, and the resultant implications for the behavior of the bidders and the ultimate developer of the deposit. In effect, the auction rules had firms submit both the option premium and the exercise price of the real option to develop the property. By allowing bidders to set both elements of the bid, the government may have substantially reduced the problem of winners' curse and motivated bidders to propose very high investment levels in the plant; however, it simultaneously increased the likelihood that the ultimate winner would walk away from the project. Furthermore, the rules created an important time-inconsistency problem, giving incentives for renegotiation after initial exploration of the property was completed.

The next section provides background data on the Antamina mine and the privatization process set up by the Peruvian government. The third section presents the valuation of the mine, using now-standard real option valuation techniques. The fourth section revisits the bidding rules put in place by the Peruvian government and the incentives brought about by these rules. The last section is a concluding postscript.

8.2 BACKGROUND ON THE ANTAMINA MINE[1]

Beginning in the early 1990s, the Peruvian government sought to return many of its state-owned companies to private ownership. The government planned privatizations that would raise $5.75 billion in cash and investment commitments during 1996–1999. One of the larger entities to be sold was Centromin, Peru's largest state-owned mining company, which controlled seven mines, a metallurgical complex, four hydroelectric plants, a railway system, port facilities, and numerous undeveloped natural resource deposits. The firm had been owned by U.S.-based Cerro de Pasco Corporation until 1974, when it was nationalized by the Peruvian government. After two decades of state ownership, the government attempted to sell the entire company in 1994 and 1995, but without success. In 1996, the plan was to sell Centromin's 11 properties piecemeal, with the first two parcels being a gold mine and the Antamina mine.

The Antamina mine, located 482 km north of Lima, Peru, was a rich polymetallic copper and zinc deposit. Based on engineering reports made public by the government as part of the auction, the property had proven and probable ore reserves estimated at 127 million metric tons of ore containing 1.7% copper and 0.8% zinc. Centromin's management had publicly stated that these figures vastly underestimated the likely reserves of the property. Although part of the ore body had been well studied by

[1] The material in this section is excerpted with modifications from the Harvard Business School case study "Bidding for Antamina," No. 297-054, prepared by Peter Tufano and Alberto Moel. Copyright (c) 1997 by the President and Fellows of Harvard College; all rights reserved.

geologists, there had been virtually no geologic study of a large portion of the deposit. As a result, there was large uncertainty about the size of the reserves.

From a practical perspective, none of the potential bidders could carry out anything but limited geological work on the property before the bids were due, and therefore they had to rely on their analysis of surveys produced by Cerro de Pasco and Centromin. In addition, the government was not willing to represent or guarantee the amount of reserves. However, based on previous experience, some industry experts estimated that the actual reserves might range from 100 to 175 million metric tons.

A feasibility study, which would largely consist of additional geological exploration through drilling, could more precisely establish the amount and quality of ore in the Antamina property. Such exploration, which would cost approximately $24 million, was expected to take about 2 years and would be completed before mine construction began. Once additional geological work had been completed, the developer of the property would be "more confident" of the expected reserves, i.e., within ±20%.

Were the subsequent geological work to suggest the mine was economically exploitable, the property would need to be developed to extract the copper and other metals. Antamina was located in a remote mountainous region in Peru at 4000 m above sea level, and 200 km from the ocean. Developing this site would require the construction of roads, mining rigs, crushing plants, and other ancillary facilities, and the purchase and transport of heavy mining equipment, and was expected to last 3 years. Based on available estimates, the capital expenditures to develop the mine (excluding the feasibility study) ranged from $581 million to $622 million (in 1996 U.S. dollars) and were a function of the amount of ore found.

Table 8.1 shows estimates of the mine's life, yearly production, capital expenditures, and operating costs for three development scenarios, corresponding to three potential outcomes for the quantity of ore in the deposit. These estimates were derived from discussions with industry experts. The *expected* scenario was thought to represent the mean or median of the distribution of possible ore reserves, the *low* scenario represented 1 to 1.5 standard deviations below the mean (corresponding to the 100 million metric tons estimate), and the *high* scenario (175 million metric tons) represented 1 to 1.5 standard deviations above the mean.

8.3 VALUATION OF THE ANTAMINA INVESTMENT OPPORTUNITY

In a "typical" *all-cash* auction, interested firms are asked to bid the amount of cash they are willing to pay up front for the right to develop the mineral resource. Some of the first applications of real options, such as Paddock et al. (1988), have dealt with this type of problem. In this section, we apply classic real option valuation methodology to value the investment opportunity, as if bidders were asked to submit standard all-cash bids.

The economic value of the Antamina mine is the value of the discounted stream of expected future sales of copper and zinc, less any development and extraction costs. It is well known that the standard valuation technique of risk-adjusted discounted cash flow (DCF) analysis fails to capture all sources of value associated with this type of

Table 8.1
Summary of Information Used to Value Antamina[a]

Scenario	Low case	Expected	High case
Reserves (million metric tons)	100	127	175
Mine life (years)	12	14	18
Copper production (million lb/year)	313	339	365
Zinc production (million lb/year)	155	168	181
Operating costs[b] (millions of 1996 U.S. $)	131	138	145
Copper treatment charge[c] (1996 U.S. dollars/lb)	0.28	0.28	0.28
Zinc treatment charge[c] (1996 U.S. dollars/lb)	0.22	0.22	0.22
Feasibility study[d]			
1996 (millions of 1996 U.S. $)	6	6	6
1997 (millions of 1996 U.S. $)	18	18	18
Capital expenditure[d]			
1998 (millions of 1996 U.S. $)	54	55	55
1999 (millions of 1996 U.S. $)	246	255	264
2000 (millions of 1996 U.S. $)	281	292	303
Per year after 2000[d] (millions of 1996 U.S. $)	8.7	9.0	9.3
Closure costs[d] (millions of 1996 U.S. $)	45	45	45

[a] Estimates of mine life, yearly production, capital expenditures, and operating costs for three development scenarios corresponding to the quantity of ore in the deposit. The expected scenario represents the mean or median of the distribution of possible ore content, the low scenario represents 1 to 1.5 standard deviations below the mean, and the high scenario represents 1 to 1.5 standard deviations above the mean.

[b] While the operating costs are expressed in U.S. dollars, less than half would be set in Peruvian Sols. These costs are expressed in real (1996) amounts, and exclude the treatment charges paid to a smelter.

[c] The treatment charges were paid by the mining company to smelters (typically in Japan) and would be set and paid in U.S. dollars. These treatment charges are set by contract with the smelter, and tend to adjust with the relative demand for smelting capacity, which tends to increase with the price of copper. From the smelter, the mining company received revenue equal to the amount of metal produced times the U.S. dollar market price of copper (or zinc) minus the treatment charge.

[d] The feasibility study, the initial and continuing capital expenditures, and the closure costs (environmental clean-up and reclamation) are expressed in real (1996) amounts. These expenses would primarily be set and paid in U.S. dollars.

investment, in that it assumes that the decision to invest is *irreversible* and *inflexible*, i.e., the investment cash flows are committed and fixed for the life of the project. A main contribution of real options analysis is to incorporate managerial flexibility inherent in the project in its valuation. Added flexibility value, overlooked in DCF analysis, comes from managerial decisions that can take advantage of mineral price movements: operating flexibility and investment timing flexibility.

Operating flexibility includes various options to vary operating parameters, including shutting down and reopening, expanding and contracting operations, abandoning operations completely, optimizing cutoff grades, and varying production rates as prices fluctuate.[2] Investment timing flexibility is the ability to delay and optimally

---

[2] Models of the operating options to shut down, reopen, and abandon a mineral resource project were developed by Brennan and Schwartz (1985a,b). Applications include those by

time the start of new property development.[3] Of course, both types of managerial flexibility can be present jointly. For example, Paddock et al. (1988) value the option to delay exploration and/or extraction of undeveloped offshore petroleum leases for up to 5 years, and then the option to shut down, reopen, or abandon once the field has been developed.[4]

In this section, we value the *right to develop* the Antamina mineral reserves, focusing on the investment options available to the winning bidder. We value the winning bidder's right to develop the property as a call option, treating the developed mine as the underlying asset and the development expenses as the exercise price of this option. Following the extant literature, we consider the developed mine as a levered claim on a traded underlying asset, where the leverage comes from operating leverage and the traded underlying is a set of forward contracts on copper and zinc. By mapping the underlying asset (the developed mine) into traded assets (metals prices), we can use the risk-neutral valuation methodology developed by Cox and Ross (1976) and Harrison and Kreps (1979).

To value Antamina, we use a Monte Carlo simulation model, implemented within the popular spreadsheet program Excel. This decision was made for three reasons. First, the European style of this option makes Monte Carlo a feasible approach. Second, the analysis is a practical approach for classroom or practitioner use, as its transparency allows users to see the assumptions used and the workings of the valuation model. Finally, it allows varying both the optimal amount of investment and the mine life based on the amount of ore found. In particular, it allows simulating a series of possible price paths for copper and zinc prices that can then be used as inputs to a DCF model to establish the distribution of values for the underlying asset (the developed mine). The model then values the real option to develop the mine after the 2-year feasibility study is completed and the related ore uncertainty is resolved. We make a number of simplifying assumptions:

1. *We focus only on the investment timing option, ignoring any operating options.* In particular, we assume that once development of the project has begun, any options to delay or speed up development, temporarily shut down, or reopen, change the production profile (e.g., speed up or slow down production) or the ore grade, or abandon the project can be ignored.

2. *The probability distribution of ore quantity can be adequately character-ized by three discrete outcomes.* In particular, we adopt the three possible

---

Palm et al. (1986), who value the option to shut down and reopen low-cost and high-cost copper mines, Cavender (1992) who values the option to shut down and reopen a small open-pit gold mine, and Mardones (1993) who analyzes flexibility to adjust cutoff grade and to stockpile work in process.

[3] The value of the option to delay development of an oil field for a finite time has been studied by Brennan and Schwartz (1985a,b), McDonald and Siegel (1986), Paddock et al. (1988), Trigeorgis (1990), Bjerksund and Ekern (1990), Laughton (1993), and Laughton and Jacoby (1991).

[4] Trigeorgis (1990) values the option to defer, expand, or cancel a nonfuel mineral project. Bjerksund and Ekern (1990) carry out a similar analysis, except the option to delay is perpetual.

quantity outcomes described in Table 8.1, each with a known probability of occurring.[5]

3. *The risk-free discount rate is known and deterministic.* We discount the mine revenues (derived from forward prices or simulated at a risk-neutral drift rate) at a constant risk-free rate, as in Brennan and Schwartz (1985a,b). They argue that if the mine owner can enter into forward contracts to sell the mine output in the future at currently agreed-on prices, the price risk would be eliminated and the relevant discount rate would be the risk-free rate. In Brennan and Schwartz (1985b), they also hypothesize known and certain costs, discounted at the risk-free rate as well.[6] We follow their treatment. Other uncertain variables, such as exchange rates and inflation rates, are also assumed to be known and deterministic.[7]

4. *Project estimates gathered from industry sources are representative.* To arrive at the information needed to value the mine given in Table 8.1, we interviewed industry experts and consultants. Although the estimated parameters are not necessarily those used by bidders for Antamina, we have been told that they are representative of those used. In addition to the assumptions made in Table 8.1, we assume working capital of 25% of net revenue (gross revenue less treatment charges), 5-year straight-line depreciation starting in 2001, a tax rate of 30%, and a long-term annual inflation rate of 3.5% for all costs.[8]

5. *Copper and zinc prices follow a joint diffusion process.* Following the work of Gibson and Schwartz (1990) and Schwartz (1997), we assume that the prices of copper and zinc and their convenience yields follow a joint diffusion process. In particular, the copper and zinc prices follow geometric Brownian motion, while their convenience yields are mean reverting. The prices of each commodity are negatively correlated with that commodity's convenience yield, while copper and zinc returns are positively correlated with each other. More formally, the dynamics of prices and convenience yields are given by the following:[9]

---

[5] We estimate that the *low* and *high* case have a 0.2 probability of occurring, while the *expected* outcome has a probability of 0.6. In reality, the quantity would be a continuous random variable (while the investment programs would be lumpy). We use a discrete version of the distribution to simplify the computational burden of the Monte Carlo model.

[6] The assumption that costs can be discounted at the risk-free rate is appropriate if costs are riskless in the sense that they have no systematic risk.

[7] The extension of commodity price modeling to include stochastic interest rates is discussed in Schwartz (1997).

[8] The project value will be sensitive to these assumptions. For example, inflation affects the operating costs, investment expenditures, and closure costs of the project; higher inflation will decrease the value of the project.

[9] We make the additional simplifying assumption that the market price of convenience yield risk λ is zero. Schwartz (1997) finds that λ for copper was not significantly different from zero in the period 1988–1995. Given our assumption that the mine can be expressed as a claim on the copper, its λ would also be zero. Although this assumption simplifies our analysis,

$$\frac{dP_c}{P_c} = (r - \delta_c)\, dt + \sigma_c\, dz_c$$

$$\frac{dP_z}{P_z} = (r - \delta_z)\, dt + \sigma_z\, dz_z \tag{8.1}$$

$$d\delta_c = k_c(\alpha_c - \delta_c)\, dt + \sigma_{\delta c}\, dz_{\delta c}$$

$$d\delta_z = k_z(\alpha_z - \delta_z)\, dt + \sigma_{\delta z}\, dz_{\delta z}$$

where Ps are prices, r is the risk-free rate, δs are convenience yields, and the subscripts c and z correspond to the copper and zinc processes, respectively. The αs are the long-term mean convenience yields, while the ks are the mean-reversion coefficients dictating the speed with which the convenience yields approach their long-term means. The dzs are correlated increments to standard Brownian processes, with correlations among their noise terms:

$$dz_c\, dz_z = \rho_{cz}\, dt$$

$$dz_c\, dz_{\delta c} = \rho_{c,\delta c}\, dt \tag{8.2}$$

$$dz_z\, dz_{\delta z} = \rho_{z,\delta z}\, dt$$

where the ρs denote the corresponding correlation coefficients between the relevant Brownian motions. The first equation relates the prices of copper and zinc, while the second and third equations relate the commodity prices to their respective convenience yields.

To obtain estimates for the relevant parameters, we used copper and zinc spot and futures market data from the London Metals Exchange for the period September 1991 to July 1996. We used the spot and 3-month futures prices of zinc and copper to determine the convenience yield, as given by Gibson and Schwartz [1990, Eq. (8.9)]:

$$\delta = r' - 4 \ln\left[\frac{F(S, 3)}{S}\right] \tag{8.3}$$

where r' is the 3-month risk-free rate, S is the spot price, and $F(S, 3)$ is the 3-month copper or zinc futures price. To determine the mean-reversion parameters k and α, we ran the regression[10]

$$\delta_t - \delta_{t-1} = \alpha + b\delta_{t-1} + \varepsilon_t \tag{8.4}$$

for both zinc and copper convenience yields, and calculated

---

we recognize its limitations. In particular, a portion of the project (the cost structure) is not a tradable asset, and therefore may have a market price of risk.

[10] The methodology used is described in Gibson and Schwartz (1990) and in Dixit and Pindyck (1994).

$$\alpha = -\frac{\hat{\alpha}}{\hat{b}}$$

$$k = -\ln(1 + \hat{b}) \qquad (8.5)$$

$$\hat{\sigma} = \hat{\sigma}_\varepsilon \sqrt{\frac{\ln(1 + \hat{b})}{(1 + \hat{b})^2 - 1}}$$

where $\hat{\sigma}_\varepsilon$ is the standard error of the regression. Table 8.2 shows the mean-reversion parameters k and α, the volatilities (calculated over a 90-day window), and the relevant correlations.

We forecast the copper and zinc prices and convenience yields monthly for the first 2 years, using a discrete-time version for the diffusion processes of Eq. (8.1), and the relevant parameters from Table 8.2. The initial spot prices and convenience yields (at the time of the bidding in mid-1996) were $1.00/pound and 20% for copper and $0.55/pound and −5% for zinc, respectively. Under the assumption that

Table 8.2
Price Process Parameter Estimates[a]

A: Convenience yield mean reversion parameters (κ and α)

κ_c	κ_z	α_c	α_z
0.8	0.6	6.0%	−0.2%

B: Copper and zinc annualized volatilities (σ)

σ_c	σ_z	$\sigma_{\delta c}$	$\sigma_{\delta z}$
22%	18%	25%	23%

C: Correlations (ρ) among copper and zinc prices (P)
and convenience yields (δ)

	P_c	P_z	δ_c	δ_z
P_c	1.00			
P_z	0.44	1.00		
δ_c	0.57		1.00	
δ_z		0.73		1.00

[a] Daily data from the London Metals Exchange for the period September 1991 to July 1996 was used to determine the metal price process parameters used in Eqs. (8.1) and (8.2). A shows the zinc and copper 3-month futures convenience yield mean reversion parameters k and α, estimated from the data using Eqs. (8.3), (8.4), and (8.5). B shows the copper and zinc annualized return volatilities calculated on the basis of the prior 90-day price changes. A year is assumed to have 250 trading days. B also shows the annualized convenience yield volatilities obtained from the third equation in (8.5). C shows the return correlations (ρ) for copper and zinc and their convenience yields. All correlations are for daily data for the period September 1991–July 1996 and are significant to 1%.

a forward market extends indefinitely into the future and that the convenience yields are mean reverting, the forward price of copper (or zinc) at time t after year 2 can be approximated by Schwartz [1997, Eqs. (18) and (20)]:

$$F_1(P, \delta, t) = P \, \exp\left[-\delta \frac{1 - e^{-kt}}{k} + A(t)\right] \tag{8.6}$$

$A(t)$ is given by

$$A(t) = \left(r - \alpha + \tfrac{1}{2}\frac{\sigma_\delta^2}{k^2} - \frac{\sigma_\delta \sigma \rho_\delta}{k}\right)t + \tfrac{1}{4}\sigma_\delta^2 \frac{1 - e^{-2kt}}{k^3}$$
$$+ \left(\alpha k + \sigma_\delta \sigma \rho_\delta - \frac{\sigma_\delta^2}{k}\right)\frac{1 - e^{-kt}}{k^2} \tag{8.7}$$

where σ is the commodity price volatility, δ is the (stochastic) convenience yield, α is the long-term mean convenience yield, k is the convenience yield mean reversion coefficient, ρ_δ is the correlation of the convenience yield with the commodity price, and σ_δ is the convenience yield volatility.[11]

Our Monte Carlo simulation generated 10,000 price and convenience yield paths from year 0 to year 2 using monthly time steps. For each run, the ending metal prices and convenience yields at year 2 are used as inputs into Eqs. (8.6) and (8.7) to generate the forward prices for copper and zinc in future periods. These forward prices are then used to derive the cash flows in three DCF scenarios, which correspond to the high, medium (expected), and low ore outcomes. As a base case, the top graph in Figure 8.1 shows the distribution of values for the Antamina mine if the mine *had to be developed* in year 2 (i.e., there was no option to delay development, and a standard DCF model applied). The mean net present value (NPV) of this "real forward contract," i.e., of a commitment to develop at the end of 2 years, is $454 million, with a wide distribution as shown in Figure 8.1.

This distribution (Figure 8.1A) shows that in about 4 of 10 outcomes the value of developing the mine at year 2 is negative. The essence of the *real option* is that at this go/no-go point, managers could optimally decide not to proceed after learning the outcome of the exploration by year 2 if the economic value of developing the mine turns out to be negative.[12] By walking away from the project these negative outcomes can be truncated, as shown in Figure 8.1B.

---

[11] Under the assumption that the term structure of convenience yields at the end of year 2 does *not* display mean reversion, the forward curve is given by the usual expression

$$F_1(P, \delta, T) = P \, \exp[(r - \delta)T] \tag{8.6'}$$

where the convenience yield (δ) is assumed constant. Schwartz (1997, especially Figure 7) shows that the incorporation of stochastic convenience yields into the calculation of the term structure has a large effect on the shape of these curves, and the effect differs across different time periods. Although the spot prices of the metals are correlated in our analysis, our calculation of the forward curves does not explicitly take metal price correlation into account in the construction of the term structure of the forward curves.

[12] In reality, the managers could postpone this decision by accepting the penalty, but we do not model this choice.

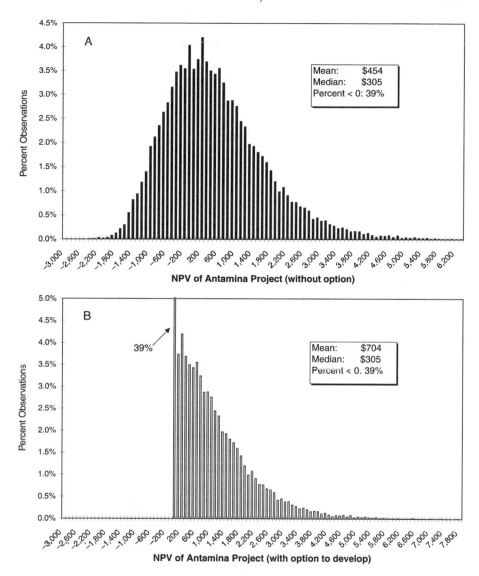

Figure 8.1 Distribution of values for antamine if winning bidder is committed to develop (A) or has an option to develop (B). (A) The results of a 10,000 run Monte Carlo simulation for the Antamina mine if the mine had to be developed at the end of year 2. The mean NPV is $454 million. The project has a negative NPV in 39% of the trials. (B) The effect of the option to abandon development on the value (expanded NPV) of the project. In this case, negative NPV outcomes are not developed, resulting in an expanded mean NPV of $704 million.

As shown in Table 8.3, the decision not to develop would be made in 23% of the high-ore scenarios, 39% of the medium-ore scenarios, and 53% of the low-ore scenarios. The mine would not be developed when metals prices are low, convenience yields are large (i.e., when the forward curves are shallow or downward sloping), or when the quantity of ore is low. Under these circumstances, the value of a developed mine is not high enough to justify the expenditure of the development charges.

Table 8.3

Characteristics of the Antamina Mine Project, Conditioned on Whether It Is Developed after Year 2[a]

	Project developed	*Project not developed*
High ore		
Copper price/convenience yield	$1.04/5.5%	$0.63/8.9%
Zinc price/convenience yield	$0.64/−0.5%	$0.47/0.5%
Percent of trials	77%	23%
Expected ore		
Copper price/convenience yield	$1.07/5.4%	$0.67/7.9%
Zinc price/convenience yield	$0.65/−0.6%	$0.50/0.4%
Percent of trials	61%	39%
Low ore		
Copper price/convenience yield	$1.10/5.3%	$0.70/7.4%
Zinc price/convenience yield	$0.70/−0.7%	$0.52/0.3%
Percent of trials	47%	53%
All outcomes		
Copper price/convenience yield	$1.07/5.4%	$0.68/7.8%
Zinc price/convenience yield	$0.65/−0.6%	$0.50/0.3%
Percent of trials	61%	39%

[a] Mean copper and zinc prices and convenience yields, conditioned on whether the project is developed at the end of year 2. The means are shown for the high, expected, and low ore outcomes, and for all outcomes combined. We also show the percent of trials in which the mine was developed for all outcomes. t tests of the differences between developed and not-developed outcomes show that all means of prices and convenience yields are significantly different from one another, with p-values exceeding 0.01 in all cases.

By being able to abandon the project at year 2, management can eliminate all negative NPV outcomes. In that case, the "expanded" mean NPV of the mine would rise to $704 million. The difference between the two mean NPVs of $250 million is the value of the development timing (or abandonment) option at year 2. This amounts to 55% of the standard DCF valuation of $454 million, which is on the high end of the findings of Davis (1996).

As with any valuation model, the outputs are only as valid as the parameters used as inputs to the model. Some executives in the mining industry suggested that these valuations might be "too high," but without access to their private assumptions we cannot ascertain whether this difference is due to our parameter inputs or other factors. Certainly, the choice of the diffusion process is an important modeling decision. Schwartz (1997) points out that the mean-reverting characteristics of metal prices have a first-order impact on valuation and the decision of when to exercise real options. Our application confirms his point. If we calculate the mine value ignoring mean reversion after year 2 (i.e., if the forward curve is given by the expression in footnote 11), the base-case NPV of the "real forward contract" is $1.3 billion, while the development timing option increases it to $1.7 billion, for a $400 million value for the option to defer development. These values are 2.5 to 3 times those resulting from the analysis using Schwartz's (1997) mean-reverting specification for the dynamics of metals' prices. Were we to ignore all volatility in both the price and convenience yields of these metals, the value of the project would be reduced to about a quarter: $112 million for the commitment and about $158 million with the option to develop.[13] Although it is obvious that the level of volatility affects the valuation of the real option, the seemingly technical choice of how to model the diffusion process of commodity prices may have just as large an impact on project valuation.

The historical data used to generate the convenience yield process parameters can also have a material impact on the valuation. In the past, copper and zinc convenience yields have been highly unstable. For example, the 3-month convenience yield of zinc oscillated between −10% and 60% in the period 1991–1996, with periods of relative stability followed by short bursts of high volatility (i.e., the distribution of convenience yields is "long-tailed" and skewed). For this reason, the choice of the window for estimation of the convenience yield parameters will influence these parameters and the resulting mine valuation.

8.4 THE INCENTIVE IMPACTS OF REAL-OPTION BIDS

The above valuation of the real option to develop the Antamina mine, while important to potential bidders, is a well-studied problem. The role of information and bidding structure on bid prices has also been extensively studied—at least under all-cash bidding rules.[14] However, the bidding rules established by the Peruvian government—and the incentives they created—are more novel than those previously studied. The auction rules themselves recognized and embodied the development timing option, asking bidders to specify both the premium and the exercise price of the option to develop the property. These rules created strong, and arguably perverse, incentives for potential bidders, leading them to promise to invest large sums in developing the property while increasing the likelihood that they would ultimately choose to walk away from the project.

8.4.1 The Rules of the Game

Bidders for Antamina were asked to submit two figures: an *initial payment* and a *pledged investment commitment*:

- The *initial payment* was the amount of cash to be paid immediately, and had to exceed $17.5 million.

---

[13] Even if there is no commodity price volatility, the option value is still positive since there is ore quantity uncertainty captured by the model.

[14] For an analysis of the role of private and public information on bids for oil and gas lease auctions using all-cash bids, see Porter (1995). The number and size of the bids received can also be influenced by elements of the bidding process itself, such as the auction mechanism, the speed of the auction process, and the number or order of assets to be auctioned. For a review of this literature, see Lopez-de-Silanes (1996).

- For the next 2 years, the winning bidder could explore the property and, under the auction rules, was obligated to spend at least $13.5 million on exploration. As exploration was projected to cost $24 million, this constraint was not binding in a real sense, except if initial exploration were to rule out all subsequent development.

- At the end of 2 years, the winner had to either:

  (1) walk away from the project, give up rights to the property, and owe the government no additional funds; or

  (2) develop the mine. If the winning bidder decided to proceed, and its investment by the end of year 5 fell short of the amount it promised to invest up front (the pledged *investment commitment*), it would owe the Peruvian government a penalty equal to 30% of this shortfall, to be paid at the end of year 5. The minimum pledged investment commitment was $135 million. The penalty was presumably put in place to prevent firms from making "false promises" regarding their intended investment plans.

- The winning bidder would be the firm proposing the largest total "bid." To establish the value of the "bid," the authorities would add the initial payment and 30% of the investment commitment, thus giving greater reward to cash payments over promises of future investment.

The actions and decisions of the winning bidder are summarized in the time line of Figure 8.2.

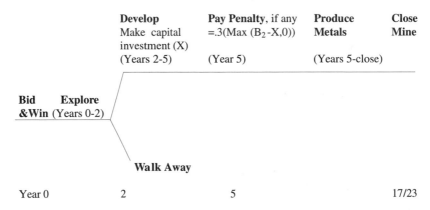

Figure 8.2 Time line of managerial decisions in Antamina auction. This figure shows the set of decisions facing a firm bidding on Antamina, focusing on the decision whether to develop the mine at the end of exploration (year 2). B_1 represents the initial cash payment made at year zero, B_2 represents the pledged investment commitment, and X represents the actual amount spent on development in years 2 through 5 (exercise price) if the firm proceeds. The penalty is paid in year 5, after development is completed. Closure takes place when the reserves are depleted, which is predicted to occur between years 17 and 23, depending on the ore found.

8.4.2 Analyzing the Government's Bidding Rules

To place these bidding rules in perspective, it is useful to contrast this auction mechanism to a more traditional one in which firms make *all-cash* bids, proposing only how much cash they will pay today for the right to develop in the future.

Under the all-cash bid, the expected value for each bidder, conditional on winning, is

$$E\{PV[Max(S - X, 0)]\} - B \tag{8.8}$$

where the actual investment cost (X) is the exercise price of the real option to develop the property, the cash bid (B) is the premium paid for the option, and the underlying asset is the value of the developed reserves (S). PV[·] is the present value operator, and E{·} represents the expectation operator.

By contrast, under the rules established to sell Antamina, firms bid both the initial payment B_1 and the promised investment commitment B_2. The expected value now is:

$$E\{PV[Max(S - X - PEN, 0)]\} - B_1 \tag{8.9}$$

where *PEN* is the penalty, given by

$$PEN = 0.3 Max(B_2 - X, 0) \tag{8.10}$$

Since bidders would always bid B_2 at least equal to X,[15] this simplifies to

$$E\{PV[Max(S - 0.7X - 0.3B_2, 0)]\} - B_1 \tag{8.11}$$

Comparing this actual bidding structure to the above all-cash scheme, the difference is that the Antamina rules have firms propose not only the option premium B_1, but also a portion $(0.3B_2)$ of the total exercise price, $0.7X + 0.3B_2$. Thus, the government has bidders propose the two option terms simultaneously.

8.4.3 Incentives for Bidding

In analyzing this auction, one can ask how the all-cash and the Antamina bidding rules compare along a variety of dimensions: the bids submitted by the firms, the likely identity of bidders, the winner's subsequent decision regarding development of the property, and the possibility of renegotiating the contract.

In setting bids under all-cash, first-price bid rules, bidders would be unwilling to offer a cash bid that would make their expected return negative, and their reservation price would equal the first term in Eq. (8.8). They face the classic winner's curse

---

[15] If X is the amount a bidder would spend to develop, conditional on proceeding, then it can make an investment commitment promise of at least X without incurring any risk of penalties. By bidding B_2 less than X, the bidder would not reduce its penalty, but would reduce the likelihood of winning the auction. Thus, $B_2 = X$ dominates $B_2 < X$, so that the penalty can be expressed as $0.3(B_2 - X)$.

problem, in that the winning bidder confronts the distinct possibility of having made the most overoptimistic valuation, and hence ex-post overpaying for the property.[16]

The Antamina bidding rules create a number of subtle complications, both with respect to a bidder's choice between the cash and investment commitment portions of their bid and with respect to their subsequent decisions. In setting the bid, a firm must figure out how to allocate its bid between the initial payment B_1 and the investment commitment B_2. Consider the relative costs and benefits of adding another dollar to each of these portions of the bid. By bidding another dollar in the initial cash payment, the bidder gets an additional dollar in "bid points" under the government's weighting scheme, but must also spend a dollar (conditional on winning). By bidding another dollar in investment commitment, the bidder gets only $0.30 in "bid points," but must pay the present value of $0.30, conditional on deciding to go forward at year 2. If we compare the bid points received to the expected cost, conditional on winning the bid, there is an incentive for firms to increase their pledged investment commitment rather than the initial cash payment, as shown in Table 8.4.

Quite simply, it is "cheaper" to bid future promises—on which one can renege— than to bid cash. At an extreme, if the initial payment were zero (and exploration expenses were also zero), a firm could bid an extraordinarily high investment commit- ment B_2 and still be assured of not losing money or suffering from the winner's curse. This is because a call option cannot have negative value, and with zero premium paid, there is no exercise price that could make buying the option worth less than zero. In this extreme case, the bidder would develop only if ore prices were very high and/or there were a sufficiently large ore deposit; otherwise, it could walk away without spending any money on the project. It could not overbid because it could walk away after exploration, but before spending any money on the project.

Table 8.4
Comparison of Increasing Initial Cash Payment versus Pledged Investment Commitment under the Antamina Bidding Rules[a]

	Bidder bids another $1 on the initial cash payment	Bidder bids another $1 on investment commitment
Number of *bid points* received	$1.00	$0.30
Expected cost, conditional on winning the bid	$1.00	$E[PV(\$0.30)] < \$0.30$
	Must pay this immediately, regardless of ultimate decision to develop	The penalty is not paid until later, and only if the project is ultimately developed
Ratio of *expected cost* to *bid points*	1	Less than 1

[a] The table shows the number of "bid points" a firm would receive by adding an additional dollar to either the initial cash payment or the pledged investment commitment, under the rules set by the Peruvian government. A "bid point" is a measure used by the Peruvian government to judge alternative bids.

[16] The first mention of winner's curse in the academic literature was in the context of bidding for oil and gas drilling rights by Capen et al. in 1971.

Actually, as the government's rules insisted that bidders invest at least $17.5 as initial payment plus another $13.5 million in exploration, there could be some winner's curse. For example, if a firm bids the minimum initial cash amount and spends $24 million on exploration, it is possible to calculate the highest exercise price (investment commitment) that it could bid and still break even (its reservation investment commitment). Figure 8.3 plots the outcome to a bidder as a function of the pledged investment commitment bid.[17] Given the low option premium (initial payment and exploration expenditures), bidders could bid up to about $18 billion in investment commitment before the value of the project turned negative. The notion that a firm might bid such a "high" investment commitment may seem puzzling at first. However, once expressed in option terms, it is less difficult to grasp: Suppose that you could buy a 2-year call option on a stock that is currently priced at $10, but that is quite volatile ($\sigma = 50\%$).[18] The call writer asks you, "How high an exercise price would you accept for paying a penny premium?" In principle, you would be willing to set the strike price as high as $80, or eight times the current stock price, in return for paying a penny for the option.

The bidding rules also affect the outcome in another way, by giving a comparative advantage to smaller, less-capitalized companies. Ultimately, only three firms submitted bids for Antamina. Two were among the largest and best capitalized in the industry. The smallest of the three, a joint venture of Rio Algom and Inmet, had a combined market capitalization of only $1.5 billion, or 10% that of the largest bidder and 33% that of the next bidder. Under an all-cash auction, the joint venture of the smaller mining companies would likely be unable to raise sufficient funds to match the bids of the larger firms.[19] However, under the Peruvian bidding rules, smaller bidders could also make future *promises* to develop the mine *without having to raise much money today*. This type of bidding structure could therefore encourage smaller players to bid aggressively, given their comparative advantage in bidding future promises.

8.4.4 Incentives for Subsequent Investment

Of course, the level of investment commitment—and hence the penalty to be paid if the property is developed—will also affect the subsequent development decision. Unlike an all-cash bid, in which the cash payment becomes an irrelevant sunk cost, under the Antamina rules the investment commitment is not a sunk cost. The property will be developed subsequently only if it is economically profitable to do so, which

---

[17] This calculation assumes that the bidder makes the minimal initial payment of $17.5 million and a $24 million exploration expenditure. We assume that once development is begun, the bidder will complete the project. In reality, the bidder could abandon the project after partial development or may underinvest (and pay a penalty if its development expenditures are less than the promised investment commitment). These features would increase the value of the project because the holder would exercise them only when it is optimal to do so.

[18] The risk-free rate is assumed to be 5% (continuously compounded) in this example.

[19] In this instance, a $1+ billion cash bid by RioAlgom/Inmet might not be feasible, as it would represent two-thirds of their market capitalization.

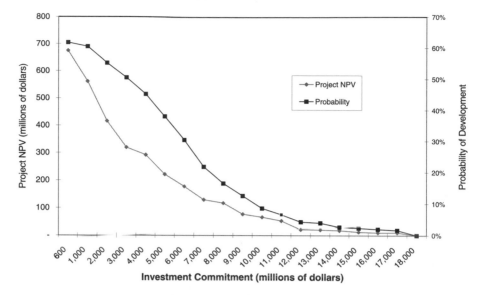

Figure 8.3   Net present value to winning bidder under the Antamina auction, and probability that the project would be developed versus size of pledged investment commitment. The left-hand scale shows the net present value of the Antamina mine as a function of the pledged investment commitment. The right-hand scale shows the probability of mine development as a function of the investment commitment. The curves intersect the x-axis (the NPV of the project turns negative) at about \$18 billion (with a probability of development of 0%). Each point on the graph represents the mean value of a 1000 run Monte Carlo simulation.

from Eq. (8.11) will occur when the value of net operating profits less 0.7 times the actual investment less 0.3 times the pledged investment commitment is greater than zero, or if

$$S - 0.7X - 0.3B_2 > 0 \tag{8.12}$$

As the pledged investment commitment (B_2) rises, it becomes harder to clear this hurdle, and the probability that the property will be developed falls. Figure 8.3 also plots (on the right scale) the probability that the mine would be developed, conditional on the winning bid pledging the investment commitment shown along the horizontal axis.[20] As the investment commitment (exercise price) increases, the cost of developing the mine and paying the penalty also increases. As a result, the call option to develop is more likely to remain unexercised at maturity. Each point represents the percentage of trials for which the firm would optimally choose not to proceed, conditional on the stated level of investment commitment. Only when the investment commitment rises above \$18 billion does the probability that the project will be developed fall to 0%. Thus, competition among bidders would tend to reduce the probability that the mine would be developed, unlike the case of an all-cash bid.

---

[20] Technically, this represents the *risk-neutral* probability that the mine would be developed, rather than the *objective* probability of its exercise.

In addition, the bidding procedure instituted by the Peruvian government might induce firms to make marginal investments that are uneconomic, rather than pay the penalty. Suppose the management of the winning bidder finds it optimal to proceed, despite the firm having bid a large investment commitment and owing a penalty to the Peruvian government. In particular, suppose it bid an investment commitment of $900 million while the necessary investment to actually develop Antamina was $600 million. If the firm invested only $600 million, it would owe the Peruvian government a penalty of $90 million, or 30% of $300 million. Alternatively, suppose it could spend another $300 million on the project, buying additional trucks, helicopters, or jets. Preferably, these "extra" investments would have some fungible value beyond that delivered to the Antamina project. As long as any losses from purchasing these assets were less than $90 million, it would be optimal for the firm to purchase these extra "flexible" assets and claim them as capital investments for Antamina to avoid the penalty; at some later date it could redeploy them to alternative uses to recoup their value. Given this disincentive, the government might need to closely monitor the type of investments made by the winning bidder. A related problem is that the winning bidder might try to use inflated transfer prices to increase its recorded investment in the project. For example, the winning bidder could hire an affiliated firm to carry out some of the development and pay it above-market rates to reduce the penalty owed to the government.[21]

8.4.5 Incentives for Renegotiation

The Antamina rules also seem to encourage ex-post renegotiation that could render the penalty moot. At the end of 2 years, suppose the winning bidder concluded that the project was not economically feasible if it must pay the penalty, but that it would be feasible without the penalty. Thus, it could either walk away from the project or appeal to the government to forgive the penalty. In response, the government could either accept this proposal, or call the firm's bluff, reacquire the property, and offer it again for sale. At that time, however, the firm that just completed the exploration would be the most informed potential bidder, and others might be reluctant to bid against it. If the information already collected by the winning bidder were revealed to the market, the government could not recover the penalty because other bidders would also know the project is not feasible if they have to make the original investment commitment. Thus, the penalty may be unenforceable in practice even when the pure development option (without the penalty) has positive intrinsic value.

This time-inconsistency problem plagued another recent auction: the Federal Communication Commission's (FCC) spectrum auction of wireless phone licenses.[22]

---

[21] Whenever contractual payoffs are determined by accounting figures, there is a temptation for firms to manipulate these reports to their advantage. There are many examples, ranging from accelerating or delaying large write-offs to maximize managers' bonuses (Healy, 1985) or underreporting earnings to avoid making payments to income bondholders (Tufano, 1997).

[22] The problem has been covered widely in the press. For example, see Bryan Gruley and Quentin Hardy, Wireless Bidders Ask to Restructure Debt, *Wall Street Journal*, June 26, 1997, p. A3. For an academic discussion of the auction rules, see McMillan (1994).

The FCC auctioned off these spectrum rights in 1996, with 89 companies bidding $10.2 billion for 493 licenses. Bidders with less than $40 million in annual revenues received attractive financing terms from the government, with no interest payable for 6 years. For a variety of reasons, the wireless business has failed to be as attractive as initially anticipated, and bidders requested the government to restructure their obligations, or else the winning bidders would default. Although one solution would be to reoffer the licenses for sale, these winning bidders could seek protection in bankruptcy courts, and it could be costly and time consuming for the FCC to gain legal access to the assets. In essence, these firms bid future promises, like the investment commitments in the Antamina example. When things did not work out, they optimally chose not to exercise the real option to proceed with development, and at that point the original contracts ceased to be binding.

8.4.6 Does the Chosen Bidding Structure Meet the Government's Stated Objectives?

Starting in the mid-1990s, the right-of-center administration of President Alberto Fujimori sought to undo decades of state intervention and to return many of Peru's state-owned firms to private ownership. The objectives of this large-scale privatization program were many, including (1) the development of projects that would generate local employment, taxable revenue, and hard currency for the country, and (2) cash proceeds for the government from the initial sale. Officials in the privatization program publically emphasized the former goal over the latter. One stated: "At the moment the treasury is not in particular need of money, but what's imperative is that we allow private companies to carry out what state entities have been doing."[23] Speaking directly about the Antamina privatization, one official said: "We obviously want to sell at an interesting price, but the principal objective is to maintain and develop the sector by attracting quality companies."[24]

Based on the above analysis, we doubt whether the proposed rules met the government's stated objectives. As discussed above, the rules encouraged weaker firms to bid large investment commitments, reducing the likelihood of actual development. The incentive to bid more in investment commitment over cash payments also meant that the government would receive less money up front. Further, given the incentives for potential renegotiation of any penalties due, their future payment is suspect. Finally, the resulting disincentives seem to require substantial ex post monitoring of the type of investments made by the winning bidder. By setting up a scheme that not only delivers little money up front, but also reduces the likelihood of development later on, the government seems unlikely to meet its stated goals.[25]

[23] Saul Hudson, Interview—Peru Upbeat on Energy and Mining, *Reuters Financial Service,* June 14, 1996.
[24] Saul Hudson, Forty Firms Qualify for Peru Copper Prospect Sale, *Reuters Financial Service*, June 21, 1996.
[25] The rules, however, may be consistent with an unstated goal of favorable public relations. A large investment commitment could be viewed positively as a signal of the government's privatization offerings.

8.4.7 Alternative Bidding Rules

To assess alternative bidding rules, it is necessary to have a clear specification of the government's objective function. In much of auction theory, the seller is assumed to maximize expected revenue. For example, the classic literature on auctions, going back to Vickrey (1961), analyzed alternative auction mechanisms on the basis of their expected revenue.[26] In Antamina's case, the government's objective is not simply to maximize expected revenue, and the option character of the bid further complicates the task of comparing alternative bidding rules.

Consider the stylized example given earlier, in which the owner of a share offers it up for "sale" via an auction in which bidders can bid any pair of option premiums and exercise prices. The shareowner is offering to write a call option on the share rather than selling it outright, and gives potential bidders the right to select any contract type they prefer. If the seller's goal were to maximize its expected revenue, it would select the bid for which the premium received exceeded the value of the call delivered, or $P - c(X)$, where P is the premium offered and $c(X)$ is the value of the call with exercise price X. There are multiple combinations of these parameters that make the seller indifferent. These are diagrammed in Figure 8.4, which shows the set of bids that has zero net expected value to both buyer and seller. Although these various bids have the same value, they present the bidder with different risk exposures; this is shown in Figure 8.4B, which plots the profit/loss to the seller at maturity for two proposed contracts. Given the seller's risk preferences, we could select from among these equal-value choices.

For Antamina, the government has stated a preference for development as a primary goal and high cash proceeds as a secondary goal. The probability of development (exercise) is inversely related to the exercise price, while cash proceeds are directly related to the option premium. Thus, while points A and B on Figure 8.4 have equal value, based on these preferences the option represented by A dominates B, in that it is more likely to be exercised as well as deliver a higher up front cash price. Taken to an extreme, this suggests that the government's interests are best served by reducing the exercise price and eliminating the penalty. Thus, it appears that an all-cash auction would seem better suited to meeting the government's objectives.

8.5 POSTSCRIPT AND CONCLUSION

The Peruvian government received three bids for Antamina and announced the winner on July 12, 1996. The largest firm that submitted a bid, RTZ-CRA Ltd., offered $17.5 million as initial payment and pledged a $900 million investment commitment. Noranda, the second largest firm, also bid $17.5 million up front, but promised a more generous $1900 million investment commitment. The winner was the small Rio Algom/Inmet partnership, which bid $20 million up front and a pledged investment commitment of $2500 million.[27]

---

[26] See Riley (1989) for an overview of this literature.

[27] See Sally Bowen, Canadians in $2.5 Billion Peruvian Copper Plan, *Financial Times*, July 16, 1996, p. 33.

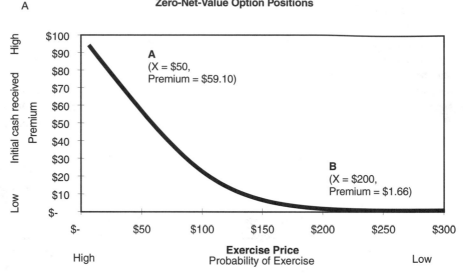

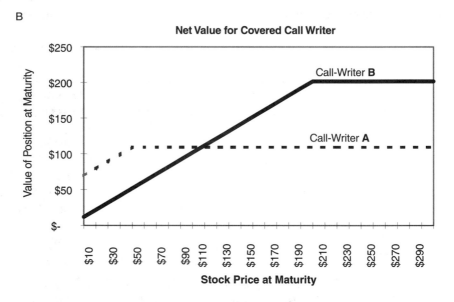

Figure 8.4 Trade-off between the premium and exercise price of a call option. (A) The combination of call option exercise prices and premiums for which the value of a 2-year European-style call option (struck at the given exercise price) less the premium paid equals zero, i.e., the set of fairly priced calls. (Assumes current stock price of $100, stock return volatility of 25%, and a risk-free rate of 10%). (B) The exposure at maturity of two covered-call writers, each of whom wrote a fairly priced option at exercise prices A and B from (A).

At a press conference later on the same day, Rio Algom Ltd. and Inmet Mining Corp. said that they intended to spend about *$1 billion* to develop their new Peruvian copper purchase. "If it does not prove viable, we just lose our up front investment," stated a Rio Algom spokesman.[28] Clearly, the joint venture partners were well aware of the options embedded in the bidding rules, signaling that they did not plan to spend the full investment commitment of $2.5 billion, but rather a more reasonable $1 billion (plus penalty) were they to proceed. They apparently wanted to convey this understanding to security analysts and make sure they were not perceived as having "overpaid" for the mine. The winning bidder clearly understood the option nature of the offering, and followed a bidding strategy consistent with what should have been predicted.[29]

The power of real option analysis—in conjunction with simple game theory—is that it promises to help us better understand not only how things are valued, but also how managers will behave when faced with flexibility and choices. In this case, a real options perspective can help us understand how firms would bid on a large capital investment project, as well as to predict what types of problems might crop up in the future.

ACKNOWLEDGMENTS

This chapter is based on the Harvard Business School teaching case, "Bidding for Antamina" (297-054) and the associated classroom note, "Copper and Zinc Markets 1996" (297-055). We would like to thank the executives of RTZ-CRA Limited, Lenos Trigeorgis, Eduardo Schwartz, Antonio Tarnawiecki, Martha Amram, and attendees of the real options workshop hosted by Analysis Group Economics and the first annual real options conference held at Columbia University in June 1997 for their useful comments on this clinical study. Finally, we thank the MBA and Executive Education students at the Harvard Business School for their classroom comments on the case. Funding for this project was provided by the Harvard Business School Division of Research as part of the Global Financial Systems project.

REFERENCES

Bjerksund, P., and S. Ekern. (1990). Managing Investment Opportunities Under Price Uncertainty: From 'Last Chance' to 'Wait and See' Strategies. *Financial Management* 19(3), 65–83.

Brennan, M., and E. Schwartz. (1985a). A New Approach to Evaluating Natural Resource Investments. *Midland Corporate Finance Journal* 3(1), 78–88.

[28] Canadian Group Hopes to Double Antamina Reserves, *Reuters Financial Service*, July 12, 1996.

[29] In the MBA classroom, students played the role of bidders for Antamina. Those who appreciated the nature of the real option apparently bid differently from those who did not, with the former offering lower initial payments and investment commitments sometimes over $15 billion.

Brennan, M., and E. Schwartz. (1985b). Evaluating Natural Resource Investments. *Journal of Business* 58(2), 135–157.

Capen, E. C., R. V. Clapp, and W. M. Campbell. (1971). Competitive Bidding in High-Risk Situations. *Journal of Petroleum Technology* 23, 641–653.

Cavender, B. (1992). Determination of the Optimum Lifetime of a Mining Project Using Discounted Cash Flow and Option Pricing Techniques. *Mining Engineering* 44, 1262–1268.

Cox, J., and S. Ross. (1976). The Valuation of Options for Alternative Stochastic Processes. *Journal of Financial Economics* 3(1 and 2), 145–166.

Davis, G. A. (1996). Option Premiums in Mineral Asset Pricing: Are They Important? *Land Economics* 72(2), 167–186.

Dixit, A. K., and R. S. Pindyck, (1994). *Investment Under Uncertainty.* Princeton, NJ: Princeton University Press.

Gibson, R., and E. Schwartz. (1990). Stochastic Convenience Yields and the Pricing of Oil Contingent Claims. *Journal of Finance* 45(3), 959–976.

Harrison, J., and D. Kreps. (1979). Martingales and Arbitrage in Multiperiod Securities Markets. *Journal of Economic Theory* 2(3), 831–408.

Healy, P. (1985). The Effect of Bonus Schemes on Accounting Decisions. *Journal of Accounting and Economics* 7(1–3), 85–107.

Laughton, D. (1993). Reversion, Timing Options, and Long-Term Decision Making. *Financial Management* 22(3), 225–240.

Laughton, D., and H. D. Jacoby. (1991). A Two-Method Solution to the Investment Timing Option. In F. J. Fabozzi (ed.), *Advances in Futures and Options Research*, Volume 5, pp. 71–87. Greenwich, CT: JAI Press.

Lopez-de-Silanes, F. (1996). Determinants of Privatization Prices. NBER Working Paper Series, No. 5494.

Mardones, J. (1993). Option Valuation of Real Assets: Application to a Copper Mine with Operating Flexibility. *Resources Policy* 19(2), 51–65.

McDonald. R., and D. Siegel. (1986). The Value of Waiting to Invest. *Quarterly Journal of Economics* 101(4), 707–727.

McMillan, J. (1994). Selling Spectrum Rights. *Journal of Economic Perspectives* 8(3), 145–162.

Paddock, J., D. Siegel, and J. Smith. (1988). Option Valuation of Claims on Real Assets: The Case of Offshore Petroleum Leases. *Quarterly Journal of Economics* 103(3), 479–508.

Palm, S. K., N. D. Pearson, and J. A. Read, Jr. (1986). Option Pricing: A New Approach to Mine Valuation. *CIM Bulletin* 79(5), 61–66.

Porter, R. H. (1995). The Role of Information in U.S. Offshore Oil and Gas Lease Auctions. *Econometrica* 63(1), 1–28.

Riley, J. G. (1989). Expected Revenue From Open and Sealed Bid Auctions. *Journal of Economic Perspectives* 3(3), 41–50.

Schwartz, E. (1997). The Stochastic Behavior of Commodity Prices: Implications for Valuation and Hedging. *Journal of Financee* 52(3) 923–973.

Trigeorgis, L. (1991). A Real-Options Application in Natural Resource Investments. In F. J. Fabozzi (ed.), *Advances in Futures and Options Research,* Volume 4, 153–164. Greenwich, CT: JAI Press.

Tufano, P. (1997). Business Failure, Judicial Intervention, and Financial Innovation: Restructuring U.S. Railroads in the Nineteenth Century. *Business History Review* 71(1), 1–40.

Vickrey, W. (1961). Counterspeculation, Auctions and Competitive Sealed Tenders. *Journal of Finance* 16(1), 8–37.

9

Agency Costs, Underinvestment, and Optimal Capital Structure

The Effect of Growth Options to Expand

DAVID C. MAUER

STEVEN H. OTT

This chapter analyzes the interaction between investment and financing decisions in a real options framework in which the firm has assets in place and a growth option to expand the scale of operations. We show that levered equityholders underinvest in the growth option by delaying exercise of the option relative to the exercise policy that maximizes total firm value. We measure this agency cost and show how it influences credit spreads on risky debt and optimal capital structure. Although financing exercise of the growth option with additional debt can reduce agency costs, shortening debt maturity or allowing equityholders to engage in strategic debt service cannot by themselves accomplish the same task. Our analysis further shows that product market competition exacerbates the underinvestment problem.

9.1 INTRODUCTION

A central concern in corporate finance is the agency costs arising from the divergence of the interests of equityholders and debtholders, the resulting suboptimal investment decisions induced by risky debt financing, and the relevance of such costs for optimal financial structure. Since the seminal works of Jensen and Meckling (1976) and Myers (1977), financial economists have successfully pinpointed the characteristics of firms that engender larger agency costs, explaining how financial contracts have evolved to mitigate such costs.[1] Nevertheless, there are few models that endogenously determine agency costs, investment policy, and optimal capital structure, allowing for a detailed analysis of the sensitivity of agency costs and credit spreads on risky debt to the characteristics of the firm and its product market environment.

---

[1] Harris and Raviv (1991) provide an excellent survey of this literature.

In this chapter we develop a contingent claims model for a firm with assets in place and a growth option to expand its scale of operations. The value of the firm is a function of the stochastic price of the commodity it produces and management's choice of optimal operating and financial policies. The optimal operating policy is characterized by two endogenously determined "trigger" prices: the price at which the firm abandons operations and the price at which it exercises its growth option to expand. The optimal financial policy involves the choice of the terms of the debt contract and endogenous bankruptcy triggers—determined both before and after exercise of the growth option. The optimal amount of debt is determined in a setting in which the tax advantage of debt is traded off against financial distress costs and an agency cost arising from a conflict of interest between equity and debt over the optimal exercise strategy for the growth option.

We show that equityholders underinvest in the growth option by delaying exercise of the option to expand relative to the exercise policy that maximizes total firm value. This occurs because equityholders bear the full cost of additional investment while sharing its benefits with debtholders. The agency cost of debt is the loss in total firm value when management chooses a growth option exercise strategy to maximize equity value instead of total firm value. We measure this cost and illustrate how it influences credit spreads on risky debt and optimal capital structure.

We show that the agency cost of underinvestment decreases sharply when the cost of exercising the growth option is partially financed with a new debt issue having the same priority in bankruptcy as the currently outstanding debt. We illustrate that a policy of maintaining a target debt ratio—by tying additional borrowing to incremental investment—can substantially reduce the agency cost of underinvestment. By contrast, the firm cannot reduce agency costs by shortening debt maturity, and strategic debt service (i.e., using the threat of costly bankruptcy to extract debt service concessions from bondholders) will not eliminate equityholders' underinvestment incentives.

Finally, we examine the effect of product market competition on equityholders' incentive to underinvest in the growth option, by allowing for the entry of a competitor who dissipates the value of the firm's growth opportunity. Although competition encourages equityholders to reduce the delay in the exercise of the growth option, it also sharply increases the agency cost of underinvestment.

Our analysis significantly extends the literature on real options by illustrating how financing decisions may influence dynamic capital-budgeting decisions. The real options literature uses contingent-claims techniques to value and determine optimal exercise policies for the firm's capital-budgeting options (see, e.g., Brennan and Schwartz, 1985; McDonald and Siegel, 1985, 1986; Dixit and Pindyck, 1994; Trigeorgis, 1996). However, with few exceptions this literature typically assumes all-equity financing, ignoring possible interactions between investment and financing decisions.

Our analysis also contributes to the literature that uses contingent claims techniques to price risky debt (see, e.g., Merton, 1974; Black and Cox, 1976; Kim et al. 1993; Leland, 1994a, b; Longstaff and Schwartz, 1995; Leland and Toft, 1996; Anderson and Sundaresan, 1996). A key assumption of this literature is that firm value follows an exogenous stochastic process with constant variance, implying that the firm's future investment decisions are unchanged by financial structure. By contrast, our analysis examines the pricing of risky debt when financial structure may affect future investment decisions.

Several other papers examine interactions of financing and investment decisions in contingent claims models. Brennan and Schwartz (1984) consider firm valuation in a setting in which bond covenants restrict financial policy and influence investment policy. Mello and Parsons (1992) compare the operating decisions of a mine under all-equity financing to those when the mine is partially debt financed and maximizes levered equity value. Trigeorgis (1993) illustrates interactions between financing and operating real options. Mauer and Triantis (1994) analyze interactions between investment and financing decisions in a setting in which debt covenants constrain the firm's choice of policies to maximize firm value. Mello et al. (1995) analyze international production flexibility and demonstrate that hedging exchange rate exposure may enhance firm value by reducing inefficiencies in operating policy caused by risky debt financing. Finally, Fries et al. (1997) examine the interaction between bond pricing, industry equilibrium, and optimal capital structure in a model in which risky debt financing may result in inefficient liquidation.

This study focuses on investment policy and the agency cost of debt when the firm has assets in place and a growth option to expand the scale of operations. In addition to examining the important question of optimal capital structure, we examine the effects of financing the growth option with additional debt, varying the maturity of debt, allowing for strategic debt service, and allowing for competition that dissipates the value of the growth option.

9.2 THE MODEL

9.2.1 Basic Assumptions

Consider a firm that produces a single commodity that is infinitely divisible and is produced continuously through time at a rate of one unit per year. The cost of producing one unit of the commodity is C, which is constant through time. As the commodity is produced, it is simultaneously sold in a perfectly competitive market at a price P per unit. The evolution of the commodity price through time follows the geometric Brownian motion:

$$\frac{dP}{P} = \alpha \, dt + \sigma \, dz \tag{9.1}$$

where the drift rate (α) and volatility (σ) are constants and dz is the increment of a standard Wiener process. The convenience yield of the commodity (δ) is assumed to be a constant proportion of its price, and the riskless security is assumed to yield a constant instantaneous interest rate of r per year.

Operating profits are also taxed instantaneously at a constant rate τ.[2] For simplicity, we do not model economic depreciation of the production facility. Furthermore, we

---

[2] Although we do not model personal taxes, it would be straightforward to include constant personal tax rates on equity and debt income.

assume a symmetric tax system with full loss offset provisions. The latter assumption is only an approximation of the current U.S. tax system that allows for a partial offset of operating losses through carryback and carryforward provisions (in effect creating a tax-option asymmetry).

The firm has two operating options. First, it can abandon operations at any time. For simplicity, we assume that the salvage value of the production facility net of closing costs is zero.[3] Second, the firm has the option to expand the scale of operations at any time by paying a fixed cost I. If the firm chooses to expand operations, the annual output of the production facility increases from one unit per year to $q > 1$ units per year. Once the firm exercises this growth option, we assume that it is prohibitively expensive to switch back to base-scale operation (one unit per year). However, the firm retains the option to abandon operations.

To value the firm and determine its optimal operating policies, we assume that the commodity price is spanned by traded securities (e.g., a futures contract on the commodity). If we further assume that investors can trade securities continuously with zero transaction costs, then it is well known that a continuously rebalanced self-financing portfolio can be constructed that replicates the value of the firm (see, e.g., Brennan and Schwartz, 1985).

9.2.2 All-Equity Financing

First consider the value of an unlevered firm *after* the growth option has been exercised. Standard risk-neutral valuation arguments require that firm value must satisfy the following differential equation:

$$\tfrac{1}{2}\sigma^2 P^2 V_{\mathrm{PP}}^{U} + (r - \delta)P V_{\mathrm{P}}^{U} - rV^{U} + (P - C)(q)(1 - \tau) = 0, \qquad P > P_{\mathrm{Aq}} \quad (9.2)$$

where P_{Aq} is the price at which the unlevered firm abandons operations. The general solution of (9.2) is

$$V_{q}^{U}(P) = \left(\frac{P}{\delta} - \frac{C}{r}\right)(q)(1 - \tau) + A_1 P^{\beta_1} + A_2 P^{\beta_2}, \qquad P > P_{\mathrm{Aq}} \quad (9.3)$$

where A_1 and A_2 are constants to be determined and

$$\beta_1 = \frac{1}{2} - \frac{(r - \delta)}{\sigma^2} + \sqrt{\left[\frac{(r - \delta)}{\sigma^2} - \frac{1}{2}\right]^2 + \frac{(2r)}{\sigma^2}} > 1$$

$$\beta_2 = \frac{1}{2} - \frac{(r - \delta)}{\sigma^2} - \sqrt{\left[\frac{(r - \delta)}{\sigma^2} - \frac{1}{2}\right]^2 + \frac{(2r)}{\sigma^2}} < 0$$

The unlevered firm value in (9.3) must satisfy three boundary conditions, namely

---

[3] A nonzero salvage value would decrease the cost of abandonment, thus providing an incentive to abandon earlier relative to the zero salvage value case. It would also increase the value of the firm, thereby increasing debt capacity.

$$\lim_{P \to \infty} V_q^U(P) = \left(\frac{P}{\delta} - \frac{C}{r} \right) (q)(1 - \tau) \tag{9.4a}$$

$$V_q^U(P_{Aq}) = 0 \tag{9.4b}$$

and

$$\left. \frac{\partial V_q^U}{\partial P} \right|_{P = P_{Aq}} = 0 \tag{9.4c}$$

Condition (9.4a) requires that the abandonment option be worthless if the commodity price gets large, and is satisfied only if $A_1 = 0$. Conditions (9.4b) and (9.4c) require, respectively, that the firm have zero net salvage value at abandonment and that the abandonment price be optimally chosen.[4] Substituting (9.3) into (9.4a)–(9.4c) gives the value of the unlevered firm as

$$V_q^U(P) = \left(\frac{P}{\delta} - \frac{C}{r} \right) (q)(1 - \tau) - \left(\frac{P_{Aq}}{\delta} - \frac{C}{r} \right) \left(\frac{P}{P_{Aq}} \right)^{\beta_2} (q)(1 - \tau) \tag{9.5}$$

where the optimal abandonment price is given by

$$P_{Aq} = \left(\frac{-\beta_2}{1 - \beta_2} \right) \frac{\delta C}{r}$$

Consider next the value of the unlevered firm *before* the growth option is exercised. The firm value must again satisfy Eq. (9.2), except that now $q = 1$. Thus the general solution is

$$V^U(P) = \left(\frac{P}{\delta} - \frac{C}{r} \right) (1 - \tau) + A_3 P^{\beta_1} + A_4 P^{\beta_2}, \quad P_A < P < P_I^U \tag{9.6}$$

where A_3 and A_4 are constants to be determined, β_1 and β_2 are given immediately below (9.3), P_A is the abandonment price before the growth option is exercised, and P_I^U is the price at which the unlevered firm exercises the growth option by investing I to expand. The unlevered firm value in (9.6) must now satisfy four boundary conditions

$$V^U(P_A) = 0 \tag{9.7a}$$

$$\left. \frac{\partial V^U}{\partial P} \right|_{P = P_A} = 0 \tag{9.7b}$$

$$V^U(P_I^U) = V_q^U(P_I^U) - I \tag{9.7c}$$

and

$$\left. \frac{\partial V^U}{\partial P} \right|_{P = P_I^U} = \left. \frac{\partial V_q^U}{\partial P} \right|_{P = P_I^U} \tag{9.7d}$$

[4] Condition (9.4c) is the standard smooth-pasting boundary, equivalent to a first-order condition requiring that P_{Aq} be chosen to maximize V_q^U.

Conditions (9.7a) and (9.7b) again require, respectively, that firm value be zero at optimal abandonment P_A and that P_A be chosen to maximize firm value. Conditions (9.7c) and (9.7d) are, respectively, the value-matching and optimality conditions that firm value must satisfy when the growth option is exercised, i.e., at P_I^U. Substituting (9.5) and (9.6) into (9.7a)–(9.7d) gives four nonlinear algebraic equations that can be numerically solved for A_3, A_4, P_A, and P_I^U.

9.2.3 Debt and Equity Financing

If the firm is partially financed with debt, then the growth-option exercise strategy that maximizes total firm value will generally differ from the policy that maximizes the value of levered equity alone. Following the previous analysis for the all-equity firm, consider first the levered firm's equity and debt values *after* the growth option is exercised. Assume initially that the firm's debt is permanent with no stated maturity. Denoting the promised coupon payment on the debt by R, the cash flow to equity now is $[(P - C)(q) - R](1 - \tau)\,dt$. The general solution for the value of *levered*-equity is now

$$E_q(P) = \left[\frac{Pq}{\delta} - \frac{(Cq + R)}{r} \right](1 - \tau) + B_1 P^{\beta_1} + B_2 P^{\beta_2}, \quad P > P_{Dq} \quad (9.8)$$

where B_1 and B_2 are constants to be determined, β_1 and β_2 are given immediately below Eq. (9.3), and P_{Dq} is the endogenously determined commodity price at which equityholders choose to default on the firm's debt.

The general solution to (9.8) must satisfy three boundary conditions:

$$\lim_{P \to \infty} E_q(P) = \left(\frac{Pq}{\delta} - \frac{(Cq + R)}{r} \right)(1 - \tau) \quad (9.9a)$$

$$E_q(P_{Dq}) = 0 \quad (9.9b)$$

and

$$\left. \frac{\partial E_q}{\partial P} \right|_{P = P_{Dq}} = 0 \quad (9.9c)$$

Condition (9.9a) holds because default becomes irrelevant as P becomes very large. Condition (9.9b) recognizes that equity has limited liability at P_{Dq}.[5] Finally, condition (9.9c) is the first-order optimality condition that requires that the default price be chosen to maximize the market value of equity. Substituting (9.8) into (9.9a)–(9.9c) gives

$$E_q(P) = \left[\frac{Pq}{\delta} - \frac{(Cq + R)}{r} \right](1 - \tau)$$

---

[5] In bankruptcy, bondholders receive the unlevered assets [given in Eq. (9.5)] net of bankruptcy costs. Condition (9.9b) could be adjusted to allow equityholders to receive a fraction of bondholders' payoff in bankruptcy, thereby allowing for a deviation from absolute priority.

$$-\left[\frac{P_{\mathrm{Dq}}q}{\delta} - \frac{(Cq+R)}{r}\right]\left(\frac{P}{P_{\mathrm{Dq}}}\right)^{\beta_2}(1-\tau) \qquad (9.10)$$

where

$$P_{\mathrm{Dq}} = \left(\frac{-\beta_2}{1-\beta_2}\right)\left(\frac{\delta(C+R/q)}{r}\right)$$

Since debt receives a permanent coupon payment of R per period in the absence of bankruptcy, the general solution for debt value is

$$D_{\mathrm{q}}(P) = \frac{R}{r} + B_3 P^{\beta_1} + B_4 P^{\beta_2}, \qquad P > P_{\mathrm{Dq}} \qquad (9.11)$$

where the constants B_3 and B_4 are determined by the requirements that

$$\lim_{P\to\infty} D_{\mathrm{q}}(P) = \frac{R}{r} \qquad (9.12a)$$

and

$$D_{\mathrm{q}}(P_{\mathrm{Dq}}) = (1-b)V_{\mathrm{q}}^{\mathrm{U}}(P_{\mathrm{Dq}}) \qquad (9.12b)$$

Condition (9.12a) says that at a high enough commodity price debtholders will almost surely receive the coupon value. Condition (9.12b) says that in bankruptcy bondholders receive the unlevered value of the firm [i.e., Eq. (9.5) evaluated at $P = P_{\mathrm{Dq}}$] net of bankruptcy costs amounting to a fraction $b(0 \le b \le 1)$ of unlevered firm value.[6] Note that $V_{\mathrm{q}}^{\mathrm{U}}(P_{\mathrm{Dq}}) > 0$ since $P_{\mathrm{Dq}} > P_{\mathrm{Aq}}$. Substituting (9.5) and (9.11) into (9.12a) and (9.12b) gives the risky debt value as

$$D_{\mathrm{q}}(P) = \frac{R}{r} + \left[(1-b)V_{\mathrm{q}}^{\mathrm{U}}(P_{\mathrm{Dq}}) - \frac{R}{r}\right]\left(\frac{P}{P_{\mathrm{Dq}}}\right)^{\beta_2} \qquad (9.13)$$

The total value of the levered firm *after* the growth option is exercised, $V_{\mathrm{q}}^{\mathrm{I}}(P)$, is simply the sum of $E_{\mathrm{q}}(P)$ in (9.10) and $D_{\mathrm{q}}(P)$ in (9.13). Thus we have

$$V_{\mathrm{q}}^{\mathrm{L}}(P) = \left(\frac{P}{\delta} - \frac{C}{r}\right)(q)(1-\tau) + \left[V_{\mathrm{q}}^{\mathrm{U}}(P_{\mathrm{Dq}}) - \left(\frac{P_{\mathrm{Dq}}}{\delta} - \frac{C}{r}\right)(q)(1-\tau)\right]$$

$$\left(\frac{P}{P_{\mathrm{Dq}}}\right)^{\beta_2} + \left(\frac{\tau R}{r}\right)\left[1 - \left(\frac{P}{P_{\mathrm{Dq}}}\right)^{\beta_2}\right] - bV_{\mathrm{q}}^{\mathrm{U}}(P_{\mathrm{Dq}})\left(\frac{P}{P_{\mathrm{Dq}}}\right)^{\beta_2} \qquad (9.14)$$

Notice that $V_{\mathrm{q}}^{\mathrm{L}}(P)$ equals the value of (unlevered) assets plus the expected discounted value of tax shields on debt minus the expected discounted value of bankruptcy costs.

We now turn to the problem of deriving firm and securityholder values *before* the growth option is exercised. The "first-best" growth option exercise strategy is chosen

---

[6] Although here we model proportional bankruptcy costs, condition (9.12b) could easily be changed to accommodate either fixed bankruptcy costs or a combination of proportional and fixed bankruptcy costs.

to maximize total firm value. However, we assume that it is prohibitively costly to write and enforce contracts that ensure management adopts a firm-value-maximizing growth option exercise policy. Therefore, management may choose a "second-best" growth option exercise strategy that maximizes levered equity value.

For the first-best policy, the general solutions for equity and levered firm values are

$$E_F(P) = \left(\frac{P}{\delta} - \frac{(C+R)}{r}\right)(1-\tau) + K_1^F P^{\beta_1} + K_2^F P^{\beta_2}, \quad P_D < P < P_I^F \quad (9.15)$$

and

$$V_F^L(P) = \left(\frac{P}{\delta} - \frac{C}{r}\right)(1-\tau) + \frac{\tau R}{r} + K_3^F P^{\beta_1} + K_4^F P^{\beta_2}, \quad P_D < P < P_I^F \quad (9.16)$$

where K_1^F, K_2^F, K_3^F, and K_4^F are constants to be determined, P_D is the endogenously determined commodity price at which equityholders default on the debt before the growth option is exercised, and P_I^F is the commodity price at which the firm exercises the growth option. Note that P_D will not, in general, be equal to P_{Dq}, since exercising the growth option will alter equityholders' decision as to when to put the firm to bondholders.

Equations (9.15) and (9.16) must satisfy the following boundary conditions:

$$E_F(P_D) = 0 \qquad\qquad (9.17a)$$

$$\left.\frac{\partial E_F}{\partial P}\right|_{P=P_D} = 0 \qquad\qquad (9.17b)$$

$$E_F(P_I^F) = E_q(P_I^F) - I \qquad\qquad (9.17c)$$

$$V_F^L(P_D) = (1-b)V^U(P_D) \qquad\qquad (9.17d)$$

$$V_F^L(P_I^F) = V_q^L(P_I^F) - I \qquad\qquad (9.17e)$$

$$\left.\frac{\partial V_F^L}{\partial P}\right|_{P=P_I^F} = \left.\frac{\partial V_q^L}{\partial P}\right|_{P=P_I^F} \qquad\qquad (9.17f)$$

Conditions (9.17a) and (9.17b) recognize that equity has limited liability at P_D and that P_D is chosen to maximize equity value, respectively. Condition (9.17c) is a continuity requirement for the value of equity at P_I^F, where the right-hand side equity value is that specified in Eq. (9.10). Condition (9.17d) specifies the requirement that at P_D levered firm value equals unlevered firm value [i.e., the value specified in Eq. (9.6) subject to conditions (9.7a)–(9.7d)] net of bankruptcy costs.[7] Finally, conditions (9.17e) and (9.17f) are the respective value-matching and optimality conditions for levered firm value at the first-best growth option exercise strategy P_I^F, where the right-hand side levered firm value is that specified in Eq. (9.14). Note in (9.17f) that P_I^F is chosen to maximize $V_F^L(P)$.

---

[7] Bankruptcy costs consist of the direct cost of bankruptcy and lost tax shields. Note that the growth option is not lost when equity defaults on the debt.

Substituting (9.6), (9.10), (9.14), (9.15), and (9.16) into (9.17a)–(9.17f) produces a system of six nonlinear algebraic equations that can be numerically solved for the constants K_1^F, K_2^F, K_3^F, and K_4^F, and the policy choices P_D and P_I^F. The first-best debt value can then be computed as $D_F(P) = V_F^L(P) - E_F(P)$.

For the second-best policy, the general solutions for equity and levered firm values are

$$E_S(P) = \left[\frac{P}{\delta} - \frac{(C+R)}{r}\right](1-\tau) + K_1^S P^{\beta_1} + K_2^S P^{\beta_2}, \quad P_D < P < P_I^S \quad (9.18)$$

and

$$V_S^L(P) = \left[\frac{P}{\delta} - \frac{C}{r}\right](1-\tau) + \frac{\tau R}{r} + K_3^S P^{\beta_1} + K_4^S P^{\beta_2}, \quad P_D < P < P_I^S \quad (9.19)$$

where the constants K_1^S, K_2^S, K_3^S, and K_4^S, and the second-best growth option exercise strategy P_I^S, are determined by the following conditions:

$$E_S(P_D) = 0 \qquad (9.20a)$$

$$E_S(P_I^S) = E_q(P_I^S) - I \qquad (9.20b)$$

$$\left.\frac{\partial E_S}{\partial P}\right|_{P=P_I^S} = \left.\frac{\partial E_q}{\partial P}\right|_{P=P_I^S} \qquad (9.20c)$$

$$V_S^L(P_D) = (1-b)V^U(P_D) \qquad (9.20d)$$

and

$$V_S^L(P_I^S) = V_q^L(P_I^S) - I \qquad (9.20e)$$

There are two differences between the sets of boundary conditions for the first- and second-best problems. First, note that the second-best problem uses as an input the solution from the first-best problem for the default price, P_D. Thus, we require in (9.20a) only that E_S be zero at P_D, and not that E_S also be maximized at P_D. Although this places a restriction on the second-best solution, it allows for a closer focus on the effects of differential first- and second-best growth option exercise policies. Second, notice in (9.20c) that the second-best growth option exercise strategy, P_I^S, is chosen to maximize the market value of *equity*, and not total firm value. This, of course, is the critical difference between the first- and second-best solutions. Substitution of (9.6), (9.10), (9.14), (9.18), and (9.19) into (9.20a)–(9.20e) gives five nonlinear algebraic equations that can be numerically solved for K_1^S, K_2^S, K_3^S, K_4^S, and P_I^S. The market value of debt is again computed as $D_S(P) = V_S^L(P) - E_S(P)$.

The agency cost of debt can now be directly measured as

$$AC(P) = V_F^L(P) - V_S^L(P), \quad P_D < P < \max(P_I^F, P_I^S) \qquad (9.21)$$

i.e., as the difference between the first- and second-best levered firm values. Thus, $AC(P)$ captures the loss in firm value when the growth option exercise strategy is chosen to maximize equity value instead of total firm value. Agency costs can be further decomposed as

$$AC(P) = \left[V_F^U(P) - V_S^U(P)\right] + [TS_F(P) - TS_S(P)]$$
$$+ [BC_S(P) - BC_F(P)] \tag{9.22}$$

where $V_F^U(P) - V_S^U(P)$ measures the loss in the unlevered component of firm value (i.e., the sum of the values of assets in place and the growth option), $TS_F(P) - TS_S(P)$ measures the loss in debt tax-shield value, and $BC_S(P) - BC_F(P)$ measures the increase in the expected value of bankruptcy costs, all as a result of the suboptimal growth option exercise strategy.

The credit spread of risky debt can be computed as $[R/D(P)] - r$, where $R/D(P)$ is the interest cost or yield of debt. The agency-induced component of the credit spread can then be measured as $\{[R/D_S(P)] - r\} - \{[R/D_F(P)] - r\}$.

9.3 ANALYSIS OF THE MODEL

9.3.1 Base-Case Example

Table 9.1 summarizes the set of base-case parameter values for our numerical simulation results. Currently, the firm's annual rate of production is one unit per year at a cost (C) of \$1 per unit. However, the firm has an option to expand capacity to three units per year (i.e., $q = 3$) upon making an additional investment expenditure (I) of \$20. The annualized riskless rate of interest (r) is 7%, and the annualized convenience yield (δ) and volatility (σ) of the output price are 7% and 15%, respectively.[8] The corporate tax rate (τ) is assumed to be 35%. Finally, we assume that debt has a promised coupon

Table 9.1
Base-Case Parameter Values for Numerical Simulations

Parameter	Value
Annual rate of production	One unit per year
Production costs	$C = \$1$ per unit
Growth-option scale factor	$q = 3$
Growth-option investment cost	$I = \$20$
Riskless interest rate	$r = 7\%$ annually
Convenience yield	$\delta = 7\%$ annually
Output price volatility	$\sigma = 15\%$ annually
Corporate tax rate	$\tau = 35\%$
Promised coupon payment	$R = \$1.75$
Bankruptcy costs	$b = 50\%$

[8] Dixit and Pindyck (1994, p. 225) use 4% for the *real* risk-free rate and for the convenience yield of copper. Like Dixit and Pindyck, we also model a commodity price; however, we use *nominal* values and returns. Our choice of parameters is similar to Leland and Toft (1996) who use a risk-free rate of 7.5% and a convenience yield of 7%.

Table 9.2
The Unlevered and Levered Firms' Growth Option and Abandonment/Default Exercise Policies[a]

A: Optimal Growth Option Exercise Policy

	Levered firm policies	
Unlevered firm policy	*First best*	*Second best*
$P_I^U = 3.06$	$P_I^F = 2.78$	$P_I^S = 3.16$

B: Optimal Abandonment/Default Policy

	Unlevered equity	*Levered equity*
Before exercise of growth option	$P_A = 0.64$	$P_D = 1.51$
After exercise of growth option	$P_{Aq} = 0.67$	$P_{Dq} = 1.06$

[a] P_I^U is the commodity price at which the unlevered firm exercises the growth option; P_I^F is the first-best levered firm growth option exercise price; P_I^S is the second-best levered firm growth option exercise price; P_A and P_{Aq} are the respective commodity prices at which unlevered equity abandons the firm before and after the exercise of the growth option; and P_D and P_{Dq} are the respective commodity prices at which levered equity defaults before and after the exercise of the growth option. The first-best growth option exercise policy maximizes total firm value; the second-best growth option exercise policy maximizes equity value.

payment (R) of $1.75 and that bankruptcy costs (b) amount to 50% of the value of unlevered assets at the time of bankruptcy.

Given these base-case parameters, Table 9.2 reports the first- and second-best growth option exercise prices, and the prices at which equity should default on debt before and after exercise of the growth option. Table 9.2A shows that equityholders underinvest in the growth option by waiting for a higher output price than the one that maximizes total firm value. Specifically, the first-best policy is to exercise the growth option at $P_I^F = \$2.78$, with the second-best policy at $P_I^S = \$3.16$. Assuming a 5% annual expected rate of appreciation in the output price (i.e., $\alpha = 0.05$), the expected time it would take for the price to reach $3.16 from $2.78 is over 3 years.[9] Clearly, equityholders significantly underinvest in the growth option.

One may interpret this result as delaying investment rather than underinvesting. However, by waiting for a higher output price, the probability that investment takes place by any future date decreases. Accordingly, the expected amount of investment by that date is lower. It is in this sense that equityholders underinvest relative to the first-best value-maximizing investment strategy.

Table 9.2B shows that exercise of the growth option leads to a significant decrease in the price at which levered equity optimally defaults on debt payments. Before the

[9] This is the expected first-passage time, $E[\tilde{t}]$, for P to reach P_I^S given that the price starts at $P_I^F \le P_I^S$ and follows geometric Brownian motion with drift $\alpha = 0.05$ and volatility $\sigma = 0.15$. From Cox and Miller (1970), the calculation is

$$E[\tilde{t}] = \frac{\ln(P_I^S) - \ln(P_I^F)}{\alpha - 0.5\sigma^2} = \frac{\ln(3.16) - \ln(2.78)}{0.05 - (0.5)(0.15)^2} = 3.31 \text{ years}$$

option is exercised, levered equity puts the firm to the bondholders when the price falls to $P_D = \$1.51$, but after the option is exercised it waits until the price falls to $P_{Dq} = \$1.06$. The reason for the significant change in policy is that operating cash flows are higher after exercise (by a factor of $q = 3$), therefore the opportunity cost of putting the firm to the bondholders is larger.

Equityholders underinvest in the growth option because, although they pay the full cost of the investment, they do not receive all of the benefits. The cost to the equityholders, which is the same whether the policy is to maximize total firm value or equity value, is the sum of the direct cost of investment, I, and the indirect cost of killing the option to wait for further resolution of uncertainty about the path of the output price. The benefits from exercise include higher cash flows (at the rate q), lower expected bankruptcy costs, and higher expected tax shields (as a result of the reduction in the probability of default). Although equity benefits from the higher operating cash flows and expected tax shields, it does not receive the full benefit of the increase in cash flows, nor does it benefit from the reduction in expected bankruptcy costs. It is the bondholders who benefit from the reduced present value of bankruptcy costs and the reduced probability of default. Therefore equityholders, taking account of the wealth transfer to bondholders, wait for a higher output price.

Of course, the deviation from the first-best exercise policy is reflected in the price that debtholders are willing to pay for the debt at issuance. The resulting higher yield on the debt is the ex-ante cost that equityholders bear for the agency problem of underinvestment. Table 9.3 tabulates the first- and second-best firm and securityholder values as a function of the output price. As expected, $V_F^L(P) > V_S^L(P)$, $E_F(P) < E_S(P)$, and $D_F(P) > D_S(P)$.

For different output prices, Table 9.4 tabulates the unlevered, tax shield and bankruptcy cost components of first- and second-best firm values, the differences between these component parts, total agency costs [the sum of the differences, or simply $V_F^L(P) - V_S^L(P)$], and total agency costs as a proportion of (second-best) firm and debt values. Focusing first on total agency costs (the last three columns in Table 9.4), observe that total costs reach a maximum of a little more than 1.5% of firm value and about 2.8% of debt value for an output price of \$2.80. Figure 9.1 shows the first- and second-best credit spreads (in basis points) as a function of the output price. The difference between these credit spreads, displayed in the figure, measures the increase in the cost of debt capital as a result of equityholders' (ex-post) incentive to underinvest in the growth option. Notice that this increased cost reaches a maximum of about 60 basis points.

Focusing next on the components of total agency costs, note in Table 9.4 that agency costs are driven by differences in the expected value of tax shields and bankruptcy costs across the first- and second-best cases. Indeed, the unlevered component of firm value (the value of an otherwise identical unlevered firm following the *levered* firm's operating policies) is actually larger under equity-value maximization than under firm-value maximization for all but the upper range of output prices in Table 9.4.[10] To see why, observe in Table 9.2A that unlevered equity prefers to wait

---

[10] Note that the difference in unlevered values is zero at a price of \$3.16 (as are the differences in the tax shield and bankruptcy cost components) because this is the price at which levered equity exercises the growth option, hence the agency conflict no longer exists.

Table 9.3
Unlevered and Levered Firm Values as a Function of the Output Price[a]

Output price P	Unlevered firm value before and after exercise of growth option		First-best levered firm value before exercise of growth option			Second-best levered firm value before exercise of growth option			Postexercise levered firm value		
	$V^U(P)$	$V_q^U(P)$	$V_F^L(P)$	$E_F(P)$	$D_F(P)$	$V_S^L(P)$	$E_S(P)$	$D_S(P)$	$V_q^L(P)$	$E_q(P)$	$D_q(P)$
1.50	7.32	15.70							18.80	4.85	13.95
1.60	8.64	18.27	6.49	0.14	6.36	6.47	0.18	6.28	22.06	6.75	15.32
1.70	10.03	20.87	9.25	0.53	8.72	9.19	0.63	8.56	25.25	8.80	16.44
1.80	11.50	23.51	11.88	1.16	10.72	11.78	1.31	10.47	28.36	10.97	17.39
1.90	13.05	26.16	14.42	1.97	12.45	14.29	2.18	12.11	31.43	13.24	18.18
2.00	14.68	28.84	16.92	2.96	13.96	16.75	3.22	13.53	34.45	15.59	18.86
2.10	16.39	31.53	19.39	4.09	15.30	19.19	4.43	14.76	37.44	18.00	19.45
2.20	18.19	34.24	21.88	5.38	16.50	21.63	5.78	15.85	40.40	20.46	19.95
2.30	20.08	36.95	24.39	6.79	17.59	24.09	7.27	16.82	43.34	22.96	20.39
2.40	22.06	39.68	26.94	8.34	18.59	26.59	8.89	17.70	46.27	25.49	20.77
2.50	24.15	42.41	29.54	10.01	19.53	29.15	10.65	18.50	49.17	28.06	21.11
2.60	26.33	45.15	32.22	11.81	20.41	31.76	12.54	19.23	52.06	30.65	21.41
2.70	28.62	47.89	34.97	13.72	21.25	34.46	14.55	19.91	54.94	33.26	21.68
2.80	31.02	50.64				37.24	16.69	20.54	57.81	35.89	21.91
2.90	33.53	53.39				40.51	18.97	21.14	60.67	38.54	22.13
3.00	36.16	56.14				43.08	21.37	21.71	63.52	41.20	22.32
3.10		58.90				46.16	23.90	22.26	66.37	43.88	22.49
3.20		61.66							69.21	46.56	22.65

[a] Blank spaces represent prices where either P is less than the price at which optimal default occurs, or alternatively, where P is greater than the price at which optimal exercise of the growth option occurs.

Table 9.4
The Agency Cost of Debt[a]

Output price	First-best levered firm value component parts			Second-best levered firm value component parts			Agency cost component parts				Total agency cost	
P	$V_F^U(P)$	$TS_F(P)$	$BC_F(P)$	$V_S^U(P)$	$TS_S(P)$	$BC_S(P)$	$V_F^U - V_S^U$	$TS_F - TS_S$	$BC_S - BC_F$	AC	% of V_S^L	% of D_S
1.51	7.38	0.00	3.69	7.38	0.00	3.69	0.00	0.00	0.00	0.00	0.00	0.00
1.60	8.61	1.10	3.22	8.63	1.07	3.24	−0.02	0.03	0.02	0.03	0.46	0.48
1.70	9.98	2.07	2.80	10.02	2.00	2.84	−0.04	0.07	0.04	0.06	0.66	0.70
1.80	11.42	2.90	2.44	11.49	2.79	2.50	−0.07	0.11	0.06	0.09	0.80	0.86
1.90	12.94	3.61	2.13	13.04	3.47	2.21	−0.09	0.14	0.08	0.13	0.90	1.07
2.00	14.54	4.23	1.86	14.66	4.05	1.96	−0.12	0.19	0.10	0.17	0.99	1.26
2.10	16.22	4.79	1.62	16.37	4.56	1.74	−0.15	0.23	0.12	0.21	1.07	1.42
2.20	17.99	5.29	1.40	18.17	5.01	1.55	−0.18	0.28	0.15	0.25	1.14	1.58
2.30	19.84	5.74	1.19	20.05	5.41	1.37	−0.21	0.33	0.18	0.29	1.22	1.72
2.40	21.79	6.16	1.01	22.03	5.77	1.21	−0.25	0.38	0.21	0.34	1.29	1.92
2.50	23.83	6.55	0.83	24.11	6.10	1.07	−0.29	0.44	0.24	0.39	1.35	2.11
2.60	25.96	6.91	0.66	26.29	6.40	0.93	−0.33	0.51	0.27	0.45	1.42	2.34
2.70	28.20	7.26	0.50	28.58	6.69	0.80	−0.37	0.58	0.31	0.51	1.49	2.56
2.80	30.64	7.54	0.37	30.97	6.95	0.68	−0.33	0.59	0.32	0.57	1.54	2.78
2.90	33.39	7.62	0.34	33.48	7.20	0.57	−0.09	0.43	0.23	0.56	1.41	2.65
3.00	36.14	7.70	0.32	36.10	7.44	0.46	0.04	0.26	0.14	0.45	1.03	2.07
3.10	38.90	7.77	0.30	38.85	7.67	0.35	0.06	0.10	0.05	0.21	0.46	0.94
3.16	40.65	7.81	0.29	40.65	7.81	0.29	0.00	0.00	0.00	0.00	0.00	0.00

[a] $V_F^U(P)$ and $V_S^U(P)$ are the first- and second-best values for the unlevered component of firm value; $TS_F(P)$ and $TS_S(P)$ are the first- and second-best values of interest tax shields; and $BC_F(P)$ and $BC_S(P)$ are the first- and second-best values of expected bankruptcy costs. Total agency cost (AC) is the sum of the differences between the first- and second-best unlevered, tax shield, and bankruptcy cost components, or simply $V_F^L - V_S^L$. The table also reports total agency cost (AC) as a percentage of levered firm value (V_S^L) and debt value (D_S).

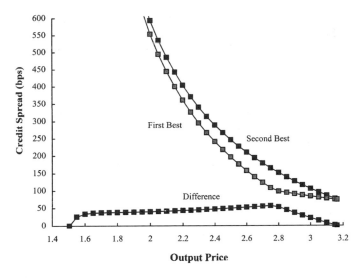

Figure 9.1 Credit spread (in basis points) as a function of output price for first- and second-best growth option exercise policies.

for a higher price before exercising the growth option than the exercise price that maximizes total levered firm value. The reason is that unlevered equity's decision is not influenced by a desire to increase the expected value of tax shields or decrease the expected value of bankruptcy costs. Consequently, the unlevered equity growth option exercise policy is much closer to that of levered equity, and therefore the unlevered component of the first-best firm value is typically smaller than the corresponding second-best component.

9.3.2 Comparative Static Properties of Agency Costs

Figure 9.2 shows agency costs (measured as a percent of firm value) as a function of output price for convenience yields (δ) of 5, 7, and 9%. All other parameters are held constant at their base-case values in Table 9.1. Agency costs sharply increase as the convenience yield increases.[11] Holding the risk-adjusted discount rate constant, a larger convenience yield means a smaller rate of price appreciation (α) and therefore a smaller firm and growth option value.[12] Accordingly, as δ increases equityholders

---

[11] Note that the agency cost graphs are only directly comparable for the range of output prices in which the firm operates (i.e., for $P > P_D$) under each of the convenience yield scenarios. This same cautionary note applies to all of the comparative static figures discussed below.

[12] Given our assumption that the commodity price is spanned by traded assets, the risk-adjusted discount rate for commodity price risk, μ_P, must satisfy the relation $\mu_P = r + \eta\rho\sigma = \alpha + \delta$, where η is the market price of risk and ρ is the instantaneous correlation of the spanning asset (or dynamic portfolio of spanning assets) with the systematic pricing factor. From this relation it is clear that if μ_P is held constant, an increase in δ must be accompanied by a decrease in α.

put the firm to the bondholders sooner (i.e., P_D increases) and wait for a higher price before exercising the growth option. This increases the probability of default, making debt considerably more risky at higher values of δ. The implication is that the difference between the first- and second-best growth option exercise prices widens, and therefore agency costs increase as δ increases.

Figure 9.3 shows agency costs as a function of price at output price volatilities (σ) of 10, 15, and 20%. Interestingly, agency costs decrease sharply as volatility increases. Note that the value of the firm's growth option increases as σ increases, as does the price at which the firm exercises that option.[13] Because the option and the firm are more valuable as σ increases, the price at which equityholders choose to default on promised debt payments, P_D, is a decreasing function of σ. The implication is that the probability of default actually decreases as σ increases; therefore, equityholders are less concerned about a wealth transfer to debtholders when the growth option is exercised. As a result, first- and second-best growth option exercise policies converge and agency costs decrease as σ increases.

Figure 9.4 shows agency costs as a function of output price for promised coupon payments (R) of $1.60, $1.75, and $1.90. As R increases, the probability of default increases (i.e., $\partial P_D / \partial R > 0$) and debt becomes riskier. Thus the firm-value maximizing policy is to exercise the growth option sooner (i.e., at a lower output price) as R increases, to offset this higher probability of default. By comparison, equityholders have no incentive to reduce the risk of debt, waiting instead for a higher exercise price as R increases. The resulting widening of the differential between the

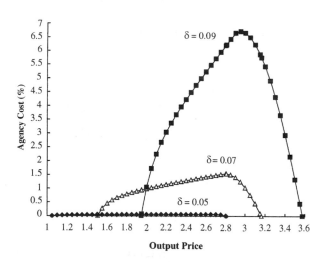

Figure 9.2 Agency cost of debt as a function of output price for different convenience yields (δ).

[13] It is a standard result from the real options literature that greater uncertainty increases the value of the firm's investment options and discourages investment by increasing the value of waiting to invest (see, e.g., McDonald and Siegel, 1986).

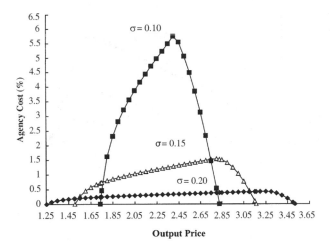

Figure 9.3 Agency cost of debt as a function of output price for different price volatilities (σ).

first- and second-best growth option exercise prices causes agency costs to increase as *R* increases.

Figure 9.5 shows agency costs as a function of output price for proportional bankruptcy costs (*b*) of 0.25, 0.50, and 0.75. Since expected bankruptcy costs increase as *b* increases, the first-best growth option investment policy is to exercise the option sooner. However, equityholders have no such incentive, and therefore the second-best exercise policy is insensitive to *b*. Hence the disparity between the first- and second-best policies is magnified; as seen in Figure 9.5, agency costs increase as *b* increases.

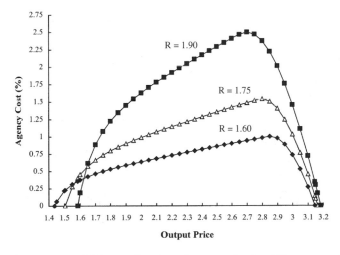

Figure 9.4 Agency cost of debt as a function of output price for different promised coupon payments (*R*).

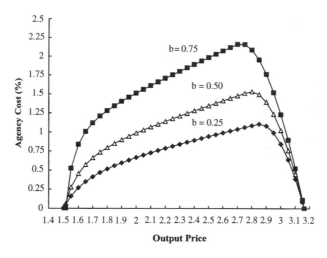

Figure 9.5 Agency cost of debt as a function of output price for different proportional bankruptcy costs (*b*).

Figure 9.6 shows agency costs as a function of output price for corporate tax rates (τ) of 15, 25, and 35%. As τ decreases (from the base case value of 35%) firm value increases (despite a lower tax shield value of debt), and options on future production are worth more. Thus both first- and second-best policy makers are encouraged to exercise the growth option sooner. As a result, the difference between the two growth option trigger prices remains relatively constant as τ decreases, and therefore agency costs are relatively insensitive to τ.

Figure 9.7 shows agency costs as a function of output price for growth option scale

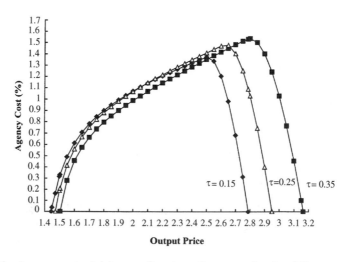

Figure 9.6 Agency cost of debt as a function of output price for different corporate tax rates (τ).

factors (q) of 2, 3, and 4 units. As q increases the expected payoff from exercising the growth option increases, and a larger share of total firm value is made up by the growth option value; therefore differences between first- and second-best exercise policies have a larger influence on firm value. The net effect, as illustrated in Figure 9.7, is that agency costs increase as q increases.

Finally, Figure 9.8 shows agency costs as a function of output price for growth option investment expenditures (I) of \$17, \$20, and \$23. As I increases, the value of the growth option decreases, and both first- and second-best policy makers delay exercise of the growth option by waiting for a higher output price. Since the option is exercised at a higher output price, there is less of a potential wealth transfer to debtholders on exercise. Thus, the divergence between first- and second-best exercise policies narrows, and agency costs decrease as I increases.

9.3.3 Optimal Capital Structure

An interesting question is whether the agency cost of underinvestment has a significant effect on optimal capital structure. In the context of our model, the determination of optimal capital structure involves finding the coupon payment R that maximizes firm value at a given output price. The optimal R is determined where the marginal expected interest tax shield equals the marginal expected bankruptcy and agency costs of debt. However, there is also a more subtle leverage-related cost associated with the loss of interest tax shields in bankruptcy. As a consequence, we should expect to find an interior optimal capital structure (i.e., debt-to-firm value ratio less than one) even when bankruptcy and agency costs are zero.

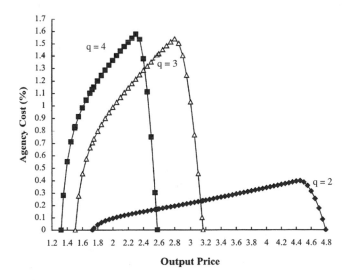

Figure 9.7 Agency cost of debt as a function of output price for different growth option scale factors (q).

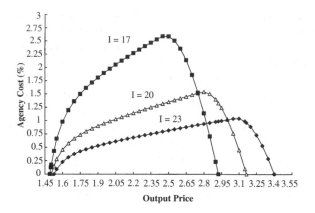

Figure 9.8 Agency cost of debt as a function of output price for different growth option investment expenditures (I).

We compare the optimal capital structures under first- and second-best growth option exercise policies to isolate the effect of agency costs on optimal capital structure. If the optimal promised coupon payment under the second-best growth option exercise policy is less than that under the first-best policy, we can conclude that the agency cost of underinvestment influences optimal capital structure.

Table 9.5A and B displays the optimal capital structures for the first- and second-best cases at an output price of $2.50 for bankruptcy costs b of zero and 50%, respectively. First observe that even when bankruptcy and agency costs are zero (i.e., the first-best case in Table 9.5A), the firm is not 100% debt financed; for this case the optimal coupon payment for the first-best policy is $2.86 and the debt-to-firm value ratio is 0.91. This reflects the loss of interest tax shields in bankruptcy that eventually overrides the interest tax shield benefit of extreme leverage. More important, however, regardless of the magnitude of bankruptcy costs, the optimal amount of leverage is significantly less under the second-best case. For example, in Table 9.5B ($b = 50\%$) the optimal promised coupon payment for the first-best policy is $2.30 and that for the second-best policy is $1.76; the leverage ratio comparison is 0.81 versus 0.64. The implication is that the agency cost of underinvestment is a significant determinant of optimal capital structure.[14]

Table 9.5C and D illustrates the effect of an increase in uncertainty on optimal capital structure by varying σ from 10 to 20%. Bankruptcy costs are held constant at 50%. Observe that the differences between the optimal coupon payments and leverage ratios for the first- and second-best cases narrow as σ increases. This reflects our earlier finding that the agency cost of underinvestment decreases as uncertainty increases. As

---

[14] One might be concerned by the high optimal leverage ratios in the model. However, recall that these calculations ignore personal taxes and assume that the firm always earns its interest tax shields outside of bankruptcy (i.e., full loss-offset provisions). For example, reducing the tax rate from 35% (base case) to 15% (reflecting the *net* tax advantage of debt relative to equity after adjusting for personal taxes) approximately halves the optimal leverage ratios reported in Table 9.5.

Table 9.5
Optimal Capital Structure for Different Bankruptcy Costs and Output Price Volatilities[a]

	Promised coupon payment	Firm value	Debt-to-firm value ratio
A: Bankruptcy costs $b = 0$			
First best	2.86	31.61	0.91
Second best	2.21	30.71	0.75
B: Bankruptcy costs $b = 50\%$			
First best	2.30	29.79	0.81
Second best	1.76	29.15	0.64
C: Output-price volatility $\sigma = 10\%$			
First best	2.07	28.51	0.89
Second best	1.38	27.47	0.62
D: Output-price volatility $\sigma = 20\%$			
First best	2.32	31.61	0.69
Second best	2.11	31.32	0.63

[a] The optimal promised coupon payment, firm value, and debt-to-firm value ratio are calculated for an output price of $2.50.

such, the optimal promised coupon payment for the second-best case sharply increases as σ increases. However, note that the corresponding optimal leverage *ratio* is less sensitive to σ, reflecting the fact that the higher debt value is almost completely offset by the larger growth option component of firm value.

9.4 RESOLVING THE AGENCY PROBLEM OF UNDERINVESTMENT

This analysis assumes that it is prohibitively costly to write and enforce bond covenants that force equityholders to choose the growth option exercise policy that maximizes total firm value. Of course, if such covenants could be written and enforced there would be no agency problem of underinvestment. However, even without such covenants, several authors have pointed out that underinvestment incentives can be controlled with other aspects of financial policy. For example, Myers (1977) argues that underinvestment incentives can be mitigated by shortening debt maturity or by financing growth options with additional debt.[15] Similarly, recent work by Anderson and Sundaresan (1996) and Mella-Barral and Perraudin (1997) suggests that inefficiencies in investment policy induced by risky debt financing may be reduced, if not eliminated, when there is scope for negotiating prior to formal bankruptcy. In

[15] Barnea et al. (1985) and Ho and Singer (1984) argue that call and sinking-fund provisions can also mitigate investment incentive effects of risky debt financing by reducing the effective maturity of debt.

this section, we first examine the impact of partially financing the growth option with additional debt financing. We then extend the model to the case of finite-maturity debt and examine whether shortening debt maturity can reduce underinvestment incentives. Finally, we consider the impact on underinvestment incentives when equityholders can act strategically by persuading debtholders to accept debt service concessions prior to formal bankruptcy proceedings.

9.4.1 Partially Financing the Growth Option with Additional Borrowing

The agency conflict arises because equityholders pay the entire cost of exercising the growth option, but receive less than 100% of the benefits. What happens when the cost of exercising the growth option is partially financed with a new debt issue?

Figure 9.9 shows agency costs as a function of output price for the base case in which the cost of exercising the option is all-equity financed, and for three cases in which the cost is partially financed with a new debt issue. The three debt issue cases have promised coupon payments, RN, of $0.50, $1.00, and $1.50. For all cases, the original debt has a promised coupon payment, R, of $1.75. We assume that the old and new debt have the same priority in bankruptcy, and apportion each debt's share of the value of firm assets in bankruptcy according to their proportional share of total coupon payments.

As seen in Figure 9.9, agency costs sharply decrease as the amount of new debt financing RN increases. Indeed, agency costs are essentially zero when $RN = $1.50. For this case, the market value of new debt at issuance is $16.99, and 85% (= 16.99/20) of the cost of exercising the growth option is financed with additional borrowing. As RN increases, a larger share of the benefits from exercising the growth option accrues

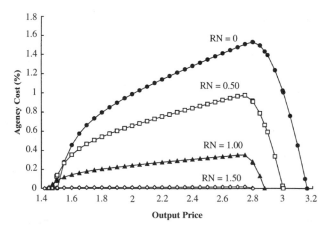

Figure 9.9   Agency cost of debt as a function of output price when the cost of exercising the growth option is partially financed with a new debt issue having promised coupon payment RN.

to equityholders because any increase in the value of old debt is partially offset by the dilution in the value of their position. Therefore, equityholders have less of an incentive to underinvest, and the divergence between the first- and second-best growth option exercise prices narrows.

This result has implications for observed debt contracts. Smith and Warner (1979) and Brick and Fisher (1987) have noted that indenture provisions typically do not provide strict "me-first" protection. Indeed, Brick and Fisher provide evidence that since about the 1950s virtually all long-term industrial bonds have been issued under open indentures that permit new issues to have at least the same seniority against the present asset base. Our analysis shows that one important benefit of open indentures is that they can help reduce underinvestment incentives.

Our analysis also suggests a possible rationale for a policy of maintaining a target debt ratio by linking additional borrowing to incremental investment. For example, in Table 9.5B the optimal debt ratio for the second-best case is 64%, which if the firm were to maintain as a target debt ratio, would require that $12.80 (= 0.64 × 20) of the cost of the investment be financed with additional borrowing. New debt with a market value of $12.80 would require a coupon (RN) of approximately $1.15. As seen in Figure 9.9, such a policy would produce minimal agency costs.

9.4.2 Shortening Debt Maturity

Myers (1977) argues that the underinvestment problem can be minimized, if not eliminated, by shortening the maturity of debt. This is clear if the firm's debt matures before the growth option is exercised, but is much less obvious in the more realistic setting in which the growth option exercise strategy is endogenous and the firm plans to maintain a leveraged capital structure through time. We examine this issue by revising our base model's assumption of infinite debt maturity to an arbitrary rollover rate.

Following Leland (1994b), we assume that the firm retires a fraction m of its outstanding debt principal F each period and replaces it with new debt having the same coupon rate, principal amount, and priority in bankruptcy as the debt retired. Although both old and new debt have the same infinite original maturity, the average maturity of debt, $M = 1/m$, can be made arbitrarily small by increasing the rate m of debt retirement. Thus, if $m = 0$ average maturity is infinite; as $m \rightarrow \infty$, average maturity approaches zero.[16]

Table 9.6 illustrates the effect of debt maturity on the agency cost of underinvestment for debt maturities ranging from 2 years ($m = 0.5$) to infinity ($m = 0$). The calculations assume an output price of $2.50 and hold capital structure constant at the optimal level for 10-year maturity debt, i.e., for $m = 0.1$. The optimal capital structure is determined by finding the coupon payment and debt principal that maximize firm value subject to the constraint that the market value of debt equals its principal amount

---

[16] A detailed derivation showing how the model can be extended to accommodate an arbitrary average maturity is available from the authors on request.

at an output price of $2.50.[17] The resulting coupon payment and principal amount are $1.35 and $14.31, respectively.[18]

Surprisingly, Table 9.6 shows that the agency cost of underinvestment increases as the firm shortens debt maturity. The reason is that as debt maturity is shortened equityholders choose to put the firm to bondholders sooner (i.e., P_D increases),[19] and thus expected bankruptcy costs increase. Note that the expected tax shields are also smaller, since there is now a larger probability of losing them in bankruptcy. The first-best solution calls for exercising the growth option sooner to offset the larger expected bankruptcy costs and lower expected tax shields. However, since equityholders ignore bankruptcy costs when making their exercise decision, the gap between the first- and second-best exercise policies widens. Thus, agency costs increase as debt maturity decreases.

For comparison, Table 9.7 performs the same experiment but allows the firm to simultaneously adjust the optimal capital structure in response to the variation in debt maturity. Interestingly, when capital structure is no longer held constant, agency costs decrease as debt maturity is shortened. To see why, recall that expected bankruptcy

Table 9.6

Agency Cost of Debt for Different Debt Maturities (Holding Capital Structure Constant)[a]

Debt maturity (years)	Agency cost (%)
2	0.93
3	0.63
5	0.50
10	0.44
20	0.41
∞	0.39

[a] Agency costs are calculated for an output price of $2.50, holding capital structure constant at its optimal level for 10-year-maturity debt. This capital structure is determined by finding the coupon rate and debt principal that maximize firm value subject to the constraint that the market value of debt equals its principal amount at an output price of $2.50.

[17] Thus, at a price of $2.50, 10-year average maturity debt could be issued at par. However, subsequent debt issues (as the firm retired and issued new replacement debt) would be issued at a premium or discount, depending on whether the price was above or below $2.50.

[18] For this coupon and debt principal, we are unable to obtain solutions for debt maturities less than 2 years. The reason, as illustrated in Table 9.7, is that debt capacity is substantially reduced as debt maturity is shortened.

[19] The general result is that $\partial P_D / \partial m > 0$. When the output price is low, new debt issued to retire old debt is likely to sell for a price below par value. Accordingly, at such prices the net cash flow accruing to equity from rolling over debt will be negative. Since the absolute value of this cash flow is increasing in m, equityholders are encouraged to put the firm to bondholders sooner as m increases.

costs increase as debt maturity decreases. As seen in Table 9.7, this encourages the firm to sharply reduce leverage, which reduces the risk of the remaining debt and thereby equityholders' incentive to deviate from the first-best growth option exercise policy. Nevertheless, observe that firm value is an increasing function of debt maturity; the lower agency costs at shorter maturities are more than offset by the reduced debt tax shield value.

The important implication of this analysis is that firms cannot control underinvestment incentives solely by shortening debt maturity. This implication is consistent with the recent empirical findings of Barclay and Smith (1996) and Stohs and Mauer (1996) that firms with large amounts of growth options tend to have both less leverage and shorter debt maturity structures.

9.4.3 Strategic Debt Service

As in most contingent claims models, there is no scope for negotiation prior to formal bankruptcy in our model. Although equityholders can endogenously choose the bankruptcy trigger prices before and after exercise of the growth option, they do not have the flexibility to negotiate with bondholders for lower debt service payments to avoid bankruptcy. Anderson and Sundaresan (1996) and Mella-Barral and Perraudin (1997) develop models in which the bankruptcy decision is endogenous and where equityholders can offer strategic debt service. In a model similar to that examined here, Mella-Barral and Perraudin demonstrate that strategic debt service can eliminate bankruptcy costs and an agency cost of debt resulting from inefficient early liquidation of the firm. However, strategic debt service significantly increases the yield spread on debt since bondholders anticipate that equityholders will use the threat of costly bankruptcy to reduce the promised coupon payment when the firm's cash flows are low.

Table 9.7
Agency Cost of Debt for Different Debt Maturities Allowing for Optimal Capital Structure Adjustments[a]

Debt maturity (years)	Coupon	Debt-to-firm value ratio	Firm value	Agency cost (%)
0.5	0.40	0.19	24.99	0.00
1	0.64	0.30	25.21	0.00
2	0.82	0.37	25.72	0.02
5	1.18	0.47	26.89	0.22
10	1.35	0.52	27.66	0.44
20	1.51	0.56	28.26	0.73
∞	1.76	0.64	29.15	1.40

[a] For each debt maturity, the optimal capital structure, firm value, and agency cost of debt are calculated for an output price of $2.50. The debt is priced so that the market value of debt equals its principal value for that output price.

An interesting question is whether strategic debt service can mitigate equity-holders' incentive to underinvest in the growth option. Although it is beyond the scope of this chapter to include an analysis of strategic debt service, we believe that strategic debt service would not eliminate equityholders' incentive to underinvest in the growth option. In our model, equityholders inefficiently delay exercise of the growth option because they pay the full cost of exercising the option but bondholders reap part of the benefits through a reduction in the probability of costly bankruptcy. Even if strategic debt service could eliminate costly bankruptcy, bond value will still be sensitive to low price outcomes because equityholders will use the threat of costly bankruptcy to lower promised coupon payments. As such, there will continue to be a divergence between the growth option exercise strategies preferred by equityholders and debtholders. Debtholders will want to exercise the growth option sooner to reduce the probability of triggering strategic debt service, while equityholders will want to exercise the growth option at a higher output price to minimize the wealth transfer to debtholders when the option is exercised.

9.5 EFFECT OF COMPETITION ON THE AGENCY COST OF DEBT

Our basic model assumes that the firm has a monopoly right to exercise the growth option. In such a setting, there is considerable value of waiting to invest because there is no chance that the firm could be preempted by a competitor. Intuitively, we would expect competition to motivate the firm to exercise the growth option sooner than it would in the absence of competition. However, it is unclear whether this effect would significantly offset equityholders' incentive to underinvest (i.e., delay investment) in the growth option.

To assess the effect of exogenous competitive entry, we extend the base-case model by introducing uncertainty about the firm's ability to profitably exercise the growth option. Specifically, we assume that elimination of the growth opportunity by competition follows a Poisson process with a constant intensity parameter $\lambda \geq 0$. That is, with probability λ per unit time the growth opportunity vanishes; the expected time to elimination is simply λ^{-1}.[20]

Figure 9.10 shows agency costs (as a percentage of firm value) as a function of the output price for competitive intensity (λ) values of zero (no competition), 0.15 and 0.30. Note that when λ is 0.15 (0.30), competition is expected to eliminate the growth opportunity in 6.67 (3.33) years. We use the base-case parameter values of Table 9.1, except that R is set equal to $1.25.[21]

Surprisingly, the figure illustrates that agency costs increase sharply as λ increases; maximum agency costs are less than 0.5% of firm value when λ is zero and increase to well over 5% of firm value when λ is 0.30. The intuition for this result is

---

[20] A detailed derivation showing how the model can be extended to handle this additional source of uncertainty is available from the authors on request.

[21] We choose $R = 1.25$ for the competitive case because firm value and debt capacity decline as λ increases.

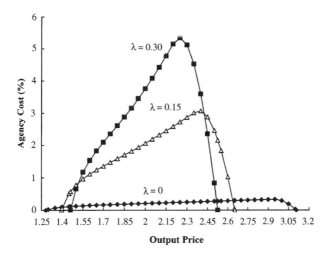

Figure 9.10 Agency cost of debt as a function of the output price for different competition intensity parameters (λ).

as follows. Since the option to wait is less valuable as λ increases, the first-best policy calls for earlier exercise of the growth option (i.e., at a lower output price than that for the no competition case). For the same reason, equityholders under the second-best policy also have an incentive to exercise the growth option earlier. In making their decision, however, equityholders also consider the wealth transfer to bondholders that occurs on exercise resulting from the reduced probability of bankruptcy. This wealth transfer is larger at lower output prices. As a result, the gap between the first- and second-best policies widens as λ increases, causing an increase in agency costs.

9.6 SUMMARY AND CONCLUSION

This chapter analyzes agency costs, investment policy, and optimal capital structure in a real options framework in which the firm has assets in place and a growth option to expand the scale of operations. We show that equityholders underinvest in the growth option by delaying exercise relative to a policy that maximizes total firm value. The divergence in the growth option exercise strategy results because equityholders bear the full cost of the investment but receive only a portion of the benefits. Risky debt captures a share of the benefits in the form of a reduction in the probability of default. We measure this agency cost and also show how it influences credit spreads on risky debt—and hence the firm's cost of debt capital—and optimal capital structure. The agency cost of underinvestment is economically significant, increasing the credit spread on risky debt by over 60 basis points for our base-case parameters.

It is argued in the literature that underinvestment incentives can be mitigated by shortening debt maturity, financing the growth option with additional debt or through strategic debt service. We also show that the agency cost of underinvestment can be significantly reduced by partially financing the growth option with new debt. By contrast, we find that agency costs actually increase as debt maturity is shortened because expected bankruptcy costs are significantly larger for shorter-maturity debt. Additionally, we argue that strategic debt service is unlikely to resolve the underinvestment problem. Although strategic debt service may eliminate bankruptcy costs, debt value will continue to be sensitive to the growth option exercise decision.

Finally, we revise the base model's assumption that the firm has a monopoly right to exercise the growth option by allowing for the random entry of a competitor who eliminates the firm's opportunity to profitably exercise the option. We show that as the probability of competitive entry increases, the agency cost of underinvestment increases significantly.

ACKNOWLEDGMENTS

We thank Paul Childs, Rob Hansen, Arnold Juster, Tim Riddiough, Michel Robe, Neil Wallace, and seminar participants at the University of Miami, and the 1996 European Finance Association and Financial Management Association meetings for helpful comments. We also thank an anonymous referee and the editors Michael Brennan and Lenos Trigeorgis for many helpful suggestions.

REFERENCES

Anderson, R. W., and S. Sundaresan. (1996). Design and Valuation of Debt Contracts. *Review of Financial Studies* 9(1), 37–68.

Barclay, M. J., and C. W. Smith. (1996). On Financial Architecture: Leverage, Maturity, and Priority. *Journal of Applied Corporate Finance* 8(1), 4–17.

Barnea, A., R. Haugen, and L. Senbet. (1985). Agency Problems and Financial Contracting. Englewood Cliffs, NJ: Prentice-Hall Book Company.

Black, F., and J. Cox. (1976). Valuing Corporate Securities: Some Effects of Bond Indenture Provisions. *Journal of Finance* 31(2), 351–367.

Brennan, M. J., and E. S. Schwartz. (1984). Optimal Financial Policy and Firm Valuation. *Journal of Finance* 39(3), 593–607.

Brennan, M. J., and E. S. Schwartz. (1985). Evaluating Natural Resource Investments. *Journal of Business* 58(2), 135–157.

Brick, I. E., and L. Fisher. (1987). Effects of Classifying Equity or Debt on the Value of the Firm under Uncertainty. *Journal of Financial and Quantitative Analysis* 22(4), 383–399.

Cox, D. R., and H. D. Miller. (1970). *The Theory of Stochastic Processes*. London, England: Methuen and Co., Ltd.

Dixit, A., and R. S. Pindyck. (1994). *Investment Under Uncertainty*. Princeton, NJ: Princeton University Press.

Fries, S., M. Miller, and W. Perraudin. (1997). Debt in Industry Equilibrium. *Review of Financial Studies* 10(1), 39–67.

Harris, M., and A. Raviv. (1991). The Theory of Capital Structure. *Journal of Finance* 46(1), 297–355.

Ho, T., and R. F. Singer. (1984). The Value of Corporate Debt with a Sinking-Fund Provision. *Journal of Business* 57(3), 315–336.

Jensen, M, and W, Meckling. (1976). Theory of the Firm: Managerial Behavior, Agency Costs, and Ownership Structure. *Journal of Financial Economics* 3(4), 305–360.

Kim, I. J., K. Ramaswamy, and S. Sundaresan. (1993). Does Default Risk in Coupons Affect the Valuation of Corporate Bonds? *Financial Management* 22(3), 117–131.

Leland, H. E. (1994a). Corporate Debt Value, Bond Covenants, and Optimal Capital Structure. *Journal of Finance* 49(4), 1213–1252.

Leland, H. E. (1994b). Bond Prices, Yield Spreads, and Optimal Capital Structure with Default Risk. Working Paper, University of California, Berkeley.

Leland, H. E., and K. B. Toft. (1996). Optimal Capital Structure, Endogenous Bankruptcy, and the Term Structure of Credit Spreads. *Journal of Finance* 51(3), 987–1019.

Longstaff, F., and E. Schwartz. (1995). A Simple Approach to Valuing Risky Fixed and Floating Rate Debt. *Journal of Finance* 50(3), 789–819.

Mauer, D. C., and A. J. Triantis. (1994). Interactions of Corporate Financing and Investment Decisions: A Dynamic Framework. *Journal of Finance* 49(4), 1253–1277.

McDonald, R., and D. R. Siegel. (1985). Investment and the Valuation of Firms When There Is an Option to Shut Down. *International Economic Review* 26(2), 331–349.

McDonald, R., and D. R. Siegel. (1986). The Value of Waiting to Invest. *Quarterly Journal of Economics* 101(4), 707–728.

Mella-Barral, P., and W. Perraudin. (1997). Strategic Debt Service. *Journal of Finance* 52(2), 531–556.

Mello, A. S., and J. E. Parsons. (1992). Measuring the Agency Cost of Debt. *Journal of Finance* 47(5), 1887–1904.

Mello, A. S., J. E. Parsons, and A. J. Triantis. (1995). An Integrated Model of Multinational Flexibility and Financial Hedging. *Journal of International Economics* 39(1), 27–51.

Merton, R. C. (1974). On the Pricing of Corporate Debt: The Risk Structure of Interest Rates. *Journal of Finance* 29(2), 449–470.

Myers, S. C. (1977). Determinants of Corporate Borrowing. *Journal of Financial Economics* 5(2), 147–175.

Smith, C. W., and J. B. Warner. (1979). On Financial Contracting: An Analysis of Bond Covenants. *Journal of Financial Economics* 7(2), 117–161.

Stohs, M. H., and D. C. Mauer. (1996). The Determinants of Corporate Debt Maturity Structure. *Journal of Business* 69(3), 279–312.

Trigeorgis, L. (1993). Real Options and Interactions with Financial Flexibility. *Financial Management* 22(3), 202–224

Trigeorgis, L. (1996). *Real Options: Managerial Flexibility and Strategy in Resource Allocation*. Cambridge, MA: The MIT Press.

Part III

Flexibility in Natural and Environmental Resource Investments

10

Valuation of Natural Resource Investments with Stochastic Convenience Yields and Interest Rates

KRISTIAN R. MILTERSEN

We apply the model of Miltersen and Schwartz (1997) to value natural resource investments. We derive a closed-form solution for the value of a simple investment project in the presence of stochastic interest rates and convenience yields. This model takes into account a possible time lag between the investment decision date and the date when the commodity is ready to be sold in the market. We provide numerical examples with realistic parameter values showing that the presence of stochastic convenience yields has a significant impact on the value of the project. We also show how our approach can simplify the valuation of more complex natural resource investments.

10.1 INTRODUCTION

In a recent paper Miltersen and Schwartz (1997) developed a model to price options on futures and forward prices. This model uses the initial term structure of commodity futures prices and the initial term structure of interest rates to derive their stochastic future movement consistent with no-arbitrage principles. Amin and Jarrow (1991) developed a similar model to price options on futures and forward prices for foreign currency. In their model the term structure of foreign bond prices conceptually plays the same role as the term structure of futures prices in the Miltersen–Schwartz model. The Miltersen–Schwartz model can be used to value various types of commodity derivatives. In this chapter we use this approach to price a natural resource investment project.

The fact that the models by Amin and Jarrow (1991) and Miltersen and Schwartz (1997) are able to price an option that matures at a date earlier than the underlying futures or forward contract is especially useful in valuing natural resource investment projects. That is because we can price an investment project in which the investment decision is taken at a date earlier than the date when the produced commodity is ready to be sold in the market. In the presence of convenience yields this time lag plays an important role in the valuation of the project.

As explained in Miltersen and Schwartz (1997), a stochastic convenience yield has a mean-reversion type of effect on option prices. Standard no-arbitrage arguments suggest that the spot convenience yield process enters the drift of the spot commodity price process under an equivalent martingale measure. For example, if the spot commodity price is positively correlated with the spot convenience yield, the drift of the spot commodity price will, on average, be reduced, when the spot commodity price goes up relative to the standard log-normal case. This is analogous to a mean-reversion effect on the spot commodity price under an equivalent martingale (or random walk) measure. Clearly, this has an impact on the valuation of the investment project.

Under the assumption of normality of continuously compounded forward interest rates and convenience yields and log normality of the spot price of the underlying commodity, we obtain closed-form solutions for the value of simple production options. This solution based on Gaussian assumptions significantly simplifies the valuation of more complex natural resource investment projects, including the valuation of compound (growth) options.

The rest of the chapter is organized as follows. Section 10.2 describes the natural resource investment project to be valued. Section 10.3 presents the model used to value the project and a useful closed form solution. Section 10.4 describes a numerical method that can be used to value the natural resource investment by simulation, and Section 10.5 provides numerical illustrations. Section 10.6 concludes. Appendix A provides a derivation of the closed-form valuation formula.

10.2 A NATURAL RESOURCE INVESTMENT PROJECT

This section describes a natural resource investment project such as the right to develop a copper mine. The investor who acquires this right basically buys a portfolio of options. Specifically, the investor has the option at date t_0 to invest k, an irreversible

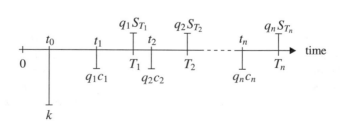

Figure 10.1   Time line of investment in a natural resource investment project.

cost of developing the copper mine for production, thereby acquiring a series of production options: If, at date t_i, the investor invests $q_i c_i$, then q_i units of copper will be ready to be sold in the market at date T_i, for $i = 1, \ldots, n$, at the prevailing unit price of S_{T_i}. The timing of investment in the natural resource investment project is summarized in Figure 10.1. We are interested in valuing the right (opportunity) to invest in this investment project at date $s \leq t_0$.

Basically, there are $n + 1$ options involved in this project. There are n production decisions at each date t_i, for $i = 1, \ldots, n$: Is it profitable to pay a cost of $q_i c_i$ at date t_i to produce q_i units of the commodity to sell at date T_i? The first option is the development option: Is it profitable to pay the cost k at date t_0 to get the portfolio of all n production options?

We are not able to obtain a closed-form solution for valuing the entire project. However, we will be able to evaluate the individual production options in closed form. This will then enable us to suggest a numerical simulation method to value the entire project efficiently.

10.3 THE VALUE OF PRODUCTION OPTIONS

Following Miltersen and Schwartz (1997) our basic inputs are zero-coupon bond prices, $P(t, T)$, for all maturities, $T \geq t$, the spot price of the underlying commodity, S_t, forward prices of the commodity, $F(t, T)$, and futures prices of the commodity, $G(t, T)$, for all maturities, $T \geq t$, at any date $t \geq 0$. Since we assume stochastic interest rates, we have to distinguish between forward and futures prices.

Following Heath et al. (1992), we employ continuously-compounded forward interest rates, $f(t, v)$, i.e., we *define* the forward interest rate, $f(t, v)$, in terms of the zero-coupon bond prices

$$P(t, T) = e^{-\int_t^T f(t,v)\, dv} \tag{10.1}$$

Hence, the term structure of interest rates can equivalently be represented either as the term structure of zero-coupon bond prices or as the term structure of forward rates. For expositional clarity reasons Heath et al. (1992) choose to model the term structure of forward rates, $f(t, v)$, explicitly and from there derive the zero-coupon bond prices using Eq. (10.1), since this gives the clearest drift restriction under an equivalent martingale measure. Similarly, the term structure of forward prices can equivalently be represented either directly as the term structure of forward prices or as the term structure of forward convenience yields, $\delta(t, v)$, defined by the following equation:

$$F(t, T) = \frac{S_t}{P(t, T)} e^{-\int_t^T \delta(t,v)\, dv} = S_t \, e^{\int_t^T [f(t,v) - \delta(t,v)]\, dv} \tag{10.2}$$

The forward convenience yield, $\delta(t, v)$, has an economic interpretation as the forward value at date t of the flow of services that accrues at date v to the holder of the physical commodity, but not to the owner of a contract for future delivery.

Unfortunately, it is not the forward prices, $F(t, T)$, but only the futures prices, $G(t, T)$, that are martingales under an equivalent martingale measure when we assume stochastic interest rates (cf. Cox et al., 1981). Therefore, it is much easier to model the term structure of futures prices than to model the term structure of forward prices. Moreover, for the same reasons as in the Heath–Jarrow–Morton analysis we explicitly model the term structure of future convenience yields, $\epsilon(t, v)$, defined by the following equation

$$G(t, T) = \frac{S_t}{P(t, T)} e^{-\int_t^T \epsilon(t,v)\, dv} = S_t\, e^{\int_t^T [f(t,v) - \epsilon(t,v)]\, dv} \tag{10.3}$$

and from there we derive the term structures of futures and forward prices. This is the same approach taken in Miltersen and Schwartz (1997). See this paper for further details.

There is not an easy economic interpretation of the future convenience yields as for the forward convenience yields. The economic interpretation for forward convenience yields does not work for future convenience yields because of the continuous resettlement payments of the futures contracts. The future convenience yield is, therefore, merely a definition. However, it is a definition that is very useful in the development of our model, because it is much easier to find the drift restriction under an equivalent martingale measure for the future convenience yields than for the forward convenience yields, since we know that it is the futures prices that are martingales under an equivalent martingale measure.

The observables of this model are zero-coupon bond prices at some date $s \leq t_0$, $P(s, T)$, for all maturities, $T \geq s$, the spot price of the underlying commodity, S_s, forward prices of the commodity, $F(s, T)$, and futures prices of the commodity, $G(s, T)$, for all maturities, $T \geq s$.

Our stochastic model of future price movements consists of three processes: The spot price of the underlying commodity, the term structure of forward interest rates, and the term structure of future convenience yields. Since our objective is to value the project by no-arbitrage arguments, we focus on the stochastic behavior of these processes under an equivalent martingale measure.[1] The stochastic differential equation (SDE) for the continuously compounded forward interest rates, f, under an equivalent martingale measure is

$$f(t, v) = f(s, v) + \int_s^t \mu_f(u, v)\, du + \sum_{k=1}^d \int_s^t \sigma_f^k(u, v)\, dW_u^k \tag{10.4}$$

where W is a standard d-dimensional Wiener process. Similarly, the SDE for the continuously compounded future convenience yields, ϵ, is given by[2]

---

[1] When the objective is pricing of derivative securities it is necessary to model the underlying stochastic processes only under an equivalent martingale measure and to use the risk-neutral valuation principle [cf., e.g., Harrison and Kreps (1979) and Harrison and Pliska (1981)].

[2] Modeling the term structure of future convenience yields explicitly separates our approach from the foreign currency approach taken in Amin and Jarrow (1991), where they are modeling the term structure of foreign forward rates explicitly.

$$\epsilon(t, v) = \epsilon(s, v) + \int_s^t \mu_\epsilon(u, v)\, du + \sum_{k=1}^d \int_s^t \sigma_\epsilon^k(u, v)\, dW_u^k \qquad (10.5)$$

Finally, the spot price of the underlying commodity follows

$$S_t = S_s + \int_s^t S_u\, \mu_S(u)\, du + \sum_{k=1}^d \int_s^t S_u\, \sigma_S^k(u)\, dW_u^k \qquad (10.6)$$

Possible correlation between the three processes comes via the specification of the diffusion terms (the σs) since the same vector Wiener process, W, is used in all three SDEs.

One advantage of modeling the term structure of forward rates compared to the term structure of zero-coupon bond prices is that the short-term interest rate (at date t) is embedded explicitly into the model as $f(t, t)$, i.e., the forward rate observed at date t for an infinitely short loan at the same date, t. Similarly, the spot convenience yield (at date t) is embedded in both the future and the forward convenience yield models as $\delta(t, t) = \epsilon(t, t)$. Proving that $\delta(t, t)$ and $\epsilon(t, t)$ are equal and, in fact, equal to the spot convenience yield prevailing at date t is outside the scope of this chapter but can be found in Miltersen and Schwartz (1997).

Given this, standard no-arbitrage restrictions [cf. Harrison and Kreps (1979) and Harrison and Pliska (1981)] imply that the drift restriction of the spot commodity price process under an equivalent martingale measure is determined as

$$\mu_S(t) = f(t, t) - \epsilon(t, t) \qquad (10.7)$$

Similarly, the Heath–Jarrow–Morton analysis implies that the drift restriction of the forward interest rate process under an equivalent martingale measure is given by

$$\mu_f(t, u) = \sum_{k=1}^d \sigma_f^k(t, u) \left[\int_t^u \sigma_f^k(t, v)\, dv \right] \qquad (10.8)$$

Finally, the no-arbitrage drift restriction for the future convenience yield process under an equivalent martingale measure is

$$\mu_\epsilon(t, u) = \sum_{k=1}^d \sigma_f^k(t, u) \left[\int_t^u \sigma_f^k(t, v)\, dv \right]$$

$$+ \sum_{k=1}^d \left[\sigma_f^k(t, u) - \sigma_\epsilon^k(t, u) \right] \left[\sigma_S^k(t) + \int_t^u \{ \sigma_f^k(t, v) - \sigma_\epsilon^k(t, v) \}\, dv \right] \quad (10.9)$$

This drift restriction is derived from the no-arbitrage condition dictating that futures prices are martingales under an equivalent martingale measure. Details can be found in Appendix A (or in Miltersen and Schwartz, 1997). This drift restriction differs from the drift restriction on the term structure of foreign forward rates derived in Amin and Jarrow (1991).

So far, the diffusion terms (the σs) have been left unspecified. However, they must fulfill certain regularity conditions such that (strong) solutions of the stated SDEs exist.[3] For the rest of this chapter we will assume that the three σ processes are deterministic functions of time. That is, we assume Gaussian continuously compounded forward interest rates and future convenience yields as well as log-Gaussian spot commodity prices. These assumptions allow us to obtain a closed form Black–Scholes/Merton type pricing formula for the value of the production option, which, in principal, is the value of a European call option written on the discounted forward price.

To evaluate the production option let us first simplify the notation. Assume that by paying the cost c at date t, the investor can produce one unit of the commodity, which will be ready to be sold at a later date T (i.e., $t \leq T$). Since the commodity will not be ready to be sold before date T, the *value* at date t of the unit to be produced at date T is given by the forward price $F(t, T)$ times the discount factor $P(t, T)$.[4] Hence, at date t, the investor will decide to produce if and only if

$$P(t, T) \, F(t, T) \geq c \tag{10.10}$$

Therefore, at some date s before date t (i.e., $s \leq t$), we can evaluate the option to produce at date t as

$$C_s^p = \hat{E}_s \left[e^{-\int_s^t f(v,v)\,dv} \, \max \{ P(t, T) \, F(t, T) - c, 0 \} \right] \tag{10.11}$$

where $\hat{E}_s$ denotes the expectation under an equivalent martingale measure conditional on the information at date s. Following Miltersen and Schwartz (1997), a closed-form expression for the value of this option (derived in Appendix A) is given by

$$C_s^p = P(s, T) \, F(s, T) \, N \left[\frac{\ln \frac{P(s,T)\,F(s,T)}{P(s,t)\,c} + \frac{1}{2}\sigma^2}{\sigma} \right]$$
$$- P(s, t) \, c \, N \left[\frac{\ln \frac{P(s,T)\,F(s,T)}{P(s,t)\,c} - \frac{1}{2}\sigma^2}{\sigma} \right] \tag{10.12}$$

where $N(\cdot)$ denotes the standard cumulative normal distribution function and the expression for σ is given by

$$\sigma^2 = \sum_{k=1}^{d} \int_s^t \left[\sigma_S^k(u) + \int_u^t \sigma_f^k(u, v)\,dv - \int_u^T \sigma_\epsilon^k(u, v)\,dv \right]^2 du \tag{10.13}$$

This formula is closely related to the celebrated formula developed by Black and Scholes (1973) and the extension to stochastic interest rates by Merton (1973).

---

[3] For more on stochastic differential equations, in general, and strong solutions, in particular, cf. Karatzas and Shreve (1988).

[4] Obviously, having one unit of the commodity for sure at date T by buying a forward contract with maturity date T is not the same as having one unit of the commodity at hand on date t, since the investor does not benefit from the convenience yield because the commodity is not available for sale until date T.

However, there are two differences worth mentioning. First, Eq. (10.12) takes the lost convenience yield from date t to date T into account by using the discounted forward price of the underlying commodity instead of the spot price. Second, σ^2 is adjusted compared to the Black–Scholes/Merton variance expression by taking the mean-reversion effect of the underlying commodity price (under an equivalent martingale measure) into account. This mean-reversion effect appears if the stochastic convenience yield is positively correlated with the commodity price as can be seen from Eq. (10.7). That is, if the underlying commodity price, S_t, increases there is a high probability that the spot convenience yield, $\epsilon(t, t)$, will also increase because of the positive correlation, implying that the drift of the underlying commodity price will decrease under an equivalent martingale measure [cf. Eq. (10.7) and vice versa]. Hence, the drift reacts as if there was mean reversion in the commodity price.

Convenience yields here play exactly the same role as dividend yields, hence, Eq. (10.12) can also be used to price a European call option on an underlying security that pays stochastic dividend rates of size $\epsilon(t, t)$.

10.4 THE VALUE OF THE NATURAL RESOURCE INVESTMENT PROJECT

The value of the entire project described in Section 10.2 prior to the initial decision date t_0 can be written as[5]

$$C_s = \hat{E}_s \left[e^{- \int_s^{t_0} f(v,v)\, dv} \, \max \left(\sum_{i=1}^{n} C_i^p - k, 0 \right) \right] \tag{10.14}$$

where C_i^p denotes the value of each individual production option, i.e.,

$$C_i^p = q_i \, \hat{E}_{t_0} \left[e^{- \int_{t_0}^{t_i} f(v,v)\, dv} \, \max \{ P(t_i, T_i)\, F(t_i, T_i) - c_i, 0 \} \right] \tag{10.11'}$$

Using the closed-form solution of Eq. (10.12) in Section 10.3, this is given by

$$C_i^p = q_i \left\{ P(t_0, T_i)\, F(t_0, T_i)\, N \left[\frac{\ln \frac{P(t_0, T_i)\, F(t_0, T_i)}{P(t_0, t_i)\, c_i} + \frac{1}{2}\sigma_i^2}{\sigma_i} \right] \right.$$
$$\left. - P(t_0, t_i)\, c_i\, N \left[\frac{\ln \frac{P(t_0, T_i)\, F(t_0, T_i)}{P(t_0, t_i)\, c_i} - \frac{1}{2}\sigma_i^2}{\sigma_i} \right] \right\} \tag{10.12'}$$

where σ_i is given by

$$\sigma_i^2 = \sum_{k=1}^{d} \int_{t_0}^{t_i} \left[\sigma_S^k(u) + \int_u^{t_i} \sigma_f^k(u, v)\, dv - \int_u^{T_i} \sigma_\epsilon^k(u, v)\, dv \right]^2 du \tag{10.13'}$$

---

[5] We can value each production option separately and use value additivity since we have no switching costs and a fixed time horizon such that we cannot exhaust the mine. Extensions to include shut down and reopening costs, hysteresis effects, etc. will destroy the value additivity property. See Dixit and Pindyck (1994, Chapters 6–7) for more on this issue.

The value of the entire investment opportunity in Eq. (10.14) can be evaluated using simulation. This is rather straightforward given our Gaussian assumptions, since we know the conditional simultaneous distribution (under an equivalent martingale measure) of

$$\left\{ e^{-\int_s^{t_0} f(v,v)\,dv}, \; [P(t_0, t_i)]_{i=1}^n, \; [P(t_0, T_i)\,F(t_0, T_i)]_{i=1}^n \right\}$$

given the information at date s. Hence, we can write

$$e^{-\int_s^{t_0} f(v,v)\,dv} = A\,e^{-X}$$

$$P(t_0, t_i) = D_i\,e^{-U_i}$$

and

$$P(t_0, T_i)\,F(t_0, T_i) = B_i\,e^{Z_i}$$

where $[A, (B_i)_{i=1}^n, (D_i)_{i=1}^n]$ are deterministic constants and $[X, (U_i)_{i=1}^n, (Z_i)_{i=1}^n]$ is jointly normal with mean zero. The variance–covariance structure is

$$\sigma_{ui}^2 = \sum_{k=1}^d \int_s^{t_0} \left[\int_{t_0}^{t_i} \sigma_f^k(u, v)\,dv \right]^2 du \tag{10.15a}$$

$$\sigma_x^2 = \sum_{k=1}^d \int_s^{t_0} \left[\int_u^{t_0} \sigma_f^k(u, v)\,dv \right]^2 du \tag{10.15b}$$

$$\sigma_{zi}^2 = \sum_{k=1}^d \int_s^{t_0} \left[\sigma_S^k(u) + \int_u^{t_0} \sigma_f^k(u, v)\,dv - \int_u^{T_i} \sigma_\epsilon^k(u, v)\,dv \right]^2 du \tag{10.15c}$$

$$\sigma_{uiuj} = \sum_{k=1}^d \int_s^{t_0} \left[\int_{t_0}^{t_i} \sigma_f^k(u, v)\,dv \right]\left[\int_{t_0}^{t_j} \sigma_f^k(u, v)\,dv \right] du \tag{10.15d}$$

$$\sigma_{uix} = \sum_{k=1}^d \int_s^{t_0} \left[\int_{t_0}^{t_i} \sigma_f^k(u, v)\,dv \right]\left[\int_u^{t_0} \sigma_f^k(u, v)\,dv \right] du \tag{10.15e}$$

$$\sigma_{uizj} = \sum_{k=1}^d \int_s^{t_0} \left[\int_{t_0}^{t_i} \sigma_f^k(u, v)\,dv \right]$$
$$\left[\sigma_S^k(u) + \int_u^{t_0} \sigma_f^k(u, v)\,dv - \int_u^{T_j} \sigma_\epsilon^k(u, v)\,dv \right] du \tag{10.15f}$$

$$\sigma_{xzi} = \sum_{k=1}^d \int_s^{t_0} \left[\int_u^{t_0} \sigma_f^k(u, v)\,dv \right]$$
$$\left[(\sigma_S^k(u) + \int_u^{t_0} \sigma_f^k(u, v)\,dv - \int_u^{T_i} \sigma_\epsilon^k(u, v)\,dv \right] du \tag{10.15g}$$

and

$$\sigma_{z_i z_j} = \sum_{k=1}^{d} \int_{s}^{t_0} \left[\sigma_S^k(u) + \int_{u}^{t_0} \sigma_f^k(u,v)\, dv - \int_{u}^{T_i} \sigma_\epsilon^k(u,v)\, dv \right]$$

$$\left[\sigma_S^k(u) + \int_{u}^{t_0} \sigma_f^k(u,v)\, dv - \int_{u}^{T_j} \sigma_\epsilon^k(u,v)\, dv \right] du \quad (10.15\text{h})$$

where the subscripts x, u, and z refer to the stochastic variables X, U, and Z, respectively, and i and j refer to the indices on the stochastic variables U and Z. The deterministic constants, $[A, (B_i)_{i=1}^{n}, (D_i)_{i=1}^{n}]$, are given by

$$A = P(s, t_0)\, e^{-\frac{1}{2}\sigma_x^2}$$

$$B_i = \frac{P(s, T_i)}{P(s, t_0)}\, F(s, T_i)\, e^{-\frac{1}{2}\sigma_{z_i}^2 + \sigma_{x z_i}}$$

and

$$D_i = \frac{P(s, t_i)}{P(s, t_0)}\, e^{-\frac{1}{2}\sigma_{u_i}^2 - \sigma_{x u_i}}$$

The entire investment opportunity can then be evaluated using Eq. (10.14) by simulating a large number of independent realizations of

$$A\, e^{-X} \max\left(\sum_{i=1}^{n} C_i^p - k, 0 \right) \quad (10.14')$$

with

$$C_i^p = q_i \left\{ B_i\, e^{Z_i}\, N\left[\frac{\ln \frac{B_i \exp Z_i}{D_i \exp - U_i\, c_i} + \frac{1}{2}\sigma_i^2}{\sigma_i} \right] \right.$$

$$\left. - D_i\, e^{-U_i}\, c_i\, N\left[\frac{\ln \frac{B_i \exp Z_i}{D_i \exp - U_i\, c_i} - \frac{1}{2}\sigma_i^2}{\sigma_i} \right] \right\} \quad (10.12'')$$

and then taking the average. Note that we are simulating under an equivalent martingale measure and that we, therefore, get an estimate of the expectation under risk-neutrality. Variance reduction techniques such as the antithetic variable technique and control variate technique[6] may be considered for valuation of large projects or for commercial use.

10.5 NUMERICAL ILLUSTRATION

In this section, we provide a numerical illustration that compares the value of both the production options and the development option using our approach with a standard Black–Scholes approach. Our numerical example is based on Miltersen and Schwartz

---

[6] See Kloeden and Platen (1992) for more on simulation and variance reduction techniques. See also Hull (1997, Chapter 15) for an easy introduction.

(1997). We assume a three-factor Gaussian model, i.e., $d = 3$, with the three deterministic diffusion terms (the σs) defined as follows:

$$\sigma_S(t) = \sigma_S \begin{pmatrix} 1 \\ 0 \\ 0 \end{pmatrix} \tag{10.16a}$$

$$\sigma_\epsilon(t, v) = \sigma_\epsilon\, e^{-\kappa_\epsilon(v-t)} \begin{pmatrix} \rho_{S\epsilon} \\ \sqrt{1 - \rho_{S\epsilon}^2} \\ 0 \end{pmatrix} \tag{10.16b}$$

and

$$\sigma_f(t, v) = \sigma_f\, e^{-\kappa_f(v-t)} \begin{pmatrix} \rho_{Sf} \\ \dfrac{\rho_{\epsilon f} - \rho_{S\epsilon}\rho_{Sf}}{\sqrt{1-\rho_{S\epsilon}^2}} \\ \sqrt{1 - \rho_{Sf}^2 - \dfrac{(\rho_{\epsilon f} - \rho_{S\epsilon}\rho_{Sf})^2}{1-\rho_{S\epsilon}^2}} \end{pmatrix} \tag{10.16c}$$

Using Eq. (10.13),

$$
\begin{aligned}
\sigma^2 =\ & \sigma_S^2(t - s) + 2\sigma_S \left\{ \sigma_f\rho_{Sf}\frac{1}{\kappa_f}\left[(t-s) - \frac{1}{\kappa_f}e^{-\kappa_f(t-s)}\left(e^{\kappa_f(t-s)} - 1\right)\right]\right. \\
& \left. -\sigma_\epsilon\rho_{S\epsilon}\frac{1}{\kappa_\epsilon}\left[(t-s) - \frac{1}{\kappa_\epsilon}e^{-\kappa_\epsilon T}\left(e^{\kappa_\epsilon(t-s)} - 1\right)\right]\right\} \\
& + \sigma_\epsilon^2\frac{1}{\kappa_\epsilon^2}\left[(t-s) + \frac{1}{2\kappa_\epsilon}e^{-2\kappa_\epsilon T}\left(e^{2\kappa_\epsilon(t-s)} - 1\right) - 2\frac{1}{\kappa_\epsilon}e^{-\kappa_\epsilon T}\left(e^{\kappa_\epsilon(t-s)} - 1\right)\right] \\
& + \sigma_f^2\frac{1}{\kappa_f^2}\left[(t-s) + \frac{1}{2\kappa_f}e^{-2\kappa_f(t-s)}\left(e^{2\kappa_f(t-s)} - 1\right)\right. \\
& \left. -2\frac{1}{\kappa_f}e^{-\kappa_f(t-s)}\left(e^{\kappa_f(t-s)} - 1\right)\right] \\
& - 2\sigma_\epsilon\sigma_f\rho_{\epsilon f}\frac{1}{\kappa_\epsilon}\frac{1}{\kappa_f}\left[(t-s) - \frac{1}{\kappa_\epsilon}e^{-\kappa_\epsilon T}\left(e^{\kappa_\epsilon(t-s)} - 1\right)\right. \\
& \left. -\frac{1}{\kappa_f}e^{-\kappa_f(t-s)}\left(e^{\kappa_f(t-s)} - 1\right) + \frac{1}{(\kappa_\epsilon + \kappa_f)}e^{-\kappa_\epsilon T - \kappa_f(t-s)}\left(e^{(\kappa_\epsilon + \kappa_f)(t-s)} - 1\right)\right]
\end{aligned}
\tag{10.13''}
$$

10.5.1 Valuation of the Production Option

To value the production option using Eq. (10.12), we use the parameter estimates for the COMEX High Grade Copper Futures data described in Schwartz (1997, Table 10), namely

$$\sigma_S = 0.266 \qquad \rho_{S\epsilon} = 0.805$$

$$\sigma_\epsilon = 0.249 \qquad \rho_{Sf} = 0.0964 \qquad \kappa_\epsilon = 1.045$$

$$\sigma_f = 0.0096 \qquad \rho_{\epsilon f} = 0.1243 \qquad \kappa_f = 0.2$$

Here we assume that we will have to pay a cost c at date $t = 1$ to be able to produce 100 ounces of copper that will be ready to be sold at date T. The current forward price for copper to be delivered at date T is $F(s, T) = \$0.95$ per ounce, for all $T = 1, 2, 3$. The price of the zero-coupon bond maturing at date T is $P(s, T) = \$e^{-0.06(T-s)}$. Table 10.1 provides comparisons of the value of the production option at date $s = 0$ for three different values of the cost of production, c, and three different delivery dates, T. We have valued the production option using two different models, labeled M–S and B–S. M–S refers to the Miltersen–Schwartz model, i.e., the valuation is done by Eq. (10.12) with σ from Eq. (10.13). B-S refers to a standard Black–Scholes modification using Eq. (10.12) with

$$\sigma^2 = \sigma_S^2 t \tag{10.13'''}$$

Hence, both models take into account the lost convenience yield of not having the commodity ready to be sold in the market before date T. The Black–Scholes modification, however, does not take into account the reduced variance due to the mean-reversion effect coming from the stochastic convenience yield of copper. Since the convenience yield is highly positively correlated with the spot price of copper ($\rho_{S\epsilon} = 0.805$), the standard Black–Scholes modification overvalues the production option relative to our model. As shown in Table 10.1, this overvaluation is relatively large, particularly when the cost of production is high (e.g., $c = 110$). Moreover, the overvaluation increases—at least in percentage terms—as the time lag between production and delivery is increased. Note, however, that the overvaluation is persistent even in the case in which there is no time lag.

Table 10.1
Comparison of the Value of the Production Option Using the Miltersen–Schwartz (M–S) Model and a Standard Black–Scholes Modification (B–S) for Different Costs of Production and Delivery Dates[a]

	c	M–S	B–S	Difference	% Difference
$s = 0$ years	80	16.03	17.53	−1.50	−9.36
$t = 1$ year	95	7.33	9.47	−2.14	−29.21
$T = 1$ year	110	2.76	4.65	−1.89	−68.61
$s = 0$ years	80	10.77	13.63	−2.87	−26.63
$t = 1$ year	95	3.35	6.82	−3.46	−103.27
$T = 2$ years	110	0.71	3.10	−2.39	−336.06
$s = 0$ years	80	7.14	10.34	−3.21	−44.94
$t = 1$ year	95	1.72	4.76	−3.04	−177.44
$T = 3$ years	110	0.27	1.99	−1.72	−637.21

[a] The value of the production option (estimated at $s = 0$) when having to pay cost c at date $t = 1$ to produce 100 ounces of copper sold at date T.

10.5.2 Valuation of the Development Option

To illustrate the valuation of the development option we use the simulation algorithm outlined in Section 10.4. To value this development option we have simulated 30,000 independent realizations (under an equivalent martingale measure) of the option value and taken the average. For this illustration we assume that we will have to pay the development cost of $100 at date $t_0 = 1$ to be able to get the opportunity to produce $q_i = 500$ ounces of copper (at a cost of c_i per unit) at dates t_1 and t_2, which will be ready to be sold at dates T_1 and T_2, respectively. Compare Figure 10.1 with $n = 2$ for an illustration. In this example we have assumed that the current forward price of copper to be delivered at date T is

$$F(s, T) = \$0.95 \, e^{0.03(T-s)}$$

and that the current price of the zero-coupon bond maturing at date T is

$$P(s, T) = e^{-0.06(T-s)}$$

We have valued the development option using our model (M–S) and a standard Black–Scholes modification (B–S). Table 10.2 provides comparisons of the value of the development option at date $s = 0$ for three different values of the cost of production, $c_1 = c_2$, and four different combinations of production dates, t_i, and delivery dates, T_i. We have again used the parameter estimates for the COMEX High Grade Copper Futures data. Once more, note the persistent overvaluation of the option value by the Black–Scholes modification, which again is most profound

Table 10.2
Comparison of the Value of the Development Option Using Our Model (M–S) and a Standard Black–Scholes Modification (B–S) for Different Costs of Production, Production Dates, and Delivery Dates[a]

	c	M–S	B–S	Difference	% Difference
$t_1 = 2$ years	0.80	126.62	164.06	−37.44	−29.57
$t_2 = 3$ years	0.95	55.23	101.21	−45.99	−83.27
$T_i - t_i = 0$ years	1.10	19.39	59.87	−40.49	−208.85
$t_1 = 2$ years	0.80	101.96	145.65	−43.69	−42.85
$t_2 = 3$ years	0.95	38.36	87.48	−49.12	−128.03
$T_i - t_i = 1$ year	1.10	11.21	50.37	−39.15	−349.18
$t_1 = 2$ years	0.80	84.00	128.62	−44.62	−53.11
$t_2 = 3$ years	0.95	28.89	75.12	−46.24	−160.08
$T_i - t_i = 2$ years	1.10	7.69	42.06	−34.37	−447.28
$t_1 = 3$ years	0.80	116.91	165.56	−48.65	−41.62
$t_2 = 4$ years	0.95	51.44	108.59	−57.15	−111.10
$T_i - t_i = 1$ year	1.10	18.39	69.13	−50.74	−275.84

[a] The development option involves paying the development cost of $100 at date $t_0 = 1$ to produce 500 ounces of copper (at Q cost of c_i per unit) at dates t_1 and t_2, to be sold at dates T_1 and T_2.

for out-of-the-money options, i.e., at high production costs. Again we see that this overvaluation is significant even with no time lag between production and delivery, but that the overvaluation increases as the time lag is increased.

10.5.3 Valuation of the Development Option: The Path-Dependent Case

The above example in Section 10.5.2 illustrated the simplest case in which an investor has the right to explore the natural resource for exactly two periods and has limited production capacity so that more than 500 ounces per period cannot be produced. To illustrate that our model can include (at least limited) path dependencies, we will show how to value the development option in the case in which the investor has increased production capacity to 1000 ounces per period. Moreover, we will impose an upper limit of 1000 ounces on the total amount of copper that the investor is allowed to explore from the natural resource during the two periods. Clearly, this changes the decision that the investor has to make at date t_1. For example, if the investor decides to produce 1000 ounces of copper at date t_1, the investor has killed the option to produce at date t_2. Hence, the valuation of the development option from Eq. (10.14) is restated as

$$C_s = \hat{E}_s\left[e^{-\int_s^{t_0} f(v,v)\,dv} \max\left(C^p - k, 0\right)\right] \tag{10.14''}$$

where C^p denotes the value of the production option, i.e.,

$$C^p = \hat{E}_{t_0}\left[e^{-\int_{t_0}^{t_1} f(v,v)\,dv} \max\left\{q_1\left[P(t_1, T_1) F(t_1, T_1) - c_1\right], C_2^p\right\}\right] \tag{10.11''}$$

where C_2^p is given from Eq. (10.12'). Note that it can never be optimal to produce in both periods; either it will be optimal to produce all 1000 ounces in period one or in period two. As opposed to Eq. (10.11'), there is no closed-form solution for Eq. (10.11''), hence it has to be evaluated by a simulation algorithm similar to the one described in Section 10.4. This value for the production option, C_p, can then be used in Eq. (10.14'') to value the development option. Numerical experiments have shown that it is sufficient to use around 100 independent realizations to evaluate the production option, C^p, from Eq. (10.11''), whereas it is still necessary to have in the range of 10,000 to 30,000 independent realizations to get a stable value for the development option, C_s, from Eq. (10.14''). Table 10.3 presents the values of the development option in the path-dependent case for the same parameter values that were used to calculate the values in Table 10.2, where the development option was valued in the path-independent case.

As may be expected, the increased flexibility in the way the natural resource can be explored has increased the development option value, ceteris paribus. Once again we see a persistent overvaluation of the option value by the Black–Scholes modification, which once again is most profound for out-of-the-money options, i.e., for high production costs. Note, in this connection, that the percentage overvaluation of the Black–Scholes modification is always lower in the path-dependent case than

Table 10.3

Comparison of the Value of the Development Option in the Path-Dependent Case Using Our Model (M–S) and a Standard Black–Scholes Modification (B–S) for Different Costs of (C) Production, Production Dates, and Delivery Dates

	c	M–S	B–S	Difference	% Difference
$t_1 = 2$ years	0.80	160.55	175.46	−14.91	−9.29
$t_2 = 3$ years	0.95	79.50	113.39	−33.89	−42.63
$T_i - t_i = 0$ years	1.10	32.60	70.89	−38.30	−117.49
$t_1 = 2$ years	0.80	115.04	156.84	−41.81	−36.34
$t_2 = 3$ years	0.95	47.58	98.99	−51.41	−108.03
$T_i - t_i = 1$ year	1.10	15.74	60.44	−44.70	−283.89
$t_1 = 2$ years	0.80	92.27	139.53	−47.25	−51.21
$t_2 = 3$ years	0.95	34.98	85.92	−50.94	−145.62
$T_i - t_i = 2$ years	1.10	10.57	51.18	−40.61	−384.31
$t_1 = 3$ years	0.80	130.19	176.12	−45.93	−35.28
$t_2 = 4$ years	0.95	61.81	119.71	−57.90	−93.66
$T_i - t_i = 1$ year	1.10	24.47	79.46	−54.99	−224.69

in the path-independent case, simply because the production option is more valuable in the path-dependent case and, hence, the development option is not as far out-of-the-money as in the path-independent case, where the production option has lower value due to less flexibility in the production decision.

In all these three examples in which we have valued opportunities to invest in different parts of the natural resource investment project, we have seen how important a factor the stochastic convenience yield is when it comes to valuation and investment decisions in realistic natural resource investment settings and for any investments where real options are considered, in general.

10.6 CONCLUSIONS

In this chapter, we used the model by Miltersen and Schwartz (1997) to value natural resource investment projects. This model takes both stochastic convenience yields and stochastic interest rates into account. The inputs to the model are the term structure of commodity forward prices and discount bond prices.

Under Gaussian assumptions, we were able to obtain closed-form solutions for the production options when there is a time lag between the date of the production decision and the date when the commodity is ready to be sold in the market. Finally, we used a simple simulation method to value the entire natural resource investment opportunity involving a compound option structure.

In this chapter we assumed that our multiple production decisions were independent and, hence, we valued them as the sum of European options. This is consistent with a situation in which an entrepreneur has a time-limited right to explore a natural resource that is so short that there is no possibility of exhausting the resource. Allowing nonzero switching costs, possible state-dependent costs of production due to exhausting the mine or other physical constraints on the amount of copper in the mine would invalidate the path-independence assumption underlying our fast simulation approach. We illustrated this in a simple example where the entrepreneur has a limit on the total amount that can be explored from the natural resource.[7] A valuation that takes these complexities into account will, as we have illustrated, be much more demanding.

Using the parameters estimated by Schwartz (1997) for copper futures, we illustrated in simple numerical examples that stochastic convenience yields can have a significant effect on the value of both the development option and the production option—especially when there is a time lag between production and product availability in the market—and, thereby, also for the decision to develop the natural resource. This is due to the very high correlation between the spot commodity price and the spot convenience yield, which induces a mean-reversion effect into the spot commodity price, in turn reducing volatility and the value of the option to develop the product.

The fact that standard Black–Scholes evaluation methods significantly overvalue natural resource investment projects in most real-life cases indicates that using these methods for decision support will lead to overinvestment in natural resource projects.[8] Moreover, the overvaluation is most significant for projects with high costs, which are exactly the most critical projects (in break-even terms), and, therefore, the projects in which it is most important that we make more careful decisions.

Appendix A

This appendix derives (a) the drift restriction for the future convenience yield under an equivalent martingale measure, i.e., Eq. (10.9); and (b) the closed-form expression for the value of the production option, i.e., Eq. (10.12).

To ease the notation, we introduce

$$Y(t, T) = e^{\int_t^T [f(t,v) - \epsilon(t,v)] dv} \tag{10.A1}$$

That is, the futures price of the commodity can be written as

$$G(t, T) = S_t Y(t, T) \tag{10.3'}$$

The same arguments that were used by Heath et al. (1992) to derive the dynamics of the zero-coupon bond prices can be used on $Y(t, T)$ from Eq. (10.A1) using both the SDEs of the forward interest rates from Eq. (10.4) and the future convenience yields from Eq. (10.5). That is,

---

[7] Valuation of the development option in the path-independent case illustrated in section 10.5.2 took less than 2 seconds on a standard PC, whereas the path-dependent version outlined in the last part of Section 10.5.3 took about 3 minutes on the same PC.

[8] That is, for almost any commodity (except for precious metals) we observe stochastic convenience yields that are positively correlated with the underlying spot commodity price.

$$Y(t, T) = Y(0, T) + \int_0^t Y(u, T) \Bigg\{ (-f(u, u) + \epsilon(u, u)$$

$$+ \int_u^T \mu_f(u, v) \, dv - \int_u^T \mu_\epsilon(u, v) \, dv$$

$$+ \frac{1}{2} \sum_{k=1}^d \left[\int_u^T \sigma_f^k(u, v) \, dv \right]^2 + \frac{1}{2} \sum_{k=1}^d \left[\int_u^T \sigma_\epsilon^k(u, v) \, dv \right]^2 \qquad (10.A2)$$

$$- \sum_{k=1}^d \left[\int_u^T \sigma_f^k(u, v) \, dv \right] \left[\int_u^T \sigma_\epsilon^k(u, v) \, dv \right] \Bigg\} \, du$$

$$+ \sum_{k=1}^d \int_0^t Y(u, T) \left[\int_u^T \sigma_f^k(u, v) \, dv - \int_u^T \sigma_\epsilon^k(u, v) \, dv \right] dW_u^k$$

Now, Itô's lemma on the expression of the futures price given by Eq. (10.13′) with the SDEs of the spot commodity price from Eq. (10.6) and $Y(t, T)$ from Eq. (10.A2) gives the dynamics (or the SDE) of the futures prices

$$G(t, T) = G(0, T) + \int_0^t G(u, T) \Bigg\{ - \int_u^T \mu_\epsilon(u, v) \, dv + \sum_{k=1}^d \left[\int_u^T \sigma_f^k(u, v) \, dv \right]^2$$

$$+ \frac{1}{2} \sum_{k=1}^d \left[\int_u^T \sigma_\epsilon^k(u, v) \, dv \right]^2 - \sum_{k=1}^d \left[\int_u^T \sigma_f^k(u, v) \, dv \right] \left[\int_u^T \sigma_\epsilon^k(u, v) \, dv \right]$$

$$\qquad (10.A3)$$

$$+ \sum_{k=1}^d \sigma_S^k(u) \left\{ \int_u^T \left[(\sigma_f^k(u, v) - \sigma_\epsilon^k(u, v) \right] dv \right\} \Bigg\} \, du$$

$$+ \sum_{k=1}^d \int_0^t G(u, T) \left\{ \sigma_S^k(u) + \int_u^T \left[\sigma_f^k(u, v) - \sigma_\epsilon^k(u, v) \right] dv \right\} dW_u^k$$

Under an equivalent martingale measure, the futures price process is a martingale (cf. Cox et al., 1981), hence

$$- \int_t^T \mu_\epsilon(t, v) \, dv + \sum_{k=1}^d \left[\int_t^T \sigma_f^k(t, v) \, dv \right]^2 + \frac{1}{2} \sum_{k=1}^d \left[\int_t^T \sigma_\epsilon^k(t, v) \, dv \right]^2$$

$$- \sum_{k=1}^d \left[\int_t^T \sigma_f^k(t, v) \, dv \right] \left[\int_t^T \sigma_\epsilon^k(t, v) \, dv \right] \qquad (10.A4)$$

$$+ \sum_{k=1}^d \sigma_S^k(t) \left\{ \int_t^T \left[\sigma_f^k(t, v) - \sigma_\epsilon^k(t, v) \right] dv \right\} = 0$$

which implies (after differentiating with respect to T) that the drift of the future convenience yield process is given by

$$
\mu_\epsilon(t, u) = \sum_{k=1}^{d} \sigma_f^k(t, u) \left[\int_t^u \sigma_f^k(t, v) \, dv \right]
$$

$$
+ \sum_{k=1}^{d} \left[\sigma_f^k(t, u) - \sigma_\epsilon^k(t, u) \right] \left\{ \sigma_S^k(t) + \int_t^u \left[\sigma_f^k(t, v) - \sigma_\epsilon^k(t, v) \right] dv \right\}
$$

(10.9′)

The following subsection derives the closed-form expression for the value of the production option, i.e., Eq. (10.12). To evaluate Eq. (10.11), we follow Miltersen and Schwartz (1997) by first evaluating

$$
C_s = \hat{E}_s \left[e^{-\int_s^t f(v,v) \, dv} \max\{P(t, T) \, G(t, T) - c, 0\} \right] \qquad (10.A5)
$$

where $G(t, T)$ is the futures price. The derivation is inspired by Brenner and Jarrow (1993), who derive a closed-form solution for a European call option written on a zero-coupon bond with a similar term structure of interest rates model. To evaluate the option price from Eq. (10.A5) first write

$$
e^{-\int_s^t f(v,v) \, dv} = A e^{-X} \qquad (10.A6)
$$

with X defined as

$$
X = \sum_{k=1}^{d} \int_s^t \int_s^v \sigma_f^k(u, v) \, dW_u^k \, dv
$$

$$
= \sum_{k=1}^{d} \int_s^t \left[\int_u^t \sigma_f^k(u, v) \, dv \right] dW_u^k
$$

and A being residually determined. Note that A is nonstochastic because of the way X is specified. Define

$$
P(t, T) = D e^{-U} \qquad (10.A7)
$$

with U defined as

$$
U = \sum_{k=1}^{d} \int_s^t \left[\int_t^T \sigma_f^k(u, v) \, dv \right] dW_u^k \qquad (10.A8)
$$

and D again being residually determined and (by construction of U) nonstochastic. Finally, write

$$
G(t, T) = F e^V \qquad (10.A9)
$$

with V defined as

$$V = \sum_{k=1}^{d} \int_{s}^{t} \left\{ \sigma_{S}^{k}(u) + \int_{u}^{T} \left[\sigma_{f}^{k}(u, v) - \sigma_{\epsilon}^{k}(u, v) \right] dv \right\} dW_{u}^{k} \quad (10.A10)$$

where F is again residually determined and (by construction of V) nonstochastic. Obviously, (U, V, X) is jointly normally distributed with mean zero. The variances and covariances are

$$\sigma_{u}^{2} = \sum_{k=1}^{d} \int_{s}^{t} \left[\int_{t}^{T} \sigma_{f}^{k}(u, v) \, dv \right]^{2} du$$

$$\sigma_{v}^{2} = \sum_{k=1}^{d} \int_{s}^{t} \left\{ \sigma_{S}^{k}(u) + \int_{u}^{T} \left[\sigma_{f}^{k}(u, v) - \sigma_{\epsilon}^{k}(u, v) \right] dv \right\}^{2} du$$

$$\sigma_{x}^{2} = \sum_{k=1}^{d} \int_{s}^{t} \left[\int_{u}^{t} \sigma_{f}^{k}(u, v) \, dv \right]^{2} du$$

$$\sigma_{uv} = \sum_{k=1}^{d} \int_{s}^{t} \left[\int_{t}^{T} \sigma_{f}^{k}(u, v) \, dv \right] \left\{ \sigma_{S}^{k}(u) + \int_{u}^{T} \left[\sigma_{f}^{k}(u, v) - \sigma_{\epsilon}^{k}(u, v) \right] dv \right\} du$$

$$\sigma_{ux} = \sum_{k=1}^{d} \int_{s}^{t} \left[\int_{t}^{T} \sigma_{f}^{k}(u, v) \, dv \right] \left\{ \int_{u}^{t} \sigma_{f}^{k}(u, v) \, dv \right\} du$$

and

$$\sigma_{vx} = \sum_{k=1}^{d} \int_{s}^{t} \left[\int_{u}^{t} \sigma_{f}^{k}(u, v) \, dv \right] \left\{ \sigma_{S}^{k}(u) + \int_{u}^{T} \left[\sigma_{f}^{k}(u, v) - \sigma_{\epsilon}^{k}(u, v) \right] dv \right\} du$$

If we define $Z \equiv V - U$, then

$$P(t, T) \, G(t, T) = D \, F \, e^{Z} \quad (10.A11)$$

Moreover,

$$\sigma_{z}^{2} = \sigma_{u}^{2} + \sigma_{v}^{2} - 2\sigma_{uv}$$

$$= \sum_{k=1}^{d} \int_{s}^{t} \left[\sigma_{S}^{k}(u) + \int_{u}^{t} \sigma_{f}^{k}(u, v) \, dv - \int_{u}^{T} \sigma_{\epsilon}^{k}(u, v) \, dv \right]^{2} du \quad (10.13'''')$$

and

$$\sigma_{xz} = \sigma_{vx} - \sigma_{ux} \quad (10.A12)$$

Define $B \equiv D \, F$. The value of the option from Eq. (10.A5) can be calculated as in Miltersen and Schwartz (1997). That is, the value of the production option from Eq. (10.A5) can now be written as

$$C_s = A \hat{E}\left[e^{-X} \max\left(B e^Z - c, 0\right)\right]$$

$$= A \hat{E}\left[\hat{E}\left[e^{-X} \mid Z\right] \max\left(B e^Z - c, 0\right)\right] \tag{10.A13}$$

using iterated expectations. Since in the Gaussian case the conditional distribution of X given Z is given as

$$X \mid Z = z \sim N\left[z \frac{\sigma_{xz}}{\sigma_z^2}, \sigma_x^2\left(1 - \frac{\sigma_{xz}^2}{\sigma_x^2 \sigma_z^2}\right)\right]$$

we can calculate the conditional expectation as

$$\hat{E}\left[e^{-X} \mid Z = z\right] = e^{-z \frac{\sigma_{xz}}{\sigma_z^2} + \frac{1}{2}\sigma_x^2\left(1 - \frac{\sigma_{xz}^2}{\sigma_x^2 \sigma_z^2}\right)}$$

Hence, Eq. (10.A13) can be rewritten as

$$C_s = A e^{\frac{1}{2}\sigma_x^2\left(1 - \frac{\sigma_{xz}^2}{\sigma_x^2 \sigma_z^2}\right)} \hat{E}\left[e^{-Z \frac{\sigma_{xz}}{\sigma_z^2}} \max\left(B e^Z - c, 0\right)\right] \tag{10.A14}$$

Introducing the indicator function $1_{\{Z > \ln c/B\}}$, Eq. (10.A14) can be written as

$$C_s = A B e^{\frac{1}{2}\sigma_x^2\left(1 - \frac{\sigma_{xz}^2}{\sigma_x^2 \sigma_z^2}\right)} \hat{E}\left[1_{(Z > \ln \frac{c}{B})} e^{Z\left(1 - \frac{\sigma_{xz}}{\sigma_z^2}\right)}\right]$$

$$\tag{10.A15}$$

$$- A c e^{\frac{1}{2}\sigma_x^2\left(1 - \frac{\sigma_{xz}^2}{\sigma_x^2 \sigma_z^2}\right)} \hat{E}\left[1_{(Z > \ln \frac{c}{B})} e^{-Z \frac{\sigma_{xz}}{\sigma_z^2}}\right]$$

Straightforward manipulations of normal densities yield

$$\hat{E}\left[1_{(Z > \ln \frac{c}{B})} e^{Z\left(1 - \frac{\sigma_{xz}}{\sigma_z^2}\right)}\right] = e^{\frac{(\sigma_z^2 - \sigma_{xz})^2}{2\sigma_z^2}} N\left(\frac{\ln \frac{B}{c} + \sigma_z^2 - \sigma_{xz}}{\sigma_z}\right)$$

and

$$\hat{E}\left[1_{(Z > \ln \frac{c}{B})} e^{-Z \frac{\sigma_{xz}}{\sigma_z^2}}\right] = e^{\frac{\sigma_{xz}^2}{2\sigma_z^2}} N\left(\frac{\ln \frac{B}{c} - \sigma_{xz}}{\sigma_z}\right)$$

Observe that

$$A e^{\frac{1}{2}\sigma_x^2\left(1 - \frac{\sigma_{xz}^2}{\sigma_x^2 \sigma_z^2}\right)} e^{\frac{\sigma_{xz}^2}{2\sigma_z^2}} = A e^{\frac{1}{2}\sigma_x^2} = \hat{E}_s\left[e^{-\int_s^t f(v,v)\,dv}\right] = P(s,t)$$

and that

$$A B e^{\frac{1}{2}\sigma_x^2\left(1 - \frac{\sigma_{xz}^2}{\sigma_x^2 \sigma_z^2}\right)} e^{\frac{(\sigma_z^2 - \sigma_{xz})^2}{2\sigma_z^2}} = A B e^{\frac{1}{2}(\sigma_x^2 + \sigma_z^2 - 2\sigma_{xz})}$$

$$= \hat{E}_s\left[e^{-\int_s^t f(v,v)\,dv} P(t,T) G(t,T)\right]$$

Moreover,

$$B \, e^{\frac{1}{2}\sigma_z^2 - \sigma_{xz}} = \frac{\hat{E}_s \left[e^{-\int_s^t f(v,v)\,dv} \, P(t,T) \, G(t,T) \right]}{P(s,t)}$$

implying that

$$\ln \frac{B}{c} + \frac{1}{2}\sigma_z^2 - \sigma_{xz} = \ln \frac{\hat{E}_s \left[e^{-\int_s^t f(v,v)\,dv} \, P(t,T) \, G(t,T) \right]}{P(s,t)\,c}$$

Finally, defining

$$G(s,t,T) = \hat{E}_s \left[e^{-\int_s^t f(v,v)\,dv} \, P(t,T) \, G(t,T) \right]$$

and substituting into Eq. (10.A15), we have that

$$C_s = G(s,t,T) \, N \left[\frac{\ln \frac{G(s,t,T)}{P(s,t)\,c} + \frac{1}{2}\sigma_z^2}{\sigma_z} \right]$$

$$- P(s,t) \, c \, N \left[\frac{\ln \frac{G(s,t,T)}{P(s,t)\,c} - \frac{1}{2}\sigma_z^2}{\sigma_z} \right] \qquad (10.A16)$$

where σ_z is defined in Eq. (10.13'''). With the normality assumption, we can calculate $G(s,t,T)$ as follows

$$G(s,t,T) = A \, D \, F \, e^{\frac{1}{2}(\sigma_x^2 + \sigma_z^2 - 2\sigma_{xz})}$$

$$= A \, D \, F \, e^{\frac{1}{2}(\sigma_x^2 + \sigma_u^2 + \sigma_v^2 - 2\sigma_{uv} - 2\sigma_{vx} + 2\sigma_{ux})}$$

$$= A \, D \, \hat{E} \left[e^{-X-U} \right] F \, \hat{E} \left[e^V \right] e^{-\sigma_{uv} - \sigma_{vx}} \qquad (10.A17)$$

$$= \hat{E}_s \left[e^{-\int_s^t f(v,v)\,dv} \, P(t,T) \right] \hat{E}_s \left[G(t,T) \right] e^{-\sigma_{uv} - \sigma_{vx}}$$

$$= P(s,T) \, G(s,T) \, e^{-\sigma_{uv} - \sigma_{vx}}$$

since the futures price, $G(\cdot,T)$, is a martingale under an equivalent martingale measure. By defining β as

$$\beta \equiv -\sigma_{uv} - \sigma_{vx}$$

$$= -\sum_{k=1}^{d} \int_s^t \left[\int_u^T \sigma_f^k(u,v)\,dv \right] \qquad (10.A18)$$

$$\left\{ \sigma_S^k(u) + \int_u^T \left[\sigma_f^k(u,v) - \sigma_\epsilon^k(u,v) \right] dv \right\} du$$

we can expand the expression for $G(s,t,T)$ from Eq. (10.A17) and thereby simplify Eq. (10.A16) to

$$C_s = P(s, T) G(s, T) e^{\beta} N \left[\frac{\ln \frac{P(s,T) G(s,T)}{P(s,t) c} + \beta + \frac{1}{2}\sigma_z^2}{\sigma_z} \right]$$

$$- P(s, t) c N \left[\frac{\ln \frac{P(s,T) G(s,T)}{P(s,t) c} + \beta - \frac{1}{2}\sigma_z^2}{\sigma_z} \right]$$

(10.A19)

This provides a closed-form expression for the price of a European call option with maturity date t and exercise price c written on the commodity futures price with maturity T discounted back to date t.

In the Gaussian case, the ratio of forward prices to futures prices can be derived as

$$F(t, T) = G(t, T) H(t, T) \tag{10.A20}$$

where $H(t, T)$ is

$$H(t, T) = e^{-\sum_{k=1}^{d} \int_t^T \left[\int_u^T \sigma_f^k(u,v) \, dv \right] \left\{ \sigma_S^k(u) + \int_u^T \left[\sigma_f^k(u,v) - \sigma_\epsilon^k(u,v) \right] dv \right\} du} \tag{10.A21}$$

which is deterministic and, therefore, known at date s. See Amin and Jarrow (1991) and Miltersen and Schwartz (1997) for details. Using this ratio, the value of the production option, C_s^p, from Eq. (10.11), can be written as

$$C_s^p = H(t, T) \hat{E}_s \left[e^{-\int_s^t f(v,v) \, dv} \right.$$

$$\left. \max \left\{ P(t, T) G(t, T) - \frac{c}{H(t, T)}, 0 \right\} \right] \tag{10.11'''}$$

We can therefore value the production option using our formula for options on futures prices from Eq. (10.A19) as

$$C_s^p = H(t, T) P(s, T) G(s, T) e^{\beta} N \left[\frac{\ln \frac{H(t,T) P(s,T) G(s,T)}{P(s,t) c} + \beta + \frac{1}{2}\sigma_z^2}{\sigma_z} \right]$$

$$- H(t, T) P(s, t) \frac{c}{H(t, T)} N \left[\frac{\ln \frac{H(t,T) P(s,T) G(s,T)}{P(s,t) c} + \beta - \frac{1}{2}\sigma_z^2}{\sigma_z} \right] \tag{10.A22}$$

where σ_z is defined in Eq. (10.13'''). Moreover,

$$H(t, T) G(s, T) e^{\beta} = \frac{H(t, T)}{H(s, T)} e^{\beta} F(s, T) = F(s, T) \tag{10.A23}$$

using the definitions of H and β from Eqs. (10.A21) and (10.A18). That is, the value of the production option from Eq. (10.A22) can be simplified to

$$C_s^p = P(s, T) F(s, T) N \left[\frac{\ln \frac{P(s,T) F(s,T)}{P(s,t) c} + \frac{1}{2}\sigma_z^2}{\sigma_z} \right]$$

$$- P(s, t) c N \left[\frac{\ln \frac{P(s,T) F(s,T)}{P(s,t) c} - \frac{1}{2}\sigma_z^2}{\sigma_z} \right] \tag{10.12'''}$$

which provides the desired closed-form expression for the value of the production option.

ACKNOWLEDGMENTS

The chapter was presented at the *Conference on Real Options: Theory Meets Practice* at Columbia University, New York, June 1997 and at the *Symposium on Real Options* at Copenhagen Business School, Copenhagen, Denmark, September 1997. I am grateful to Michael Brennan, Eduardo S. Schwartz, Lenos Trigeorgis, two anonymous referees, and seminar participants for valuable comments. The author gratefully acknowledges the financial support of the Danish Natural and Social Science Research Councils and Den Danske Bank.

REFERENCES

Amin, K. I., and R. A. Jarrow. (1991). Pricing Foreign Currency Options Under Stochastic Interest Rates. *Journal of International Money and Finance* 10, 310–329.

Black, F., and M. Scholes. (1973). The Pricing of Options and Corporate Liabilities. *Journal of Political Economy* 81(3), 637–654.

Brenner, R. J., and R. A. Jarrow. (1993). A Simple Formula for Options on Discount Bonds. In *Advances in Futures and Options Research*, Volume 6, pp. 45–51. Greenwich, CT: JAI Press, Inc.

Cox, J. C., J. E. Ingersoll, Jr., and S. A. Ross. (1981). The Relation between Forward Prices and Futures Prices. *Journal of Financial Economics* 9, 321–346.

Dixit, A. K., and R. S. Pindyck. (1994). *Investment under Uncertainty.* Princeton NJ: Princeton University Press.

Harrison, M. J., and D. M. Kreps. (1979). Martingales and Arbitrage in Multiperiod Securities Markets. *Journal of Economic Theory* 20, 381–408.

Harrison, M. J., and S. R. Pliska. (1981). Martingales and Stochastic Integrals in the Theory of Continuous Trading. *Stochastic Processes and Their Applications* 11, 215–260. Addendum: Harrison and Pliska (1983).

Heath, D., R. A. Jarrow, and A. J. Morton. (1992). Bond Pricing and the Term Structure of Interest Rates: A New Methodology for Contingent Claims Valuation. *Econometrica* 60(1), 77–105.

Hull, J. (1997). *Options, Futures, and Other Derivatives,* 3rd edition. Upper Saddle River, NJ: Prentice-Hall.

Karatzas, I., and S. E. Shreve. (1988). *Brownian Motion and Stochastic Calculus,* Number 113 in *Graduate Texts in Mathematics*. New York: Springer-Verlag.

Kloeden, P. E., and E. Platen. (1992). *Numerical Solutions of Stochastic Differential Equations,* Universitext. Berlin: Springer-Verlag.

Merton, R. C. (1973). Theory of Rational Option Pricing. *Bell Journal of Economics and Management Science* 4, 141–183. Reprinted in Merton (1990, chapter 8).

Merton, R. C. (1990). *Continuous-Time Finance,* Padstow, Great Britain: Basil Blackwell Inc.

Miltersen, K. R., and E. S. Schwartz. (1997). Pricing of Options on Commodity Futures with Stochastic Term Structures of Convenience Yields and Interest Rates. Finance Working Paper #5-97, The John E. Anderson Graduate School of Management at UCLA. *Journal of Financial and Quantitative Analysis*, 1998.

Schwartz, E. S. (1997). The Stochastic Behavior of Commodity Prices: Implications for Valuation and Hedging. *The Journal of Finance* 52(3), 922–973.

11

A Compound Option Model for Evaluating Multistage Natural Resource Investments

GONZALO CORTAZAR

JAIME CASASSUS

This chapter develops a natural resource investment evaluation model that considers multistage production decisions as compound options. The model allows for multiple stages with finite resource and finite capacity output levels at each stage. Numerical solutions for the two-stage case are presented, showing that the lower the remaining resources and the higher the intermediate inventory, the higher the critical production prices. The optimal operating policy is dependent on the natural resource life cycle, inducing more first-stage production and inventory accumulation during the early years, and more second-stage production and inventory depletion as reserves decline.

11.1 INTRODUCTION

An extensive literature deals with the use of option theory to evaluate real assets.[1] In a seminal paper, Brennan and Schwartz (1985) solve for the value and optimal production policy of a natural resource investment, contingent on the price of a commodity with a futures market. By assuming there are no arbitrage opportunities available in trading in the real (the natural resource) and the financial (the futures market) assets, the value and optimal operating policy of the investment as a function of the commodity price can be determined. The production policy is defined by the schedules of prices at which production is delayed, resumed, or abandoned.

Other models have been developed to take into account different aspects of real options. For example, Majd and Pindyck (1989) include the effect of a learning

---

[1] For a review of real options see Dixit and Pindyck (1994) and Trigeorgis (1996).

curve by assuming that accumulated production reduces unit costs. Trigeorgis (1993) examines various real options and their interactions with financial flexibility. Others, like McDonald and Siegel (1986) and Majd and Pindyck (1987), have taken as the control variable the investment rate, instead of the production rate. He and Pindyck (1992) include two production level controls for two different products, while Cortazar and Schwartz (1993) consider a two-stage production system. The source of uncertainty may be a commodity price (Paddock et al., 1988), exchange rates (Dixit, 1989), or costs (Pindyck, 1993). Finally, models have been tailored to specific assets such as copper mines (Brennan and Schwartz, 1985), oil reserves (Ekern, 1988; Paddock et al., 1988), research and development (Schwartz and Moon, this volume), environmental technologies (Cortazar et al., 1998), flexible production processes (He and Pindyck, 1992), and multinational facility locations (Kogut and Kulatilaka, 1994; Dasu and Li, 1997).

If real option models are to be used to value particular real assets and not just to describe general economic phenomena, we should try to capture their complexity as much as possible. This chapter exemplifies this effort by presenting a model that, while remaining simple, captures the essential elements of a rather complex multistage production process.

Multistage production processes are a common feature of many real investments. For example, the output of a mining investment is typically required to go through several stages, including extraction, milling, smelting and refinery. Each of these stages takes its input from the previous stage and involves additional costs before going to the next stage. Paddock et al. (1988) state that the exploitation of petroleum leases involves three stages: exploration, development, and extraction. These are but only two examples in which real asset valuation benefits from multistage modeling.

A stylized two-stage production process has been presented in Cortazar and Schwartz (1993). In their model, the value of an infinite-resource real asset is contingent on a commodity price and the production process allows for stocking of work-in-process inventories. The firm is modeled as having a two-stage production process which may operate independently in such a way as to maximize firm value. If for some price level stage 1 produces while stage 2 does not, intermediate inventories are stocked for use in the future. In order to obtain analytical solutions, an infinite second-stage production capacity is assumed.

The present paper can be seen as an extension of Brennan and Schwartz (1985) by allowing for a production process with more than one stage or, alternatively, as an extension of Cortazar and Schwartz (1993) by relaxing the infinite resource and infinite second-stage capacity restrictions and by extending the two-stage production process to n stages.

We present a numerical solution to the two-stage production model, which includes three state variables and two controls and may thus be solved without extensive computer power. We derive the critical first-stage and second-stage prices over which it is optimal to produce, and show that the lower the remaining resources and the higher the intermediate inventory, the higher the critical prices. The optimal operating policy is dependent on the natural resource life-cycle, inducing more first-stage production and inventory accumulation during the early years, and more second-stage production and inventory depletion as reserves decline.

We also analyze the economic value of allowing in each stage to decide independently whether to produce or not, showing that it may significantly increase investment value as long as commodity prices are not too high (in which case both stages will be producing) or not too low (in which case both stages will be closed). Finally, the model is extended to *n* stages with suggestions on how it can be solved numerically.

The paper is organized as follows. The next section presents a two-stage finite resource model. Section 11.3 presents results of the numerical solution to the two-stage model. Section 11.4 generalizes the model to *n* stages, and Section 11.5 concludes. The Appendix provides details of the numerical solution.

11.2 THE TWO-STAGE PRODUCTION AND INVENTORY MODEL

11.2.1 Valuation Framework

Following Cortazar and Schwartz (1993), we model the technology of the investment project as two sequential processes, each with an independent decision variable representing the output rate. To solve their model, Cortazar and Schwartz (1993) required the second stage process to have infinite capacity and imposed an infinite resource constraint, while we allow resources and output capacity to be finite. In later sections we solve numerically and extend our model to *n*-stage sequential processes.

We assume that a non-renewable natural resource investment can be modeled as a two-stage production process with finite resources, as described in Figure 11.1. We use the following notation:

S	Commodity spot price
Q	Available resources
I	Intermediate inventory of work-in-process
t	Time
$F(S,t)$	Commodity futures price
$H(S,Q,I,t;\phi)$	Natural resource investment value
ϕ	Operating policy (output levels as a function of spot prices)
$\overline{q}_1$	First-stage output capacity
$\overline{q}_2$	Second-stage output capacity
q_1	First-stage output level
q_2	Second-stage output level
A_1	Average first-stage unit cost

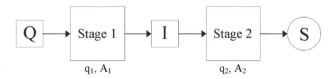

Figure 11.1   Two-stage production and inventory model.

A_2	Average second-stage unit cost
ρ	Riskless nominal interest rate
κS	Convenience yield on holding one unit of finished output[2]
μ	Instantaneous return on investing in commodity S
σ	Standard deviation of returns from investing in commodity S
dz	Increment to a standard Gauss–Wiener process
$dI = (q_1 - q_2)\, dt$	Change in work-in-process inventory

We assume commodity prices follow a standard Brownian motion:

$$\frac{dS}{S} = \mu\, dt + \sigma dz \tag{11.1}$$

By requiring that no arbitrage opportunities exist by trading in H and F, it can be shown (by forming a riskless portfolio and assuming its return must be the riskless interest rate, ρ) that the value of the natural resource investment must satisfy the following differential equation:

$$\frac{1}{2}\sigma^2 S^2 H_{SS} + (\rho - \kappa)SH_S - q_1 H_Q + (q_1 - q_2)H_I + H_t$$
$$+ [q_2(S - A_2) - q_1 A_1] - \rho H = 0 \tag{11.2}$$

This equation must hold for *any* operating policy. To compute the value of the investment we assume it is operated under a value-maximizing policy and solve the following optimization problem:[3]

$$Max_{q_1, q_2} \left\{ \frac{1}{2}\sigma^2 S^2 H_{SS} + (\rho - \kappa)SH_S - q_1 H_Q + (q_1 - q_2)H_I + H_t \right.$$
$$\left. + [q_2(S - A_2) - q_1 A_1] - \rho H \right\} = 0 \tag{11.3}$$

subject to

$$q_1 \leq \bar{q}_1 \tag{11.4}$$

$$q_2 \leq \bar{q}_2 \tag{11.5}$$

$$q_1, q_2 \geq 0 \tag{11.6}$$

$$q_1 = 0 \quad \text{if} \quad Q = 0 \tag{11.7}$$

$$q_2 \leq q_1 \quad \text{if} \quad I = 0 \tag{11.8}$$

The last two conditions impose nonnegative restrictions on inventories and reserves.

---

[2] Convenience yield is usually defined as the flow of services that accrues to an owner of the physical commodity but not to the owner of a futures contract for delayed delivery of the commodity. The existence of a significant convenience yield induces one-stage firms with finite resources not to defer production even if prices are low. Also, this convenience yield induces finite-resource multistage firms to produce if prices and/or inventories are sufficiently high by inducing a decreasing marginal benefit of accumulated inventories.

[3] For the value of the investment to be a linear function of the production rates, we assume that average unit costs are independent of q_1 and q_2.

This problem does not have an analytical solution and must be solved using numerical methods. In the next section we show how to obtain the required boundary conditions to solve the two-stage model, and how to extend it to an *n*-stage production process.

11.2.2 Optimal Policy and Value

Assuming that average first-stage and second-stage unit costs, A_1 and A_2, are not a function of output levels, q_1 and q_2, optimal operating policy has a bang-bang solution defined by two critical spot prices (S_1^*, S_2^*), one for each production stage. Whenever the spot price falls below the critical value of either of the production stages, output for that stage should stop, otherwise it should be equal to that stage's capacity. These critical spot prices may be a function of the other state variables, Q, I, and t.

We define V as the investment value under the optimal operating policy if it is optimal to be producing in both stages, Z if it is optimal to be producing only in stage 1, Y if it is optimal to be producing only in stage 2, and W if it is optimal not to be producing in either stage.

Depending on which of the critical spot prices, S_1^* or S_2^*, is smaller, either Z or Y will be feasible while the other is not. Figures 11.2 and 11.3 show the investment value contingent on commodity prices under the optimal operating policy, with the critical prices for which it is optimal to modify production levels at either stage.

11.2.3 The Model (in Real Terms) and Boundary Conditions[4]

Following Brennan and Schwartz (1985), we assume a constant rate of inflation affecting all costs. This allows us to simplify the model and eliminate its time dependency by expressing all variables in real terms.

The following new notation is used:

s Commodity spot price, expressed in real terms

$v(s, Q, I)$ Natural-resource investment value in real terms when it is optimal to produce in both stages $[s \geq Max(s_1^*, s_2^*)]$

$z(s, Q, I)$ Natural-resource investment value in real terms when it is optimal to produce only in the first stage $(s_1^* \leq s \leq s_2^*)$

$y(s, Q, I)$ Natural-resource investment value in real terms when it is optimal to produce only in the second stage $(s_2^* \leq s \leq s_1^*)$

---

[4] We follow Brennan and Schwartz (1985) and Cortazar and Schwartz (1993) in presenting the model as a system of equations with common boundary conditions. Alternatively, we could have recognized that the three differential equations are actually the same, and only the control variables adopt different values. This latter approach is used in the later sections of this chapter where we generalize the model to *n* stages. The former approach, used in this section, has the merits of eliciting more clearly that this chapter can be seen as an extension of Cortazar and Schwartz (1993) and, more importantly, of lending the model more easily to incorporate opening and closing costs (as in Brennan and Schwartz, 1985), which were not included in this model for simplicity.

$w(s, Q, I)$	Natural-resource investment value in real terms when it is optimal to produce in either stage $[0 \leq s \leq Min(s_1^*, s_2^*)]$
a_1	Average first-stage unit cost in real terms
a_2	Average second-stage unit cost in real terms
r	Riskless interest rate in real terms

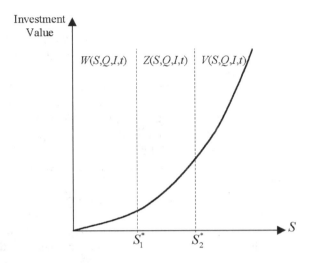

Figure 11.2   Value of the investment for critical spot prices $S_1^* < S_2^*$. The figure shows the value of the investment under the optimal operating policy when the critical spot price of the first stage is less than that of the second stage.

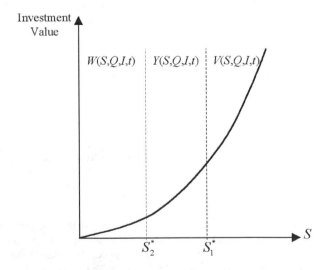

Figure 11.3   Value of the investment for critical spot prices $S_2^* < S_1^*$. The figure shows the value of the investment under the optimal operating policy when the critical spot price of the second stage is less than that of the first stage.

Even though the ranking of both critical prices may vary throughout the life of the investment, depending on the level of reserves and inventories, at any point in time either one or the other will be smaller, inducing z or y not to be feasible.

For presentation purposes, we assume that for given reserves and inventory levels the critical first-stage price, s_1^*, is smaller than the corresponding second-stage price, s_2^*, making it never optimal to produce only in the second stage. Thus, the model can be described in terms of only $w(s, Q, I)$, $z(s, Q, I)$, and $v(s, Q, I)$:

$$\frac{1}{2}\sigma^2 s^2 w_{ss} + (r - \kappa)s w_s - rw = 0 \qquad (11.9)$$

$$\frac{1}{2}\sigma^2 s^2 z_{ss} + (r - \kappa)s z_s - \bar{q}_1 z_Q + \bar{q}_1 z_I + \{-\bar{q}_1 a_1\} - rz = 0 \qquad (11.10)$$

$$\frac{1}{2}\sigma^2 s^2 v_{ss} + (r - \kappa)s v_s - \bar{q}_1 v_Q + (\bar{q}_1 - \bar{q}_2)v_I +$$
$$[\bar{q}_2(s - a_2) - \bar{q}_1 a_1] - rv = 0 \qquad (11.11)$$

To solve the model we require the following boundary conditions on the value function for the three state variables, s, Q, and I:

Boundary Conditions for the State Variable Price (s)

$$w(s_1^*, Q, I) = z(s_1^*, Q, I) \qquad (11.12)$$

$$z(s_2^*, Q, I) = v(s_2^*, Q, I) \qquad (11.13)$$

$$w_s(s_1^*, Q, I) = z_s(s_1^*, Q, I) \qquad (11.14)$$

$$z_s(s_2^*, Q, I) = v_s(s_2^*, Q, I) \qquad (11.15)$$

$$w(0, W, I) = 0 \qquad (11.16)$$

$$\lim_{s \to \infty} \frac{v(s, Q, I)}{s} < \infty \qquad (11.17)$$

Equations (11.12) and (11.13) are the value-matching conditions that guarantee the continuity of the natural-resource investment value at both critical spot prices, s_1^* and s_2^*. Equations (11.14) and (11.15) are the high-order contact or smooth-pasting conditions ensuring that the solution of the model is optimal.[5] Equations (11.16) and (11.17) impose conditions on the investment value if the state variable s reaches zero or gets very high (Brennan and Schwartz, 1985; Dixit and Pindyck, 1994).

Boundary Conditions for the Reserves (Q)

If reserves are exhausted ($Q = 0$) the only feasible first-stage output is zero ($q_1 = 0$), and the model reduces to that of Brennan and Schwartz (1985), in which there is only one stage of production with our inventory variable (I) taking the place of Brennan

---

[5] In Section 11.4 when we generalize to n stages of production we find it convenient to use an alternative model (see footnote 3) and replace these equations by first-order conditions.

and Schwartz's resources (Q).[6] We can solve this numerically using our Eqs. (11.9) and (11.11) and setting the first-stage output to zero.

Boundary Conditions for Inventory (I)

If inventories reach zero $(I = 0)$ the second-stage output is bounded by the first-stage output level. Therefore, if the optimal first-stage output level is zero, the second-stage output level must also be zero and Eq. (11.9) holds. On the other hand, if the optimal first-stage output level is $\overline{q}_1$, then the optimal second-stage output must either be zero [in which case Eq. (11.10) holds], or equal to $\overline{q}_1$ [in which case a simplified Eq. (11.11), with $(\overline{q}_1 - \overline{q}_2) = 0$ holds].

Simultaneous Conditions for Inventory (I) and Reserves (Q)

If both inventories and reserves are zero, the investment value must be zero:

$$w(s, 0, 0) = z(s, 0, 0) = v(s, 0, 0) = 0 \tag{11.18}$$

11.3 AN EXAMPLE AND NUMERICAL RESULTS OF THE TWO-STAGE MODEL

In this section we provide an example and report the results of the numerical implementation of the two-stage inventory and production model described in Section 11.2. A brief description of the numerical solution is given in Appendix A. Our intent is to elucidate some of the features of this model and highlight the importance of multistage models in valuing natural-resource investments.

To illustrate our results we consider a copper mine modeled as a two-stage process. Its operating characteristics and economic parameters are summarized in Table 11.1. We solve for the value of the above mine using three approaches. First, we disregard the option value of opening and closing the mine in response to copper price fluctuations and determine what we call the *No Option Value*. Second, we use the Brennan–Schwartz (1985) approach, which treats the entire mine operation as having one stage, by considering only one decision variable that allows both stages to be simultaneously either open or closed (imposing $q_1 = q_2$).[7] Finally, we use our proposed model, which we label *Cortazar–Casassus*, allowing the mine to have none, one, or both of the stages open, depending on commodity prices. To make the results of all three approaches comparable, we consider initial inventory to be zero $(I = 0)$.

Figure 11.4 shows the value of the copper mine using these three alternative valuation models. As a richer operating policy is allowed in response to changing commodity prices, the value of the investment project increases as expected. The difference between the *Brennan–Schwartz* model and *No Option Value* can be attributed

---

[6] Without opening, closing, and maintenance costs.
[7] We do not consider opening, closing, and maintenance costs.

Table 11.1
Operating and Economic Parameters for a Two-Stage Copper Mine

	Parameter	*Value*
Interest rate	r	10% / year
Convenience yield	κ	4% / year
Price (return) volatility	σ	8% / year
First-stage output capacity	$\overline{q}_1$	5 million lb / year
Average first-stage unit cost	a_1	0.1 U.S. $ / lb
Second-stage output capacity	$\overline{q}_2$	30 million lb / year
Average second-stage unit cost	a_2	0.9 U.S. $ / lb
Available resources	Q	100 million lb

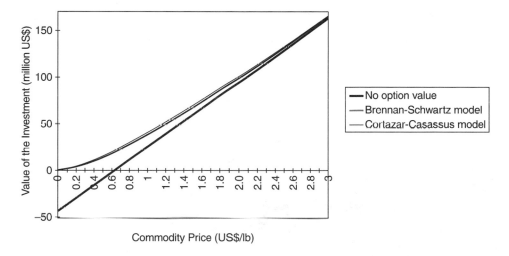

Figure 11.4 Value of a copper mine using three alternative models.

to the *opening and closure* options. *Cortazar–Casassus* adds to this value a *storage* option due to the capability of storing as work-in-process inventories any unfinished output from the first stage.

Figure 11.5 shows the value of these two operating options as a function of commodity prices. It can be seen that while the value of *opening and closure* options decreases as copper prices increase, the *storage* option is more valuable at mid-range prices. The reason for the latter is that for very low copper prices it is optimal to close down both stages, while for very high prices it is optimal to keep both open, without storing intermediate inventories. A *storage* option is valuable if prices exceed first-stage critical levels while being lower than second-stage critical prices.

The economic relevance of the *storage* option in our example can be illustrated in Figure 11.6 where the total mine value is decomposed into (1) the *no option value*, (2) the *opening/closure option*, and (3) the *storage* option. For normal copper prices of about U.S. \$1/lb the *storage* option incorporated in our model represents around 5% of total value.

The value of the *storage* option as a function of reserves can be seen in Figure 11.7. For any commodity price, s, as reserves (Q) increase the *storage* option converges to a finite value, which for very high second-stage capacity levels, q_2, equals the analytic solution presented in Cortazar and Schwartz (1993).[8]

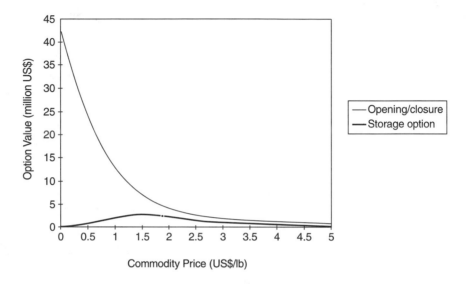

Figure 11.5   Option values as a function of commodity prices.

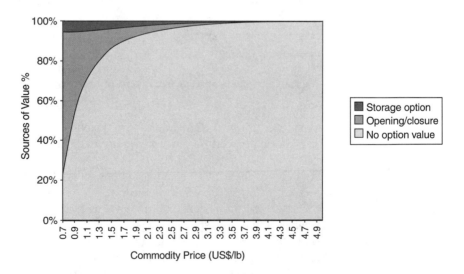

Figure 11.6   Sources of mine value as a function of copper prices.

[8] Recall that Cortazar and Schwartz (1993) require $\overline{q}_2$ and Q to be infinite in order to solve analytically.

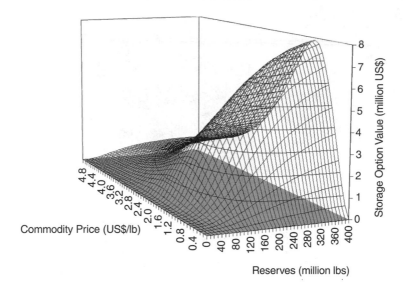

Commodity Price (US$/lb)

Reserves (million lbs)

Storage Option Value (million US$)

Figure 11.7   Value of *storage* option as a function of commodity price and reserves.

The optimal operating policy, described by the critical prices for each of the two stages, can be determined as a function of the state variables. For example, Figure 11.8 presents the critical copper price above which it is optimal to produce in the first stage. It shows that the lower the remaining reserves and the higher the intermediate inventories, the higher the critical first-stage price that induces first-stage closure.[9]

The optimal operating policy in a multistage model would allow for independent opening and closure decisions at each stage. Moreover, the critical prices for each stage would vary throughout the life of the mine. This can be seen in Figure 11.9 where the difference between first-stage and second-stage critical prices is plotted against inventories and reserves. At the beginning of the mine's life, when reserves are high, the first-stage critical price is low compared to the second-stage price (the difference is negative), inducing the mine to produce and stock inventories. On the other hand, as the reserves of the mine decline, the first-stage critical price increases compared to the second-stage critical price, inducing the mine to shut down first-stage operations and reduce inventories.

11.4 A GENERAL *n*-STAGE NATURAL-RESOURCE INVESTMENT MODEL

As noted earlier, many real-world natural resource investments could fruitfully be modeled as a series of sequential decisions, where the completion of each stage can be seen as the exercise of an option to go into the next stage, while a decision not to complete any stage stops the whole upstream sequence of stages.

---

[9] The closure of the stage takes place when the copper price falls below the critical level.

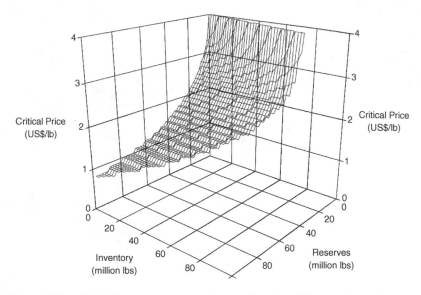

Figure 11.8   Critical first-stage copper price as a function of inventories and reserves.

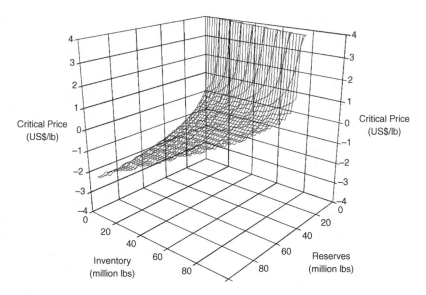

Figure 11.9   Difference between first-stage and second-stage critical prices.

Depending on the nature and the possibilities of discontinuing ongoing production at different levels of progression, the optimal number of model stages can be determined. To obtain a value-maximizing operating strategy that optimally reacts to changes in market conditions we need a model that, while recognizing the multistage production characteristics of natural resource investments, keeps complexity sufficiently low as to allow a solution without an exceedingly high effort.

Figure 11.10 modifies Figure 11.1 to include n stages of production. Each stage uses resources from an inventory of units produced by the previous stage. To simplify notation (and model structure) we treat the initial finite resources, Q, and the inventory I_1 from which stage 1 draws its units. The only special feature of I_1 is that there is no previous stage to increase the number of available units.[10]

Let us define $v(s, I_1, \ldots, I_n)$ as the value of the natural-resource investment under the value-maximizing operating policy, as a function of the commodity spot price (in real terms) s and n inventory levels, I_1 to I_n. Extending the no-arbitrage arguments used previously in the two-stage model to the n-stage case and rearranging, we obtain

$$Max_{q_1,\ldots,q_n}[\frac{1}{2}\sigma^2 s^2 v_{ss} + (r - \kappa)s v_s + \sum_{i=1}^{n-1} q_i(v_{I_{i+1}} - v_{I_i} - a_i)$$

$$+ q_n(s - v_{I_n} - a_n) - rv] = 0 \qquad (11.19)$$

subject to

$$q_i \leq \overline{q}_i \qquad \text{for } i = 1 \text{ to } n \qquad (11.20)$$

$$q_i \geq 0 \qquad \text{for } i = 1 \text{ to } n \qquad (11.21)$$

$$q_1 = 0 \qquad \text{if } I_1 = 0 \qquad (11.22)$$

$$q_i \leq q_{i-1} \quad (\text{for } i = 2 \text{ to } n) \quad \text{if } I_i = 0 \qquad (11.23)$$

The last two restrictions indicate that if inventory reaches zero, then the next-stage output level is also bounded by the previous-stage output level. To solve this model it is more convenient to present it as a single differential equation in which decision variables take different values rather than a system of multiple equations related by boundary conditions.[11] We can solve this model numerically by imposing the following additional boundary conditions:

$$v(s, 0, \ldots, 0) = 0 \qquad (11.24)$$

$$v(0, I_1, \ldots, I_n) = 0 \qquad (11.25)$$

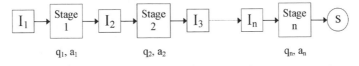

Figure 11.10 The general n-stage natural resource investment model.

[10] Actually, in the case of a mine, we could consider exploration activities as an earlier stage that can increase initial resources. In this case, the model could consider the exploration phase as stage 1 where initial unproven reserves are transformed into proven ones.

[11] See footnotes 5 and 6.

$$\lim_{s \to \infty} \frac{v(s, I_1, \ldots, I_n)}{s} < \infty \tag{11.26}$$

At the critical prices, s_i^*, the following conditions must apply:

$$v_{I_{i+1}}(s_i^*, I_1, \ldots, I_n) - v_{I_i}(s_i^*, I_1, \ldots, I_n) - a_i = 0 \tag{11.27}$$

$$s_n^* - v_{I_n}(s_n^*, I_1, \ldots, I_n) - a_n = 0 \tag{11.28}$$

which amount to

$$q_i = \begin{cases} \bar{q}_i & \text{for } s \geq s_i^* [\text{valid only for} \\ & \qquad v_{I_{i+1}}(s, I_1, \ldots, I_n) - v_{I_i}(s, I_1, \ldots, I_n) - a_i \geq 0] \\ 0 & \text{otherwise} \end{cases} \tag{11.29}$$

$$q_n = \begin{cases} \bar{q}_n & \text{for } s \geq s_n^* [\text{valid only for } s - v_{I_n}(s, I_1, \ldots, I_n) - a_n \geq 0] \\ 0 & \text{otherwise} \end{cases} \tag{11.30}$$

With the above specification, a numerical solution of the multistage model can be implemented without too much complexity. We have successfully implemented a three-stage model using this formulation. This model makes a contribution to bridging the gap between theory and practice by presenting a model approach for multistage finite-resource investments where operational flexibility accounts for a sizable amount of investment value. More details and a brief description for the n-stage numerical algorithm are provided in Appendix B.

11.5 CONCLUSIONS

We have presented a natural-resource investment evaluation model that explicitly considers multistage production decisions, viewing investments as compound options. This model extends previous literature by incorporating multiple stages and allowing for finite resource and capacity output levels at each stage. We provided a numerical implementation of the two-stage model and determined the critical first-stage and second-stage prices that define the optimal operating policy, showing that the lower the remaining resources and the higher the intermediate inventory, the higher these critical prices. Optimal operating policy is also dependent on the natural-resource life cycle, inducing more first-stage production and inventory accumulation during the early years, and more second-stage production and inventory depletion as reserves decline.

Allowing for a richer operating policy as a response to variations in commodity prices, by permitting to determine independently in each stage whether to produce or not, may significantly increase investment value. Finally, the model is extended to n stages and suggestions are given on how it can be solved numerically.

Possible extensions include analyzing the effects of imposing limitations and/or costs on inventory levels. The model could easily accommodate storage costs as a function of the accumulated inventory state variable, I, and impose a finite inventory capacity restriction by considering an arbitrarily high cost of storage if accumulated inventories exceed a given amount. Other possible extensions include the addition of opening and closure costs for each production stage, and a more sophisticated risk-adjustment process for commodity prices. Although these extensions would add more complexity to the model, they should not alter our basic results.

Appendix A

Numerical Solution of the Two-Stage Model

The two-stage production and inventory model presented above can be solved using implicit finite-difference numerical methods, discretizing Eqs. (11.9), (11.10), and (11.11) for operating states $w(s, Q, I)$, $z(s, Q, I)$, and $v(s, Q, I)$, respectively. For illustration purposes, we only discretize Eq. (11.11) for $v(s, Q, I)$:

$$\frac{1}{2}\sigma^2 s^2 v_{ss} + (r - \kappa)sv_s - \bar{q}_1 v_Q + (\bar{q}_1 - \bar{q}_2)v_I$$

$$+ [\bar{q}_2(s - a_2) - \bar{q}_1 a_1] - rv = 0 \tag{11.A1}$$

$$v(s, Q, I) = v(i\Delta s, j\Delta Q, k\Delta I) \equiv v_{i,j,k} \tag{11.A2}$$

$$s = i\Delta s \qquad \text{for } i = 0\ldots N^s \tag{11.A3}$$

$$Q = j\Delta Q \qquad \text{for } j = 0\ldots N^Q \tag{11.A4}$$

$$I = k\Delta I \qquad \text{for } k = 0\ldots N^I \tag{11.A5}$$

where N^s, N^Q, N^I is the number of discretized intervals for state variables s, Q, and I, respectively. The discretization of these three state variables generates a three-dimensional grid corresponding to the domain of the function v. For numerical purposes, we assume that $N^Q = N^I$ and $\Delta Q = \Delta I$, thus $I_{\text{max}} = N^I \cdot \Delta I + N^Q \cdot \Delta Q$.[12]
We define the following derivatives:

$$v_s = \frac{v_{i+1,j,k} - v_{i-1,j,k}}{s\Delta s} \tag{11.A6}$$

$$v_{ss} = \frac{v_{i+1,j,k} - 2v_{i,j,k} + v_{i-1,j,k}}{(\Delta s)^2} \tag{11.A7}$$

$$v_I = \frac{v_{i,j,k} - v_{i,j,k-1}}{\Delta I} \tag{11.A8}$$

$$v_I - v_Q = \frac{v_{i,j-1,k+1} - v_{i,j,k}}{\Delta I} \tag{11.A9}$$

Replacing these discretized derivatives in Eq. (11.A1) and incorporating the boundary conditions for the price variable (s), we have N^s equations (one for each price step)

---

[12] I_{max} captures the addition of the initial available levels of reserves (Q) and inventory (I) and represents the maximum feasible level of inventory.

that relate the interior points of the grid. These equations may be written as the following tridiagonal system whose solution is the value of the investment for all possible prices at specific levels of reserves ($Q = j\Delta I$) and inventories ($I = k\Delta I$):

$$
\begin{bmatrix}
1 & & & & & & \\
\alpha_1 & \beta_2 & \gamma_1 & & & & \\
\vdots & \vdots & \vdots & & & & \\
& & \alpha_1 & \beta_2 & \gamma_1 & & \\
& & \vdots & \vdots & \vdots & & \\
& & & \alpha_{N^s-1} & \beta_{N^s-1} & \gamma_{N^s-1} & \\
& & & & \alpha_{N^s} - c_{N^s} & \beta_{N^s} - \gamma_{N^s}
\end{bmatrix}
\begin{bmatrix}
v_{0,j,k} \\
v_{1,j,k} \\
\vdots \\
v_{i,j,k} \\
\vdots \\
v_{N^s-1,j,k} \\
v_{N^s,j,k}
\end{bmatrix}
=
\begin{bmatrix}
0 \\
\delta_{1,j,k} \\
\vdots \\
\delta_{i,j,k} \\
\vdots \\
\delta_{N^s-1,j,k} \\
\delta_{N^s,j,k}
\end{bmatrix}
$$

where the coefficients α, β, γ, and δ are given by

$$\alpha_i = \frac{i}{2}[i\sigma^2 - (r - \kappa)] \tag{11.A10}$$

$$\beta_i = -i^2\sigma^2 - \frac{\overline{q}_1}{\Delta I} - \frac{\overline{q}_2}{\Delta I} - r \tag{11.A11}$$

$$\gamma_i = \frac{i}{2}[i\sigma^2 + (r - \kappa)] \tag{11.A12}$$

$$\delta_{i,j,k} = -\frac{\overline{q}_1}{\Delta Q}v_{i,j-1,k+1} - \frac{\overline{q}_2}{\Delta I}v_{i,j,k-1} - [\overline{q}_2(i\Delta s - a_2) - \overline{q}_1 a_1] \tag{11.A13}$$

Although δ depends on the value of v, when we solve for $v_{i,j,k}$ we already know the values of the investment at $v_{i,j-1,k+1}$ and $v_{i,j,k-1}$. To determine the optimal production policy, we simultaneously solve the four tridiagonal systems that represent the possible operating states and choose the maximum value for each step of s. The steps of the numerical solution can be summarized as follows:

Appendix B

An Overview of the Numerical Solution for the n-Stage Model

To illustrate how to numerically solve the n-stage model we present the solution algorithm for the three-stage model. Extensions to higher-order models are possible by extrapolating the procedure explained here.

Just as in the two-stage model, the numerical solution of the three-stage model is obtained using implicit finite-difference numerical methods. Having a natural-resource investment with three stages implies that there are eight possible operating states, obtained by considering that at each stage i we can either wait ($q_i = 0$) or produce at full capacity ($q_i = \overline{q}_i$).

First, we solve the grid for all levels of inventories assuming that $Q = 0$. As the picture to the right shows, we use the boundary condition for $Q = 0$ to solve from $I = 0$ to $I = I_{max}$; we continue with the next grid in $Q = \Delta I$, again from $I = 0$, but this time to $I = I_{max} - \Delta I$. The arrows show the values we need to know when we are solving for the value $v_{i,j,k}$.

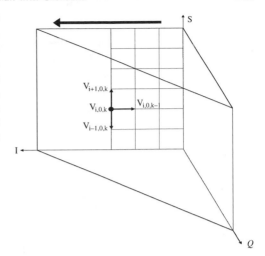

After we have solved the grid for a certain level of reserves, $Q = j\Delta I$, we call the boundary condition for the inventory ($I = 0$), using information from known points in the grid.

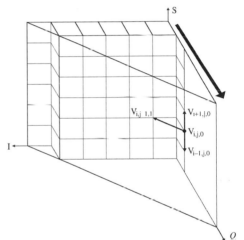

For interior points, we use the tridiagonal system shown above. To conclude the solution, we continue iterating until we complete the three-dimensional grid.

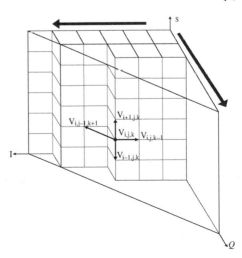

The value of the investment, $v(s, I_1, I_2, I_3)$, depends on the price of the output commodity, s, and on each of the three inventories. For numerical purposes, the discretization of the four state variables generates a four-dimensional grid corresponding to the domain of the function v. We discretize each one of the equations that represent the eight operation states, just as we did for the two-stage model. By discretizing the derivatives and considering a specific level of the three inventories, we obtain a tridiagonal system whose solution is the value of the investment for each discrete output price. To maximize the value of the natural resource, it is necessary to consider the highest value of all the operating states.

To determine the value of the entire grid, we start iterating assuming the first inventory is zero ($I_1 = 0$). The value of the investment at this point is equal to that of the two-stage model since setting $I_1 = 0$ is similar to assuming that only the last two stages of the three-stage model can operate. After we have solved the grid for $I_1 = 0$, the next step is to proceed with $I_1 = \Delta I$. We continue the iteration process for different levels of inventories in I_1 until we complete the four-dimensional grid, giving the value of the multistage investment.

11.6 ACKNOWLEDGMENTS

This research has been supported by FONDECYT, FONDEF, CODELCO, and ENAP. The authors would like to thank Eduardo Schwartz, Michael Brennan, an anonymous referee, and participants at the Conference *Real Options: Theory Meets Practice*, June 12–13, 1997, New York, for helpful comments.

REFERENCES

Brennan, M. J., and E. S. Schwartz. (1985). Evaluating Natural Resource Investments. *Journal of Business* 58(2), 135–157.

Cortazar, G., and E. S. Schwartz. (1993). A Compound Option Model of Production and Intermediate Inventories. *Journal of Business* 66(4), 517–540.

Cortazar, G., E. S. Schwartz, and M. Salinas. (1998). Evaluating Environmental Investments: A Real Options Approach. *Management Science*, 44(8), 1059–1070.

Dasu, S., and L. Li. (1997). Optimal Operating Policy in the Presence of Exchange Rate Variability. *Management Science* 43(5), 705–722.

Dixit, A. (1989). Entry and Exit Decisions Under Uncertainty. *Journal of Political Economy* 97(3), 620–638.

Dixit, A., and R. Pindyck. (1994). *Investment Under Uncertainty*. Princeton, NJ: Princeton University Press.

Ekern, S. (1988). An Option Pricing Approach to Evaluating Petroleum Projects. *Energy Economics* 10(April), 91–99.

He, H., and R. Pindyck. (1992). Investment in Flexible Production Capacity. *Journal of Economic Dynamics and Control* 16(3), 575–599.

Kogut, B., and N. Kulatilaka. (1994). Operating Flexibility, Global Manufacturing, and the Option Value of a Multinational Network. *Management Science* 40(1), 123–139.

Majd, S., and R. Pindyck. (1987). Time to Build, Option Value, and Investment Decisions. *Journal of Financial Economics* 18(1), 7–27.

Majd, S., and R. Plidyck. (1989) The Learning Curve and Optimal Decisions Under Uncertainty. *Rand Journal of Economics* 20(3), 331–343.

McDonald, R., and D. Siegel. (1986). The Value of Waiting to Invest. *Quarterly Journal of Economics* 101(4), 707–727.

Paddock, J., D. Siegel, and J. Smith. (1988). Option Valuation of Claims on Physical Assets: The Case of Offshore Petroleum Leases. *Quarterly Journal of Economics* 103(3), 479–508.

Pindyck, R. (1993). Investments of Uncertain Cost. *Journal of Financial Economics* 34(1), 53–76.

Trigeorgis, L. (1993). Real Options and Interactions with Financial Flexibility. *Financial Management* 22(3), 202–224.

Trigeorgis, L. (1996). *Real Options: Managerial Flexibility and Strategy in Resource Allocation*. Cambridge, MA: The MIT Press.

12

Optimal Extraction of Nonrenewable Resources When Costs Cumulate

JOSEPH A. CHERIAN

JAY PATEL

ILYA KHRIPKO

Recent advances have considerably improved the prescriptions for the extraction of resources. The classic analyses, going back to Hotelling (1931), assumed price certainty with the emphasis on increasing marginal costs. Recent work has addressed the uncertainty in resource prices, but assumed a constant marginal cost of extraction. We frame and solve the nonrenewable resource extraction problem (in the context of a typical mine) that jointly accounts for price uncertainty as well as the dependence of extraction costs on the cumulative amount extracted and the extraction rate. We find that ignoring cumulating costs when determining extraction policy can lead to significant loss of value. We also establish the general tools to pursue, for instance, the optimal taxation policy of the natural resource sector.

12.1 INTRODUCTION

Prices of nonrenewable resources (such as copper, petroleum, and zinc) are highly uncertain: standard deviations of annual growth rates in mineral prices during the past three decades range from 10 to 25%, which is comparable to the volatility of equity returns. Mining-dependent countries often find their national well-being at risk. During the early 1980s, for example, their natural resource sectors experienced large unforeseen declines in the real prices at which they could sell their output. The unfortunate declines in real mineral prices, compounded by inadequate risk management, led to significant fiscal and social crises.

The literature on the efficient extraction of natural resources (and related public policy issues such as optimal taxation) explicitly began addressing the stochastic nature of mineral prices in the wake of the price shocks in the early 1970s (e.g., see Weinstein and Zeckhauser, 1975; Lewis, 1977; Pindyck, 1981; Brennan and

Schwartz, 1985). However, in the solutions proposed in this work, a constant marginal cost of extraction was assumed for tractability. Such solutions may not be robust in practice since they ignore the actual experience in many mine settings where marginal costs increase significantly with cumulative extraction (hereafter cumulating costs). Indeed, the classic extraction literature based on deterministic prices incorporated cumulating costs—see Hotelling (1931), Burness (1976), Conrad and Hool (1981). We take up the challenge to jointly account for the two empirically important characteristics of stochastic prices and cumulating costs in developing an optimal extraction program. Assuming a complete market setting, we cast the optimal extraction problem as a two-state stochastic control problem in the spirit of Brennan and Schwartz (1985). Our model is similar to the model with learning (where costs decline with production) developed by Majd and Pindyck (1989).[1] However, the distinct features of our setting include a finite project life and the dependence of marginal costs on the instantaneous production rate. The solution of the control problem provides insights into the importance of cost cumulation for optimal extraction.

The paper is organized as follows. Section 12.2 discusses the importance of stochastic prices and cumulating costs for resource extraction. The optimal control problem is formulated in Section 12.3 using the valuation method developed in Appendix A. Section 12.4 examines general properties of the solution, while Section 12.5 presents an example with a numerical solution to offer intuition into the results. Section 12.6 concludes.

12.2 STOCHASTIC PRICES AND CUMULATING COSTS

We begin by reviewing the stochastic nature of mineral prices in practice. Consider oil and the eight other important minerals produced by developing countries: zinc, iron, copper, silver, phosphates, manganese, nickel, and tin.[2] Figure 12.1 traces the time-series paths of their prices over the past 40 years.[3] Any presumption of known prices for typical mining lease-life horizons of 5–15 years appears grossly inappropriate. Figure 12.1 clearly underscores the fact that an optimal extraction policy needs to account for uncertain resource prices.

We next consider the mining cost function, which encompasses economic and geological factors.[4] Before making any significant initial investment, a rational mining

---

[1] Also see Dixit and Pindyck (1994, Chapter 10).

[2] Three other important minerals, bauxite, diamonds, and gold, are not included in our empirical examination for the following reasons: reliable bauxite prices are available only since 1965; diamond sales are controlled by the De Beers cartel, which precludes reliable market prices; gold prices were pegged till the early 1970s under the Bretton Woods agreement of a fixed exchange rate system. Also, gold is not a pure commodity but is held by many investors as an inflation hedge.

[3] The average annual nominal prices in U.S. dollars (f.o.b.) are obtained from the International Financial Statistics Yearbooks of the International Monetary Fund.

[4] The following discussion draws extensively on Shukla (1992).

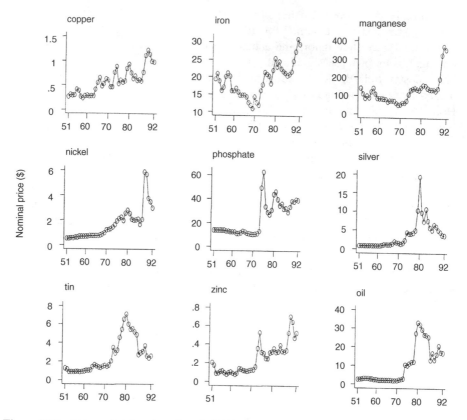

Figure 12.1   Prices of eight minerals and oil (1951–1992). The average annual nominal prices in U.S. dollars (f.o.b.) are obtained from the International Financial Statistics Yearbooks of the International Monetary Fund.

operator makes preliminary evaluations to assess the deposit size and its grade configuration in order to optimize the equipment and engineering approach. Then an initial capital investment (usually a significant multiple of the subsequent annual extraction costs) determines the scale of extraction costs. We assume that the exploratory and initial investment costs have already been made (i.e., are sunk costs), and focus on the costs related to the levels of actual extractions of an operating mine.

Unprocessed ore is rarely sold in the world market. Some processing is typically carried out by the mining firm before selling to a customer. However, information on cost functions is not generally available by stages of production. We, therefore, model a single cost function that covers both the extraction and processing stages. Slade (1984) discusses this common practice in resource economics.

If the resource body is in the form of a loose unconsolidated deposit such as alluvial gravel or mineral sands, surface mining techniques are employed to extract the mineral. In this case, the operating cost depends only on the quantity of ore extracted in a period, and not on the cumulated amount extracted to date. In this particular case, the cost function exhibits constant marginal costs and the approach of the stochastic price literature heretofore proves adequate.

However, in many common cases where the ore deposit is large, mining has to extend downward and outward such that costs rise with the amount extracted to date. With pit mining techniques, which are the most common for this type of ore body, more and more dirt has to be removed to get to the ore. The stripping ratio increases with the depth of the ore body, and the marginal cost increases with the rate of extraction and with the amount of ore extracted to date (cumulation).

A similar dependency on cumulated extraction arises with ore bodies that have significant vertical dimensions, and where underground metalliferous (vein) or bedded mining techniques have to be employed. In such cases, a good deal of underground development and techniques such as stoping and room and pillar have to be employed, and the cumulation effect becomes substantial.

Although we ignore the complication of heterogeneous ore grades in the mine, under some simplifying assumptions this issue can be made isomorphic to that of cumulating costs.[5] Briefly, with heterogeneous ore grades in the mine but with marginal costs independent of the grade being extracted, optimal grade selection by the miner under constant refined ore prices (or stochastic prices with zero drift) implies that the highest available quality of ore will be mined first. Thus, the extraction problem with heterogeneous grades becomes equivalent to one with homogeneous grades by an adjustment of the marginal cost's dependency on cumulated extraction.

A model from which the extraction policy can be obtained should, therefore, incorporate the stochastic behavior of mineral prices and the explicit dependence of extraction costs on the amount of resource extracted. Such a model is developed in the next section.

12.3 THE OPTIMAL EXTRACTION PROBLEM

Consider a prototypical mining firm, such as a multinational corporation (MNC) that maximizes the value of its equity and has a fixed-period mining lease. The mine is in operation with startup capital already invested (sunk), and will revert to the government at the lease expiration. The MNC holds no inventory of the extracted ore[6] and sells the mine's output in the spot market at an exogenous world price (i.e., the MNC is a price taker).[7]

Assuming that the mining project has no strategic dependencies with other projects, the MNC chooses the extraction policy to maximize the value of the cash flows (or profits) from ore sales over the life of the lease. Our objective is to find the

[5] See Solow and Wan (1976) or Levhari and Liviatan (1977).

[6] For optimal extraction of a firm that maintains inventory in multiple stages see Cortazar and Casassus (this volume).

[7] The copper industry was once an oligopoly, but it has become much less concentrated and is now considered to be competitive—see Foley and Clark (1982). Today, with the exception of diamonds, world prices of most minerals that are major products of developing countries can be reasonably considered exogenous to MNC's extraction decisions.

optimal extraction policy and to compute the optimal value of the lease, given the following empirically observed features:

1. Commodity prices are stochastic.
2. The extraction costs increase with cumulated resource extracted (i.e., the cost function is decreasing in the amount of remaining resource).
3. The marginal costs depend on the extraction rate.
4. The amount of resource available and the lease duration are finite.

The above MNC's extraction problem can be interpreted as a stochastic optimal control problem with a finite horizon and two state variables: the resource price, P, and the quantity of the resource remaining in the mine, Q. To formulate such a problem we need an appropriate valuation technique that would express the lease value in an expected-value form. We obtain such a representation using the general arbitrage valuation scheme for assets with cash flows contingent on commodity prices. The valuation scheme is developed in Appendix A. Briefly, we assume the existence of a futures contract on the resource (or other type of resource-linked security). The resource price process P is assumed to be adapted to the filtration generated by the futures price process, which means that the current value of P (and other adapted processes) can be determined from the history of the futures price. This allows the cash flows to be replicated by trading in the futures. The details are provided in Appendix A.

The control variable is the extraction rate, q, which can be varied between 0 and a maximum rate $\bar{q}$. To focus on the effects of the (numbered) features above, we ignore issues such as taxes, switching costs, and the risk of expropriation.[8] The initial available resource in the mine, Q_0, and the extraction cost function, $C(t, Q, q)$, which depends on time, the resource remaining, and the rate of extraction, are assumed to be known.

Let T denote the lease expiration date (which is less or equal to the expiration date of the security). For an initial resource $Q_0 > 0$ and an adapted extraction process q with values in $[0, \bar{q}]$ the adapted process for the resource Q is given by

$$Q_t = Q_0 - \int_0^t q_s \, ds \qquad (12.1)$$

The control problem terminates at time τ when the total resource is exhausted or the lease expires:

$$\tau = \min \left(t \in [0, T] : Q_t = 0 \text{ or } t = T \right)$$

Since all processes are considered only up to time τ, all the assumptions, including those about the existence of a futures contract and about the state dynamics, effectively need to be made only for $t \leq \tau$. For large or infinite T, some of the assumptions may

---

[8] Taxes can be easily incorporated. The switching costs between a closed mine ($q = 0$) and an open mine ($q > 0$) and the possibility of expropriation can also be modeled but would require a more complicated control theory setup.

become unrealistic if considered up to T, but remain reasonable if τ^*, the termination time corresponding to the optimal control, is "small."

The lease provides a stream of cash flows (or profits) at the rate

$$g(t, P_t, Q_t, q_t) = P_t q_t - C(t, Q_t, q_t), \qquad t \le \tau$$

where the (measurable) cost function $C(\cdot)$ gives the cost of extraction per unit time. For $t > \tau$ the lease has zero value. Since processes P, Q, and q are adapted and $C(\cdot)$ is measurable, the profit flow is also adapted. Hence, from Appendix A, the unique arbitrage-free value of the lease at time t under control process q is

$$V_t^q = \widetilde{E}_t \left[\int_t^\tau e^{-r(s-t)} g(s, P_s, Q_s, q_s) \, ds \right] \tag{12.2}$$

Although an optimal control problem could be formulated using such adapted q and V^q, the problem would be very hard to analyze because of the nontrivial dependence of q and V on the history of the state processes. To apply standard optimal control theory based on dynamic programming, we have to restrict our attention to state processes with Markov dynamics. In particular, we need the state process of the control problem to be a (Markov) diffusion under the equivalent martingale measure, $\widetilde{P}$. As discussed in Appendix A, there are two ways to proceed. The first approach, which provides a general formulation within a Markov setting, requires an expansion of the state process (both P and the futures price, F, have to be included as state variables of the control problem) as well as an explicit specification of the drift and diffusion functions for P and F.

The second approach, used here, is to include only P in the state process, and to assume that P by itself is a known diffusion under $\widetilde{P}$. It should be kept in mind, though, that a specific functional relation between the spot and futures prices is implicitly assumed under this formulation—see the Proposition in Appendix A. Let P be a strong solution of the stochastic differential equation

$$dP_t = \widetilde{\mu}(t, P_t) \, dt + \sigma(t, P_t) \, d\widetilde{W}_t, \qquad P_0 > 0 \tag{12.3}$$

where $\widetilde{W}$ is a standard Brownian motion under $\widetilde{P}$, and the drift and diffusion functions $\widetilde{\mu}(\cdot)$ and $\sigma(\cdot)$ are such that the solution is unique in probability law.[9]

A *Markov* (feedback) control is a measurable function $\mathbf{q}(t, P, Q) : [0, T] \times \mathbb{R} \times \mathbb{R}_+ \to [0, \overline{q}]$. For a Markov control $\mathbf{q}(\cdot)$ the resource process Q is a solution of the integral equation

$$Q_t = Q_0 - \int_0^t \mathbf{q}(s, P_s, Q_s) \, ds$$

To ensure that Q is well defined, we restrict our attention to the set of *admissible* controls $\mathbf{U}$ that consists of Markov controls for which, given any $Q_0 > 0$, the above

---

[9] Although the existense of a *weak* solution is usually sufficient for control problems not involving valuation, here the existense of a *strong* solution is important since P must be adapted to the given filtration.

equation has a unique solution for almost all paths of P. Thus, for an admissible control, the joint stochastic differential equation for (P, Q) has a strong solution unique in probability law.[10] Since the equation for Q has no Brownian motion term, it remains unchanged under the change of measure. However, the distribution of Q under the new measure is generally different from that under the original measure because Q depends on P through the control $\mathbf{q}$.

For an admissible control $\mathbf{q}$, both the state process (P, Q) and the profit flow with $q_t = \mathbf{q}(t, P_t, Q_t)$ are adapted, and as before, the value of the lease under control $\mathbf{q}$ at time t is

$$V_t^{\mathbf{q}} = \tilde{E}_t \left[\int_t^{\tau} e^{-r(s-t)} g[s, P_s, Q_s, \mathbf{q}(s, P_s, Q_s)] \, ds \right]$$

However, when an admissible control $\mathbf{q}$ is applied, the state process (P, Q) is Markov under $\tilde{\mathbf{P}}$, and the profit flow is a function of time and the current state. Therefore, $V_t^{\mathbf{q}}$ can be expressed as a function of time and the current state only:

$$V_t^{\mathbf{q}} = V^{\mathbf{q}}(t, P_t, Q_t)$$

$$V^{\mathbf{q}}(t, P, Q) = \tilde{E} \left[\int_t^{\tau} e^{-r(s-t)} g\left[s, P_s, Q_s, \mathbf{q}(s, P_s, Q_s)\right] ds \mid P_t = P, Q_t = Q \right]$$

The *optimal value function*, giving the maximum value of the lease, is obtained by taking the supremum over all admissible controls:

$$V(t, P, Q) = \sup_{\mathbf{q} \in U} V^{\mathbf{q}}(t, P, Q)$$

An admissible control $\mathbf{q}^*$ is *optimal* if $V^{\mathbf{q}^*}(t, P, Q) = V(t, P, Q)$ for all t, P, and Q.

12.4 PROPERTIES OF THE SOLUTION

In this section we explore the general properties of the optimal lease value function V and the optimal extraction policy $\mathbf{q}^*$. To better understand the characteristics of the optimal policy, we also study two simple suboptimal strategies: the maximum-extraction strategy $\bar{\mathbf{q}}$ that always extracts at the maximum possible rate, and a "myopic" strategy $\hat{\mathbf{q}}$ that ignores interdependencies between periods. Specifically,

$$\bar{\mathbf{q}}(t, P, Q) \equiv \bar{q}, \qquad \hat{\mathbf{q}}(t, P, Q) \in \arg\max_{[0, \bar{q}]} g(t, P, Q, q)$$

Many mining firms in practice appear to actually pursue such strategies.[11] If the resource is large enough so that $\tau = T$ and costs do not cumulate [i.e., $C(t, Q, q) =$

---

[10] We use standard terminology where the solution of a stochastic *differential* equation must in fact satisfy the corresponding *integral* equation. In our context the distinction is important since the integral equation for Q may have a solution when the corresponding differential equation does not. Such situations are typical for discontinuous controls $\mathbf{q}$ that are often of interest.

[11] From conversations with two owner-operators of mines, one in each of two developing countries (Guyana and India), a myopic strategy of maximizing instantaneous profits appears to be followed.

$C(t, q)$ for all possible values of Q], a myopic strategy is optimal and $V \equiv V^{\widehat{q}}$.[12] For our purposes, $\overline{\mathbf{q}}$ and $\widehat{\mathbf{q}}$ provide convenient benchmarks for the optimal performance and they help to understand the relative importance of optimal extraction for different values of t, P, and Q.

For a given admissible control $\mathbf{q}$, the corresponding value function $V^{\mathbf{q}}(\cdot)$ can be found, in certain cases explicitly, with probabilistic or analytical techniques. The probabilistic method directly uses the definition of the value function as an expected value, while the analytical method consists of solving the linear partial differential equation (PDE) which must be satisfied by $V^{\mathbf{q}}(t, P, Q)$.[13] We use the probabilistic method to characterize $V^{\overline{q}}(t, P, Q)$. Computing $V^{\widehat{q}}(t, P, Q)$ is more difficult, and an explicit expression rarely can be found.

When the control does not depend on P, the dynamics of Q is deterministic. In particular, under $\overline{q}$, $Q_s = Q_t - \overline{q}(s-t)$ and $\tau = \min\{t + Q_t/\overline{q}, T\}$ for any $t \leq s \leq \tau$. Thus $\overline{\mathbf{q}}$ is always admissible. Changing the order of integration (Fubini theorem),

$$V^{\overline{q}}(t, P, Q) = \widetilde{E}_{t,P,Q}\left[\int_t^\tau e^{-r(s-t)}[P_s\overline{q} - C(s, Q_s, \overline{q})]\,ds\right] \tag{12.4}$$

$$= \int_t^{\min\{t+Q/\overline{q},T\}} e^{-r(s-t)}\left\{m(t, s, P)\overline{q} - C[s, Q - \overline{q}(s-t), \overline{q}]\right\}ds$$

where $\widetilde{E}_{t,P,Q}$ is the expectation under $\widetilde{P}$ given $P_t = P$ and $Q_t = Q$, and $m(t, s, P) \equiv \widetilde{E}_{t,P}(P_s)$ is the expectation of P_s under $\widetilde{P}$ given $P_t = P$. The form of the dependence of $V^{\overline{q}}$ on P is determined by $m(\cdot)$ [which in turn is set by the drift and diffusion functions $\widetilde{\mu}(\cdot)$ and $\sigma(\cdot)$], while $C(\cdot)$ determines the dependence of $V^{\overline{q}}$ on Q. The min in the upper limit of integration makes $V^{\overline{q}}$ a nonlinear, nondifferentiable function of t and Q.

Example 1 (Linear drift). *If $\widetilde{\mu}(\cdot)$ is linear in P, then both $m(\cdot)$ and $V^{\overline{q}}(\cdot)$ do not depend on $\sigma(\cdot)$ and are also linear in P. Let $\widetilde{\mu}(t, P) = \mu_0(t) + \mu_1(t)P$. Then the expected price is given by*

$$m(t, s, P) = m_0(t, s) + m_1(t, s)P$$

where $m_1(t, s) = \exp\left[\int_t^s \mu_1(v)\,dv\right]$ and $m_0(t, s) = \int_t^s m_1(u, s)\mu_0(u)\,du$. The lease value for the maximum-extraction strategy becomes

$$V^{\overline{q}}(t, P, Q) = W_0(t, Q) + W_1(t, Q)P$$

where

$$W_0(t, Q) = \int_t^{\min\{t+Q/\overline{q},T\}} e^{-r(s-t)}\{m_0(t, s)\overline{q} - C[s, Q - \overline{q}(s-t), \overline{q}]\}\,ds$$

and

---

[12] In this case Q is not a relevant state variable and the state process, P, is unaffected by control.

[13] The PDE for $V^{\mathbf{q}}$ has the same form as the Bellman equation (12.5) below, but with $q = \mathbf{q}(t, P, Q)$ instead of the maximization with respect to q. In general, $V^{\mathbf{q}}$ satisfies such a PDE only under strong regularity conditions, including the continuity of $\mathbf{q}(\cdot)$.

$$W_1(t, Q) = \overline{q} \int_t^{\min(t+Q/\overline{q},T)} e^{-r(s-t)} m_1(t, s) \, ds$$

$V^{\overline{q}}$ is the same for any Ito process P with linear drift, even if the diffusion coefficient is path dependent or identically equal to zero (deterministic dynamics for P). However, this is true only when the control does not depend on P, and $\widetilde{\mu}(\cdot)$ is linear in P. For example, if P is modeled under $\widehat{\mathbf{P}}$ as a geometric Ornstein–Uhlenbeck process, such as in Schwartz (1997), then both $\widetilde{\mu}(\cdot)$ and $V^{\overline{q}}$ are nonlinear in P. Since under quite general conditions V converges to $V^{\overline{q}}$ as P increases, in such a model the optimal value function will not have a linear asymptote.

The limiting cases in which either the resource or the time-horizon is infinite (the latter representing a perpetual lease or ownership of the mine) have already been considered in the literature. Under certain conditions the arbitrage valuation procedure can be justified even when $T = \infty$, and the value functions in such limiting problems are generally finite so that the problems are well defined. However, in the case where both Q and T are infinite, $V^{\overline{q}}$ and V can also become infinite for some choices of $\widetilde{\mu}(\cdot)$.

To provide a general characterization of the solution, we make certain reasonable assumptions about the functions $\widetilde{\mu}(t, P)$, $\sigma(t, P)$, and $C(t, Q, q)$, namely:

- $\widetilde{\mu}(t, 0) = \sigma(t, 0) \equiv 0$ (i.e., the process P is absorbed at zero); $\widetilde{\mu}(t, P) < rP$ [i.e., the term structure of futures prices $F_t(T)$ lies under the curve $P_t e^{r(T-t)}$][14] and $\widetilde{\mu}, \sigma \in C^1$ with bounded first-order partial derivatives on $[0, T] \times (0, \infty)$.
- $C(t, Q, 0) \equiv 0$ (i.e., zero output results in zero costs, for convenience); C is continuous, positive, and decreasing in Q on $[0, T] \times [0, \infty) \times [0, \overline{q}]$.[15]

Under these assumptions, there exists an admissible myopic strategy $\widehat{\mathbf{q}}$. All admissible myopic strategies have the same value function $V^{\overline{q}}$ so that $V^{\overline{q}}$ is well defined. If $C(\cdot)$ is strictly convex in q, then $\widehat{\mathbf{q}}$ is unique and continuous. The solution $(V, \mathbf{q}^*)$ exhibits a number of interesting general properties for $(t, P, Q) \in [0, T] \times [0, \infty) \times [0, \infty]$. These properties are presented below along with certain features of $(V^{\overline{q}}, \overline{\mathbf{q}})$ and $(V^{\widehat{q}}, \widehat{\mathbf{q}})$ that help to understand the behavior of the optimal solution $(V, \mathbf{q}^*)$.

1. $\max\{V^{\overline{q}}, 0\} \leq V^{\widehat{q}} \leq V$.[16] This relationship can be interpreted in terms of the intrinsic value and the prices of different baskets of options. In fact, the lease under

---

[14] Except for rare instances, this assumption is supported empirically. It ensures that optimal extraction increases with price. When the assumption does not hold, a high price may create an incentive to wait for even higher price, and the optimal extraction policy is not monotone in price.

[15] Terms such as positive and decreasing are used in the weak sense, i.e., $C \geq 0$, and $Q_1 \geq Q_2$ implies $C(Q_1) \leq C(Q_2)$.

[16] In our setup the cash flows from an optimal or myopic strategy are always nonnegative. The maximum-extraction policy, however, will produce negative cash flows for low values

$\bar{q}$ is essentially a sequence of commodity forward contracts (i.e., a commodity swap) that requires at period $t \leq \min\{Q_0/\bar{q}, T\}$ to buy $\bar{q}$ units of the commodity at cost $C(t, Q_0 - \bar{q}t, \bar{q})$.

Myopic or optimal extraction can be understood as if the lease represents a basket of commodity options with different expiration dates.[17] Exercise of the currently expiring option affects the exercise prices and number of remaining options. In the case of a myopic policy, the exercise decision is based only on the current payoff as if there were no intertemporal dependencies between options, whereas optimal extraction takes into account the fact that the lease offers a set of interdependent options.

2. V is strictly increasing in $T - t$ (for $P, Q > 0$). $V(T, P, Q) \equiv 0$, and as $T - t$ goes to zero, V becomes asymptotically equivalent to $V^{\hat{q}}$:

$$\forall P, Q: \quad V(t, P, Q) / \widehat{V^q}(t, P, Q) \underset{t \to T}{\longrightarrow} 1$$

Thus, as the lease expiration approaches, the gain from employing an optimal policy instead of a myopic one goes to zero both in absolute and in relative terms.

As $T - t$ goes to infinity, under certain regularity conditions in the time dependence of $\tilde{\mu}(\cdot), \sigma(\cdot)$, and $C(\cdot)$ [e.g., $\tilde{\mu}(\cdot)$ and $\sigma(\cdot)$ are time invariant and $C(t, Q, q) = e^{\pi t}C(Q, q)$ for a constant inflation rate π], V converges to a finite value, which proves to be the optimal value function of the infinite horizon problem representing the value of owning the mine.

3. V is strictly increasing and convex in P (for $t < T, Q > 0$); $V(t, 0, Q) \equiv 0$. As P goes to infinity, V grows without bound and becomes asymptotically identical to the value function of the maximum-extraction strategy:

$$\forall t, Q: \quad V(t, P, Q) \underset{P \to \infty}{\longrightarrow} \infty$$

$$V(t, P, Q) - V^{\bar{q}}(t, P, Q) \underset{P \to \infty}{\longrightarrow} 0$$

Since $V^{\bar{q}} \leq V^{\hat{q}} \leq V$, asymptotically all three value functions coincide. Thus, for large P little is lost by adopting $\bar{q}$ or $\hat{q}$ permanently until τ, instead of pursuing an optimal policy.

4. V is increasing in Q; $V(t, P, 0) \equiv 0$. V increases in Q for two reasons: a larger resource allows a potentially longer stream of profits and, at the same time,

---

of P. Note that $V^{\hat{q}} \geq V^{\bar{q}}$ does not follow simply from the instantaneously optimizing nature of $\hat{q}$. If the cost function was increasing in Q for some values of the arguments, the maximum-extraction policy could become superior to a myopic one.

[17] Since both P and Q are stochastically evolving, these are not pure call or put options, but rather options to exchange two assets. In each period $t \leq \tau$, there is an option to exchange $q \in [0, \bar{q}]$ units of one asset with total price $C(t, Q_t, q)$ for the same quantity of another asset with total price $P_t q$.

provides lower costs of extraction. As Q goes to infinity, V converges to a finite value, the optimal value function for the infinite resource problem:

$$\forall\, t, P : \quad V(t, P, Q) \xrightarrow[Q \to \infty]{} V(t, P, \infty)$$

For $Q = \infty$, the optimal and myopic policies coincide, and $V(t, P, \infty) \equiv V^{\widehat{q}}(t, P, \infty)$. Thus, V is asymptotically identical to $V^{\widehat{q}}$. When Q is large, a permanent switch to $\widehat{\mathbf{q}}$ would capture most of the value.

Properties 3 and 4 above demonstrate that the absolute gain from optimal extraction versus a myopic one, $V - V^{\widehat{q}}$, vanishes both for very large and for very small P and Q, and therefore achieves its maximum at intermediate values of P and Q. The relative gain, $(V - V^{\widehat{q}})/V^{\widehat{q}}$, decreases to zero as P and Q grow to infinity, but does not vanish as P and Q decrease to zero. In fact, the relative gain monotonically decreases in Q, and is the highest for small values of Q.

5. V is absolutely continuous. The partial derivatives V_t, V_P, V_Q exist almost everywhere. V is bounded in t and Q, and satisfies a linear growth condition in P. In particular, $V(t, P, Q) \le MP$ for a constant M.

6. There exists an optimal policy $\mathbf{q}^*$. All optimal and myopic policies satisfy

$$\mathbf{q}^*(t, P, Q) \in \arg \max_{q \in [0, \bar{q}]} \left[qP - C(t, Q, q) - q\, V_Q(t, P, Q) \right]$$

$$\mathbf{q}^*(t, P, Q) \le \widehat{\mathbf{q}}(t, P, Q)$$

$$\mathbf{q}^*(t, P, Q) - \widehat{\mathbf{q}}(t, P, Q) \xrightarrow[t \to T]{} 0$$

$$\mathbf{q}^*(t, P, Q) - \widehat{\mathbf{q}}(t, P, Q) \xrightarrow[Q \to \infty]{} 0$$

$$P > \overline{P} \;\rightarrow\; \mathbf{q}^*(t, P, Q) = \widehat{\mathbf{q}}(t, P, Q) = \bar{q}$$

for almost all t, P, and Q, and some $\overline{P} < \infty$.

A myopic policy fails to account for the value-reducing effects of current extraction: an increase in future costs and a reduction of the available resource. This leads to overextraction relative to an optimal policy. When the lease expiration is very close or the resource is very large, those effects (represented by V_Q) become negligible so that $\mathbf{q}^*$ and $\widehat{\mathbf{q}}$ converge. On the other hand, when the commodity price is sufficiently large, the maximum extraction rate is selected both under optimal and myopic extraction.

7. V is increasing in $\tilde{\mu}$ and σ, and decreasing in C:

$$\tilde{\mu}_1 \le \tilde{\mu}_2, \quad \sigma_1 \le \sigma_2, \quad C_1 \ge C_2 \;\Longrightarrow\; V_1 \le V_2$$

The dependence of V on $\tilde{\mu}$ and C is quite trivial, while its dependence on σ is less obvious and more important. It corresponds to the general property of options to increase in value when the volatility of the underlying assets increases.

Although most of these properties are quite intuitive, the proofs for some of them under the general assumptions of this section are quite complicated. Note that there is no monotone relation between the time left $\tau - t$ and the gains from optimal extraction. An increase in $\tau - t$ due to a change in $T - t$ when Q is held fixed makes both absolute and relative gains larger. But a similar increase in $\tau - t$ due to a change in Q when $T - t$ is held fixed lowers the relative gain, while its effect on the absolute gain is ambiguous.[18]

We conclude this section with a discussion of the relation between the optimal value function and the Bellman equation. In the present case of optimal control of diffusion processes, the Bellman equation is a second-order nonlinear PDE. In our problem it takes the following form:

$$
\begin{aligned}
& V_t + \widetilde{\mu}(t, P)V_P + \frac{1}{2}\sigma^2(t, P)V_{PP} \\
& + \sup_{q \in [0, \bar{q}]} \left[qP - C(t, Q, q) - qV_Q \right] - rV = 0
\end{aligned}
\tag{12.5}
$$

The *verification theorem* of optimal control theory states that if a function $V(t, P, Q)$ of class $C^{1,2,2}$ solves the Bellman equation (with the appropriate boundary conditions) and satisfies a polynomial growth condition, then it is the optimal value function. Further, if given such a function there is an admissible policy $\mathbf{q}^*$ that performs the maximization in the Bellman equation, then $\mathbf{q}^*$ is an optimal control.[19] Thus, a smooth solution of the Bellman equation is a sufficient condition for the optimal value function and optimal control policy.

The verification theorem is useful when one can obtain an analytical solution of the Bellman PDE, or the existence of a smooth solution can be shown. Unfortunately, in our case neither result is available even with the simplest choice of $\widetilde{\mu}(\cdot)$, $\sigma(\cdot)$, and $C(\cdot)$. When there are binding constraints on the allowable control values and the state process is controlled, the Bellman equation effectively becomes a system of nonlinear PDEs with free boundaries between the domains. It is very unlikely that such a system can be solved analytically.[20] Our problem is an example of such a situation, since the control variable q is naturally constrained to be nonnegative and a component of the state process, Q, is controlled. On the other hand, in continuous-time problems the optimal value function is not necessarily a solution of the Bellman equation, at least in the classical sense.[21] The value function may have nondifferentiable "kinks" and the Bellman PDE may have no smooth solution. This is typical for problems like ours, where the state process includes degenerate diffusions with no Brownian motion term.

---

[18] In the infinite horizon problem, such as the one treated by Brennan and Schwartz (1985), the value function does not depend on t, and an increase in $\tau - t$ can be caused only by an increase in Q.

[19] For example, see Theorem VI.4.1 in Fleming and Rishel (1975).

[20] A parallel can be drawn to the problem of American option valuation. Although that problem involves only a single linear PDE with a free boundary, no analytical solution has been found.

[21] This is in contrast to the discrete-time formulations where the Bellman equation is generally a necessary condition for the value function.

In such situations one can often show that the optimal value function is a solution of the Bellman PDE in some generalized sense. For example, with additional assumptions about differentiability of $\tilde{\mu}(\cdot)$, $\sigma(\cdot)$, and $C(\cdot)$, it can be proved that V satisfies (12.5) for almost all t, P, and Q, or that V is a viscosity solution of (12.5). Although such results are useful for the analysis, generalized PDE solutions often are not unique.[22] The use of the Bellman PDE for numerical solutions will be discussed in the next section where we apply our framework to an example.

12.5 EXAMPLE ILLUSTRATING SOLUTION PROPERTIES

To gain further insight into the general properties of the solution presented in the previous section, we consider an illustrative example and solve it numerically. Consider the time-invariant functions $\tilde{\mu}(t, P) = \mu P$, $\mu < r$, and $\sigma(t, P) = \sigma P$. This form of $\tilde{\mu}(\cdot)$ is equivalent to a constant proportional cost-of-carry relation between the spot and futures commodity prices (see Appendix A).[23] In principle, $\tilde{\mu}(\cdot)$ could be inferred from futures prices, while $\sigma(\cdot)$ can be estimated from the spot price data. However, since the emphasis of this chapter is on general qualitative properties of the solution, we use the constant proportional functions that provide a reasonable first-order approximation within a one-factor model.

The existing literature on nonrenewable resources considers cost functions with time-invariant marginal costs (zero, constant, increasing in the extraction rate) as well as marginal costs that increase with the ore extracted to date (cumulation effect). The classic natural resources literature [see Neher (1990) and references therein] assumes that the marginal cost function, $C_q(\cdot)$, is increasing in the extraction rate, q, and decreasing in the level of resource, Q. A representative cost function could be based on empirical analyses with cost data from several mines. This, however, is difficult for two reasons. First, mining companies keep cost data a closely guarded secret. Second, whatever cost data are publicly available are in a highly aggregated form. They typically include both the cost of mining and the cost of capital replacement.[24]

Consider the following representative cost function:

$$C(t, Q, q) = e^{\pi t} \left[c(Q) q + \gamma q^2 \right] \tag{12.6}$$

$$c(Q) = \delta + (\alpha - \beta Q)^+, \quad \alpha, \beta, \delta \geq 0; \quad \gamma \geq -\delta/\overline{q}$$

---

[22] See Fleming and Soner (1993) Section II.2 for simple examples of nondifferentiability of the value function and nonuniqueness of generalized solutions, Section IV.10 for the characterization in the almost-everywhere sense, and Chapter V for the characterization of the value function as a unique viscosity solution of the Bellman PDE.

[23] This relation is also known as a constant proportional net convenience yield.

[24] No reliable study is available about how the nature and shape of the operating and marginal cost curves change with increasing rates or levels of extraction for different types of mines. The Bureau of Mines (Department of Interior, Government of USA) has looked at the extraction of phosphate rocks and has concluded that the marginal cost in some range is flat but is generally upward sloping. For pit mining, the Bureau has prepared a set of tables giving various elements of cost (labor, equipment etc.) as exponents of capacity (Circular No. IC 9298, 1991).

where $x^+ \equiv \max[0, x]$, and $\alpha, \beta, \gamma, \delta, \pi$ are known parameters. The cost function is decreasing in the resource Q, and is nonlinear in the current extraction rate, q (i.e., the marginal costs depend on q). Thus, we retain both features of cost functions found in the classic literature on the subject. Also, the cost function is positive and continuous, as required.

For convenience we set $\delta = \pi = 0$. Thus, we have $C(t, Q, q) = (\alpha - \beta Q)^+ q + \gamma q^2$ with $\alpha, \beta, \gamma \geq 0$. If $\beta > 0$, then C does not depend on Q for $Q \geq \alpha/\beta$. Moreover, when $Q \geq \alpha/\beta + \overline{q}(T - t)$, C will be independent of Q for all relevant values of the arguments, and the resource will be unrestricted [$Q \geq \overline{q}(T - t)$ so that $\tau = T$]. Therefore, for $Q \geq \alpha/\beta + \overline{q}(T - t)$, the value functions $V^{\overline{q}}$, $V^{\widehat{q}}$, and V do not depend on Q, and $V \equiv V^{\overline{q}}$. On the other hand, if $Q < \alpha/\beta + \overline{q}(T - t)$ for an interior point ($t < T$, $P > 0$, $Q > 0$) then costs will cumulate for some Q values, and therefore the value function of any nonzero policy strictly increases in Q and $V > V^{\widehat{q}}$.

The choice of $\widetilde{\mu}(\cdot)$ and $C(\cdot)$ implies $m(t, s, P) = e^{\mu(s-t)} P$ and

$$V^{\overline{q}}(t, P, Q) = W_0(t, Q) + W_1(t, Q)P \qquad (12.7)$$

where

$$W_1(t, Q) = \overline{q} \int_0^{\min(Q/\overline{q}, T-t)} e^{-(r-\mu)s} ds$$

$$= \frac{\overline{q}}{r - \mu} \left(1 - e^{-(r-\mu)\min(Q/\overline{q}, T-t)}\right)$$

$$W_0(t, Q) = -\int_0^{\min(Q/\overline{q}, T-t)} e^{-rs} \left[(\alpha - \beta Q + \beta \overline{q}s)^+ \overline{q} + \gamma \overline{q}^2\right] ds$$

$$= -\frac{\overline{q}}{r} \left\{\left[I(t, Q) + \gamma \overline{q}\right] - e^{-r\min(Q/\overline{q}, T-t)} \left[J(t, Q) + \gamma \overline{q}\right]\right\}$$

$$I(t, Q) \equiv \begin{cases} \alpha - \beta Q + \frac{\beta \overline{q}}{r} & \text{if } \alpha - \beta Q > 0 \\ \frac{\beta \overline{q}}{r} \exp\left[\frac{r}{\beta \overline{q}}(\alpha - \beta Q)\right] & \text{if } -\beta \overline{q}(T - t) < \alpha - \beta Q \leq 0 \\ 0 & \text{if } \alpha - \beta Q \leq -\beta \overline{q}(T - t) \end{cases}$$

$$J(t, Q) \equiv \begin{cases} \alpha - \beta(Q - \overline{q}(T - t))^+ + \frac{\beta \overline{q}}{r} & \text{if } \alpha - \beta Q > -\beta \overline{q}(T - t) \\ 0 & \text{if } \alpha - \beta Q \leq -\beta \overline{q}(T - t) \end{cases}$$

Note that $V^{\overline{q}}$ does not depend on σ, is linear in P, and highly nonlinear in t and Q. Also, $V^{\overline{q}}$ is continuous but nondifferentiable with respect to t and Q, for example at the points where $Q = \overline{q}(T - t)$. As Q or $T - t$ goes to infinity, $V^{\overline{q}}$ converges to a finite limit.[25]

A myopic policy must satisfy

---

[25] If we allowed $\mu \geq r$, and let both Q and $T - t$ go to infinity, then W_1 would diverge so that $V^{\overline{q}}$ would become infinite for any $P > 0$.

$$\widehat{\mathbf{q}}(t, P, Q) \in \arg \max_{[0,\bar{q}]} \left\{ \left[P - (\alpha - \beta Q)^+ \right] q - \gamma q^2 \right\}$$

If $\gamma > 0$, then C is strictly convex in q, and the myopic policy is unique and continuous:

$$\widehat{\mathbf{q}}(t, P, Q) = \widehat{\mathbf{q}}(P, Q) = h[\widehat{\mathbf{q}}_0(P, Q)]$$

where $\widehat{\mathbf{q}}_0(P, Q)$ is the unconstrained maximizer setting marginal cost equal to price:

$$\widehat{\mathbf{q}}_0(P, Q) = \frac{1}{2\gamma} \left[P - (\alpha - \beta Q)^+ \right]$$

and $h(\cdot)$ is the "constraint" function:

$$h(x) = \begin{cases} 0 & \text{if } x < 0 \\ x & \text{if } 0 \le x < \bar{q} \\ \bar{q} & \text{if } x \ge \bar{q} \end{cases}$$

Both $\widehat{\mathbf{q}}_0$ and h are Lipschitz continuous, time-invariant, piecewise linear and increasing, and h is bounded. Therefore, $\widehat{\mathbf{q}}$ is Lipschitz continuous and bounded (showing admissibility),[26] time-invariant, piecewise linear and increasing in P and Q. If $\gamma = 0$, there are multiple myopic policies, all of which are discontinuous. In this case the admissibility can be established using the results on existence and uniqueness of solutions for integral equations of Volterra type.[27]

An optimal policy $\mathbf{q}^*$ satisfies (almost everywhere)

$$\mathbf{q}^*(t, P, Q) \in \arg \max_{q \in [0, \bar{q}]} \left\{ \left[P - (\alpha - \beta Q)^+ - V_Q(t, P, Q) \right] q - \gamma q^2 \right\}$$

For $\gamma > 0$ there is a unique maximizer, and for almost all t, P, and Q,

$$\mathbf{q}^*(t, P, Q) = h[\mathbf{q}_0^*(t, P, Q)]$$

$$\mathbf{q}_0^*(t, P, Q) = \frac{1}{2\gamma} \left[P - (\alpha - \beta Q)^+ - V_Q(t, P, Q) \right]$$

The "overextraction" property of the myopic policy $(\widehat{\mathbf{q}} \ge \mathbf{q}^*)$ is obvious from $V_Q \ge 0$.

For numerical illustration we select the following set of (annualized) parameter values: $\mu = 0.05$, $r = 0.07$, and $\sigma = 0.10$. The price P and the resource Q are considered in the normalized range from 0 to 100, the time to lease expiration $T - t$ is varied from 0 to 20 years, and the maximum extraction rate $\bar{q}$ is set at 5. The cost function parameters are $\alpha = 50$, $\beta = 1$, $\gamma = 4$. Thus, the linear term of the cost function has the coefficient $c(Q) = 50 - Q$ for $0 \le Q < 50$ and zero for $Q > 50$,

---

[26] $f(x)$ is called Lipschitz continuous if $|f(x_1) - f(x_2)| \le L |x_1 - x_2|$ for all x_1, x_2 and a constant L. If $\mathbf{q}(t, P, Q)$ is continuous and bounded (in all arguments), and Lipschitz continuous in Q, then given $Q(0)$ and a continuous $P(t)$, the equation $Q(t) = - \int_0^t \mathbf{q}[s, P(s), Q(s)] ds$ has a unique solution.

[27] See Gripenberg et al. (1990, Chapters 12–13).

and the linear and quadratic terms have on average about the same contribution to the total costs. The optimal and myopic value functions coincide at an interior point if and only if $Q \geq 50 + 5(T - t)$.

When the optimal value function can be characterized as a unique solution of the Bellman PDE (possibly in some generalized sense), one may be able to show that a numerical solution of the PDE converges to the value function. Standard numerical techniques, such as finite differences, can then be applied to solve the PDE (see Fleming and Soner, 1993, Chapter IX). However, such a characterization and the convergence of the solutions usually require smoothness of the functions. This would include the cost function $C(\cdot)$ being differentiable with respect to Q, which is not the case for the cost function used in our example.

An alternative is to use a method that does not directly use the analytical properties of the value function, such as the Markov chain approximation technique proposed by Kushner (1977; Kushner and Dupuis, 1992). This method is robust and can even be used to treat discontinuous functions. It also avoids the problems caused by degeneracies in the state process while still using the intuition obtained from the Bellman PDE. We therefore use this method to solve our example. Briefly, the Markov chain approximation methodology is as follows. The continuous-time problem is discretized and the original state process is approximated by a finite Markov chain that can be viewed as a multinomial tree with probabilities dependent on the state and control. The discrete-time problem is then solved by standard techniques of dynamic programming. The Markov chain is constructed in such a way that it satisfies certain consistency properties that guarantee the convergence of the numerical solution to the solution of the original problem, as the time and state intervals go to zero. There is substantial freedom in the choice of an approximating chain. The simple form that we employ uses a finite-difference approximation of the differential operator of the state process. Thus, the method is quite similar to a numerical solution of the Bellman PDE. However, this analogy is informal, and the method remains valid even in situations when the value function is not a unique solution of the PDE.

A numerical solution, of course, has to be performed on a bounded state space. In particular, we have to bound P by some maximum value $\overline{P}$ and either assume a reflection of the price process at $\overline{P}$ or assign a boundary value to V (or its derivative) at $\overline{P}$. We use the asymptotic Property 3 from the previous section, and set $V(t, \overline{P}, Q) = V^{\overline{q}}(t, \overline{P}, Q)$.[28] This boundary condition also has an economic justification: if there are any nonzero costs associated with making the optimal control decisions and adjusting the extraction rate, then there will be some large, finite value of P at which the simple policy $\overline{q}$ should be adopted permanently until the lease expiration.

The results of the numerical solution are straightforward to analyze. The optimal and suboptimal extraction policies and their corresponding performance are shown in Figures 12.2–12.4. Figure 12.5 shows the absolute and relative gains from employing an optimal policy versus a myopic one. The over-extraction property of the myopic

---

[28] In the presented results $\overline{P}$ is set to 200, while the solutions are shown for $P \leq 100$. Further increase in $\overline{P}$ does not lead to any significant change of the solutions in the region $P \leq 100$.

policy is evident for all levels of price, resource, and time. For a low enough commodity price P and resource Q, nothing is extracted, both in the optimal and myopic case. However, the optimal extraction rate stays at zero for larger values of P and Q. Similarly, for high enough commodity prices and resource levels, full extraction $\bar{q}$ is achieved, with the myopic policy hitting full extraction at lower values of P and Q. The suboptimality of the myopic policy is clearly seen, however the degree of suboptimality varies dramatically.

Figure 12.2 plots the extraction rates and the lease values as functions of time-to-lease-expiration for several settings of P and Q. The myopic and optimal extraction rates (left column panels) and the corresponding value functions (right column panels) coincide near the lease expiration and diverge as $T - t$ increases. As lease life goes to infinity, all functions converge to their corresponding infinite-horizon limits, which are finite. The myopic policy is time invariant while the optimal extraction rate decreases in $T - t$. The optimal and myopic value functions are strictly increasing, but the value of the maximum-extraction policy is not monotone. The latter becomes negative for some or even all values of $T - t$ when P is small, as seen in Figure 12.2B and D.

Figure 12.3 shows the behavior of the solution as a function of the mineral price. The optimal and myopic extraction rates as well as their corresponding value functions start at zero and increase with P. The spreads between optimal and myopic, both extraction rates and value functions, first increase up to some level of price and thereafter fall back to zero. (This feature of the value functions becomes clearly apparent in Figure 12.5C.) The myopic and optimal value functions are convex in price, and both converge to the linear value function of the maximum-extraction policy as P increases. This pattern illustrates the interpretation of the lease under myopic and optimal extraction as a portfolio of commodity options (see Property 1 in Section 12.4).

Figure 12.4 illustrates the properties of the extraction policies and lease value functions versus the available resource. The optimal and myopic extraction rates and value functions are increasing in Q, and the difference between optimal and myopic behavior (both in terms of q and V) vanishes as Q becomes large. As Q goes to zero, the myopic and optimal value functions converge (to 0), whereas the two extraction rates remain very distinct, provided P is not very low or very high. The distinction between optimal and myopic behavior for low Q is further emphasized in Figure 12.5F.

Figure 12.5 compares the performance of the optimal and myopic extraction policies. The graphs clearly show that optimal extraction provides a substantial improvement in lease value. When measured in absolute terms, this benefit is especially important when the lease has a long life and when the price and resource remaining take on intermediate values. When measured in relative terms, the gains again attain a maximum for high values of $T - t$ and mid-range values of P. In contrast, whereas the relative gain is positive for the entire range of Q values, it monotonically decreases in Q with the maximum being achieved at low Q.

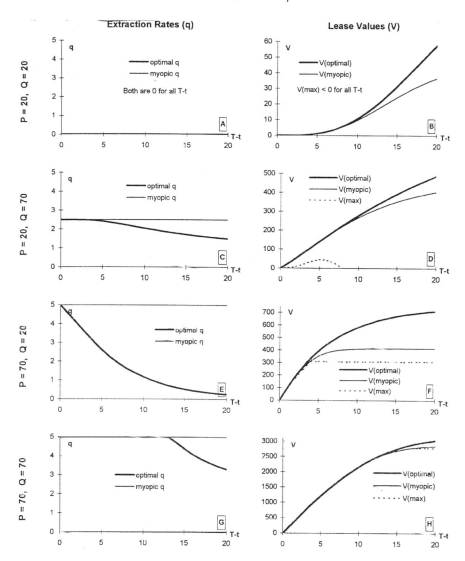

Figure 12.2 Extraction rate and lease value as functions of time to expiration. This figure (A–H) plots the extraction rates (q) and the lease values (V) as functions of time-to-lease-expiration ($T - t$) for several settings of the price (P) and resource level (Q). The myopic and optimal extraction rates (left column panels) and the corresponding value functions (right column panels) coincide near lease expiration and diverge as $T - t$ increases. As lease life goes to infinity, all functions converge to their infinite-horizon limits. The myopic policy is time invariant while the optimal extraction rate decreases in $T - t$. The value of the maximum-extraction policy is not monotone and becomes negative when P is small.

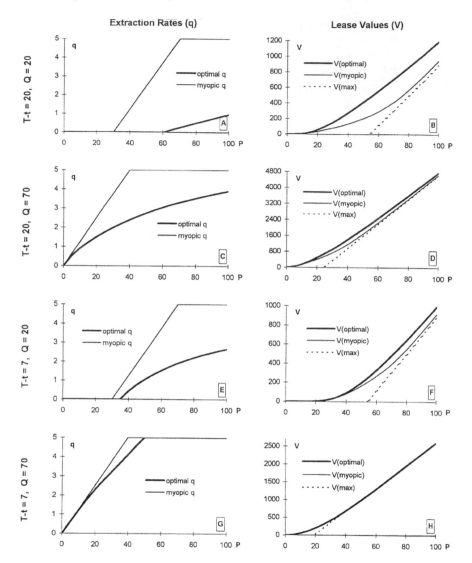

Figure 12.3 Extraction rate and lease value as functions of mineral price. This figure (A–H) shows the extraction rates (q) and the lease values (V) as functions of mineral price (P) for several settings of the time to expiration ($T - t$) and resource level (Q). The optimal and myopic extraction rates as well as their corresponding value functions start at zero and increase with P. The difference between optimal and myopic behavior, both in terms of extraction rates and value functions, first increases up to some level of price and thereafter falls back to zero. The myopic and optimal value functions are convex in price, and both converge to the linear value function of the maximum-extraction policy as P increases.

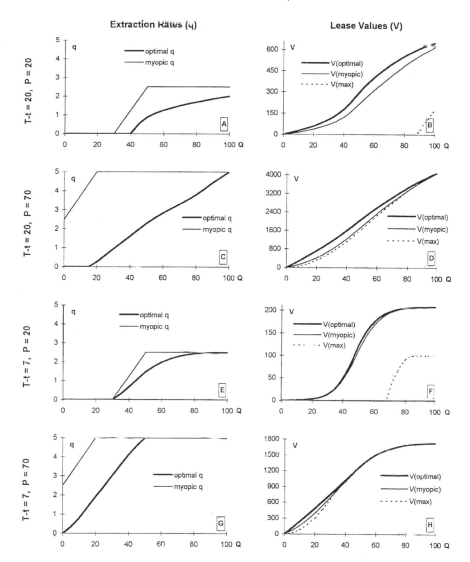

Figure 12.4 Extraction rate and lease value as functions of available resources. This figure (A–H) shows the extraction rates (q) and the lease values (V) as functions of available resource (Q) for several settings of the time to expiration ($T-t$) and mineral price (P). The optimal and myopic extraction rates and value functions are increasing in Q, and the difference between optimal and myopic behavior (both in terms of extraction rates and value functions) vanishes as Q becomes large. As Q goes to zero, the myopic and optimal value functions aslo converge to zero, whereas the two extraction rates remain very distinct, provided P is not very low or very high.

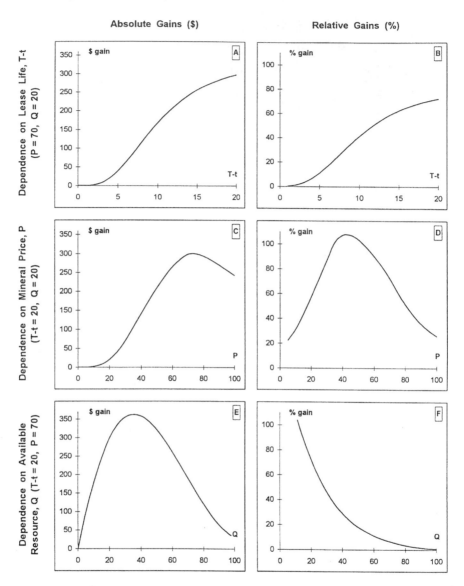

Figure 12.5   Absolute and percentage gains from optimal extraction relative to myopic extraction. This figure (A–F) compares the performance of the optimal and myopic extraction policies. The graphs clearly show that optimal extraction provides a substantial improvement in lease value. When measured in absolute terms, this benefit is especially important when the lease life $(T-t)$ is long and when the price (P) and resource remaining (Q) take on intermediate values. Measured in relative terms, the gains again attain a maximum at high values of $T-t$ and mid-range values of P. In contrast, the relative gain monotonically decreases in Q with the maximum being achieved at low levels of resources.

12.6 CONCLUSION

We have provided a comprehensive analysis of the problem of optimal extraction of nonrenewable resources. Our framework accounts for stochastic prices as well as marginal costs that increase both in cumulative extraction and the extraction rate. The framework unifies the vast literature on natural resource extraction that heretofore has only addressed these issues separately. The analysis demonstrates that appropriate consideration of cumulating costs in extraction policies can provide a significant increase in value, especially for longer lease lives and at mid-range values of the mineral price. The gain in dollar terms is largest for mid-range amounts of the available resource, while the percentage gain is highest for low resource quantities. Thus, mining practice that seeks to raise firm value can benefit from the approach developed here.

The stochastic control framework that we considered should prove to have more general applications. For example, it can be applied to (1) studying the optimal tax policy for the natural resource sector, (2) formulating environmental policy, and (3) addressing issues related to the renewable resources industry when path dependency becomes important (as in the case of overfishing or the overharvesting of forests).

We have taken only a small step in interpreting our solution in terms of the optimal management of a portfolio of real options. Further and more complete developments of this approach may increase insights into the solutions as well as facilitate their acceptance by managers.

Appendix A

This Appendix presents a general arbitrage valuation scheme for contingent claims on commodities in the presence of futures contracts, and provides some interesting results for the case when the commodity price is assumed to be a diffusion under the changed probability measure. The scheme can be modified to accommodate situations where, instead of futures, other types of commodity-linked securities are traded in the market. The method allows one to finesse the issues of proper discounting of risky cash flows and specifying the drift of the commodity price process. These features make it particularly useful for applications, such as the control problem analyzed in this chapter. To cast the asset value maximization as a stochastic optimal control problem, we need to express the objective functional, i.e., the asset value, in an expected-value form. In a complete market setting such a representation can be easily obtained using arbitrage pricing techniques.[29] In particular, the representation

---

[29] When markets are incomplete, an expected-value expression for the value of a contingent claim can still be obtained, but there is no unifying approach as in the complete market case. Methods range from utility-based general equilibrium models (e.g., Cox et. al., 1985) to attempts to relate the value of a claim to some observable data (e.g., Wang, 1997).

follows directly from the general results on the relation between arbitrage and equivalent martingale measures, originated by Harrison and Kreps (1979).[30] We use the continuous-time framework since it is economically plausible and provides elegant and intuitive results. Certain technical conditions that have no economic interpretation are purposely left out in order to present the main ideas in a reasonably simple form.

12.A1 VALUATION OF COMMODITY CONTINGENT CLAIMS

We start from a summary of the basic result. Suppose in a stochastic market model there is a security with no intermediate dividends and a well-behaved price process B.[31] Define the discount factor between time t and s by $\delta(t, s) = B_t/B_s$. Then in the absence of (approximate) arbitrage there exists an equivalent probability measure such that, for any security with a cumulative dividend process D and a price process S, the sum of the discounted dividends and price, $\int_0^t \delta(0, s) \, dD_s + \delta(0, t) \, S_t$, is a martingale (provided that the integral is defined). Therefore,

$$S_t = \widetilde{E}_t \left[\int_t^T \delta(t, s) \, dD_s + \delta(t, T) \, S_T \right]$$

where $\widetilde{E}_t$ is the expectation under the new probability measure conditional on the underlying filtration.

This representation holds both for nonredundant securities and redundant contingent claims. However, in order to apply this result, one needs to know the underlying processes under the new measure. Hence, additional structure is needed. We consider a one-factor market model where the uncertainty is generated by a single Brownian motion. The whole methodology readily extends to a multifactor setting.

Assume that there exists a commodity futures contract with delivery at time T, continuous resettlement, and futures price following an Ito process:

$$F_t = F_0 + \int_0^t \mu_s^F \, ds + \int_0^t \sigma_s^F \, dW_s, \quad 0 \le t \le T$$

where W is a standard Brownian motion.[32] Note that the futures price F is *not* the value of the futures contract. Under continuous resettlement, the futures contract is a security with zero price and cumulative dividends $D_t = F_t - F_0$.

---

[30] An alternative approach is based on the construction of the partial differential equation (PDE), which must be satisfied by the value of a contingent claim in the absence of arbitrage. In that case, an expected-value representation can be obtained using the Feynman–Kac formula. However, that approach is indirect, works only in the Markov diffusion setting, and requires strong regularity conditions. Duffie (1996) presents a detailed exposition of both methods.

[31] To be "well behaved," it is sufficient for B to be bounded above and away from zero, i.e., $0 < \underline{B} \le B_t \le \overline{B} < \infty$ for $t \in [0, T]$. Below we consider the special case of a bond with constant interest rate.

[32] By an *Ito process* we mean a continuous semimartingale of the form $X_t = X_0 + \int_0^t \mu_s \, ds + \int_0^t \sigma_s \, dW_s$ for adapted processes μ and σ such that the integrals are well defined. We use μ and σ to denote processes, functions, and constants whose precise meaning must be clear from the context.

We assume that $\sigma_t^F \neq 0$ (almost everywhere), and μ^F, σ^F are such that F does not permit arbitrage and the (augmented) filtration $\{\mathcal{F}_t\}$ generated by F coincides with the filtration generated by the Brownian motion W. Thus, all the relevant information is contained in the history of the futures price process. The equality of filtrations holds in the case of diffusions (see Proposition 1 in Harrison and Kreps, 1979) as well as in many other cases of interest. The commodity spot price process P is assumed to be adapted to $\{\mathcal{F}_t\}$.

Finally, we assume for simplicity that the continuously compounded interest rate $r > 0$ is constant so that the price of a risk-free security is $B_t = B_0 e^{rt}$. Then the absence of arbitrage implies the existence of an equivalent probability measure $\widetilde{\mathbf{P}}$ under which $\int_0^t e^{-rs} dF_s$ is a martingale.[33] Furthermore, the market is complete in the following sense: the cash flows of any contingent claim with adapted cumulative dividends $\widehat{D}_t$, $t \leq T$, and $\mathcal{F}_T$-measurable time-T value V_T, can be replicated by trading in the futures contract combined with borrowing and lending at the risk-free rate. The unique arbitrage-free value V_t of the claim equals the value of the replicating trading strategy, and $\int_0^t e^{-rs} d\widehat{D}_s + e^{-rt} V_t$ is a $\widetilde{\mathbf{P}}$-martingale. Therefore,

$$V_t = \widetilde{E}_t \left[\int_t^T e^{-r(s-t)} d\widehat{D}_s + e^{-r(T-t)} V_T \right]$$

In particular, this is true when $\widehat{D}_t$ and V_T are arbitrary measurable functions of the entire history of P, F, and other adapted processes.

Strictly speaking, V_t is the unique arbitrage-free value of the claim only if the claim can be bought and sold short by some market participants. If the claim is in limited supply and it is possible to buy it but not sell it short (which is usually the case for mine leases considered in this chapter), then the absence of arbitrage guarantees only that V_t is a lower bound for the price of the claim. However, since the claim has no separate convenience value, no rational agent would buy the claim for a price higher than V_t since this is the cost of replicating the cash flows of the claim. Therefore, if all buyers are rational, the actual transaction price must be V_t.

Note that the replication and valuation of a claim with cash flows on the entire interval $[0, T]$ do not require the existence of futures contracts with various delivery dates. A single contract with delivery at T and known price dynamics is sufficient. The futures contract can be replaced by another security for which the sum of the price and cumulative dividends follows an arbitrary (known) nondegenerate Ito process.

The fact that $\int_0^t e^{-rs} dF_s$ is a $\widetilde{\mathbf{P}}$-martingale implies that F_t itself is a $\widetilde{\mathbf{P}}$-martingale. Therefore, there exists a process $\widetilde{W}$ that is a standard Brownian motion under $\widetilde{\mathbf{P}}$ and

$$F_t = F_0 + \int_0^t \sigma_s^F d\widetilde{W}_s \tag{12.A1}$$

If the spot price P follows an Ito process under the original measure:

$$dP_t = \mu_t^P dt + \sigma_t^P dW_t$$

---

[33] Under certain integrability conditions $\widetilde{\mathbf{P}}$ can be constructed explicitly using Girsanov's theorem, but it is not necessary for our purposes.

then P is also an Ito process under $\widetilde{\mathbf{P}}$, with

$$dP_t = \widetilde{\mu}_t^P \, dt + \sigma_t^P \, d\widetilde{W}_t, \qquad \widetilde{\mu}_t^P = \mu_t^P - \frac{\mu_t^F}{\sigma_t^F} \sigma_t^P \qquad (12.A2)$$

12.A2 THE CASE OF DIFFUSIONS

The preceding argument is very general and is valid for arbitrary Ito processes as well as some other types of semimartingales. In applications, it is often convenient to restrict the attention to (Markov) diffusion processes, where drift and diffusion coefficients can be expressed in terms of time and the current value of the process. One can start from a joint diffusion for (P, F) under the original measure, i.e., take $\mu_t^P, \sigma_t^P, \mu_t^F$, and σ_t^F equal to some functions of t, P_t, and F_t. If these functions allow a solution of the resulting stochastic differential equation for (P, F), and F satisfies the assumptions made above, then the joint diffusion for (P, F) under $\widetilde{\mathbf{P}}$ follows immediately from Eqs. (12.A1) and (12.A2).

If, however, one would like P by itself to be a diffusion under $\widetilde{\mathbf{P}}$, then additional assumptions are needed. Clearly, $\sigma_t^P = \sigma(t, P_t)$ must be true for a well-behaved function $\sigma(\cdot)$. This condition is testable since σ^P, although not directly observed, can be statistically tracked quite well. The second assumption, that $\widetilde{\mu}_t^P = \widetilde{\mu}(t, P_t)$ for some function $\widetilde{\mu}(\cdot)$, has no direct statistical or economic interpretation but turns out to be equivalent to the assumption of a specific functional relation between the spot and futures prices (independent of the original drift μ^P). This equivalence allows testing the hypotheses about the existence and the specific form of the function $\widetilde{\mu}$, as well as its estimation using the spot and futures price data.

Since F is a $\widetilde{\mathbf{P}}$-martingale and the futures price is equal to the spot price on the delivery date, we have $F_t = \widetilde{E}_t(F_T) = \widetilde{E}_t(P_T)$. If P is a Markov process under $\widetilde{\mathbf{P}}$, then $F_t = \widetilde{E}_t(P_T) = f(t, P_t)$ where $f(t, P) = \widetilde{E}(P_T \mid P_t = P)$. In the case of a diffusion process we can be more specific and establish the relation between the functions f, $\widetilde{\mu}$, and σ. The following proposition shows that for any given $\sigma(\cdot)$ there is (up to technical conditions) a one-to-one correspondence between $\widetilde{\mu}(\cdot)$ and $f(\cdot)$. As usual, subscripts of a function denote the corresponding partial derivatives.

Proposition 1. *(i) Suppose P satisfies the stochastic differential equation*

$$dP_t = \widetilde{\mu}(t, P_t) \, dt + \sigma(t, P_t) \, d\widetilde{W}_t$$

and $\widetilde{\mu}$, $\widetilde{\mu}_P$, $\widetilde{\mu}_{PP}$, σ, σ_P, σ_{PP} are continuous and satisfy a polynomial growth condition in P. Then $F_t = f(t, P_t)$ where f is the unique solution of the equation

$$f_t(t, P) + \widetilde{\mu}(t, P) f_P(t, P) + \frac{1}{2}\sigma^2(t, P) f_{PP}(t, P) = 0, \quad t < T \quad (12.A3)$$

$$f(T, P) = P$$

in the class of $C^{1,2}$ functions that satisfy a polynomial growth condition in P.
   (ii) Suppose $\sigma_t^P = \sigma(t, P_t)$ and $F_t = f(t, P_t)$ for $f \in C^{1,2}$ with $f_P \neq 0$. Then $\widetilde{\mu}_t^P = \widetilde{\mu}(t, P_t)$ where $\widetilde{\mu}(\cdot)$ is determined by (12.A3).

In general, f has a third argument, T, but in our case T is fixed and the dependence on T can be suppressed. If $F_t = f(t, P_t)$ for $f \in C^{1,2}$, then from Ito's Lemma, $\sigma_t^F = \sigma(t, P_t) f_P(t, P_t)$. Thus, for $\sigma_t^F \neq 0$ (which is needed for market completeness) both $\sigma(t, P_t)$ and $f_P(t, P_t)$ must be nonzero. Also f must obviously satisfy $f(T, P) = P$.

Proof. (i) As a diffusion process, P is Markov under $\widetilde{\mathbf{P}}$. From our previous discussion, $F_t = \widetilde{E}_t(P_T) = f(t, P_t)$ where $f(t, P) = \widetilde{E}(P_T \mid P_t = P)$. The rest follows from Theorem 2.9.10 in Krylov (1980).

(ii) From Eq. (12.A1) and Ito's Lemma,

$$0 = \widetilde{\mu}_t^F = f_t(t, P_t) + \widetilde{\mu}_t^P f_P(t, P_t) + \frac{1}{2}\sigma^2(t, P_t) f_{PP}(t, P_t)$$

Since $f_P(t, P_t) \neq 0$,

$$\widetilde{\mu}_t^P = \widetilde{\mu}(t, P_t) = -\left[f_t(t, P_t) + \frac{1}{2}\sigma^2(t, P_t) f_{PP}(t, P_t)\right] / f_P(t, P_t) \;\blacksquare$$

Example 2 (Geometric Ornstein–Uhlenbeck process) *If P is a geometric Ornstein–Uhlenbeck process (i.e., $\ln P$ is an OU process) under $\widetilde{\mathbf{P}}$, then*

$$\widetilde{\mu}(t, P) = \alpha(\delta - \ln P)P, \quad P > 0; \quad \widetilde{\mu}(t, 0) = 0$$

$$\sigma(t, P) = \sigma P$$

for constant $\alpha > 0$, $\sigma \neq 0$ and δ. The corresponding f is given by

$$f(t, P) = f_0(t) P^{f_1(t)}, \quad P \geq 0$$

where

$$f_0(t) = \exp\left[\delta + e^{-\alpha(T-t)}(2\beta - \delta) - (1 + e^{-2\alpha(T-t)})\beta\right], \quad \beta = \sigma^2/(4\alpha)$$

$$f_1(t) = e^{-\alpha(T-t)}$$

This is Model 1 of Schwartz (1997). Although f satisfies a growth condition in P and is a solution of (12.A3) for $P > 0$, $\widetilde{\mu}$ does not satisfy the conditions of part (i). As a result, $f \notin C^{1,2}$ (f_P and f_{PP} are discontinuous at $P = 0$) and we cannot use the proposition to establish the uniqueness of the solution to (12.A3).

Under the assumption that $F_t = f(t, P_t)$, the drift of P under the new measure is completely determined by the functions $f(\cdot)$ and $\sigma(\cdot)$, independently of the original drift of P. Such formulation avoids the question of what is the correct drift of the commodity price process. This feature is especially convenient since there is no agreement on the drift in the literature, and statistical estimation cannot provide a definite answer.[34] Since the original drift μ^P can be an almost arbitrary adapted process, we allow for very general, possibly non-Markov, dynamics of the commodity price under the original measure.

In the linear case the correspondence between $\tilde{\mu}$ and f is more precise and can be established independently of both the original drift and the diffusion coefficient [$\sigma_t^P = \sigma(t, P_t)$ is not necessary].

Corollary 1 (Linear case). $\tilde{\mu}_t^P = \tilde{\mu}(t, P_t) = \mu_0(t) + \mu_1(t)P_t$ *for continuous* μ_0, μ_1 *if and only if* $F_t = f(t, P_t) = f_0(t) + f_1(t)P$ *for* f_0, $f_1 \in C^1$, *and* $f_1 \neq 0$. *The functions are related by*

$$f_0(t) = \int_t^T \exp\left[\int_u^T \mu_1(v)\,dv\right]\mu_0(u)\,du, \qquad f_1(t) = \exp\left[\int_t^T \mu_1(u)\,du\right]$$

$$\mu_0(t) = -\frac{f_0'(t)}{f_1(t)}, \qquad \mu_1(t) = -\frac{f_1'(t)}{f_1(t)}$$

Here $f \in C^{1,2}$ is equivalent to f_0, $f_1 \in C^1$, $f_P \neq 0$ corresponds to $f_1 \neq 0$, and $f(T, P) = P$ is equivalent to $f_0(T) = 0$ and $f_1(T) = 1$.

Proof. (i) Suppose $\tilde{\mu}_t^P = \mu_0(t) + \mu_1(t)P_t$ for continuous μ_0 and μ_1. The linear stochastic differential equation

$$dP_t = (\mu_0(t) + \mu_1(t)P_t)\,dt + \sigma_t^P d\tilde{W}_t$$

has a unique (strong) solution given by

$$P_t = d(0, t)P_0 + \int_0^t d(u, t)\mu_0(u)\,du + \int_0^t d(u, t)\sigma_u^P d\tilde{W}_u$$

where $d(t, s) = \exp\left[\int_t^s \mu_1(u)\,du\right]$. (See Karatzas and Shreve, 1991, Section 5.6.C.) The conditional mean is easily computed and is equal to

$$\tilde{E}_t(P_s) = m(t, s, P_t) = m_0(t, s) + d(t, s)P_t$$

where $m_0(t, s) = \int_t^s d(u, s)\mu_0(u)\,du$. In particular, $F_t = \tilde{E}_t(P_T) = m_0(t, T) + d(t, T)P_t$, which is easily seen to be the required result. Continuity of μ_0 and μ_1 and the definition of d and m_0 imply that f_0, $f_1 \in C^1$, and $f_1 \neq 0$. To relate to the previous proposition, note that f is a $C^{1,2}$ solution of (12.A3) satisfying

---

[34] In the context of stock prices, Merton (1980) showed that a reliable estimation of the drift is very difficult, even in the simplest parametric form.

[35] Even when $\sigma_t^P \neq \sigma(t, P_t)$, f satisfies (12.A3) since $f_{PP} \equiv 0$ and the last term cancels. The conditions on coefficients used in the previous proposition were needed to guarantee the existence of a solution to (12.A.3). Conditions for uniqueness are much weaker and it is sufficient that $\sigma(\cdot)$ satisfies a linear growth condition in P—see Friedman (1975, Corollary 6.4.4).

a growth condition in P, and such solution is unique when $\sigma_t^P = \sigma(t, P_t)$ for a $\sigma(\cdot)$ that satisfies mild regularity conditions [35]

(ii) Suppose $F_t = f_0(t) + f_1(t)P$ for f_0, $f_1 \in C^1$, and $f_1 \neq 0$. Repeating as in part (ii) of the proposition, we obtain

$$f_0'(t) + f_1'(t)P_t + f_1(t)\widetilde{\mu}_t^P = 0$$

which gives the desired form of $\widetilde{\mu}$ in terms of f_0 and f_1. The conditions on f_0 and f_1 guarantee that μ_0 and μ_1 are well defined and continuous. ∎

Example 3 (Constant coefficients). *The assumption that $\widetilde{\mu}_t^P = \mu_0 + \mu_1 P_t$ for constant μ_0 and μ_1 is equivalent to the assumption that*

$$F_t = \frac{\mu_0}{\mu_1}\left(e^{\mu_1(T-t)} - 1\right) + e^{\mu_1(T-t)}P_t, \quad \text{if} \quad \mu_1 \neq 0$$

and

$$F_t = \mu_0(T - t) + P_t, \quad\quad \text{if} \quad \mu_1 = 0$$

[Note that $\widetilde{\mu}$ is continuous; $f \in C^{1,2}$ and satisfies $f_P(t, P) \neq 0$, $f(T, P) = P$.]

One example is the mean-reverting drift $\widetilde{\mu}_t^P = \alpha(\overline{P} - P_t)$ for constant long-run mean $\overline{P}$ and rate of reversion $\alpha > 0$. The corresponding futures price is a convex combination of P and $\overline{P}$:

$$F_t = e^{-\alpha(T-t)}P_t + [1 - e^{-\alpha(T-t)}]\overline{P}$$

Another example is $\widetilde{\mu}_t^P = \mu P_t$, which is equivalent to $F_t = e^{\mu(T-t)}P_t$. This form of f is interpreted as a constant proportional cost of carry for the commodity. If in addition $\sigma_t^P = \sigma P_t$ for a constant $\sigma \neq 0$, then P is a geometric Brownian motion under the new measure, with parameters μ and σ:

$$dP_t = \mu P_t dt + \sigma P_t d\widetilde{W}_t, \quad P_0 > 0$$

Starting with a strictly positive value, the geometric Brownian motion stays strictly positive so that $\sigma(t, P_t) \neq 0$ as required. Under the original measure, P can be an arbitrary Ito process with constant proportional diffusion coefficient $\sigma_t^P = \sigma P_t$ (e.g., geometric Brownian motion or geometric Ornstein–Uhlenbeck process with arbitrary drift parameters).[36]

It is convenient in modeling to start directly from a specific diffusion process for P under the new measure by specifying functional forms of $\widetilde{\mu}(t, P)$ and $\sigma(t, P)$ based on some economic or mathematical criteria. However, since observation of P (under the original measure) provides no information about $\widetilde{\mu}$, this approach is hard

---

[36] ln P must have a constant diffusion coefficient σ. Also, since P is strictly positive with probability one under an equivalent measure, this property must hold under the original measure as well.

to justify unless there is empirical support for the implied function f. The popular practice of defining the process under the original measure and then assuming that "the market price of risk is constant" seems inappropriate. Since a functional relation between spot and futures prices is already implicitly assumed, the adequate choice of $\tilde{\mu}(\cdot)$ must be consistent with (if not dictated by) the form of $f(\cdot)$ observed in the data. This also applies to multifactor models, interest rate models, and generally any situation in which the underlying process is not a price of a financial asset.

ACKNOWLEDGMENTS

We thank Michael Brennan, Eduardo Schwartz, Lenos Trigeorgis, Raman Uppal, Richard Zeckhauser, and participants at the 9th INFORMS Applied Probability Conference, the NBER Luncheon Seminar Series, and the 2nd Annual Conference on Real Options for their helpful comments.

REFERENCES

Brennan, M. J., and E. S. Schwartz. (1985). Evaluating Natural Resource Investments. *Journal of Business* 58, 135–157.

Burness, H. S. (1976). On the Taxation of Nonreplenishable Natural Resources. *Journal of Environmental and Economic Management* 3, 289–311.

Conrad, R. F., and R. B. Hool. (1981). Resource Taxation with Heterogenous Quality and Endogenous Reserves. *Journal of Public Economics* 16, 17–33.

Cox, J. C., J. E. Ingersoll, and S. A. Ross. (1985). An Intertemporal General Equilibrium Model of Asset Prices. *Econometrica* 53, 363–384.

Dixit, A. K., and R. S. Pindyck. (1994). *Investment under Uncertainty*. Princeton, N.J.: Princeton University Press.

Duffie, D. (1996). *Dynamic Asset Pricing Theory*, 2nd edition. Princeton, N.J.: Princeton University Press.

Fleming, W. H., and R. W. Rishel. (1975). *Deterministic and Stochastic Optimal Control*. New York: Springer-Verlag.

Fleming, W. H., and H. M. Soner. (1993). *Controlled Markov Processes and Viscosity Solutions*. New York: Springer-Verlag.

Foley, P. T., and J. P. Clark. (1982). The Effects of State Taxation on U.S. Copper Supply. *Land Economics* 58, 153–180.

Friedman, A. (1975). *Stochastic Differential Equations and Applications*, Volume 1. New York: Academic Press.

Gripenberg, G., S.-O. Londen, and O. Staffans. (1990). *Volterra Integral and Functional Equations*. Cambridge: Cambridge University Press.

Harrison, J. M., and D. M. Kreps. (1979). Martingales and Arbitrage in Multiperiod Securities Markets. *Journal of Economic Theory* 20, 381–408.

Hotelling, H. (1931). The Economics of Exhaustible Resources. *Journal of Political Economy* 39, 137–175.

Karatzas, I., and S. E. Shreve. (1991). *Brownian Motion and Stochastic Calculus*, 2nd edition. New York: Springer Verlag.

Krylov, N. V. (1980). *Controlled Diffusion Processes*. New York: Springer-Verlag.

Kushner, H. J. (1977). *Probability Methods for Approximations in Stochastic Control and for Elliptic Equations*. New York: Academic Press.

Kushner, H. J., and P. G. Dupuis. (1992). *Numerical Methods for Stochastic Control Problems in Continuous Time*. New York: Springer-Verlag.

Levhari, D., and N. Liviatan. (1977). Notes on Hotelling's Economics of Exhaustible Resources. *Canadian Journal of Economics* 10, 177–192.

Lewis, T. R. (1977). Attitude towards Risk and the Optimal Exploitation of an Exhaustible Resource. *Journal of Environmental and Economic Management* 4, 111–119.

Majd, S., and R. S. Pindyck. (1989). The Learning Curve and Optimal Production under Uncertainty. *RAND Journal of Economics* 20, 331–343.

Merton, R. C. (1980). On Estimating the Expected Return on the Market: An Exploratory Investigation. *Journal of Financial Economics* 8, 323–361.

Neher, P. (1990). *Natural Resource Economics: Conservation and Exploitation*. Cambridge: Cambridge University Press.

Pindyck, R. S. (1981). The Optimal Production of an Exhaustible Resource When Price Is Exogenous and Stochastic. *Scandinavian Journal of Economics* 87, 277–288.

Schwartz, E. S. (1997). The Stochastic Behavior of Commodity Prices: Implications for Valuation and Hedging. *Journal of Finance* 52, 923–973.

Shukla, G. (1992). Taxation of Exhaustible Natural Resources with Stochastic Prices. Ph.D. dissertation, Harvard University.

Slade, M. E. (1984). Tax Policy and the Supply of Exhaustible Resources: Theory and Practice. *Land Economics* 60, 133–147.

Solow, R. M., and F. Y. Wan. (1976). Extraction Costs in the Theory of Exhaustible Resources. *Bell Journal of Economics* 7, 359–370.

Wang, L. (1997). Using Risk-Premium Information from Firms to Value New Securities in an Incomplete Market. Working Paper, Stanford University.

Weinstein, M. C., and R. J. Zeckhauser. (1975). The Optimal Consumption of Depletable Natural Resources. *Quarterly Journal of Economics* 89, 371–392.

13

Real Options and the Timing of Implementation of Emission Limits under Ecological Uncertainty

JEAN-DANIEL M. SAPHORES
PETER CARR

Using real options, we analyze the timing of implementation of emission limits for a pollutant when its stock varies because of random environmental effects. Two types of irreversibility are present: ecological irreversibility, which results from long-term environmental damages, and investment irreversibility, which comes from sunk investments in pollution abatement. With reference to the deterministic case, we find that a small level of uncertainty may either delay or advance a reduction in pollutant emissions, depending on the cost of reducing emissions relative to the gain of reducing expected social costs. Thus, we cannot know a priori the bias introduced by neglecting low levels of uncertainty in environmental problems. When environmental uncertainty is "high enough," however, we find that pollutant emissions should be curbed immediately because of the prevalence of environmental damage. These results illustrate the importance of explicitly modeling uncertainty in environmental problems.

13.1 INTRODUCTION

The impact of uncertainty and irreversibility on environmental policy has long been a subject of debate among economists and policy makers, which has not yet been resolved. In the context of pollution, irreversibility has two basic sources. First, environmental damage may be so large that it becomes permanent or the amount of pollution may be so large that it leads to long-term damages. Second, investments to control or reduce a stock externality are often (at least partially) sunk. An example is the installation of scrubbers by a utility.

The extensive resources devoted to improving our understanding of environmental issues (e.g., global climate change, hazardous waste, or acid rain) highlight the pervasive nature and importance of uncertainty in environmental problems. There are two aspects to uncertainty, which are not always distinguished: one is associated with risk aversion and the other with the arrival of information over time. In this chapter, we are concerned only with the latter.

A preoccupation with the combined effect of irreversibility and uncertainty led Weisbrod (1964) to introduce the concept of option value. He argues that if a decision has irreversible consequences, then the flexibility ("the option") to choose the timing of that decision should be included in a cost–benefit analysis. Weisbrod uses the case of a national park where total operating costs cannot be recovered. In this case, he argues, it could be socially detrimental to shut down the park and cut down its trees because many people would be willing to make a financial contribution in order to preserve the possibility for themselves or their children to visit the park in the future.

Weisbrod's work has led to two competing interpretations of option value. The first, due to Cicchetti and Freeman (1971) and Schmalensee (1972), views option value as a risk premium paid by risk-averse consumers to reduce the impact of uncertainty in the supply of an environmental good. The second interpretation, advanced independently by Arrow and Fisher (1974) and Henry (1974), stresses the intertemporal aspect of irreversibility and the arrival of new information over time. This has lead them to introduce the concept of "quasioption value," which is akin to a shadow tax on development to correct benefits from development in a traditional cost–benefit analysis. Although quite useful, this view has led to a debate not only on the magnitude of option value, but also on its sign.

Many papers in the quasioption literature are based on two-period discrete time models. A standard result (e.g., see Arrow and Fisher, 1974, or Henry, 1974) is that, in the presence of environmental irreversibility, a standard cost–benefit analysis is biased against conservation. Freixas and Laffont (1984) generalize this result, and Conrad (1980) links option value to the expected value of information. More recently, Kolstad (1996), in a study of pollution stock effects and sunk emission control capital, shows that there is an irreversibility effect only when there is excess stock pollutant. However, Hanemann (1989) shows that conclusions drawn from this simple framework cannot be carried over when the benefit function is nonlinear or when the decision maker faces a continuum of irreversible development.

In this chapter, we use another approach, which returns to Weisbrod's original intuition about option value. Since we are concerned with the value of flexibility in the presence of irreversibilites, we rely on the theory of real options from finance. A real option can be defined as the value of being able to choose some characteristics (e.g., the timing) of a decision with irreversible consequences, which affects a real asset (as opposed to a financial asset). This approach has been applied fruitfully in the growing real options literature.

One of the first papers on real options is by Brennan and Schwartz (1985); it analyzes the operation of a mine, which can be temporarily closed. Later, Paddock et al. (1988) propose a model to value offshore petroleum leases as a function of the market price of oil. More recently, Clarke and Reed (1990) study the preservation of natural wilderness reserves. For a good introduction to investment under uncertainty using real options, see Dixit and Pindyck (1994) and Trigeorgis (1996).

In this chapter we revisit the problem of pollution reduction under environmental uncertainty in the presence of economic and environmental irreversibilities, which was recently considered by Kolstad (1996). However, instead of a discrete-time setting with two periods, we use a more general, continuous-time model. To obtain manageable closed-form results, we adopt a quadratic damage function and consider a class of square-root diffusions for the process followed by the stock of pollutant.

In Section 13.2, we introduce our simple continuous-time model, which features a single stock externality. The pollution control problem is formulated as a stopping problem where a risk-neutral social planner has to make a one-time decision on when and how much to reduce the emissions of a pollutant. In Section 13.3, we solve the corresponding deterministic problem to get a benchmark for the impact of randomness in the stock of pollutant. In Section 13.4, we tackle the stochastic case. Uncertainty is measured by the infinitesimal variance of the diffusion process of the stock of pollutant. Because it is difficult to analyze in general the impact of uncertainty, we look at vanishingly "small" and "large" uncertainty. A numerical application is provided in Section 13.5. The last section summarizes our conclusions.

13.2 MODELING POLLUTANT STOCK UNCERTAINTY

In this section, we consider a stylized model with one environmental pollutant, which decays at rate $\alpha \geq 0$. If $\alpha > 0$, we say that we have a decaying pollutant. A decaying pollutant is one for which the environment has some absorptive capacity (e.g., organic wastes discharged in oxygen-rich waters). On the other hand, if $\alpha = 0$ we say that we have a nondecaying pollutant. Examples of nondecaying pollutants include persistent synthetic chemicals such as polychlorinated biphenyls.

Let X denote the stock of this pollutant and E_1 its rate of emission. To focus solely on the impact of the variability of X, we assume that E_1 is constant. Because of the randomness of the physical and chemical processes that lead to changes in pollutant stock, we assume that X follows the diffusion process:

$$dX = (E_1 - \alpha X) \, dt + \sqrt{vX} \, dz = \alpha(x_{1c} - X) \, dt + \sqrt{vX} \, dz \qquad (13.1)$$

The parameter $v \geq 0$ characterizes the volatility of the process followed by the stock of pollutant and dz is an increment of a standard Wiener process. Thus, the infinitesimal variance of the process, which equals vX here, increases linearly with X. This specification seems a good compromise between a model with a fixed variance (which does not seem realistic), and a model where the infinitesimal variance of X varies with X^2, as for the geometric Brownian motion. Since diffusions have continuous trajectories, X remains nonnegative and tends to revert to $x_{1c} \equiv E_1/\alpha$, so the decay rate, α, also characterizes the speed of reversion. The initial stock of pollution, which is assumed known, is denoted $X(0)$.

We further assume that the flow of social costs resulting from pollution damage, noted $C(X)$, is the quadratic form:

$$C(X) = -cX^2 \qquad (13.2)$$

where $c > 0$ is a valuation parameter. We adopt the convention that costs are negative.

The emission of pollution can be decreased from E_1 to a constant $E_2 < E_1$, at a cost K, which may depend on E_1 and the change $E_1 - E_2$. We suppose that K is completely sunk, which is reasonable for many pollution control measures (e.g., the installation of scrubbers by utilities). After the emission reduction investment is made, X follows the new process:

$$dx = (E_2 - \alpha X)\, dt + \sqrt{vX}\, dz = \alpha(x_{2c} - X)\, dt + \sqrt{vX}\, dz \qquad (13.3)$$

where $x_{2c} \equiv E_2/\alpha$.

To eliminate risk aversion from the problem, we consider a risk-neutral social planner whose goal is to simultaneously select $E_2 (0 \leq E_2 \leq E_1)$, the rate to which pollutant emission should be reduced, and T, the socially optimal time of doing so, in order to maximize (with respect to T and E_2) the present value function:

$$J(T, E_2) = \varepsilon_0 \int_0^\infty -cX^2 e^{-rt} dt - e^{-rt} K(E_2, E_1 - E2) \qquad (13.4)$$

subject to Eq. (13.1) for $0 \leq t \leq T$ and to Eq. (13.3) for $t > T$, given $X(0)$. Here, ε_0 is the expectation operator based on information available at time $t = 0$ and r is the social discount (risk-free) rate.

This optimization problem can be solved in two steps. First, for an arbitrary value of E_2, such that $0 \leq E_2 < E_1$, we calculate the critical (threshold) stock of pollutant, denoted x^*, at which the rate of pollution emission should be reduced from E_1 to E_2. Once x^* is known, we can find $\varepsilon_0 T(x^*; E_2)$, the expected time at which the stock of pollutant reaches x^* for the first time, given an initial stock of $X(0)$. When $v > 0$, X is a random variable and $T(x^*; E_2)$ is a (first-passage) stopping time. For E_2 fixed, $X < x^*$ defines the so-called "continuation region," or region 1, where the optimal decision is to wait. As soon as $X > x^*$, which defines the so-called "stopping region," or region 2, the rate of pollutant emissions should be reduced to E_2. The second step consists in finding the value of E_2 that will maximize the objective function J.

In this chapter we want to analyze the impact of uncertainty on the timing of the decision to make a sunk investment K to reduce pollution emissions, for arbitrary functional forms of K. Hence, we focus on the determination of x^* as a function of v for a fixed E_2, and we ignore the determination of the optimal value of T that comes into play in the determination of E_2.

We thus have a standard stopping problem that bears similarities with an optimal investment problem. We solve the problem by stochastic dynamic programming. Let $V_i(x)$ be the value function in region "i." The corresponding Hamilton–Jacobi–Bellman equation is

$$rV_i = -cx^2 + (-\alpha x + E_i)\frac{dV_i}{dx} + \frac{vx}{2}\frac{d^2 V_i}{dx^2}, \qquad i = 1, 2 \qquad (13.5)$$

The left side of Eq. (13.5) can be interpreted as a return; the first term on the right side is the flow of social pollution costs; and the other terms, which result from Ito's Lemma (see Karlin and Taylor, 1975), represent capital gains.

Equation (13.5) is a linear second-order equation. Its solution is thus the sum of a particular solution, denoted $P_i(x)$, and the general solution of the associated homogeneous equation, denoted $\varphi(x)$. We pick $P_i(x)$ to represent the expected social costs from continuing to emit the pollutant at rate E_i forever, given a current stock of pollutant of x. $\varphi(x)$ is the value of the option to choose the timing for reducing emissions. By construction, it has nonnegative value. In this context, waiting reduces the present value of the cost of cutting pollution emissions while reducing emissions earlier decreases the present value of pollution damages. In financial terms, $\varphi(x)$ is a perpetual American option.

When we consider a one-time reduction in pollutant emissions, there is no option term after pollutant emissions have been cut to E_2, so the solutions of Eq. (13.5) in regions 1 and 2, respectively, are

$$V_1(x) = \varphi(x) + P_1(x), \qquad V_2(x) = P_2(x) \tag{13.6}$$

To find x^*, we need two additional conditions (for a heuristic proof, see Dixit and Pindyck, 1994; for a more rigorous treatment see Brekke and Oksendal, 1991). First, at x^*, the value of the option plus the social cost of polluting forever at rate E_1 should equal the social cost of polluting forever at rate E_2 plus the cost of reducing emissions from E_1 to E_2. This gives the continuity condition:

$$\varphi(x^*) + P_1(x^*) = P_2(x^*) - K \tag{13.7}$$

The second condition, called "smooth-pasting," says that when the option to reduce emissions should be exercised, a marginal change in the value of the option equals the marginal change in the difference of social pollution costs:

$$\frac{d\varphi(x^*)}{dx} = \frac{dP_2(x^*)}{dx} - \frac{dP_1(x^*)}{dx} \tag{13.8}$$

By combining these two conditions, we obtain a "stopping rule": for this problem, it is an equation whose smallest nonnegative root defines the critical stock of pollutant at which pollution emissions should be reduced from E_1 to E_2.

13.3 SOLUTION OF THE DETERMINISTIC CASE

We implement the above formulation in a deterministic setting ($v = 0$) to illustrate the concept of real option. In this context, the real option term gives the value of being able to choose the timing and magnitude of a one-time investment to reduce pollution emissions. In this case, there is no arrival of information over time so the option term measures the value of the flexibility of a decision with irreversible consequences. Equations (13.1), (13.3), and (13.5) degenerate to first-order linear differential equations. Integrating Eq. (13.1) gives

$$X(t) = \frac{E_1}{\alpha} + \left[X(0) - \frac{E_1}{\alpha} \right] e^{-\alpha t} \tag{13.9}$$

This shows that if pollutant emission rates are unchanged, X converges asymptotically towards $x_{1c} \equiv E_1/\alpha$, from above if $X(0) > x_{1c}$, and from below otherwise. In this case, x_{1c} is a barrier. Next, we calculate the present value of social pollution costs.

Lemma 1: *If the rate of pollutant emission is fixed at E_i and the initial stock of pollutant is x, the present value of social pollution costs is*

$$P_i(x) = -\frac{cx^2}{(r+2\alpha)} - \frac{2cE_i x}{(r+\alpha)(r+2\alpha)} - \frac{2cE_i^2}{r(r+\alpha)(r+2\alpha)} \qquad (13.10)$$

To prove Lemma 1, simply calculate $\int_0^{+\infty} -cX^2 e^{-rt} dt$ with $X(t) = [x - (E_i/\alpha)] e^{-\alpha t} + (E_i/\alpha)$.

The option term for this case is

$$\varphi(X) = \text{Max}\,[\widetilde{\varphi}(X), 0] \qquad (13.11)$$

where $\widetilde{\varphi}(x)$ is the solution of the homogeneous equation associated to Eq. (13.5):

$$\widetilde{\varphi}(x) = \begin{cases} A_0 |\alpha x - E_1|^{-r/a}, & \text{if } \alpha > 0 \\ \widetilde{\varphi}(x) = A_0 e^{(r x/E_1)}, & \text{if } \alpha = 0 \end{cases} \qquad (13.12)$$

In Eq. (13.12), A_0 is a nonnegative constant to be determined jointly with x_0^*, the critical stock of pollutant at which it is optimal to reduce pollution emissions from E_1 to E_2.

To obtain x_0^*, we substitute Eqs. (13.10), (13.11), and (13.12) into the continuity and smooth-pasting conditions and take their ratio to get rid of unknown parameter A_0. We find

$$x_0^* = \frac{r(2\alpha + r)K}{2c(E_1 - E_2)} - \frac{E_2}{\alpha + r} \qquad (13.13)$$

As expected, x_0^* increases with K, α, and r, and decreases when c or E_1 increase. Also note that x_0^* can be negative if the cost of adoption is "low," in which case the emission reduction policy should be adopted immediately.

However, if $x_0^* > x_{1c}$, the smooth-pasting condition cannot be met and Eq. (13.13) is not valid. Indeed,

$$\frac{d\widetilde{\varphi}(x)}{dx} = \frac{r}{E_1 - \alpha x} \widetilde{\varphi}(x) \quad \text{so} \quad \frac{d\widetilde{\varphi}(x)}{dx}$$

the left side of the smooth-pasting condition, is positive if $x < E_1/\alpha$ and negative otherwise. From Equation (13.10), $\forall x \geq 0$,

$$\frac{d P_{2,m}(x)}{dx} - \frac{d P_{1,m}(x)}{dx} > 0$$

which is the right-hand side of the smooth pasting condition. Hence, when $x_0^* > E_1/\alpha$, the option value is zero, so making a sunk investment to reduce pollution emissions is a "now or never" proposition: we should invest now in pollution reduction if $J(0, E_2) > J(+\infty, E_2)$, and never otherwise. Using Eqs. (13.4) and (13.10), we find that this condition is equivalent to the rule: when $x_0^* > E_1/\alpha$, invest now if $x > [(r+\alpha)x_0^* - E_1]/r$, where x is the current stock of pollutant, and never otherwise.

Once $x_0^* < x_{1c}$ is known, we can calculate the first-passage time T^* by inverting Eq. (13.9). We find

$$T^* = \begin{cases} \frac{1}{\alpha} \ln\left(\dfrac{E_1 - \alpha x_0}{E_1 - \alpha x_0^*}\right), & \text{if } \alpha > 0 \\ (x_0^* - x_0)/E_1, & \text{if } \alpha = 0 \end{cases} \tag{13.14}$$

Finally, we can derive explicitly the option term:

$$\widetilde{\varphi}(x) = \begin{cases} \dfrac{2c(E_1 - E_2)}{r(\alpha + r)(2\alpha + r)}(E_1 - \alpha x_0^*)\left|\dfrac{E_1 - \alpha x_0^*}{E_1 - \alpha x}\right|^{r/\alpha}, & \text{if } \alpha > 0 \\ \dfrac{2c(E_1 - E_2)E_1}{r^3}e^{(r/E_1)(x - x_0^*)}, & \text{if } \alpha = 0 \end{cases} \tag{13.15}$$

Once x_0^* is known for all values of E_2 of interest, the optimal level of pollution reduction E_2^* can be calculated by a simple optimization.

The expressions of T^* and x_0^* can also be obtained by solving the social planner's problem directly. In that case, the second-order condition for a maximum confirms that when $x_0^* > E_1/\alpha$, we should invest now in pollution reduction if $J(0, E_2) > J(+\infty, E_2)$, and never otherwise.

13.4 THE STOCHASTIC CASE

In this section, we assume that the variance parameter of the stock of pollutant, v, is greater than 0.

Lemma 2: *The expected social costs from continuing to pollute at rate E_i forever, given an initial pollutant stock x, are*

$$P_i(x) = -\frac{cx^2}{(r + 2\alpha)} - \frac{c(2E_i + v)x}{(r + \alpha)(r + 2\alpha)} - \frac{cE_i(2E_i + v)}{r(r + \alpha)(r + 2\alpha)} \tag{13.16}$$

To prove this result, we need to calculate the moment generating function of the process followed by X. Calculations are shown in Appendix A. From this expression for $P_i(x)$, it is clear that an increase in v augments the expected social costs of pollution. As before, P_i increases when r (or α) decreases, and it increases when E_i increases. Moreover, since $P_1(x) < P_2(x)$ (recall that $E_1 > E_2$), the smooth-pasting condition requires the option term to be increasing in x. Because the expression of the option term differs between the cases $\alpha = 0$ and $\alpha > 0$, we treat decaying and nondecaying pollutants separately.

13.4.1 The Case of a Decaying Pollutant

In this case ($\alpha > 0$), we have:

Lemma 3: *For a decaying pollutant, the stochastic option term is given by Eq. (13.11) with:*

$$\widetilde{\varphi}(x) = B_0 \Phi \left(\frac{r}{\alpha}, \frac{2E_1}{v}; \frac{2\alpha}{v}x \right) \tag{13.17}$$

See Appendix B for a proof. In the above, B_0 is a constant to be determined jointly with x^*, and $\Phi(a, b; y)$ is the confluent hypergeometric function with argument y and parameters a and b (see Lebedev, 1972).

Substituting Eqs. (13.16) and (13.17) into the continuity and smooth-pasting conditions (Eqs. 13.7 and 13.8), we find that x^* is the smallest nonnegative real value which verifies:

$$\left[\Phi \left(\frac{r}{\alpha}, \frac{2E_1}{v}; \frac{2\alpha}{v}x^* \right) \right] \bigg/ \left[\frac{r}{E_1} \Phi \left(\frac{r}{\alpha}+1, \frac{2E_1}{v}+1; \frac{2\alpha}{v}x^* \right) \right] =$$
$$x + \frac{E_1 - (r+\alpha)x_0^*}{r} + \frac{v}{2r} \tag{13.18}$$

Since

$$\frac{[P_2(x^*) - P_1(x^*) - K]}{\left[P_2'(x^*) - P_1'(x^*) \right]} = x + \frac{E_1 - (r+\alpha)x_0^*}{r} + \frac{v}{2r}$$

Equation (13.18) says that, at x^*, the net savings from reducing emissions from E_1 to E_2 divided by the corresponding marginal savings equals the ratio of the option term to its marginal value. This relationship defines x^* as a function of v.

In general, it is not possible to find an explicit expression for x^*, and it is quite difficult to examine how x^* changes with v because of the complexity of the derivative of $\Phi[(r/\alpha), (2E_1/v); (2\alpha/v)x]$ with respect to v. We thus examine how x^* changes for large values of v and for v close to zero. Considering first "large" values of v, we have

---

Proposition 1. *For "large enough" values of the pollutant stock volatility v, x^* decreases to zero. If $x_0^* > 0$, then the value of v for which $x^* = 0$ is $\tilde{v}$ such that*

$$\tilde{v} = 2(r+\alpha)x_0^* \tag{13.19}$$

If $x_0^* \leq 0$, pollution emissions should be reduced to E_2 right away.

This result is intuitive because an increase in v augments expected social costs, as we remarked above, but leaves investment K unchanged. For large enough values of v, environmental irreversibility prevails over sunk pollution control costs and it becomes optimal to act immediately.

Proof of Proposition 1. Equation (13.19) is obtained from Eq. (13.18) by setting x^* to zero and simplifying. If $x_0^* \leq 0$, we have seen above that the sunk investment needed for curbing emissions down to E_2 is so small relative to the expected social gains from a cleaner environment that pollution emissions should be curbed right away.

We next investigate how x^* changes when v goes to zero.

Proposition 2. *Let $\tilde{x}_0^* = \lim_{v \to 0+} x^*(v)$, where $x^*(v)$ is the solution of Eq. (13.18). When $x_0^* < E_1/\alpha$, $\tilde{x}_0^* = x_0^*$. However, when $x_0^* > E_1/\alpha$, $\tilde{x}_0^*$, differs from x_0^* given by Eq. (13.13) and, just as in the deterministic case, we find*

$$\tilde{x}_0^* = \frac{(r+\alpha)x_0^* - E_1}{r} > x_0^* \qquad (13.20)$$

The limit of the stochastic case as the volatility of the stock of pollutant goes to zero gives the deterministic results.

Proof of Proposition 2. When $\tilde{x}_0^* < E_1/\alpha$, it can be shown (see Appendix C) that

$$\lim_{v \to 0} \Phi\left(\frac{r}{\alpha} + k, \frac{2E_1}{v} + k; \frac{2\alpha x^*}{v}\right) = \left(1 - \frac{\alpha \tilde{x}_0^*}{E_1}\right)^{(r/a)k}$$

with $k = 0$ or 1. Inserting these results into Eq. (13.18) yields Eq. (13.13).
    However, when $\tilde{x}_0^* > E_1/\alpha$,

$$\lim_{v \to 0} \Phi\left(\frac{r}{\alpha}, \frac{2E_1}{v}; \frac{2\alpha}{v}x^*\right) \Big/ \Phi\left(\frac{r}{\alpha} + 1, \frac{2E_1}{v} + 1; \frac{2\alpha}{v}x^*\right) = 0$$

which leads to Eq. (13.20).

Let us now examine how $x^*(v)$ changes when v increases from 0.

Proposition 3. *For small values of v, the variance parameter of the process followed by the stock of pollutant, x^*, may be larger or smaller than $\tilde{x}_0^*$, depending on the cost of reducing emissions relative to the expected social gains from reducing the emissions of pollution. If we define: $x^*(v) = \tilde{x}_0^* = Dv + o(v)$, then*

$$D = \begin{cases} \dfrac{(2\alpha + r)x_0^* - E_1}{2(\alpha + r)(E_1 - \alpha x_0^*)}, & \text{if } \tilde{x}_0^* < \dfrac{E_1}{\alpha} \\[3ex] \dfrac{(\alpha - r)\tilde{x}_0^* - E_1}{2r(E_1 - \alpha \tilde{x}_0^*)}, & \text{if } \tilde{x}_0^* > \dfrac{E_1}{\alpha} \end{cases} \qquad (13.21)$$

Proof of Proposition 3. To derive this result, we substitute the first-order expansion of $x^*(v)$ as a function of v into the expression of the stopping frontier, given by Eq. (13.18). Details are provided in Appendix C.

From Eq. (13.21), we see that, if $x_0^* < E_1/(2\alpha + r)$ then $D < 0$, while $E_1/(2\alpha + r) < x_0^* < E_1/\alpha$ implies $D > 0$. If we recall the expression of x_0^*, the first case corresponds to relatively small values of K, so the environmental irreversibility dominates. An increase in v augments the expected social costs, so action is required earlier than in the deterministic case. If K (and thus x_0^*) is larger, sunk investment costs dominate. When $x_0^* > E_1/\alpha$, the sign of D depends on the value of r (the social discount rate) compared to that of α (the pollutant rate of decay). A little algebra shows that if $\alpha < r$ (i.e., the pollutant decays faster than the social discount rate), then $D > 0$. If $\alpha > r$, however, D is positive for $E_1/\alpha < \tilde{x}_0^* < E_1/(\alpha - r)$ and negative for $\tilde{x}_0^* > E_1/(\alpha - r)$.

13.4.2 The Case of a Nondecaying Pollutant

For completeness, we now deal with the case of a nondecaying pollutant ($\alpha = 0$). Proceeding as above, we obtain qualitatively the same results as for a decaying pollutant in the region $x_0^* < x_{1c}$ (when $\alpha = 0, x_{1c} = +\infty$). More specifically, we find that:

> **Lemma 4:** *For a nondecaying pollutant ($\alpha = 0$), the stochastic option term is given by Eq. (13.11) with*

$$\tilde{\varphi}(x) = D_0 \Theta\left(\frac{2E_1}{v}; \frac{2r}{v}x\right) \tag{13.22}$$

(See Appendix D for a proof.) As before, D_0 is a constant that has to be evaluated jointly with x^*, and Θ is given by

$$\Theta(a; y) = \sum_{n=0}^{+\infty} \frac{1}{(a)_n} \frac{y^n}{n!} = \Gamma(a)y^{(1-a)/2}I_{a-1}(2\sqrt{y}) \tag{13.23}$$

$I_v(z)$ is the modified Bessel function of order v. Equation (13.16), which gives $P_i(x)$, is still valid after setting α to zero. Substituting Eqs. (13.22) and (13.16) (with $\alpha = 0$) into the continuity and smooth-pasting conditions [Eqs. (13.7) and (13.8)], we find that x^* is the smallest nonnegative root of

$$\left[\Theta\left(\frac{2E_1}{v}; \frac{2r}{v}x\right)\right] \Big/ \left[\frac{r}{E_1}\Theta\left(\frac{2E_1}{v} + 1; \frac{2r}{v}x\right)\right] = x = \frac{E_1 - rx_0^*}{r} + \frac{v}{2r} \tag{13.24}$$

This equation has the same interpretation as Eq. (13.18). Proposition 1, the first part of Proposition 2 (here $\alpha = 0$ so $x_{1c} = \infty$), and Proposition 3 remain valid for this case after setting α to zero. For small values of v, we find that $x^*(v)$ decreases when v increases if x_0^* is "small," which happens when environmental irreversibility dominates. Conversely, $x^*(v)$ increases with v when x_0^* is "large," which happens when sunk costs from pollution control are larger.

13.5 A NUMERICAL APPLICATION

A numerical illustration is presented in Figure 13.1A and B and in Table 13.1. Figure 13.1A and B shows how x^*/x_0^* [the critical stock of pollutant in the stochastic case, also noted $x^*(v)$, normalized by its deterministic value] changes as a function of $\sqrt{v}$ over a range of parameter values for α and r, respectively. Table 13.1 gives the value of the critical stock of pollutant, $x^*(v)$, and option value at $x^*(v)$ per unit cost K (noted φ^*/K), for small values of v and for a wide range of values of α and r. Results in Table 13.1 are for $E_1 = 1$ and $E_2 = 0.7$, which corresponds to a 30% reduction in pollutant emissions.

From the figures, observe that $x^*(v)$ goes to zero for large enough values of $\sqrt{v}$, as shown in Proposition 1. In that case, expected environmental damages, which increase with v, dominate sunk pollution control investments. Moreover, α and r appear to have symmetric effects on the determination of $x^*(v)$. This is expected

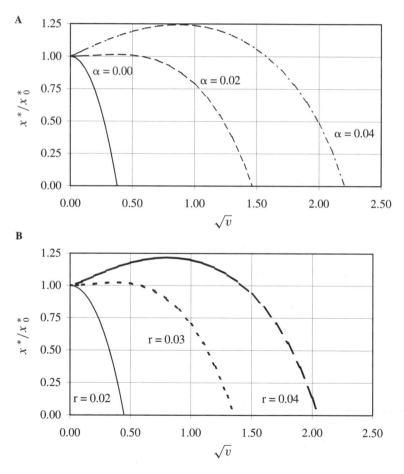

Figure 13.1 (A) Variations of x^*/x_0^* with $\sqrt{v}$ and α for $r = 0.06$, $E_1 = 1$, $E_2 = 0.75$, and $K/c = 1900$. (B) Variations of x^*/x_0^* with $\sqrt{v}$ and r for $\alpha = 0.03$, $E_1 = 1$, $E_2 = 0.7$, and $K/c = 6000$. x^* is the critical stock of pollutant; α is the pollutant rate of decay; r is the social discount rate; v is the volatility of X; K is the sunk investment needed to reduce pollution emissions from E_1 to E_2; and c is the coefficient of valuation of pollution.

Table 13.1

Critical Pollutant Stock (x^*) and Standardized Option Value at x^{*a}

α	$\sqrt{v}$	$r = 0.02$		$r = 0.03$		$r = 0.04$		$r = 0.05$	
		x^*	$\varphi^*/K(\%)$	x^*	$\varphi^*/K(\%)$	x^*	$\varphi^*/K(\%)$	x^*	$\varphi^*/K(\%)$
$K/c = 20000$									
0.00	0.00	< 0	—	6.67	111.1	35.83	46.9	69.33	24.0
	0.05	< 0	—	6.63	111.1	35.85	47.0	69.39	24.1
	0.10	< 0	—	6.53	111.2	35.89	47.2	69.57	24.4
0.01	0.00	3.33	120.8	32.50	33.8	66.00	8.5	106.00[b]	0.0
	0.05	3.30	120.9	32.53	33.9	66.21	8.7	107.09	0.8
	0.10	3.18	121.1	32.61	34.2	66.76	9.4	108.55	1.9
$K/c = 6000$									
0.02	0.00	< 0	—	7.00	81.9	20.33	30.9	35.00	9.5
	0.05	< 0	—	6.99	82.0	20.36	31.0	35.12	9.8
	0.10	< 0	—	6.94	82.2	20.42	31.3	35.45	10.4
0.03	0.00	2.00	117.5	15.33	33.3	30.00	3.6	54.00[b]	0.0
	0.05	1.98	117.6	15.35	33.4	30.29	4.0	54.08	0.1
	0.10	1.91	117.9	15.39	33.7	30.88	5.0	54.32	0.5
0.04	0.00	8.33	55.6	23.00	3.5	53.50[b]	0.0	83.00[b]	0.0
	0.05	8.33	55.7	23.27	3.9	53.53	0.1	83.02	0.0
	0.10	8.31	55.9	23.81	4.7	53.61	0.2	83.08	0.2

[a] x^* is the critical stock of pollutant; α is the pollutant rate of decay; r is the social discount rate; v is the volatility of X; K is the sunk investment needed to reduce pollution emissions from E_1 to E_2; c is the coefficient of valuation of pollution; and ϕ^*/K is the option value at x^* normalized by K.
[b] Indicates that $\tilde{x}_0^*$ differs from x_0^* given by Eq. (13.13).

since a decrease in α increases future levels of the stock of pollutant, everything else being the same, and thus increases expected social pollution costs. A decrease in r has the same effect, although more directly. For small values of v, $x^*(v)$ can either increase or decrease with v, as shown in Proposition 3. However, for relatively large values of α and r, the expected social costs of pollution are given less weight and irreversibility linked to pollution control dominates.

The evolution of $x^*(v)$ when v is small is examined in more detail in Table 13.1, which provides values for the relative magnitude of the option value at the critical stock of pollutant $x^*(v)$. First, we see that option value can be larger than K. Ignoring it (as would be done in a conventional cost–benefit analysis) is likely to yield suboptimal decisions. We also observe that option value increases with v, which makes sense because an increase in v augments expected environmental damages while leaving K unchanged. The flexibility to reduce expected social costs then becomes more valuable. As expected, for $\tilde{x}_0^* > E_1/\alpha$, we see that option value is close to zero when v is small since there is no option value when $x_0^* > E_1/\alpha$ in the deterministic case. Finally, Table 13.1 illustrates the large sensitivity of x^* to α and r.

13.6 CONCLUSIONS

In this chapter, we use the theory of real options to examine the tension between ecological irreversibility and investment irreversibility (sunk pollution control costs), in the presence of ecological uncertainty. This uncertainty is represented by the stochastic variations of a stock of pollutant, which result from natural fluctuations in its absorption or production by ecosystems (as in the case of some greenhouse gases, for example). After developing a simple deterministic model to obtain a benchmark for the impact of uncertainty, we analyze a stochastic model in which the infinitesimal variance of the pollutant stock, denoted vX, varies linearly with X. When uncertainty is low, we show that a small level of uncertainty may either delay or advance a reduction in pollutant emissions, depending on the cost of reducing pollution relative to the expected social gains from reducing pollution. This is because at low levels of uncertainty, either ecological (through natural damage) or investment (through sunk investments needed to reduce emissions) irreversibility may prevail. Thus, we cannot know a priori the bias introduced by neglecting low levels of uncertainty in environmental problems. Moreover, we show that when uncertainty is high enough, expected environmental damages become dominant and pollutant emissions should be reduced immediately.

These results illustrate the need to model uncertainty explicitly in environmental problems as uncertainty may have a key impact both on the timing and intensity of pollution reduction measures. In particular, our results may be useful in the debate on global warming where it is often argued that action on curbing emission of greenhouse gases should be delayed to wait for the arrival of new information on the effect of global warming.

Finally, this chapter shows that the theory of real options provides a natural framework to analyze environmental policy because irreversibility and uncertainty are dominant features of many environmental problems. Indeed, the theory of real options embodies Weisbrod's original intuition on option value, and it does not suffer from some of the conceptual problems that plague the concept of option value in the environmental economics literature.

Appendix A

Let $M(\theta, t)$ be the moment generating function of $X(t)$ with $\alpha > 0$:

$$M(\theta, t) = \varepsilon(e^{-\theta x}) = \int_{-\infty}^{+\infty} \phi(x_0, t_0; x, t) E^{-\theta x} dx \qquad (13.A1)$$

where $\phi(x_0, t_0; x, t)$ is the probability density function of x at t, given that $x(t_0) = x_0$. Then

$$\frac{\partial M}{\partial t} = \int_{-\infty}^{+\infty} \frac{\partial \phi}{\partial t} e^{-\theta x} dx \qquad (13.A2)$$

The Kolmogorov forward equation for this process (see Cox and Miller, 1965) is

$$\frac{\partial \phi}{\partial t} = \frac{vx}{2} \frac{\partial^2 \phi}{\partial x^2} + (v + \alpha x - E_1) \frac{\partial \phi}{\partial x} + \alpha \phi \qquad (13.A3)$$

We substitute (13.A3) into (13.A2) and integrate to obtain

$$\frac{\partial M}{\partial t} = -\theta(\alpha + \frac{v}{2}\theta) \frac{\partial M}{\partial \theta} - E_1 \theta M \qquad (13.A4)$$

This partial differential equation must be solved subject to the boundary conditions

$$M(0, t) = 1, \quad \frac{\partial M(0, 0)}{\partial \theta} = -x_0, \quad \frac{\partial^2 M(0, 0)}{\partial \theta^2} = x_0^2 \qquad (13.A5)$$

We find

$$M(\theta, t) = \left(1 + \frac{v\theta}{2\alpha}\right)^{(2E/v)} \left[1 + C_1 \frac{2\theta e^{-\alpha t}}{2\alpha + \theta v} + C_2 \left(\frac{2\theta e^{-\alpha t}}{2\alpha + \theta v}\right)^2\right] \qquad (13.A6)$$

with

$$C_1 = E - \alpha x_0, \quad C_2 = \frac{1}{2}\left[\left(E - \alpha x_0 + \frac{v}{2}\right)^2 - \frac{v}{2}\left(E + \frac{v}{2}\right)\right] \qquad (13.A7)$$

We then use the relationship

$$\frac{\partial^n M(0, t)}{\partial \theta^n} = (-1)^n \varepsilon(x_t^n) \qquad (13.A8)$$

and integrate with respect to time to obtain Eq. (13.16).

Appendix B

In this Appendix, we obtain the option term of the stochastic problem. It must be defined at $X = 0$, be nonnegative, and increasing with X. Let $Y = 2\alpha X/v$, and define $W(Y) \equiv V(X)$. With this change of variables, the homogeneous equation corresponding to Eq. (13.5) becomes

$$Y\frac{d^2 W}{dY2} + \left(\frac{2E_1}{v} - Y\right)\frac{dW}{dY} - \frac{r}{\alpha}W = 0 \qquad (13.B1)$$

This is Kummer's Equation (see Lebedev, 1972), a second-order ordinary differential equation. A general solution of Eq. (13.B1) can be written as

$$W(Y) = B_0 \Phi\left(\frac{r}{\alpha}, \frac{2E_1}{v}; Y\right) + B_1 z^{1-b} \Phi\left(1 + \frac{r}{\alpha} - \frac{2E_1}{v}, 2 - \frac{2E_1}{v}; Y\right) \qquad (13.B2)$$

where Φ is the confluent hypergeometric function of the first kind, and B_0 and B_1 are two unknown constants. Φ has the series representation

$$\Phi(a, b; z) = \sum_{k=0}^{+\infty} \frac{(a)_k}{(b)_k} \frac{z^k}{k!} \qquad (13.B3)$$

As $z \to 0$, the derivative of the second solution tends to $+\infty$, and for v small enough, the second solution itself tends to $+\infty$. We thus retain only the term in $B_0 \Phi$ as our solution. In the above

$$(b)_0 = 1, \ (b)_k = \frac{\Gamma(b+k)}{\Gamma(b)} = b(b+1)\ldots(b+k-1) \quad \text{for } k \geq 1 \ (13.B4)$$

and Γ is the Gamma function. To find the stopping frontier, we need the derivative of Φ. From its series expansion, it is easy to see that

$$\frac{d\Phi(a, b; z)}{dx} = \frac{a}{b}\Phi(a+1, b+1; z) \qquad (13.B5)$$

Appendix C

In this Appendix we derive a first-order approximation to $x^*(v)$ when v is close to zero. When $v \to 0$, we have the formal convergence

$$\Phi\left[\frac{r}{\alpha}, \frac{2E_1}{v}; \frac{2\alpha}{v}x^*(v)\right] \to S(\tilde{x}_0^*) \equiv \sum_{n=0}^{+\infty}\left(\frac{r}{\alpha}\right)_n \frac{1}{n!}\left(\frac{\alpha\tilde{x}_0^*}{E_1}\right)^n \qquad (13.C1)$$

This series converges provided $\alpha\tilde{x}_0^*/E_1 < 1$, or $\tilde{x}_0^* < E_1/\alpha \equiv x_{1c}$, where $\tilde{x}_0^* = \lim_{v\to 0} x^*(v)$. When this condition does not hold, $S(\tilde{x}_0^*) = +\infty$. We thus distinguish between two cases:

Case 1: $\tilde{x}_0^* < x_{1c}$

In this case, we can use Eq. (4.3.7) in Slater (1960):

$$\Phi(a, b; by) = (1-y)^{-a}\left[1 - \frac{a(a+1)}{2b}\left(\frac{y}{1-y}\right)^2 + O(|b|^{-2})\right] \ (13.C2)$$

This expression is valid for a and y bounded complex variables and b real and "large." Then

$$\Phi(a+1, b+1; by) = (1-ky)^{-a-1}$$

$$\left[1 - \frac{(a+1)(a+2)}{2(b+1)}\left(\frac{ky}{1-ky}\right)^2 + O(|b|^{-2})\right] \qquad (13.C3)$$

with $k \equiv b/(b+1)$. Here, $a = r/\alpha$, $b = 2E_1/v$, $z = 2\alpha x^*/v$, so $y = \alpha x^*/E_1$ and $k = 2E_1/(2E_1 + v)$. Using repeatedly $(1 + \varepsilon)^r = 1 + r\varepsilon + o(\varepsilon)$ where ε is small, we find

$$\text{As } v \to 0+, \quad \left[\Phi\left(\frac{r}{\alpha}, \frac{2E_1}{v}; \frac{2\alpha x^*}{v}\right)\right]\left[\Phi\left(\frac{r}{\alpha}+1, \frac{2E_1}{v}+1; \frac{2\alpha x^*}{v}\right)\right]$$

$$= \left(1 - \frac{\alpha x^*}{E_1}\right)\left[1 + \frac{\alpha + r}{2}\frac{x^* v}{(E_1 - \alpha x^*)^2} + o(v)\right] \tag{13.C4}$$

Case 2: $\tilde{x}_0^* > x_{1c}$

In this case, we extend (9.12.8) in Lebedev (1972) to obtain:

$$\Phi(a; b; by) = \frac{\Gamma(b)}{\Gamma(a)}e^{by}(by)^{a-b}\left[\left(1 - \frac{1}{y}\right)^{a-1} + o(1)\right] \tag{13.C5}$$

so, after substituting and simplifying

$$\text{As } v \to 0+, \quad \left[\Phi\left(\frac{r}{\alpha}, \frac{2F_1}{v}; \frac{2\alpha}{v}x^*\right)\right]\left[\Phi\left(\frac{r}{\alpha}+1, \frac{2E_1}{v}+1; \frac{2\alpha}{v}x^*\right)\right]$$

$$= \frac{rx^* v}{2E_1(\alpha x^* - E_1)} + o(v) \tag{13.C6}$$

Using this result into Eq. (13.18) leads to Eq. (13.20).

To derive the results of Proposition 3, we start by substituting the expression

$$x^*(v) = \tilde{x}_0^* + Dv + o(v) \tag{13.C7}$$

into the right-hand side (noted RIIS) of Eq. (13.18). We obtain

$$\text{RHS} = 1 + \frac{r\tilde{x}_0^*}{E_1} - \frac{r+\alpha}{E_1}x_0^* + \left(\frac{rD}{E_1} + \frac{1}{2E_1}\right)v + o(v) \tag{13.C8}$$

Combining this result with Eqs. (13.C4) and (13.C6) yields Eq. (13.21).

Appendix D

To find the option term when $\alpha = 0$, we need to find a solution to the following equation (which is positive, increasing, and well defined for x nonnegative):

$$rV = E\frac{dV}{dx} + \frac{vx}{2}\frac{d^2V}{dx^2} \tag{13.D1}$$

Trying a series solution we find

$$V(x) = D_0 \Theta \left(\frac{2E_1}{v}; \frac{2rx}{v} \right) \equiv D_0 \sum_0^{+\infty} \frac{1}{(2E_1/v)_n} \frac{1}{n!} \left(\frac{2rx}{v} \right)^n \quad (13.\text{D}2)$$

where D_0 is a constant. Equation (13.D1) is a second-order ordinary differential equation so we need to find another independent solution. A simple calculation shows that

$$\Omega(x) \equiv x^{1-(2E_1/v)} \Theta \left(\frac{2E_1}{v}; \frac{2rx}{v} \right) = x^{1-(2E_1/v)} \sum_0^{+\infty} \frac{1}{(2E_1/v)_n} \frac{1}{n!} \left(\frac{2rx}{v} \right)^n \quad (13.\text{D}3)$$

is also a solution of Eq. (13.D1). We discard this solution, however, because its derivative is infinite at 0 (and it may not be well defined at $x = 0$ when v is small).

ACKNOWLEDGMENTS

We thank Michael Brennan, Lenos Trigeorgis, Jon Conrad, and Neha Khanna for helpful comments on various versions of this paper. We are of course responsible for all remaining errors.

REFERENCES

Arrow, K. J., and A. C. Fisher. (1974). Environmental Preservation, Uncertainty, and Irreversibility. *Quarterly Journal of Economics* 88, 312–319.

Brekke, K. A., and B. Oksendal. (1991). The High Contact Principle as a Sufficiency Condition for Optimal Stopping. In D. Lund and B. Oksendal (eds.), *Stochastic Models and Option Values*, pp. 187–208. Amsterdam: North Holland.

Brennan, M. J., and E. S. Schwartz. (1985). Evaluating Natural Resources Investments. *Journal of Business* 58 (January), 135–157.

Cicchetti, C. J., and A. M. Freeman III. (1971). Option Demand and Consumer Surplus: Comment. *Quarterly Journal of Economics* 85, 523–527.

Clarke, H. R., and W. J. Reed. (1990). Land Development and Wilderness Conservation Policies under Uncertainty: A Synthesis. *Natural Resources Modeling* 4, 11–37.

Conrad, J. M. (1980). Quasi-Option Value and the Expected Value of Information. *Quarterly Journal of Economics* 95, 813–820.

Cox, D. R., and H. D. Miller. (1965). *The Theory of Stochastic Processes*. London: Chapman and Hall.

Dixit, A. K., and R. S. Pindyck. (1994). *Investment under Uncertainty*. Princeton, NJ: Princeton University Press.

Freixas, X., and J.-J. Laffont. (1984). The Irreversibility Effect. In M. Boyer and R. Khilstrom (eds.), *Bayesian Models in Economic Theory*. Amsterdam: North Holland.

Hanemann, W. M. (1989). Information and the Concept of Option Value. *Journal of Environmental Economics and Management* 16, 23–37.

Henry, C. (1974). Investment Decisions under Uncertainty. *American Economic Review* 64, 1006–1012.

Karlin, S., and H. M. Taylor. (1975). *A First Course in Stochastic Processes*, 2nd ed. New York: Academic Press.

Kolstad, C. D. (1996). Fundamental Irreversibilities in Stock Externalities. *Journal of Public Economics* 60, 221–233.

Lebedev, N. N. (1972). *Special Functions and Their Applications*. R. A. Silverman, trans. New York: Dover Publications.

Malliaris, A. G., and W. A. Brock. (1982). *Stochastic Methods in Economics and Finance*. Amsterdam: North Holland.

Paddock, J. L., D. R. Siegel, and J. L. Smith. (1988). Option Valuation of Claims on Real Assets: The Case of Offshore Petroleum Leases. *Quarterly Journal of Economics* 103 (August), 479–508.

Schmalensee, R. (1972). Option Demand and Consumer Surplus: Valuing Price Changes under Uncertainty. *American Economic Review* 62, 814–824.

Slater, L. J. (1960). *Confluent Hypergeometric Functions*. Cambridge: Cambridge University Press.

Trigeorgis, L. (1996). *Real Options: Managerial Flexibility and Strategy in Resource Allocation*. Cambridge, MA: MIT Press.

Weisbrod, B.A. (1964). Collective-Consumption Services of Individualized-Consumption Goods. *Quarterly Journal of Economics* 78, 471–477.

Part IV

Strategic Options and Product Market Competition

14

Equilibrium with Time-to-Build

A Real Options Approach

STEVEN R. GRENADIER

In most real options models of investment, it is assumed that investment strategies can be formulated in isolation and that investment is instantaneous. In this chapter, both of these assumptions are relaxed. A real options approach is utilized to derive a dynamic competitive equilibrium for a market subject to time-to-build. Such an equilibrium is complicated by a potentially infinite state space, as future prices depend not only on completed supply, but also on the previous entry times of units in the supply pipeline. The equilibrium processes for prices, quantities, and asset values are fully characterized. Several interesting aspects of the equilibrium are discussed. In particular, equilibrium asset values are path dependent, and equilibrium entry strategies are always conditional on a finite transformation of the original state space.

14.1 INTRODUCTION

Two fundamental characteristics of many real-world investment decisions are that investment takes time to build, and that investment strategies take place in a competitive context and cannot be formulated in isolation. For example, consider a real estate developer contemplating the construction of an office building. Because construction may take over 2 years from initiation until completion, the agent must exercise his development option conditional on his expectation of rents prevailing at the completion of construction. In addition, while this developer contemplates the optimal construction time, so too do his competitors. The developers realize that the construction decisions of their competitors will impact both equilibrium rents and building values. However, with few exceptions, real options models of investment under uncertainty assume that investment is instantaneous and that investment payoffs are unaffected by the actions of competitors. In this chapter, a model is developed that combines the time-to-build feature with a competitive industry equilibrium. By using a real options approach, the model is able to fully characterize equilibrium entry, prices, and asset values.

Time-to-build is an important characteristic of many real investment markets. Examples of investments with significant construction lags abound. In commercial real estate development, the construction of large office towers or superregional shopping malls can often take more than 2 years to complete (Wheaton, 1987). In mining and natural resource extraction, the construction of an underground mine can require at least 5 or 6 years (Majd and Pindyck, 1987). For these markets with time-to-build, investors must optimally take into account in their investment decisions the potential market fluctuations that may ensue over the intervening construction period. The inclusion of a time-to-build feature in real options models has thus far been confined to models of individual firm (rather than industry equilibrium) investment strategies. Real options models with time-to-build include Majd and Pindyck (1987), Grenadier (1995a, 1996), and Bar-Ilan and Strange (1996).

The impact that the forces of competition have on investment outcomes has also been relatively neglected in real options models. In the majority of both financial as well as real options models, the starting point is an exogenous process for underlying asset values (e.g., the stock price in the Black–Scholes framework) or cash flows [e.g., Brennan and Schwartz (1985) or McDonald and Siegel (1986)]. In essence, this assumption allows agents to ignore their competitors' investment strategies while formulating their own. However, for many real investment contexts, the payoffs from a firm's investment are fundamentally affected by the investment strategies of its competitors. In the model developed in this chapter, I take the industry equilibrium structure to be perfectly competitive. Real options models that utilize a competitive equilibrium structure (but with no time-to-build) include Leahy (1993), Dixit (1989a, 1991), and Grenadier (1995b).[1]

The general framework of the model is the real options approach to investment under uncertainty in a competitive industry subject to continuous-time demand shocks. Investment requires an initial lump sum construction cost and a time-to-build period of δ years. At any point in time, firms that have completed construction sell their existing supply of a single, homogeneous good. Market clearing ensures that the spot price adjusts so that current supply equals (stochastic) demand. In addition, there are firms currently undergoing construction, as units in the pipeline await completion. If the industry's prospects become sufficiently favorable, new firms will find it optimal to begin constructing new units of the asset and enter the industry. The decision to enter the industry is analogous to the decision to exercise a call option on an asset δ years from completion, where the relevant exercise price is the cost of construction.

Although firms pursue individually optimal entry strategies, the forces of competition lead to a competitive determination of equilibrium prices, supply, and asset

---

[1] For models of real options with an oligopolistic industry equilibrium, see Grenadier (1996, 1999), Kulatilaka and Perotti (1998), and Smit and Trigeorgis (1997). For examples of strategic option exercise behavior in the context of warrants and convertible securities, see Emanuel (1983), Constantinides (1984), and Spatt and Sterbenz (1988).

values. Individual firms choose entry strategies in a framework of irreversible investment under uncertainty. However, whenever the value of entering the industry rises to the level of the construction cost, new firms will enter ensuring that there are no excess profits from entry.

The difficulty of deriving a competitive industry equilibrium with time-to-build is that the state space of the industry can be of infinite dimension. Unless the model can be converted to one of finite dimensionality, the standard solution techniques that require a Markov state space cannot be employed. Consider the relevant variables that are needed to describe the current state of the industry. At any time t, the current state of demand and the number of completed units on the market determine the current level of output prices. However, agents must also condition their information on the number of units currently in the pipeline as well as the times at which these units will be completed. The amount and arrival times of units currently in the pipeline are relevant because they will impact the prices over the ensuing δ years of construction. However, to know the arrival times of units under construction, agents need knowledge of the historical path of entry over the previous δ years.

The solution approach employed in this chapter is to solve for an equilibrium in an "artificial" industry in which all units currently in the pipeline are assumed to be completed. Thus, in this artificial industry there are only two relevant state variables: the current level of demand and the total supply of "committed capacity." The essential feature of this artificial industry is that the equilibrium entry strategies will be identical to those in the true industry. The intuition is quite simple. Because a firm entering construction will not receive cash flows for δ years, the firm is concerned only with the supply of assets δ years in the future and beyond. As all of the current units under construction will have been completed by then, they are treated the same as all currently completed units. Given the derived equilibrium entry strategies, the true equilibrium prices are then determined by market clearing. Finally, equilibrium asset values can be determined from the discounted expected value of future equilibrium prices, net of the cost of construction.

The equilibrium processes for supply, prices, and asset values are fully characterized. Closed-form solutions for asset values as well as the conditional probability density functions for future supply and prices are presented. Several interesting features of the equilibrium are apparent. First, current asset values depend not only on current supply and demand, but also on the path of previous construction, i.e., on the times at which units currently in the pipeline will complete construction. This path dependency is a consequence of the time-to-build feature. Second, in contrast to the standard real options result that investment occurs only when net present values are positive, in a competitive equilibrium the option to wait is eliminated under competitive pressure. Third, in contrast to the standard real options competitive equilibrium where the equilibrium price process follows a regulated diffusion process, in this model with construction lags it is the expected price prevailing at completion δ years in the future that follows a regulated diffusion process.

The chapter proceeds as follows. Section 14.2 outlines the basic model and assumptions. Section 14.3 derives the competitive equilibrium entry strategies. Section 14.4 analyzes the equilibrium processes for supply, output prices, and asset values. Section 14.5 concludes.

14.2 MODEL AND ASSUMPTIONS

Consider a competitive industry with a large number of firms producing a single, homogeneous good. For convenience, I assume that each firm owns one unit of the underlying asset. Thus, one can use the terms "firm" and "asset" interchangeably.[2] In addition, I assume that the units are small enough and the number of firms large enough that the current total supply of completed output may be represented as a continuum whose mass at time t is $C(t)$.

At each point in time, the price per unit of output, $P(t)$, evolves in order to clear the market. Assume that the market inverse demand function is of the constant-elasticity form:

$$P(t) = X(t) C(t)^{-1/\gamma} \tag{14.1}$$

where $\gamma > 0$.[3] Such a market is characterized by evolving uncertainty in the state of demand for the good. At each point in time, even demand at the next instant is uncertain. $X(t)$ represents a multiplicative demand shock that evolves as a geometric Brownian motion:

$$dX = \alpha_x X dt + \sigma_x X dz_x \tag{14.2}$$

where α_x is the instantaneous conditional expected percentage change in X per unit time, σ_x is the instantaneous conditional standard deviation per unit time, and dz_x is an increment of a standard Wiener process.

Firms may add to the supply of assets by incurring a one-time construction cost of K, proportional to the quantity of new units supplied, which are assumed irreversibly committed thereafter. Although completed supply earns an instantaneous profit per unit time of $P(t)$, there is a lag between the initiation of construction (entry) and completion. Let us denote the time-to-build by δ, where $\delta \geq 0$. That is, a firm entering at time t will begin receiving operating cash flows only at time $t + \delta$.

With such construction lags, at any point in time t there may be both completed output, $C(t)$, and units that are currently under construction. Let $N(t)$ denote the mass of units that are currently under construction, i.e., $N(t)$ is the mass of units that began construction during the interval $(t - \delta, t]$ and are currently "in the pipeline." Let $Q(t)$ denote "committed capacity" where $Q(t) = C(t) + N(t)$. Note that new supply enters only at points in time at which $Q(t)$ is strictly increasing.[4] In addition, because any unit that is completed today must have been part of committed capacity δ years ago, one can always write $C(t) = Q(t - \delta)$.

---

[2] The model will yield identical results if firms are permitted to own more than one unit of the asset, provided no single firm wields significant market power.

[3] In addition to the cost of construction, one could also include variable costs of operation. However, we can interpret the inverse demand function as being a reduced-form profit function. An explicit consideration of operating costs would complicate the model's presentation without altering any of its fundamental insights.

[4] At times t at which there is no new entry, but when units are just being completed, $dQ(t) = 0$ because $dC(t) = -dN(t)$.

The aim is to construct a competitive equilibrium in which firms have rational expectations. Specifically, such an equilibrium involves the simultaneous determination of prices and entry strategies of firms. Investment strategies, the price process, and expectations are all interdependent and must be mutually consistent in equilibrium. Firms choose investment strategies so as to maximize the discounted present value of profits less the construction costs, given their expectations concerning the probability law governing prices. These strategies, in conjunction with the exogenous demand shocks, determine the actual realization of prices and supply in the industry. If expectations are indeed rational, then the price process with which firms form their strategies and the actual price process will be the same function of the current state variables. Finally, to qualify as a competitive equilibrium, the present discounted value of equilibrium profits (beginning δ years after the initiation of construction) at any point of entry must equal the cost of construction at that time.

Such a rational expectations competitive equilibrium can be determined as the solution to a specific maximization problem. As in Lucas and Prescott (1971) or Dixit (1989a, 1991), the equilibrium evolves *as if* to maximize the expected present discounted value of social welfare in the form of consumer surplus. That is, the equilibrium path of prices and quantities can be derived from the social planner's perspective.

The social planner's problem is to choose the path of new supply so as to maximize the value of the flow of consumer surplus. This is precisely the same as choosing the path of $Q(t)$, since the points of increase in $Q(t)$ are the points of new construction. The total flow rate of social surplus, $S[X(t), C(t)]$, is equal to the area under the demand curve:

$$S[X(t), C(t)] = \int_0^{C(t)} \left[X(t) q^{-1/\gamma} \right] dq = \frac{\gamma}{\gamma - 1} X(t) C(t)^{(\gamma-1)/\gamma} \quad (14.3)$$

I assume that agents are risk neutral, and thus the appropriate discount rate is the risk-free rate of interest, r. This seemingly restrictive assumption can easily be relaxed by adjusting the drift rate, α_x, by a risk premium in the manner of Cox and Ross (1976).

Let the state of the industry at time t be denoted by the set $\Omega(t)$, with the current state at time zero being Ω_0. The social planner's problem is to choose the path $Q(t)$ so as to solve the following optimal control problem:

$$J(\Omega_0) = \max_{[Q(s):s>0]} E\left[\int_0^\infty e^{-rt} S[X(t), Q(t-\delta)] \, dt \right.$$

$$\left. - \sum_t K e^{-rt} \Delta Q_t \, | \Omega(0) = \Omega_0 \right] \quad (14.4)$$

where ΔQ_t denotes the increment in capacity at instants t when investment is made, and the sum is taken over all those instants when capacity additions take place. The solution to the planner's problem is denoted by the Bellman value function, $J(\Omega_0)$.

Consider now the information needed to determine the current state of the industry at time t, $\Omega(t)$. This is the information on which the central planner conditions his expectation of the future path of industry surplus. At any time t, the planner needs to know the current state of demand, $X(t)$, and the number of completed units on the market, $C(t)$, because both $C(t)$ and $X(t)$ determine the current level of surplus. However, the planner must also condition his information on both the number of units currently in the pipeline, $N(t)$, and the times at which these units will be completed and enter the market. The amount and arrival times of units currently in the pipeline are relevant to the planner because they will impact the surplus flow over the ensuing δ years. Of course, to know the arrival times of units under construction, the planner must have knowledge of the historical path of entry over the previous δ years. Thus, the state of the industry at any time t is summarized by

$$\Omega(t) = [X(t), C(t), N(t), \Lambda(t)] \tag{14.5}$$

where the set $\Lambda(t) \equiv \{\tau \in [t - \delta, t) : Q(\tau) > Q(\tau^-)\}$ specifies all the times during the previous δ years at which new construction was initiated.[5] Thus, the planner simply adds the time-to-build δ to determine the arrival times.

The apparent difficulty of finding such an equilibrium in a model with lags is due to the complexity of the state of the industry, $\Omega(t)$. Most notably, inclusion of the set $\Lambda(t)$ leads to the potential infinite dimensionality of the state space. If there is no time-to-build, the entire state of the industry can be summarized by the current value of the demand shock, $X(t)$, and the current supply, $C(t)$.[6] By allowing for construction lags, the state of the system may become one of infinite dimensionality. In the next section, it is shown that the equilibrium path of new supply additions can be derived by transforming the problem into one in which only two state variables are needed.

14.3 DETERMINATION OF COMPETITIVE EQUILIBRIUM

In this section I use the techniques of option-pricing analysis to solve for the competitive industry equilibrium. To derive the equilibrium prices, quantities, and asset values, one must solve the stochastic control problem (14.4) subject to the information set (14.5) and the dynamics of the demand shock (14.2).

This is a problem of irreversible investment under uncertainty. A fundamental result of papers on individual firm behavior under such conditions (Dixit, 1989b; Pindyck, 1988; McDonald and Siegel, 1986) is that there exists a potentially valuable "option to wait" to invest; firms delay investment past the point of zero net present value and enter only when investment yields substantial positive value. The option to invest is analogous to a perpetual call option since the firm holds an option to purchase the project δ years from completion at an exercise price equal to the cost of construction. Because waiting to invest is equivalent to holding an option, the true

---

[5] Because firms are assumed uniform in size, there is no need to introduce the size of future capacity increments into the state space.

[6] Even if a model with instantaneous construction is extended to multidimensional exogenous uncertainty, the state of the system remains finite, provided there is a finite number of exogenous state variables.

economic cost of investment is not just the construction cost, but also the cost of extinguishing the option. The greater the value of the underlying option to wait, the greater the threshold value needed to trigger investment.

In the case of perfectly competitive equilibrium, however, the net present value of entry must be zero. Thus, the value of the option to wait, at the optimal point of entry, must be zero. Therefore, the central planner's solution must balance the individual interests of firms to delay investment, with the competitive pressure to squeeze out any potential value from delay.

To solve the central planner's optimal control problem, I first show that the relevant state space for determining equilibrium entry strategies can be considerably simplified by a slight reformulation of the problem. Specifically, I demonstrate that knowledge of only the current levels of the demand shock, $X(t)$, and of committed capacity, $Q(t)$, is sufficient for determining equilibrium new entry. That is, the future course of entry depends not on the distinction between completed and in-the-pipeline output, but only on total committed capacity.[7]

To demonstrate the state space transformation, I first rewrite the maximization problem in (14.4) broken up into two parts:

$$J(X_0, C_0, N_0, \Lambda_0) = E\left[\int_0^\delta e^{-rt} S\left[X(t), Q(t-\delta)\right] dt \,\Big|\, \Omega_0 = (X_0, C_0, N_0, \Lambda_0)\right] +$$

$$\max_{[Q(s):s>0]} E\left[\int_\delta^\infty e^{-rt} S\left[X(t), Q(t-\delta)\right] dt - \sum_t Ke^{-rt}\, \Delta Q_t \,\Big|\, \Omega_0 = (X_0, C_0, N_0, \Lambda_0)\right]$$

$$(14.6)$$

Note that the choice of the optimal path of $Q(t)$ does not influence the surplus flow over the interval from $(0, \delta)$ because of the construction lag.

It is important to note that although the expectation in the first term of (14.6) depends on the path of entry over the period $[-\delta, 0)$, or Λ_0, the expectation in the second term (where the optimization is performed) depends only on the current value of committed capacity, Q_0. This holds because the flow of surplus at time δ depends only on the amount of current committed capacity since all units currently under construction will be completed by time δ. Therefore, the optimized path of future entry conditional on the current state $\Omega_0 = (X_0, C_0, N_0, \Lambda_0)$ is identical to that under the modified state $\Omega_0 = (X_0, C_0 + N_0, 0, \varnothing) = (X_0, Q_0, 0, \varnothing)$, where all current in-the-pipeline units are now assumed to have been completed. Thus, Eq. (14.6) can be equivalently expressed as

$$J(X_0, C_0, N_0, \Lambda_0) = E\left[\int_0^\delta e^{-rt} S\left[X(t), Q(t-\delta)\right] dt \,\Big|\, \Omega_0 = (X_0, C_0, N_0, \Lambda_0)\right] +$$

$$\max_{[Q(s):s>0]} E\left[\int_\delta^\infty e^{-rt} S\left[X(t), Q(t-\delta)\right] dt - \sum_t Ke^{-rt}\, \Delta Q_t \,\Big|\, \Omega_0 = (X_0, Q_0, 0, \varnothing)\right]$$

$$(14.7)$$

---

[7] This transformation of the state space was demonstrated by Bar-Ilan et al. (1992) in a model of production capacity with time-to-build.

where $Q_0 = C_0 + N_0$. Using the definition of J in (14.6), Eq. (14.7) can be rewritten in the following equivalent form:

$$J(X_0, C_0, N_0, \Lambda_0) = J(X_0, Q_0, 0, \emptyset) \tag{14.8}$$

$$+ E\left[\int_0^\delta e^{-rt} S[X(t), Q(t-\delta)] \, dt \mid \Omega_0 = (X_0, C_0, N_0, \Lambda_0)\right]$$

$$- E\left[\int_0^\delta e^{-rt} S[X(t), Q(t-\delta)] \, dt \mid \Omega_0 = (X_0, Q_0, 0, \emptyset)\right]$$

Equation (14.8) demonstrates that the solution to the original optimization problem $J(X_0, C_0, N_0, \Lambda_0)$ is equivalent to the solution of a simpler optimization problem $J(X_0, Q_0, 0, \emptyset)$, plus two terms over which no optimization is required. Therefore, to solve for the industry equilibrium, one actually needs only to solve for $J(X_0, Q_0, 0, \emptyset)$, and then use (14.8) to solve for $J(X_0, C_0, N_0, \Lambda_0)$. Solving for $J(X_0, Q_0, 0, \emptyset)$ is much simpler than the original problem, because the initial state space now depends only on X_0 and Q_0. To emphasize this simple two-dimensional dependence, I subsequently let $V(X, Q) \equiv J(X, Q, 0, \emptyset)$.

Thus, the original optimization problem has been transformed into a much simpler, finite-state problem. In essence, one can proceed to solve the central planner's problem by solving the same optimization program for an *artificial economy* that is identical to the original economy with the sole exception that it is assumed that all units in the pipeline are completed. That is, one uses the same level of committed capacity as in the original economy, but assumes that all committed capacity is completed.

I next proceed to derive $V(X, Q)$. Because construction costs are assumed proportional, this becomes a problem of "optimal instantaneous control."[8] This form of optimal control problem implies that it is optimal for the industry to grow in a continuous path, rather than in discrete jumps, i.e., the stochastic process $Q(t)$ will be continuous, and ΔQ_t will be an infinitesimal increment denoted by dQ_t.[9]

The solution to this dynamic programming problem can be derived using the methods of option pricing, using the following analogy. Over the range in which Q is not changing, $V(X, Q)$ can be envisioned as the value of an industry with a mass of Q completed units whose dividend flow is $S(X, Q)$. However, this set of Q units also contains an option to enter an additional increment into the pipeline, at an exercise price of $K \, dQ$. In addition, once that option is exercised, another option is presented in which Q can again be incremented. This is more complicated than the standard option pricing problem in which exercise yields the value of an underlying security. In this case, every option's exercise yields the value of another option. The value of each option depends on the value of an infinite stream of future options. Thus, there is an infinite number of lagged entry options that must be solved simultaneously.

---

[8] See Harrison and Taksar (1983) and Dumas (1991).

[9] The process for $Q(t)$ evolves as follows. Starting at $Q(t) = Q$, $Q(t)$ will rise to the level $Q + h$, for any $h > 0$, at the first instant $X(t)$ hits an upper trigger $X^*(Q + h)$.

Consider the instantaneous return on $V(X, Q)$ over a region in which no new entry occurs. By Itô's Lemma, the instantaneous change in V is

$$dV = \left(\frac{1}{2}\sigma_x^2 X^2 V_{XX} + \alpha_x X V_X\right) dt + \sigma_x X V_x dz_x \tag{14.9}$$

In addition to the capital gain, the current supply yields the dividend flow rate (in the form of consumer surplus) of $S(X, Q)$. Therefore, the total expected return on V per unit time, α_v, is

$$\alpha_v \equiv E\left[\frac{dV + S(X, Q)dt}{V} \frac{1}{dt}\right]$$

$$= \frac{1}{V}\left[\frac{1}{2}\sigma_x^2 X^2 V_{XX} + \alpha_x X V_X + S(X, Q)\right] \tag{14.10}$$

In equilibrium, the expected return on any asset is set equal to r.[10] Setting α_v equal to r and simplifying, yields the following equilibrium differential equation:

$$0 = \frac{1}{2}\sigma_x^2 X^2 V_{XX} + \alpha_x X V_X - rV + S(X, Q) \tag{14.11}$$

The general solution to differential Eq. (14.11) can be shown to be

$$V(X, Q) = A(Q)X^{-\alpha} + B(Q)X^\beta + \left(\frac{X}{r - \alpha_x}\right)\left(\frac{\gamma}{\gamma - 1}\right) Q^{(\gamma-1)/\gamma}$$

where

$$-\alpha = \frac{-(\alpha_x - \frac{1}{2}\sigma_x^2) - \sqrt{(\alpha_x - \frac{1}{2}\sigma_x^2)^2 + 2r\sigma_x^2}}{\sigma_x^2} \quad (< 0) \tag{14.12}$$

$$\beta = \frac{-(\alpha_x - \frac{1}{2}\sigma_x^2) + \sqrt{(\alpha_x - \frac{1}{2}\sigma_x^2)^2 + 2r\sigma_x^2}}{\sigma_x^2} \quad (> 1)$$

with $r > \alpha_x$ assumed for convergence. The functions $A(Q)$ and $B(Q)$, along with the optimal points of entry, are determined by appropriate boundary conditions.

Consider the value function $V(X, Q)$ at a point of entry. The first condition that V must satisfy is the "value-matching" condition. Recall that $V(X, Q) = J(X, Q, 0, \emptyset)$. At the time at which entry occurs, one increment of capacity is added to the pipeline. That is, at the moment of entry, the value function with a mass of Q units of completed supply must equal the value function with a mass of Q units of completed supply plus an additional increment of capacity just entering the pipeline, minus the cost of construction $K\,dQ$. Thus, the value-matching condition implies that

---

[10] Although this value function is not an asset per se, its value to risk-neutral investors is determined by discounting expected future cash flows by r.

$$V(X^*, Q) = J(X^*, Q, dQ, \emptyset) - K\,dQ \tag{14.13}$$

where X^* denotes the level of $X(t)$ at which new supply optimally arrives.[11] One can then use (14.8) to substitute for the J function above:

$$V(X^*, Q) = V(X^*, Q + dQ) + E\left[\int_0^\delta e^{-rt}S[X(t), Q]\,dt|X(0) = X^*\right] \tag{14.14}$$

$$- E\left[\int_0^\delta e^{-rt}S[X(t), Q + dQ]\,dt|X(0) = X^*\right] - K\,dQ$$

Evaluating the expectations, simplifying, and writing this in derivative form yields

$$\frac{\partial V(X^*, Q)}{\partial Q} = \frac{X^*Q^{-1/\gamma}}{r - \alpha_x}\left[1 - e^{-(r-\alpha_x)\delta}\right] + K \tag{14.15}$$

The second condition that V must satisfy is an optimality condition that ensures that the trigger value X^* is determined optimally. In the theory of optimal instantaneous control, Dumas (1991) calls this the "super-contact" condition. This is analogous to the more commonly known "high-contact" condition in the standard option pricing literature.[12] Because the first-order condition now takes the form of restrictions on the second-order derivative, the new terminology seems appropriate. Thus, X^* must satisfy the following second-order derivative condition:

$$\frac{\partial^2 V(X^*, Q)}{\partial X \partial Q} = \frac{Q^{-1/\gamma}}{r - \alpha_x}\left[1 - e^{-(r-\alpha_x)\delta}\right] \tag{14.16}$$

The third boundary condition that $V(X, Q)$ must satisfy is

$$\lim_{X \to 0} V(X, Q) = 0 \tag{14.17}$$

This condition reflects the fact that because $X(t)$ has an absorbing barrier at zero, if demand ever reaches zero it will remain there forever. In this case the industry will yield zero profits in perpetuity. Boundary condition (14.17) implies that $A(Q) = 0$, $\forall\, Q \geq 0$.

The fourth and final boundary condition is

$$\lim_{Q \to \infty} \frac{V(X, Q)}{Q^{(\gamma-1)/\gamma}} = \frac{\gamma}{(\gamma - 1)(r - \alpha_x)}X \tag{14.18}$$

This condition ensures that, as supply goes to infinity, the probability of new entry approaches zero. Therefore, the value of existing supply approaches that of the

---

[11] This is a function of Q, $X^*(Q)$.

[12] Consider the following heuristic derivation of the super-contact condition. Using the discretized version of the value-matching condition in (14.14), one can apply the standard high-contact condition that requires that the derivatives with respect to X^* of each side of the equality are equal. Then by taking limits (as $dQ \to 0$) and writing the expression in derivative form, one obtains the super-contact condition.

perpetuity value of $S(X, Q)$. In other words, the value of all expansion options goes to zero.

Finally, appending boundary conditions (14.15), (14.16), (14.17), and (14.18) to the general solution (14.12) yields the following solution to the Bellman value function for the *artificial* economy $V(X, Q)$, as well as the trigger level $X^*(Q)$ at which new construction is initiated:

$$V(X, Q) = \frac{-\gamma \cdot K}{(\beta - 1)(\gamma - \beta)} \left[\frac{\beta (r - \alpha_x) e^{(r-\alpha_x)\delta}}{\beta - 1} K \right]^{-\beta} Q^{(\gamma-\beta)/\gamma} X^\beta$$

$$+ \frac{X}{r - \alpha_x} \frac{\gamma}{\gamma - 1} Q^{(\gamma-1)/\gamma} \tag{14.19}$$

$$X^*(Q) = \frac{\beta K (r - \alpha_x)}{\beta - 1} e^{(r-\alpha_x)\delta} Q^{1/\gamma}$$

The equilibrium pattern of entry into the industry is characterized by the trigger function $X^*(Q)$ presented in Eq. (14.19) above. The Qth unit of new supply will be initiated the first moment $X(t)$ rises to the trigger level $X^*(Q)$. Although the equilibrium entry strategy appears similar to the standard real options trigger strategy, it is actually fundamentally different. This is immediately apparent from two aspects of the equilibrium exercise trigger. First, it depends on the level of committed capacity, Q, and not on price or supply. Second, the time-to-build parameter δ is explicitly considered.

To give a rather simple, intuitive characterization of the equilibrium exercise strategy, consider first the standard real options exercise strategy. With monopolistic and instantaneous construction, the optimal trigger strategy is to exercise the first moment that $P(t)$ hits the trigger λ, where $\lambda = \{[\beta(r - \alpha_x)]/[\beta - 1]\}K$. Now, in the present equilibrium model with time-to-build, the entry strategy is to exercise when the discounted expected value of the price in δ years equals the trigger λ. To see this, incrementing Eq. (14.1) by δ years implies that $P(t+\delta) = [X(t+\delta)][C(t+\delta)^{-1/\gamma}]$. Taking the expectation at time t, and noting that $C(t + \delta) = Q(t)$, the expected price can be written as $E_t[P(t + \delta)] = X(t)e^{\alpha_x \delta} Q(t)^{-1/\gamma}$. Finally, rewriting the expression for $X^*(Q)$ in (14.19), the equilibrium trigger strategy implies exercise the first moment that $e^{-r\delta} E_t[P^*(t + \delta)] = \lambda$. Therefore, the impact of time-to-build and competitive equilibrium leads investors to modify their exercise strategies by simply replacing the current price with the discounted expected equilibrium price prevailing at the end of construction. In the following section, I demonstrate that this implies that the expected equilibrium price δ years in the future also follows a regulated geometric Brownian motion.

Using the equilibrium entry strategies and output price processes, equilibrium asset values are simply the discounted expected value of the equilibrium cash flow stream. These equilibrium relationships are fully characterized in the following section.

14.4 ANALYSIS OF COMPETITIVE EQUILIBRIUM WITH TIME-TO-BUILD: SUPPLY, PRICES, AND ASSET VALUES

The solution to the central planner's problem should be seen only as a means to an end. What is really important is not some Bellman value function for the industry, but the equilibrium processes it implies for prices, supply, and asset values. In this section, these equilibrium processes are derived and analyzed.

14.4.1 Equilibrium Supply and Entry Strategies

As shown in the previous section, equilibrium construction will begin according to a trigger value strategy. The $\bar{Q}$th unit of new supply will be initiated the first moment $X(t)$ rises to the trigger level $X^*(\bar{Q})$. At that moment, equilibrium committed capacity, $Q^*(t)$, rises to $\bar{Q}$. Because construction takes δ years to complete, equilibrium completed supply, $C^*(t)$, rises to $\bar{Q}$ in δ years from that point.

Mathematically, let $T(\bar{Q}; X, Q)$ denote the equilibrium time at which the $\bar{Q}$th unit of construction is initiated, when the current levels of $X(0)$ and $Q(0)$ are X and Q, respectively, with $Q \le \bar{Q}$. Therefore, $T(\bar{Q}; X, Q)$ can be written as the first passage time of $X(t)$:

$$T(\bar{Q}; X, Q) = \inf \left[t > 0 : X(t) \ge X^*(\bar{Q}) \right] \quad \text{for } \bar{Q} > Q \quad (14.20)$$

Thus, the time at which equilibrium completed supply first reaches the level $\bar{Q}$ is simply $T(\bar{Q}; X, Q) + \delta$.

In Appendix A, the density function (conditional on time-zero information) for equilibrium supply, $C^*(t)$, is derived in closed form. For $t \le \delta$, $C^*(t)$ is a known constant and is simply the value of committed capacity at time $t - \delta$, $Q(t - \delta)$. For the more interesting case of $t > \delta$, the density function for $C^*(t)$, denoted as $h_t(c)$, can be written as

$$
h_t(c) =
\begin{cases}
0 & c < Q(0) \\[2mm]
\Phi\left[\frac{\bar{M} - \mu(t-\delta)}{\sigma_x\sqrt{t-\delta}}\right] - \exp\left(\frac{2\mu\bar{M}}{\sigma_x^2}\right)\Phi\left[\frac{-\bar{M} - \mu(t-\delta)}{\sigma_x\sqrt{t-\delta}}\right] & c = Q(0) \\[4mm]
\dfrac{n\left[\frac{h_1(c) - \mu(t-\delta)}{(\sigma_x\sqrt{t-\delta})}\right]}{c\gamma\sigma_x\sqrt{t-\delta}} + \dfrac{\exp\left[2\mu h_1(c)/\sigma_x^2\right]}{c\gamma\sigma_x\sqrt{t-\delta}} & c > Q(0) \\[4mm]
\left\{n\left[\frac{h_1(c) - \mu(t-\delta)}{\sigma_x\sqrt{t-\delta}}\right] - \frac{2\mu\sqrt{t-\delta}}{\sigma_x} n\left[\frac{-h_1(c) - \mu(t-\delta)}{\sigma_x\sqrt{t-\delta}}\right]\right\}
\end{cases}
\quad (14.21)
$$

where

$$h_1(c) = \ln\left[\frac{\beta(r - \alpha_x)K}{(\beta - 1)e^{-(r-\alpha_x)\delta}X(0)}c^{1/\gamma}\right]$$

$$\mu = \alpha_x - \frac{1}{2}\sigma_x^2$$

$$\bar{M} = \ln\left[\frac{\beta(r - \alpha_x)}{\beta - 1}e^{(r-\alpha_x)\delta}\frac{K}{X(0)Q(0)^{-1/\gamma}}\right]$$

with $n(\cdot)$ denoting the standard normal density function and $\Phi(\cdot)$ denoting the cumulative standard normal distribution function.

Using this distribution of equilibrium supply, many of its properties can be derived. A notion that may be of interest is the likelihood that supply in the industry will grow to any level $\bar{C}$ in the future. Two characterizations of this notion are provided: the probability that $\bar{C}$ will ever be reached and the expected time until $\bar{C}$ is reached.

Suppose the current levels of $X(0)$ and $Q(0)$ are X and Q, respectively, where $Q \leq \bar{C}$. Let $PC(\bar{C}; X, Q)$ denote the probability that $\bar{C}$ will ever be reached, conditional on the current values of X and Q. $PC(\bar{C}; X, Q)$ can be expressed as

$$PC(\bar{C}; X, Q) = \begin{cases} \left[\frac{\beta(r-\alpha_x)}{(\beta-1)e^{-(r-\alpha_x)\delta}} \frac{K}{X} \bar{C}^{1/\gamma} \right]^{2\mu/\sigma_x^2} & \text{if } \mu < 0 \\ 1 & \text{if } \mu \geq 0 \end{cases} \quad (14.22)$$

The sign of μ conveys a notion of the relative sizes of the expected growth in demand, α_x, and the volatility of demand, σ_x. Therefore, if the growth rate is large relative to volatility ($\mu \geq 0$), then supply will *eventually* reach any finite level in the future. However, if the growth rate is small relative to volatility ($\mu < 0$), supply may not ever grow to a given level in the future.

Define $TC(\bar{C}; X, Q)$ as the expected time until $\bar{C}$ is first reached. $TC(\bar{C}; X, Q)$ can be expressed as

$$TC(\bar{C}; X, Q) = \begin{cases} \infty & \text{if } \mu < 0 \\ \frac{1}{\mu} \ln\left[\frac{\beta(r-\alpha_x)}{(\beta-1)e^{-(r-\alpha_x)\delta}} \frac{K}{X} \bar{C}^{1/\gamma} \right] + \delta & \text{if } \mu \geq 0 \end{cases} \quad (14.23)$$

14.4.2 Equilibrium Output Prices

Given the equilibrium supply process, the equilibrium price process is relatively simple to characterize. From Eq. (14.1), the equilibrium price, $P^*(t)$, can be written as

$$P^*(t) = X(t)C^*(t)^{-1/\gamma} = X(t)Q^*(t-\delta)^{-1/\gamma} \quad (14.24)$$

Thus, the equilibrium price is equal to the product of a log-normal random variable, $X(t)$, and a simple function of $C^*(t)$ whose distribution was derived above in (14.21).

It is next demonstrated that the process followed by the expected equilibrium price δ years in the future is a regulated geometric Brownian motion process. From Eq. (14.19), equilibrium entry will increase $Q^*(t)$ by an infinitesimal increment dQ whenever the process $X(t)$ hits the upper threshold $X^*(Q)$. This can be expressed equivalently as supply increasing by dQ whenever $X(t)e^{\alpha_x\delta}Q^*(t)^{-1/\gamma}$ hits the upper threshold $\phi = \{[\beta(r - \alpha_x)]/[\beta - 1]\}e^{r\delta}K$. Because $E_t[P^*(t+\delta)] = X(t)e^{\alpha_x\delta}Q^*(t)^{-1/\gamma}$, this expectation follows a geometric Brownian motion regulated at the upper barrier ϕ.

In Appendix A, the density function (conditional on time-zero information) for equilibrium prices, $P^*(t)$, is derived in closed form. For $t \leq \delta$, $C^*(t)$ is a known constant and so $P^*(t)$ will be distributed log normally, as it is equal to the product of a constant and the log-normal random variable $X(t)$. For the more interesting case of $t > \delta$, the density function for $P^*(t)$, denoted as $j_t(p)$, can be written as

$$j_t(p) = a_t(p) \sum_{j=1}^{2} g_t^j(p) + b(p) \sum_{j=3}^{4} g_t^j(p) \quad (14.25)$$

where

$$a_t(p) = \frac{1}{p\sigma_x\sqrt{t}} \exp\left\{\left(\frac{\mu}{\sigma_x^2}\right)\left[c(p) - \frac{\mu t}{2}\right]\right\}$$

$$g_t^1(p) = n\left[\frac{c(p)}{\sigma_x\sqrt{t}}\right]\Phi\left[\frac{[\bar{M} - c(p)](t - \delta) + \delta\bar{M}}{\sigma_x\sqrt{t\delta(t - \delta)}}\right]$$

$$g_t^2(p) = -n\left[\frac{2\bar{M} - c(p)}{\sigma_x\sqrt{t}}\right]\Phi\left[\frac{[\bar{M} - c(p)](t - \delta) - \delta\bar{M}}{\sigma_x\sqrt{t\delta(t - \delta)}}\right]$$

$$g_t^3(p) = \left(\frac{1}{\sigma_x\sqrt{t}}\right)n\left[\frac{2\bar{M} - c(p) - \mu t}{\sigma_x\sqrt{t}}\right]\Phi\left[\frac{[\bar{M} - c(p)](t - \delta) - \delta\bar{M}}{\sigma_x\sqrt{t\delta(t - \delta)}}\right]$$

$$b(p) = \left(\frac{2}{p}\right)\exp\left\{\frac{2\mu(c(p) - \bar{M})}{\sigma_x^2}\right\}$$

$$g_t^3(p) = \left(\frac{1}{\sigma_x\sqrt{t}}\right)n\left[\frac{2\bar{M} - c(p) - \mu t}{\sigma_x\sqrt{t}}\right]\Phi\left[\frac{[\bar{M} - c(p)](t - \delta) - \delta\bar{M}}{\sigma_x\sqrt{t\delta(t - \delta)}}\right]$$

$$g_t^4(p) = \left(\frac{\mu}{\sigma_x^2}\right)\left\{\Phi\left[\frac{\bar{M} - c(p) - \delta\mu}{\sigma_x\sqrt{\delta}}\right]\right.$$
$$\left. - N_2\left[\frac{\bar{M} - c(p) - \delta\mu}{\sigma_x\sqrt{\delta}}, \frac{2\bar{M} - c(p) - \mu t}{\sigma_x\sqrt{t}}, \sqrt{\frac{\delta}{t}}\right]\right\}$$

$$c(p) = \ln\left[\frac{p}{X(0)Q(0)^{-1/\gamma}}\right]$$

$$\mu = \alpha_x - \frac{1}{2}\sigma_x^2$$

$$\bar{M} = \ln\left[\frac{\beta(r - \alpha_x)}{\beta - 1}e^{(r - \alpha_x)\delta}\frac{K}{X(0)Q(0)^{-1/\gamma}}\right]$$

Again, $n(\cdot)$ denotes the standard normal density function and $\Phi(\cdot)$ denotes the cumulative standard normal distribution function. $N_2(x_1, x_2, \rho)$ denotes the bivariate cumulative standard normal distribution function, i.e., the area under a standard bivariate normal distribution function covering the range from $-\infty$ to x_1 and $-\infty$ to x_2, where the two random variables have correlation ρ.

14.4.3 Equilibrium Asset Values

The final key component of the competitive equilibrium is the valuation of existing assets. Let $W(\Omega_0)$ denote the value of a *completed* asset, when the current state of the industry is summarized by Ω_0. Because the value of a completed asset is simply the discounted expected value of future equilibrium output prices, I can write $W(\Omega_0)$ as

$$W(\Omega_0) = E\left[\int_0^\infty e^{-rt}P^*(t)\,dt\,|\,\Omega(0) = \Omega_0\right] \tag{14.26}$$

where $P^*(t)$ has the density $j_t(p)$ expressed in Eq. (14.25).

The above integral representation of asset values can be simplified to the following form:

$$W(\Omega_0) = Xe^{-(r-\alpha_x)\delta} \int_{-\delta}^{0} e^{-(r-\alpha_x)s} Q(s)^{-1/\gamma} ds$$

$$+ Xe^{-(r-\alpha_x)\delta} \frac{Q^{-1/\gamma}}{r-\alpha_x} - A(Q)X^\beta \tag{14.27}$$

where

$$A(Q) = \frac{e^{-(r-\alpha_x)\delta}}{\beta(r-\alpha_x)} \left[\frac{\beta(r-\alpha_x)}{\beta-1} e^{(r-\alpha_x)\delta} K \right]^{1-\beta} Q^{-\beta/\gamma}$$

The equilibrium solution for $W(\Omega_0)$ has the following intuition. The first term is the present value of the future stream of cash flows from time 0 to δ. The second term is the present value of the future stream of cash flows from time δ to infinity, assuming that supply remains constant over the period. The final term subtracts out the loss of value from future increases in market supply over the period from δ to infinity.

The path dependency of equilibrium asset values is evident from Eq. (14.27). The first term in the expression for $W(\Omega_0)$ depends on the levels of committed capacity over the period $[-\delta, 0)$. Equilibrium values depend not only on current supply and demand, but also on the time path of entry over the previous δ years.

Given the value of a completed asset, the value of an asset at the beginning of construction is simple to derive. Because the asset under construction will not receive cash flows over the period from time 0 to δ, the first term of Eq. (14.27) is no longer included. In addition, the construction cost is subtracted from the option value. Letting $G(X, Q)$ denote the value of an asset just beginning construction, this value can be written as

$$G(X, Q) = Xe^{-(r-\alpha_x)\delta} \left(\frac{Q^{-1/\gamma}}{r-\alpha_x} \right) - A(Q)X^\beta - K \tag{14.28}$$

Since in equilibrium entry occurs only at the trigger values $X^*(Q)$, the *equilibrium* value of the Qth entry is $G[X^*(Q), Q]$.

It is important to emphasize the equilibrium context that differentiates this asset value from that typically obtained in standard real options models. Most importantly, the net present value of an asset (option) upon entry (exercise) is precisely zero. This is easy to verify since $G[X^*(Q), Q] = 0$ for all Q. By pursuing an optimal entry strategy, the best a firm can do is to invest in a zero-NPV project. By investing any earlier or later than optimal, a firm would incur a loss in value. The observation that in a competitive equilibrium firms exercise options only when they have zero net present value is strikingly different from the standard result that real options are exercised only when they have substantial net present value. Given that investment is equivalent to exercising an option to purchase an asset, firms will be reluctant to extinguish a valuable option unless properly compensated. Thus, firms would prefer not to invest in an asset whose value is just enough to compensate them for the cost of construction; they also demand to be compensated for giving up an option to wait and see if prospects are even better tomorrow. As stated in Pindyck (1988),

> This aspect of investment has been explored in an emerging literature, and most notably by Robert McDonald and Daniel Siegel (1986). They show that with even moderate levels of uncertainty, the value of this opportunity cost (the cost of extinguishing the option to wait) can be large, and investment rules that ignore it will be grossly in error. Their calculations, and those in related papers by Michael Brennan and Eduardo Schwartz (1985) and Saman Majd and Robert Pindyck (1987), show that in many cases projects should be undertaken only when their present value is at least double their direct cost.

Although this phenomenon may be consistent with what firms would *want* to do in the absence of competition, it is not consistent with what firms *can* do when facing competitive pressure. In this model of competitive equilibrium, the individual optimizing behavior of competitive firms leads to entry precisely at a point of zero net present value. In this sense, the urgency of potential entrants results in an option to wait with zero value; the fear of competitors usurping one's investment opportunity squeezes out all of the potential value from delay.

I conclude this section with a simulation illustration of equilibrium. Given the initial state of an industry, the equilibrium paths of entry, output prices, and asset values can be simulated using a particular sample path of the exogenous process $X(t)$. Figure 14.1 provides such a simulation for two hypothetical industries. These industries are identical [as is the path of $X(t)$], with the sole exception that their previous paths of entry differ. Specifically, although each industry has an identical initial committed capacity $Q(0)$, industry 1's capacity is completed whereas industry 2's capacity is at varying degrees of completeness. Although the equilibrium paths of output, prices, and asset values are identical after δ years, the paths differ over the initial period up to time δ. This initial divergence is a result of the path-dependent state space underlying the industry equilibrium. It is not enough to know the level of capacity (or completions) at time zero. One must also know the process of entry over the previous δ years to fully characterize the equilibrium.

In Figure 14.1, the paths of committed capacity, output prices, and asset values are simulated over a 5-year period. The assumed construction period is 1 year. Curves labeled as "industry 1" have initial (time-zero) capacity of 125 units, all of which are assumed to be completed. Curves labeled as "industry 2" have initial (time-zero) capacity of 125 units, some of which are still under construction. Figure 14.1A plots the path of $Q(t)$ over the region from the previous year to 5 years out in the future. Figure 14.1B plots the equilibrium path of output prices, $P(t)$. Although the paths are identical after 1 year, over the initial year the output price of industry 2 is greater than or equal to that of industry 1. Figure 14.1C plots the equilibrium path of asset values, $W(t)$. Once again, although the path of asset values is identical after 1 year, over the initial year the asset value of industry 2 is greater than or equal to that of industry 1.

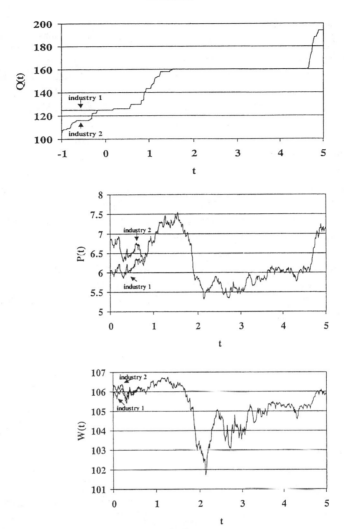

Figure 14.1 Simulation of equilibrium entry, output prices, and asset values. These graphs show simulated paths of entry, output prices, and asset values for two industries that differ only according to the previous time path of construction. The simulations reveal a path dependency: equilibrium output prices and asset values depend on the history of construction activity over the previous δ years, where $\delta = 1$. The relevant state space is thus very large. For the curves labeled "industry 1," the industry at time zero has 125 units of committed capacity, all of which are completed. For the curves labeled "industry 2," the industry at time zero also has 125 units of committed capacity; however, the units are at varying stages of completion. The evolution of uncertainty, $X(t)$, and the underlying parameter values are identical for each industry. (A) The time path of committed capacity, $Q(t)$, for the two industries. Although the initial state, $Q(0)$, is identical for both industries, the path of previous entry differs. (B) The time path of output prices, $P(t)$, for the two industries. Over the first year, industry 2 has higher prices than in industry 1. (C) The time path of asset values, $W(t)$, for the two industries. Over the first year, assets in industry 2 have greater value than in industry 1. The assumed parameter values are $\alpha_x = 0.02$, $\sigma_x = 0.1$, $r = 0.05$, $\gamma = 1.2$, $\delta = 1$, $K = 100$, $X(0) = 332.45$, and $Q(0) = 125$.

14.5 CONCLUSION

This chapter demonstrates the power of the real options approach in characterizing realistic and complex investment environments. Although standard applications of real options analysis to investment decisions assume monopolistic and instantaneous investment, the approach may be extended to a competitive equilibrium with time-to-build. This chapter permits the full determination of rational expectations equilibrium processes for prices, quantities, and asset values. Several interesting features of the equilibrium are apparent. First, current asset values depend not only on current supply and demand, but also on the path of previous construction. This path dependency is a consequence of the time-to-build feature. Second, in contrast to the standard real options result that investment occurs only when net present values are positive, in a competitive equilibrium the option to wait is eliminated under competitive pressure. Third, in contrast to the standard real options competitive equilibrium where the equilibrium price process follows a regulated diffusion process, in this model with construction lags it is the expected price prevailing at completion δ years in the future that follows a regulated diffusion process. A particularly interesting application of this analysis would be to determine whether this more general approach is better able to explain the empirical regularities of actual real asset markets.

Appendix A

In this Appendix, the equilibrium distributions of future prices and supply, conditional on current state variables, are derived. Since the derivations are quite involved, only the basic calculations are sketched out.

To facilitate the derivations, it is useful to define the following random variables:

$$Y(t) \equiv \ln \left[\frac{X(t)}{X(0)} \right]$$

$$M(t) \equiv \sup [Y(s) : 0 \le s \le t] \qquad (14.A1)$$

$$\bar{M} \equiv \bar{M}[X(0), Q(0)] \equiv \ln \left[\frac{\beta (r - \alpha_x)}{\beta - 1} e^{(r - \alpha_x)\delta} \frac{K}{X(0) Q(0)^{-1/\gamma}} \right]$$

The equilibrium supply and price processes are denoted as $C^*(t)$ and $P^*(t)$, respectively. I shall focus primarily on the case in which $t > \delta$, because for $t \le \delta$ equilibrium supply is precisely known. For $t \le \delta$, $C^*(t)$ is simply equal to the observed level of committed capacity δ years in the past. From the demand curve in Eq. (14.1), $P^*(t) = X(t)C^*(t)^{-1/\gamma}$. For $t \le \delta$, with $C^*(t)$ known, $P^*(t)$ will follow a log-normal distribution.

Thus, in the remainder of the Appendix I concentrate on the more interesting case in which $t > \delta$. In this case, $C^*(t)$ can be written as

$$C^*(t) = \max\left\{\left[\frac{(\beta-1)\,e^{-(r-\alpha_x)\delta}}{\beta\,(r-\alpha_x)}\frac{X(0)}{K}e^{M(t-\delta)}\right]^\gamma, Q(0)\right\} \quad (14.\text{A}2)$$

and $P^*(t)$ as

$$P^*(t) = \begin{cases} X(t)Q(0)^{-1/\gamma} & \text{if } M(t-\delta) \le \bar{M} \\ \left[\frac{\beta(r-\alpha_x)}{\beta-1}e^{(r-\alpha_x)\delta}\frac{K}{X(0)}\right]X(t)e^{-M(t-\delta)} & \text{if } M(t-\delta) > \bar{M} \end{cases} \quad (14.\text{A}3)$$

14.A1 DISTRIBUTION OF EQUILIBRIUM PRICES

Define the distribution function

$$J_t(p) \equiv \Pr\left[P^*(t) \le p\right] \quad (14.\text{A}4)$$

where "Pr" represents probabilities conditional on all current information.

By the law of total probability, $J_t(p)$ can be broken up into two parts:

$$J_t(p) = \Pr\left[P^*(t) \le p, M(t-\delta) \le \bar{M}\right] + \Pr\left[P^*(t) \le p, M(t-\delta) > \bar{M}\right] (14.\text{A}5)$$

Through algebraic manipulation, the above expression can be rewritten as

$$J_t(p) = \Pr\left\{Y(t) \le \ln\left[\frac{p}{X(0)Q(0)^{-1/\gamma}}\right], M(t-\delta) \le \bar{M}\right\}$$

$$+ \Pr\left\{Y(t) \le M(t-\delta) + \ln\left[\frac{p}{X(0)Q(0)^{-1/\gamma}}\right] - \bar{M}, M(t-\delta) > \bar{M}\right\} \quad (14.\text{A}6)$$

Letting $v_t(y, m)$ denote the joint (conditional) density function of $Y(t)$ and $M(t-\delta)$, $J_t(p)$ can be expressed as

$$J_t(p) = \int_0^{\bar{M}} \int_{-\infty}^{\ln\left\{p/\left[X(0)Q(0)^{-1/\gamma}\right]\right\}} v_t(y, m)\,dy\,dm$$

$$+ \int_{\bar{M}}^{\infty} \int_{-\infty}^{m+\ln\left\{p/[X(0)Q(0)^{-1/\gamma}]\right\}-\bar{M}} v_t(y, m)\,dy\,dm \quad (14.\text{A}7)$$

The probability density function (PDF) of equilibrium prices can be obtained by differentiating $J_t(p)$. Letting $j_t(p)$ denote the PDF of $P^*(t)$,

$$j_t(p) = \int_0^{\bar{M}} \left(\frac{1}{p}\right) v_t\left\{\ln\left[\frac{p}{X(0)Q(0)^{-1/\gamma}}\right], m\right\} dm$$

$$+ \int_{\bar{M}}^{\infty} \left(\frac{1}{p}\right) v_t\left\{m + \ln\left[\frac{p}{X(0)Q(0)^{-1/\gamma}}\right] - \bar{M}, m\right\} dm \quad (14.\text{A}8)$$

To derive a closed-form solution to $j_t(p)$, one must first derive the joint PDF of $Y(t)$ and $M(t-\delta)$, $v_t(y, m)$. To accomplish this, one may proceed in four stages. First, obtain the joint distribution of $Y(t-\delta)$ and $M(t-\delta)$, as in Harrison (1985, Section 1.8). Second, define the random variable $N(t) = Y(t) - Y(t-\delta)$. By the independent increments property of the Brownian motion process, $N(t)$ is independent of $Y(t-\delta)$. $N(t)$'s independence of $Y(t-\delta)$ [and therefore of $M(t-\delta)$ also] allows one to derive the joint density of $Y(t-\delta)$, $M(t-\delta)$, and $N(t)$ by merely multiplying the joint density of $Y(t-\delta)$ and $M(t-\delta)$ with the marginal density of $N(t)$. Third, because $Y(t) = N(t) + Y(t-\delta)$, the distribution of $Y(t-\delta)$, $M(t-\delta)$, and $Y(t)$ is obtained using the change of variables procedure. Finally, integrating with respect to $Y(t-\delta)$ over the region $-\infty$ to m, one derives the distribution $v_t(y, m)$.

Using the distribution $v_t(y, m)$, one can perform the integration in Eq. (14.A8) to derive a closed-form solution to the density function of $P^*(t)$. The solution is quite complicated, but can be written as

$$j_t(p) = a_t(p) \sum_{j=1}^{2} g_t^j(p) + b(p) \sum_{j=3}^{4} g_t^j(p) \tag{14.A9}$$

where the terms are defined in Eq. (14.25).

14.A2 DISTRIBUTION OF EQUILIBRIUM SUPPLY

Define the distribution function

$$H_t(c) \equiv \Pr\left[C^*(t) \le c\right] \tag{14.A10}$$

where again "Pr" represents probabilities conditional on all current information.

From the definition of equilibrium supply in Eq. (14.A2), the distribution of $C^*(t)$ is truncated below at $Q(0)$. The density function is continuous for all $c > Q(0)$, but with a probability mass at the point $Q(0)$.

First, let $c > Q(0)$. $H_t(c)$ can then be expressed as

$$H_t(c) \equiv \Pr\left(C^*(t) \le c\right)$$

$$= \Pr\left\{\left[\frac{(\beta - 1)\,e^{-(r-\alpha_x)\delta}}{\beta\,(r-\alpha_x)}\frac{X(0)}{K}e^{M(t-\delta)}\right]^{\gamma} \le c\right\}$$

$$= \Pr\left\{M(t-\delta) \le \ln\left[\frac{\beta\,(r-\alpha_x)}{(\beta - 1)\,e^{-(r-\alpha_x)\delta}}\frac{K}{X(0)}c^{1/\gamma}\right]\right\} \tag{14.A11}$$

$$= \Phi\left[\frac{h_1(c) - \mu(t-\delta)}{\sigma_x\sqrt{t-\delta}}\right] - \exp\left[\frac{2\mu h_1(c)}{\sigma_x^2}\right]\Phi\left[\frac{-h_1(c) - \mu(t-\delta)}{\sigma_x\sqrt{t-\delta}}\right]$$

where

$$h_1(c) = \ln\left[\frac{\beta\,(r-\alpha_x)}{(\beta - 1)\,e^{-(r-\alpha_x)\delta}}\frac{K}{X(0)}c^{\frac{1}{\gamma}}\right]$$

$$\mu = \alpha_x - \tfrac{1}{2}\sigma_x^2$$

The derivation in the fourth line comes from Harrison (1985, Chapter 1, Section 8). For the case $c = Q(0)$, $H_t(c)$ can be written as

$$H_t[Q(0)] = \Pr[C^*(t) \le Q(0)]$$

$$= \Pr[M(t - \delta) \le \bar{M}] \qquad (14.A12)$$

$$= \Phi\left[\frac{\bar{M} - \mu(t - \delta)}{\sigma_x\sqrt{t - \delta}}\right] - \exp\left(\frac{2\mu\bar{M}}{\sigma_x^2}\right)\Phi\left[\frac{-\bar{M} - \mu(t - \delta)}{\sigma_x\sqrt{t - \delta}}\right]$$

The density function for $C^*(t)$, denoted as $h_t(c)$, can now be derived by differentiating the distribution function $H_t(c)$, while allowing for a discrete probability mass at the point $Q(0)$. The solution for $h_t(c)$ appears in Eq. (14.21).

ACKNOWLEDGMENTS

I am grateful for the comments of Michael Brennan, Lenos Trigeorgis, and an anonymous referee.

REFERENCES

Bar-Ilan, A., and W. C. Strange. (1996). Investment Lags. *American Economic Review* 86(3), 611–622.

Bar-Ilan, A., A. Sulem, and A. Zanello. (1992). Time to Build and Capacity Choice. Working Paper, Dartmouth College and Tel-Aviv University.

Brennan, M. J., and E. Schwartz. (1985). Evaluating Natural Resource Investments. *Journal of Business* 58(2), 135–157.

Constantinides, G. M. (1984). Warrant Exercise and Bond Conversion in Competitive Markets. *Journal of Financial Economics* 13(3), 371–397.

Cox, J. C., and S. A. Ross. (1976). The Valuation of Options for Alternative Stochastic Processes. *Journal of Financial Economics* 3(1), 145–166.

Dixit, A. (1989a). Hysteresis, Import Penetration, and Exchange Rate Pass-Through. *Quarterly Journal of Economics* 104(2), 205–228.

Dixit, A. (1989b). Entry and Exit Decisions Under Uncertainty. *Journal of Political Economy* 97(3), 620–638.

Dixit, A. (1991). Irreversible Investment with Price Ceilings. *Journal of Political Economy* 99(3), 541–557.

Dumas, B. (1991). Super Contact and Related Optimality Conditions. *Journal of Economic Dynamics and Control* 15(4), 675–695.

Emanuel, D. C. (1983). Warrant Valuation and Exercise Strategy. *Journal of Financial Economics* 12(2), 211–235.

Grenadier, S. R. (1995a). The Persistence of Real Estate Cycles. *Journal of Real Estate Finance and Economics* 10(2), 95–119.

Grenadier, S. R. (1995b). Valuing Lease Contracts: A Real-Options Approach. *Journal of Financial Economics* 38(3), 297–331.

Grenadier, S. R. (1996). The Strategic Exercise of Options: Development Cascades and Overbuilding in Real Estate Markets. *Journal of Finance* 51(5), 1653–1679.

Grenadier, S. R. (1997). Information Revelation Through Option Exercise. Review of Financial Studies 12(1), 95–129.

Harrison, J. M. (1985). *Brownian Motion and Stochastic Flow Systems.* New York: Wiley.

Harrison, J. M., and M. Taksar. (1983). Instantaneous Control of Brownian Motion. *Mathematics of Operations Research* 8(3), 439–453.

Kulatilaka, N., and E. Perotti. (1998). Strategic Growth Options. *Management Science* 44, 1021–1031.

Leahy, J. V. (1993). Investment in Competitive Equilibrium: The Optimality of Myopic Behavior. *Quarterly Journal of Economics* 108(4), 1105–1133.

Lucas, R. E., Jr., and E. C. Prescott. (1971). Investment Under Uncertainty. *Econometrica* 39(5), 659–681.

Majd, S., and R. Pindyck. (1987). Time to Build, Option Value, and Investment Decisions. *Journal of Financial Economics* 18(1), 7–28.

McDonald, R., and D. Siegel. (1986). The Value of Waiting to Invest. *Quarterly Journal of Economics* 101(1), 707–727.

Pindyck, R. S. (1988). Irreversible Investment, Capacity Choice, and the Value of the Firm. *American Economic Review* 79(5), 969–985.

Smit, H., and L. Trigeorgis. (1997). Flexibility and Competitive R&D Strategies. Working Paper, Columbia University.

Spatt, C. S., and F. P. Sterbenz. (1988). Warrant Exercise, Dividends, and Reinvestment Policy. *Journal of Finance* 43(2), 493–506.

Wheaton, W. (1987). The Cyclic Behavior of the National Office Market. *Journal of the American Real Estate and Urban Economics Association* 15(4), 281–299.

15

Strategic Sequential Investments and Sleeping Patents

BART LAMBRECHT

This chapter derives the optimal investment thresholds for two symmetric investors who hold an option to invest in a two-stage sequential investment and who have incomplete information on each other's profits. In stage 1, the investors are competing to obtain a patent that gives its holder an option to proceed to the second stage. The latter stage consists of the commercialization of the invention. The optimal investment trigger for the first stage is stationary and implies a trade-off between the benefit of waiting to invest and the cost of being preempted. We determine the conditions under which inventions are likely to be patented without being put immediately to commercial use. Sleeping patents are more likely to occur when interest rates are low, profit volatility is high, or the first-stage cost is small relative to the second-stage cost. Interestingly, the strategic trigger is a *decreasing* function of profit volatility for the sleeping patent case.

15.1 INTRODUCTION

In the past decade much attention in the financial economics literature has been devoted to the option valuation approach of investments (see, for example, Brennan and Schwartz, 1985; McDonald and Siegel, 1986; Dixit, 1989; Ingersoll and Ross, 1992; Dixit and Pindyck, 1994; Miller and Zhang, 1996; Trigeorgis, 1996). This approach is usually applied to investments that share the following three characteristics: the investment is partially or completely irreversible, the future payoffs are uncertain, and there is some leeway about the timing of the investment. Dixit and Pindyck (1994) demonstrated that the traditional theory of investment has not recognized the important qualitative and quantitative implications of the interaction between the above three dimensions. In particular, the net present value (NPV) rule, which considers an irreversible investment as a "now or never" decision, ignores investors' ability to delay. A firm with an opportunity to invest actually holds an option. Just as with financial options, part of the value of this option is attributed to a time premium corresponding to the value of the flexibility to delay the investment. Taking account of this value in the investment decision may substantially alter the investment triggers.

While investment decisions under uncertainty have been extensively discussed for the two extreme market structures, namely perfect competition and monopoly, little attention has been devoted to the oligopolistic case. A few exceptions are Smets (1991), Spencer and Brander (1992), Smit and Ankum (1993), Lambrecht and Perraudin (1994, 1996), Baldursson (1996), Grenadier (1996), Trigeorgis (1996), Smit and Trigeorgis (1997), Kulatilaka and Perotti (1998), and Lambrecht (1998), who recently introduced a strategic dimension into the real options literature. According to Dixit and Pindyck (1994, p. 309), the reason for this is practical rather than fundamental: "Oligopolistic industries in our stochastic setting present formidable difficulties. The development of stochastic game theory for such applications is quite recent, and tractable models using that theory are rarer still." Strategic considerations in an oligopolistic framework can indeed substantially complicate investment decisions: on the one hand, uncertainty and irreversibility imply an option value of waiting, but on the other hand, fear of preemption by a rival suggests the need to act quickly.[1]

What is the nature of this competitive threat in an oligopolistic environment? Schumpeter (1975) has stressed the importance of competition through innovation and uncertainty. According to him, competition through innovation is more important than price competition because it is a more decisive means of gaining competitive advantage. Galbraith (1952) states that it is also more prevalent because of tacit agreement among firms in oligopolistic markets not to engage in price competition. Firms face uncertainty about the profitability of their own and of competitors' innovations, with potential rivals (known and unknown) presenting another major source of uncertainty for firms in this milieu.

Without exclusive rights (e.g., patents), however, firms are reluctant to engage in costly development of new products or processes.[2] This is a major reason for the existence of patents. Patents also have an important effect on market structure. For a new firm, a patent can be an entry ticket into the market. For an incumbent firm, patents on similar products can be used to fill up all possible niches in the market to ensure that no other firm enters. In this spirit, previous work has explored the implications of patenting for the persistence of monopoly (see, for example, Gilbert and Newbery, 1982; Reinganum, 1983; Harris and Vickers, 1985; and Leininger, 1991). In particular, Newbery (1978) considers sleeping patents obtained by a monopolist as part of a defensive strategy of deterring potential rivals from entering the industry. Fudenberg and Tirole (1985) study the adoption of a new technology and illustrate the effects of preemption in games of timing. Related work has explored more generally how profits, costs, and the intensity of rivalry determine the speed of development of an

---

[1] The threat of preemption is also referred to as the "competitive threat" by Beath et al. (1989).

[2] Kamien and Schwartz (1982) note that a general Accounting Office study in the United States indicated that not a single pharmaceutical developed with National Institutes of Health support ever reached the public because they lacked exclusive rights. This claim prompted the Department of Health, Education, and Welfare to grant such rights in 1968. In the subsequent 10 years, at least 70 important discoveries were developed by private pharmaceutical manufacturers.

innovation. Loury (1979), Dasgupta and Stiglitz (1980), Lee and Wilde (1980), and Reinganum (1981) focus, for instance, on the impact of technological uncertainty, while Fudenberg et al. (1983), Harris and Vickers (1985), and Beath et al. (1989) examine strategic interaction in contexts containing no technological uncertainty.[3]

Harris and Vickers (1987) present a model that captures both features. Anderson and Harris (1986) develop a continuous-time model of innovation in an oligopoly. Their model allows for uncertainty in future product demand and incorporates an advantage for the first mover. Pakes (1986) explores the concept of patents as options on inventions with uncertain returns and presents empirical evidence on the impact of patent renewal fees.

This chapter extends this literature by valuing patents as "strategic" real options. This is accomplished by introducing strategic behavior into the contingent claims analysis. In particular, the chapter focuses on the determinants of sleeping patents and product innovation in a duopolistic setting in which two investors compete for a patent that secures for its holder exclusive and perpetual patent protection. Our model has the following features. First, it allows for a general form of uncertainty in the future profitability of the innovation (following a geometric Brownian motion). Second, there is incomplete information with respect to the rival's profits. Third, there is no technological uncertainty, i.e., at any moment the firm can decide to innovate by paying the investment costs. The model's assumptions imply that the optimal investment strategies consist of investing the first time that the investor's stochastic profit flow exceeds a fixed trigger level.

The model is designed to analyze the phenomenon of patent suppression, commonly known as "sleeping patents." Sleeping patents arise when an invention for which a patent has been secured is not put immediately to public commercial use. In effect, it is the "shelving" of an invention that others would like to manufacture or use. Sleeping patents are a widespread phenomenon. Vaughan (1956) gives some historical evidence on sleeping patents related to important inventions, such as telephone and telegraph.[4]

Analyzing the sleeping patent phenomenon involves consideration of the optimal timing of two sequential investment decisions: patenting and commercialization of the product innovation. The first-stage decision is whether to take a patent on a product by paying a fixed patent fee. The patent gives its holder the exclusive right (but not the obligation) to move on to the second stage, which consists of the actual launching of the product, also at some predetermined cost. We show that when there is no competition both stages will be executed simultaneously, i.e., the rights on the product are bought only when it is also profitable to launch the product. However,

---

[3] Technological uncertainty refers to uncertainty in the relationship between R&D efforts and the progress toward success.

[4] "American Telephone, after obtaining thousands of patents upon various alternate methods of accomplishing specific results, used some of them and let the others lie dormant. In 1935, this company owned 46% of the patents classified as 'telephone' by the Patent Office and 62% were unused. Corresponding percentages for its telegraph patents were 45 and 65; for radio, 15 and 58; and for sound recordings and reproducing, 17 and 50. There is nothing to indicate any important change in these figures in more recent years" (Vaughan, 1956, p. 235).

this is not necessarily the case when there is a possibility of preemption. We show that strategic considerations cause the two firms to speed up their decision to take the patent. Having taken the patent, the patentholder will either proceed immediately to the second stage or postpone commercialization of the product until the profitability of the product innovation has increased. It is worthwhile to note that even though this chapter concentrates on sleeping patents, the model could easily be applied to similar types of sequential investments, such as the acquisition and exploitation of oil leases.[5]

This chapter is organized as follows. In Section 15.2 we solve the strategic investment problem when there is only one investor interested in acquiring the patent, and then derive the investor's optimal investment strategy when there is a rival whose investment behavior is exogenously given by a distribution over its first-stage investment trigger. In Section 15.3 we endogenize the patenting strategy for the case in which both investors have incomplete information about their opponent's profitability. Section 15.4 presents some closed-form solutions for the agents' equilibrium investment triggers and uses these to assess the effectiveness of two regulatory policies against sleeping patents. The first policy consists of the regulator charging a patent fee that rules out sleeping patents, without slowing down the introduction of the innovation. The second policy entails a refundable patent fee charged when the patent is acquired, but returned as soon as the innovation is put to commercial use.

15.2 A TWO-STAGE SEQUENTIAL INVESTMENT MODEL

In many situations investment decisions are made sequentially, and in a particular order. An investment in a new drug by a pharmaceutical company, for example, begins with research that may lead to a new drug, which can then be patented. Afterward production facilities need to be constructed, and ultimately the drug may be launched on the market.

Dixit and Pindyck (1994, Chapter 10) describe a simple model to value a two-stage investment by means of sequential (compound) options. Their "anticlimactic" result for the two-stage problem is that once the firm decides to start the investment, it will complete both stages of the project at the same moment (assuming both investments can be completed instantaneously). The merit of that model was that it provided us with a valuation of (and triggers for) the two separate stages of the project. This may be useful when, for instance, one firm wants to sell a partially completed project (e.g., the patent) to another firm.

In this section we show, using a similar set-up and assumptions as Dixit and Pindyck (1994) (e.g., instantaneous completion),[6] that in a two-stage investment project with potential preemption in the first stage, strategic considerations lead a firm to try to preempt its competitor in the first stage and afterward either postpone or immediately execute the second stage.

---

[5] I thank Marcus Miller for pointing this out.

[6] Majd and Pindyck (1987) and Grenadier (this volume) consider investment policies when it takes "time-to-build." The solution of their model provides a rule for optimal sequential investment that accounts for the time required to actually undertake the investment.

15.2.1 Individual Firm Behavior without Preemption

We start with a short review of the original two-stage sequential investment problem, and then develop a sequential investment model with preemptive behavior. We start with the following setup.

ASSUMPTION 1. *A firm is faced with a two-stage sequential investment. In the first stage, a patent of infinite duration can be acquired at a known cost, C.*[7,8] *Execution of this stage allows the investor to proceed to the second stage, the exploitation of the patent, which requires a further investment cost, K. Once the second stage is completed, and the product is introduced on the market, profits start flowing in at a rate πx_t, where π is a positive constant and x_t is a geometric Brownian motion of the form*[9]

$$dx_t = \mu x_t\, dt + \sigma x_t\, dZ_t \qquad (15.1)$$

where $\mu(< r)$ and $\sigma(> 0)$ are constants and Z_t is a standard Wiener process.

We next derive the value of the sequential investment opportunity and calculate the optimal triggers, $\bar{x}_p$ and $\bar{x}_c$, at which the product innovation is patented and commercialized, respectively, when the investor ignores strategic considerations. The following main question is to be addressed: will an investor who has taken a patent on a product let the patent sleep (i.e., $\bar{x}_p < \bar{x}_c$), or immediately proceed to the commercialization (i.e., $\bar{x}_p \geq \bar{x}_c$)? The derivation of the investment rule for this two-stage sequential investment is discussed in Dixit and Pindyck (1994, Chapter 10). We merely state the result here, and include the proof in Appendix A.

Proposition 1. *Assuming that investors are risk neutral and that there exists a risk free asset yielding a constant interest rate, r, the value of the investment prior to commercialization (but after patenting the product innovation), $V(x_t)$, and the value of the investment prior to patenting, $U(x_t)$, respectively, are*

$$V(x_t) = \begin{cases} \left(\frac{\pi \bar{x}_c}{r - \mu} - K\right)\left(\frac{x_t}{x_c}\right)^\beta & \text{for } x_t < \bar{x}_c \\ \frac{\pi x_t}{r - \mu} - K & \text{for } x_t \geq \bar{x}_c \end{cases} \qquad (15.2)$$

---

[7] In the United States, patents are granted for a term of 17 years (14 years for design patents). Since the model developed in this chapter uses option pricing techniques to value patents, patents can safely be regarded as infinite maturity (perpetual) options. Moreover, the additional complexity required of finite maturity models is not warranted by the small gain in accuracy.

[8] C includes costs such as patent fees, the present value of future patent maintenance fees (due at 3.5, 7.5, and 11.5 years from the date the patent is granted), services of a patent attorney or agent, and invention costs that do not depend on technological uncertainty. Note that patentholders may at some point decide not to renew the patent when the maintenance fees come due. The interested reader is referred to Pakes (1986) on this issue.

[9] x_t could, for instance, correspond to a multiplicative consumer taste shock.

$$U(x_t) = \begin{cases} [V(\bar{x}_p) - C] \left(\frac{x_t}{x_p}\right)^{\beta} & \text{for } x_t < \bar{x}_p \\ V(x_t) - C & \text{for } x_t \geq \bar{x}_p \end{cases} \tag{15.3}$$

where β is the positive root to the characteristic equation $\beta(\beta - 1)\sigma^2/2 + \mu\beta = r$ given by

$$\beta = \frac{-\mu + (\sigma^2/2) + \sqrt{[\mu - (\sigma^2/2)]^2 + 2r\sigma^2}}{\sigma^2}$$

and where

$$\bar{x}_p = \frac{\beta(C + K)(r - \mu)}{(\beta - 1)\pi} > \frac{\beta K(r - \mu)}{(\beta - 1)\pi} = \bar{x}_c$$

are the nonstrategic option triggers of the first (patent) and second (commercialization) stages, respectively.

The above illustrates how the option valuation approach leads to investment triggers that are drastically different from the neoclassical Marshallian trigger, defined by Dixit and Pindyck (1994) as follows:

Definition 1: *The Marshallian trigger is the trigger at which the total expected income flow just equals the cost of investment (i.e., NPV = 0).*

The Marshallian triggers for the first and second investment stages, $\bar{x}_{pm}$ and $\bar{x}_{cm}$, are, respectively, defined by

$$V(\bar{x}_{pm}) - C = 0 \quad \text{and} \quad \frac{\pi \bar{x}_{cm}}{r - \mu} - K = 0 \tag{15.4}$$

Equivalently,

$$\bar{x}_{pm} = \begin{cases} \bar{x}_c \left[\frac{C(\beta - 1)}{K}\right]^{1/\beta} & \text{for } \bar{x}_{pm} < \bar{x}_c \\ \frac{(C + K)(r - \mu)}{\pi} & \text{for } \bar{x}_{pm} \geq \bar{x}_c \end{cases} \tag{15.5}$$

$$\bar{x}_{cm} = \frac{K(r - \mu)}{\pi} \tag{15.6}$$

Comparing the nonstrategic option triggers with the corresponding Marshallian triggers, we see that uncertainty makes the investor delay for, since $\beta > 1$ and $C, K > 0$, the nonstrategic option triggers are higher than the Marshallian triggers : $\bar{x}_p > \bar{x}_{pm}$ and $\bar{x}_c > \bar{x}_{cm}$.

Proposition 1 also implies that, since the second-stage nonstrategic option trigger is below the first-stage trigger ($\bar{x}_p > \bar{x}_c$), the second stage will be executed at $\bar{x}_p$ (immediately after the first stage) and not at $\bar{x}_c$. Hence, when there are no strategic considerations it is not optimal to let patents sleep. Indeed, the investor could do better by putting the patent fee in the bank to earn interest. The optimal investment rule consists of taking the patent and launching the underlying product immediately afterward. Note that the trigger rule for the first stage has the same form as for the second stage, with the only difference being that the exercise price is now $C + K$ rather than C. Intuitively, the exercise trigger for stage 1 should be situated above the trigger for stage 2 since the higher the sunk cost required to obtain a risky payoff, the higher the critical price necessary to trigger investment. Finally, although it is *optimal* for the investor not to let the patent sleep without preemption, this does not necessarily preclude sleeping patents from still being *profitable*, as shown next.

Proposition 2. *The Marshallian trigger for the first investment stage, $\bar{x}_{pm}$, and the nonstrategic option trigger for the second investment stage, $\bar{x}_c$, satisfy the following conditions:*

$$\bar{x}_{pm} < \bar{x}_c \iff (\beta - 1) < \frac{K}{C}$$

$$\bar{x}_{pm} \geq \bar{x}_c \iff (\beta - 1) \geq \frac{K}{C} \qquad (15.7)$$

Hence, if $(\beta - 1) < K/C$, then all first-stage triggers in the open interval $]\bar{x}_{pm}, \bar{x}_c[$ lead to a situation of sleeping patents. Although these triggers are suboptimal, they still are profitable.

15.2.2 Individual Firm Behavior with Preemption

Consider now the problem in which two competing firms consider investing in the above two-stage project, but in which only the first one to complete the first (patent) stage is entitled to continue with the second stage of commercialization. We further assume that there is incomplete information between the two firms. More specifically, we make the following assumptions:

ASSUMPTION 2. *Only the first firm to acquire the patent is entitled to proceed to the second stage.*

ASSUMPTION 3. *A firm i with profit rate $\pi_i x_t$ considers the opportunity to invest in the sequential investment described in Assumption 1. It knows, however, that another firm j may acquire the patent first. Firm i conjectures that firm j will invest in the patent when x_t first crosses some level $\bar{x}_{jps}$, and that $\bar{x}_{jps}$ is an independent draw from a distribution $F_j(\bar{x}_{jps})$ that has a continuously differentiable density $F'(\bar{x}_{jps})$ with positive support on the interval $[\bar{x}_L, \bar{x}_U]$.*

We refer to $\bar{x}_{jps}$ ($\bar{x}_{ips}$) as firm j's (i's) strategic first-stage (patent) trigger. We will now derive the optimal investment rule for firm i, taking firm j's behavior, $F_j(\bar{x}_{jps})$, as exogenously given. In the next section we also endogenise firm j's behavior.

Ignoring any strategic behavior, firm i would calculate its first-stage trigger as described above, fully enjoying its option to delay the investment. However, as soon as strategic considerations come into play, firm i will select its optimal trigger, $\bar{x}_{ips}$, taking into account the possibility that it may be preempted by a rival. We suppose, as in Assumption 3, that firm i has rational conjectures about the distribution of the other firm's trigger. Furthermore, as time goes by, firm i will update its conjecture. In particular, whenever x_t hits a new high and firm j does not act, firm i learns that firm j's trigger lies in a smaller, higher interval, updating its conjecture about firm j's trigger distribution accordingly. Let $F_j(\bar{x}_{jps}|\hat{x}_t)$ denote firm i's conjecture about firm j's trigger, $\bar{x}_{jps}$, conditional on the information available at time t. A sufficient statistic that captures this information is given by $\hat{x}_t$, which denotes the maximum level reached so far by x_t without one of the firms having acted, i.e., $\hat{x}_t \equiv \max(x_\tau|0 \leq \tau \leq t)$. The support of $F_j(\bar{x}_{jps}|\hat{x}_t)$ is given by $[\hat{x}_t, \bar{x}_U]$ and, as $\hat{x}_t$ increases, Bayesian updating takes the following simple form:

$$1 - F_j(\bar{x}_{jps}|\hat{x}_t) = \frac{1 - F_j(\bar{x}_{jps})}{1 - F_j(\hat{x}_t)} \tag{15.8}$$

The value of firm i's claim before anybody has taken any action can be written as

$$W_{it} = E_t\left[\left(V_i(\bar{x}_{T_i}) - C\right)e^{-r(T_i-t)}\left(1 - \text{Prob}\left(T_j < T_i\right)\right)\right] \tag{15.9}$$

where $T_i \equiv \inf(\tau|x_\tau \geq \bar{x}_{ips})$ is the first time that x_t hits $\bar{x}_{ips}$. Intuitively, the total value, W_{it}, equals the expected discounted value of firm i's payoff at T_i times the probability that firm i acts first. Note that $\bar{x}_{jps}$, the trigger level for firm j, is a random variable as far as firm i is concerned. Conditioning on the other firm's trigger level, one may evaluate the above expression directly as given in the following proposition:

Proposition 3. *The value of the sequential investment opportunity for firm i prior to investment by either firm, and conditional on the other firm's trigger level, is given by*

$$W_i(x_t, \hat{x}_t) = \left[V_i(\bar{x}_{ips}) - C\right]\left(\frac{x_t}{\bar{x}_{ips}}\right)^\beta\left[1 - F_j(\bar{x}_{ips}|\hat{x}_t)\right] \tag{15.10}$$

where firm i's optimal choice of $\bar{x}_{ips}$ satisfies:

$$\left[-V_i(\bar{x}_{ips}) + C\right]h_j(\bar{x}_{ips}) + \bar{x}_{ips}\frac{\partial V_i(\bar{x}_{ips})}{\partial \bar{x}_{ips}} - \beta\left[V_i(\bar{x}_{ips}) - C\right] = 0 \tag{15.11}$$

with $h_j(\bar{x}_{ips}) = [F_j'(\bar{x}_{ips})\bar{x}_{ips}]/[1 - F_j(\bar{x}_{ips})].[10]

Figure 15.1 plots the value of the sequential investment opportunity to firm i.[11] The graph shows how the value of the strategic claim depends not only on x_t but also

---

[10] Equivalently, $\bar{x}_{ips}$ is the point at which the envelope $W_i(\hat{x}_t, \hat{x}_t)$ smoothpastes to the exercise line $[V_i(x_t) - C]$.

[11] The figure is based on the following parameter values: $r = 0.03$, $\mu = 0$, $\sigma = 0.1$, $C = 0.5$, $K = 10$, $\pi = 0.3$, $F_j(\bar{x}_{jps}) = 1 - (4/5\bar{x}_{jps})^{0.5}$.

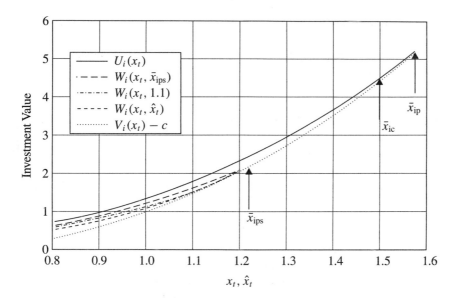

Figure 15.1 Value of sequential investment opportunities. The figure plots the value of the nonstrategic investment claims, $V_i(x_t)$ and $U_i(x_t)$, and the strategic investment claim, W_i, $(x_t, \hat{x}_t)$, as a function of the state variables x_t, at various levels of the state variable $\hat{x}_t$. x_t refers to the profit level at time t, whereas $\hat{x}_t$ denotes the highest profit level reached so far. $\bar{x}_{ip}$ and $\bar{x}_{ic}$ denote, respectively, firm i's first-stage (patent) and second-stage (commercialization) nonstrategic option trigger whereas $\bar{x}_{ips}$ denotes firm i's first-stage strategic option trigger. C denotes the first-stage investment cost.

on $\hat{x}_t$: each time the state variable hits a new maximum the claim value shifts along the "envelope" $W_i(x_t, \hat{x}_t)$ to a higher level, reflecting the fact that as $\hat{x}_t$ goes up it becomes more likely that firm i will not be preempted. Firm i will act at $\bar{x}_{ips}$, where the envelope is tangent to the exercise line $V_i(x_t) - C$, which is the value of the investment in the second stage after subtracting the patent cost. The nonstrategic sequential investment claim is shown to smoothpaste at $\bar{x}_{ip}$, which is situated well above the strategic trigger, $\bar{x}_{ips}$. The second-stage trigger, $\bar{x}_{ic}$, marks the point at which the function $V_i(x_t) - C$ [see Eq. (15.2)] changes from a power function into a straight line.

Consider now the first-stage strategic investment trigger, $\bar{x}_{ips}$. Although the value of the investment critically depends on both x_t and $\hat{x}_t$, the trigger $\bar{x}_{ips}$ does not because $h_j(x)$ is independent of both state variables. By definition, $h_j(x)$ is the hazard rate[12] multiplied by x, proxying for the likelihood that firm j will act at x given that it has not acted (preempted) yet. The hazard rate is zero when there is no fear of preemption at all, and goes to $+\infty$ when $\hat{x}_t \to \bar{x}_U$. Indeed, as $\hat{x}_t \to \bar{x}_U$ and patenting has not taken place yet, firm i knows that the other firm will act almost certainly in the next few instants, which causes the hazard of being preempted to explode. The trigger rule

---

[12] The hazard rate is defined as the likelihood of an event occurring in the next instant, given that the event has not occurred yet. It is given by $f_j(x)/1 - F_j(x)$.

for firm i therefore strikes a balance between the option benefit of waiting an instant longer at $\overline{x}_{ips}$ and the cost of being preempted an instant after $\overline{x}_{ips}$.

The following proposition illustrates the effect of the preemption hazard rate on the strategic option trigger.

Proposition 4. *The first-stage strategic trigger,* $\overline{x}_{ips}$, *is situated between the Marshallian trigger,* $\overline{x}_{ipm}$, *and the nonstrategic option trigger,* $\overline{x}_{ip}$, *i.e.,*

$$\overline{x}_{ipm} \leq \overline{x}_{ips} \leq \overline{x}_{ip} \tag{15.12}$$

The upper bound is reached as $h_j(x) \to 0$, *while the lower bound is reached as* $h_j(x) \to \infty$.

In brief, it is clear from the optimal trigger rule of Proposition 3 that firm i's strategic trigger, $\overline{x}_{ips}$, depends on the firm's own parameters as well as its conjecture about the opponent's trigger. Using the terminology of Beath et al. (1989), we can say that the point of patenting is determined by two different forces: the "profit incentive" and "competitive threat." The profit incentive is the incentive to invest as if the firm had no competitors. As discussed in Section 15.2.1, this leads to the identification of two triggers, the nonstrategic option trigger, $\overline{x}_p$, and the Marshallian trigger, $\overline{x}_{pm}$, depending on whether uncertainty and irreversibility are taken into account. The second force determining the decision to patent comes from the recognition that the firm is in a race against its rival, leading to the identification of the strategic trigger, $\overline{x}_{ps}$.

We consider next the relationship between the first- and second-stage triggers, $\overline{x}_{ips}$ and $\overline{x}_{ic}$.[13] Rearranging the first-order condition (15.11) and substituting for $V_i(x_t)$, we can derive a result analogous to Proposition 2.

Proposition 5. *If firm j's trigger distribution is given by $F_j(\overline{x}_{jps})$, firm i's investment triggers for the first and second stage, $\overline{x}_{ips}$ and $\overline{x}_{ic}$, satisfy the following decision rule:*

$$\overline{x}_{ips} < \overline{x}_{ic} \iff \frac{[\beta + h_j(\overline{x}_{ips})](\beta - 1)}{h_j(\overline{x}_{ips})} < \frac{K}{C} \tag{15.13}$$

$$\overline{x}_{ips} \geq \overline{x}_{ic} \iff \frac{[\beta + h_j(\overline{x}_{ips})](\beta - 1)}{h_j(\overline{x}_{ips})} \geq \frac{K}{C} \tag{15.14}$$

Since sleeping patents arise when $\overline{x}_{ips} < \overline{x}_{ic}$, Proposition 5 allows us to analyze the determinants of sleeping patents. First is the size of the second stage cost, K, relative to the patent fee, C. This makes intuitive sense. Think of the extreme case in which

---

[13] Note that there is no strategic aspect to the choice of the second-stage trigger since the holder of the patent faces no competitive threat.

the patent can be obtained costlessly. In this case, it is clearly optimal for firm i to grab the patent immediately and to let it sleep ($\bar{x}_{ips} < \bar{x}_{ic}$) until it is optimal to proceed with its exploitation. By doing this the competitor is preempted at no cost. As the cost of patenting increases, it becomes more expensive to let the patent sleep. On the other hand, if the second-stage investment cost, K, is zero there will be no reason for sleeping patents at all ($\bar{x}_{ips} \geq \bar{x}_{ic}$) because, given our payoff structure, the patentholder would forgo free profits.

A second set of factors determining the occurrence of sleeping patents is the price volatility, σ, the interest rate, r, and the profit growth rate, μ. As volatility increases, β converges toward 1, causing the condition for sleeping patents to be satisfied. Similarly, sleeping patents are more likely to occur when interest rates are low and profit growth rates are high. Another crucial determinant of sleeping patents is the competitive threat given by $h_j(\cdot)$. Proposition 5 confirms our previous result (from Proposition 1) that as the competitive threat disappears [$h_j(\cdot) \to 0$], the patent will not be taken out until the product is to be launched. A somewhat surprising result is that the profit parameter, π, does not appear in Proposition 5. However, we will see that when the hazard rate $h_j(\bar{x}_{ips})$ is endogenously determined, the sleeping patent phenomenon can also be influenced by the profit parameter, π.

It is also interesting to compare the nonstrategic first-stage trigger, $\bar{x}_{ip}$, with the strategic trigger, $\bar{x}_{ips}$. Since, $\bar{x}_{ip} > \bar{x}_{ic}$, the case for which $\bar{x}_{ips} < \bar{x}_{ic}$ implies that $\bar{x}_{ips} < \bar{x}_{ip}$. This means that we observe preemptive behavior in the first stage, while the execution of the second stage is postponed. Due to a combination of the above-mentioned reasons, the state variable is not yet favorable enough to justify the second-stage investment, but for strategic reasons we already decided to activate the first stage of the project. Do we also have accelerated investment behavior in the case in which $\bar{x}_{ips} > \bar{x}_{ic}$? Preemptive behavior requires that

$$\bar{x}_{ips} = \frac{(C+K)[h_j(\bar{x}_{ips}) + \beta]}{\pi_i[h_j(\bar{x}_{ips}) + \beta - 1]} < \frac{(C+K)\beta}{\pi_i(\beta-1)} = \bar{x}_{ip} \qquad (15.15)$$

or equivalently $h_j(\bar{x}_{ips}) > 0$. Considering the definition of $h_j(\bar{x}_{ips})$, this is always the case. Accelerated action, therefore, occurs also in this case, but to a lesser extent than in the previous case. These results are summarized in Table 15.1.

Table 15.1
Decision Rule for the Occurrence of Sleeping Patents[a]

	$\frac{[h_j(\bar{x}_{ips}) + \beta](\beta-1)}{h_j(\bar{x}_{ips})} < \frac{K}{C}$	$\frac{[h_j(\bar{x}_{ips}) + \beta](\beta-1)}{h_j(\bar{x}_{ips})} \geq \frac{K}{C}$
Stage 1	$\bar{x}_{ips} < \bar{x}_{ic} < \bar{x}_{ip}$ (preemptive behavior)	$\bar{x}_{ic} < \bar{x}_{ips} < \bar{x}_{ip}$ (preemptive behavior)
Stage 2	Postponed until x_t reaches $\bar{x}_{ic}$	Immediate execution (if feasible)

[a] $\bar{x}_{ip}$ and $\bar{x}_{ic}$ are, respectively, firm i's nonstrategic option trigger for the first (patent) and second (commercialization) investment stage. $\bar{x}_{ips}$ is firm i's strategic option trigger for the first (patent) investment stage. C and K are, respectively, the first-stage and second-stage investment cost, $h_j(x)$ is the hazard of preemption by firm j at trigger level x.

15.3 FIRM BEHAVIOR IN A COMPETITIVE EQUILIBRIUM FRAMEWORK

In this section we use the analysis of individual firm investment behavior from the previous section to derive the strategic investment rule for *both* firms within an equilibrium framework when there is incomplete information with respect to the profit parameter, π. Solving this problem leads to the identification of a symmetric Bayesian Nash equilibrium.[14] We first introduce the following assumptions:

ASSUMPTION 4. *Consider two symmetric firms (i = 1, 2) that have the opportunity to invest in the sequential investment described in Assumptions 2 and 3. Only the firm that executes stage 1 first can proceed to the second stage. If the firms act simultaneously, then with probability 1/2, one firm receives the patent while the other gets nothing.*

ASSUMPTION 5. *Both firms are identical, except for their profit parameter π. The ith (i = 1, 2) firm observes its own profit parameter π_i, but knows only that π_j (j $\neq$ i) is an independent draw from a distribution $G(\pi)$, which is public knowledge. $G(\pi)$ has a continuously differentiable density $G'(\pi)$, with strictly positive support on an interval $[\pi_L, \pi_U]$.*

In what follows, $\bar{x}_{ips}(\pi)$ (i = 1, 2) denote the equilibrium mappings from firm i's profit parameter, π_i, to its optimal first-stage strategic investment trigger, $\bar{x}_{ips}$. Once we have determined these mappings, it is relatively straightforward to derive the equilibrium trigger distributions, $F_i(\bar{x}_{ips})$, using the following transformation rule:

$$F_i(\bar{x}_{ips}) = 1 - G[\pi_{is}(\bar{x})] \quad \text{and} \quad F_i'(\bar{x}_{ips}) = -G'[\pi_{is}(\bar{x})]\pi_{is}'(\bar{x}) \quad (15.16)$$

where $\pi_{is}(\bar{x})$ is the inverse of $\bar{x}_{ips}(\pi)$.

From the previous section we know that the optimal trigger rules must satisfy the first-order conditions given by Eq. (15.11). Using the fact that

$$h_j(x) = \frac{x F_j'(x)}{1 - F_j(x)} = \frac{-x G'(\pi)\pi_{js}'(x)}{G(\pi)} \quad (15.17)$$

one obtains a system of differential equations in $\pi_{js}(x)$ (j = 1, 2). Exploiting the symmetry of the problem leads to the following proposition:

---

[14] It is rather straightforward to characterize the equilibrium when there is complete information. If the agents are identical, the only pure-strategy Nash equilibrium is full preemption: the firms apply for the patent as soon as their first-stage Marshallian trigger is hit. If the firms are not identical, then the more profitable firm will act at the smaller of either its rival's Marshallian trigger (also referred to as "epsilon preemption") or its own nonstrategic trigger. Real options models within a complete information framework have been discussed by Smets (1991) and Grenadier (1996), among others.

Proposition 6. *The symmetric equilibrium* $\pi_{is}(x) = \pi_{js}(x) \equiv \pi_s(x)$ *is the solution to*

$$
\pi_s'(x) = \begin{cases}
\dfrac{-G[\pi_s(x)]}{xG'[\pi_s(x)]} \left\{ \dfrac{\beta C}{\phi K^{1-\beta}[\pi_s(x)x]^\beta - C} \right\} & \text{for } x_t < \bar{x}_c \\[4mm]
\dfrac{-G[\pi_s(x)]}{xG'[\pi_s(x)]} \left\{ \dfrac{\pi_s(x)x - \beta[\pi_s(x)x - (r-\mu)(C+K)]}{\pi_s(x)x - (r-\mu)(C+K)} \right\} & \text{for } x_t \geq \bar{x}_c
\end{cases}
\tag{15.18}
$$

subject to $\pi_s(x_U) = \pi_L$, *where*

$$
\bar{x}_U = \begin{cases}
\dfrac{1}{\pi_L} \left(\dfrac{C}{\phi K^{1-\beta}} \right)^{1/\beta} & \text{if } \dfrac{K}{C} \geq \beta - 1 \\[4mm]
\dfrac{(C+K)(r-\mu)}{\pi_L} & \text{if } \dfrac{K}{C} < \beta - 1
\end{cases}
\tag{15.19}
$$

$\phi = (\beta - 1)^{\beta-1}[\beta(r - \mu)]^{-\beta}$, *and where* $[\bar{x}_L, \bar{x}_U]$ *is the support of* $F_1(x) = F_2(x) \equiv F(x)$.

Figure 15.2 plots the strategic first-stage trigger, $\bar{x}_{ps}$, for the case in which the profit parameter distribution is given by[15]

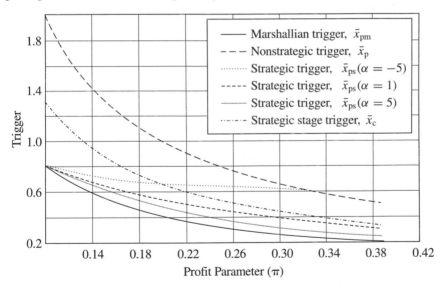

Figure 15.2 Trigger mappings versus profit (π) and competitive threat (α). The figure plots the trigger mappings as a function of the profit parameter, π, at various levels of the competitive threat proxied by the profit distribution parameter, α, where $G(\pi) = (\pi/\pi_U)^\alpha$ is the profit parameter distribution. An increase in α corresponds to an increase in the competitive threat by the opponent. $\bar{x}_p$ and $\bar{x}_c$ denote, respectively, the first-stage (patent) and second-stage (commercialization) nonstrategic option trigger, whereas $\bar{x}_{ps}$ denotes the first stage strategic option trigger. $\bar{x}_{pm}$ denotes the first-stage Marshallian (break-even) investment trigger. π_U is the upper bound of the profit parameter distribution.

[15] The plot is drawn using the following parameter values: $r = 0.03$, $\mu = 0$, $\sigma = 0.2$, $\pi_L = 0.1$, $\pi_U = 0.39$, $C = 1$, $K = 2$.

$$G(\pi) = \frac{\pi^\alpha - \pi_L^\alpha}{\pi_U^\alpha - \pi_L^\alpha} \quad \text{for } \pi \in [\pi_L, \pi_U] \tag{15.20}$$

where $0 < \pi_L < \pi_U < \infty$ and $\alpha \neq 0$

Differential Eq. (15.18) is solved numerically using backward differences. Note that the case for which α equals one corresponds to the uniform distribution. Figure 15.2 shows that when competitive threat is low (α is low),[16] the trigger values shift toward the nonstrategic solution. As preemption fear increases, the solution gradually converges to the Marshallian threshold. Figure 15.2 further illustrates that the profit scaling parameter π can also determine whether we have sleeping patents. When the profit scaling parameter, π, is low, firms tend to take the patent without putting it to commercial use until profits have gone up. As the profit parameter increases, we eventually end up in a situation in which $\bar{x}_{ps} > \bar{x}_c$ for which it is not optimal to let patents sleep.

15.4 MODEL WITH ISOELASTIC PROFIT DISTRIBUTION

15.4.1 Analytical Trigger Solutions and Sensitivity Analysis

In this section we derive a closed-form solution to (15.18) for the case in which $G(\pi) = (\pi/\pi_U)^\alpha$. This distribution, more generally known as the Pareto distribution, has the property that the elasticity $\pi G'(\pi)/G(\pi)$ is constant and equal to α.[17]

Proposition 7. For $G(\pi) = (\pi/\pi_U)^\alpha$ and $\alpha > 0$, the optimal strategic trigger $\bar{x}_{ps}(\pi)$ is given by

$$\bar{x}_{ps}(\pi) = \begin{cases} \dfrac{1}{\pi} \left[\dfrac{(\alpha+\beta)C}{\alpha \phi K^{(1-\beta)}} \right]^{1/\beta} & \text{for } x < \bar{x}_c \\[4mm] \dfrac{1}{\pi} \left[\dfrac{(\alpha+\beta)(C+K)(r-\mu)}{\alpha+\beta-1} \right] & \text{for } x \geq \bar{x}_c \end{cases} \tag{15.21}$$

This simple closed-form solution allows us to analyze the optimal first-stage triggers in a straightforward way.

Figure 15.3 shows the triggers as a function of the main model parameters μ, σ, α, K, and C.[18] Figure 15.3A shows the Marshallian ($\bar{x}_{pm}$), the strategic ($\bar{x}_{ps}$), and the nonstrategic ($\bar{x}_p$) triggers for the first stage as a function of the competitive threat,

---

[16] Lowering α shifts the probability weight toward the lower end of the profit parameter support.

[17] In a study on the profit distribution of patented inventions in Germany, Scherer (1997) finds that the profit distribution is very skewed (with only a few inventions turning out to be extremely profitable) and closely fits a Pareto distribution.

[18] The following parameter values were used for Figure 15.3: $r = 0.03$, $\mu = 0$, $\sigma = 0.2$, $\pi = 0.3$, $\pi_U = 0.5$, $\alpha = 1$.

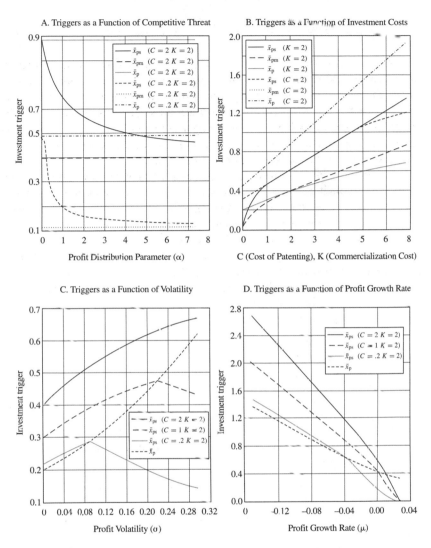

Figure 15.3 Sensitivity analysis of investment trigger values to competitive threat (A), investment costs (B), volatility (C), and profit growth rate (D).

α. When there is no preemption fear ($\alpha = 0$), the strategic trigger, $\overline{x}_{ps}$, coincides with the nonstrategic option trigger, $\overline{x}_p$. The solid line corresponds to the case for which $\overline{x}_{ps} \geq \overline{x}_c$ (i.e., $\beta - 1 \geq K/C = 2/2$) while the dashed line corresponds to the case for which $\overline{x}_{ps} < \overline{x}_c$ (i.e., $\beta - 1 < K/C = 2/0.2$). As α increases, the strategic trigger gradually converges to the Marshallian trigger. In other words, as preemption fear increases, all the option value of delaying the investment is eventually destroyed. Thus,

$$\lim_{\alpha \to \infty} \overline{x}_{ps}(\pi) = \frac{1}{\pi} \left[\frac{\beta C}{\phi K^{(1-\beta)}} \right]^{1/\beta} = \overline{x}_{pm} \text{ for } x < \overline{x}_c$$

$$\lim_{\alpha \to \infty} \overline{x}_{\mathrm{ps}}(\pi) = \frac{1}{\pi} \left[\frac{(C+K)(r-\mu)}{\beta - 1} \right]^{1/\beta} = \overline{x}_{\mathrm{pm}} \text{ for } x \geq \overline{x}_{\mathrm{c}} \qquad (15.22)$$

Figure 15.3B shows the first-stage triggers as a function of the first- and second-stage investment costs, C and K. For the first three cases K is held constant while C varies, whereas for the next three cases the opposite is true. All triggers are, as expected, monotonically increasing in both the first- and second-stage costs. Less standard is that both the Marshallian and the strategic trigger are strictly concave functions in the case of sleeping patents ($\overline{x}_{\mathrm{ps}} < \overline{x}_{\mathrm{c}}$). Note also that since the nonstrategic trigger, $\overline{x}_{\mathrm{p}}$, is symmetric in C and K, both curves for $\overline{x}_{\mathrm{p}}$ coincide.

Figure 15.3C presents the strategic trigger as a function of profit volatility for three different combinations of investment costs. The fourth curve shows that the nonstrategic trigger, $\overline{x}_{\mathrm{c}}$, is an increasing function of σ, a well-known standard result. For $\overline{x}_{\mathrm{ps}} \geq \overline{x}_{\mathrm{c}}$ the strategic trigger is increasing, but for the case of sleeping patents it is a *decreasing* function of volatility! A similar result was found by Kulatilaka and Perotti (1998) who analyze the optimal timing of a real investment under uncertainty, complete information, and imperfect competition. They find that increased uncertainty favors early investment because the first mover's claim value is more convex in the state variable than the claim of the late entrant.

The limiting behavior of our triggers is

$$\lim_{\alpha \to 0} \overline{x}_{\mathrm{c}}(\pi) = \frac{rK}{\pi} \qquad \text{for } \mu \geq 0$$

$$\lim_{\alpha \to 0} \overline{x}_{\mathrm{c}}(\pi) = \frac{(r-\mu)K}{\pi} \qquad \text{for } \mu < 0$$

$$\lim_{\alpha \to +\infty} \overline{x}_{\mathrm{c}}(\pi) = +\infty \qquad (15.23)$$

The last equation means that if volatility is infinite, firms would never execute the second stage. The corresponding limiting cases for the strategic trigger in the sleeping patent case ($\overline{x}_{\mathrm{ps}} < \overline{x}_{\mathrm{c}}$) are

$$\lim_{\sigma \to 0} \overline{x}_{\mathrm{ps}}(\pi) = \exp\{\frac{1}{r}[\mu \ln(\alpha\mu + r) + \mu \ln(C) - 2\mu \ln(\mu) - \mu \ln(\alpha)]\}$$

$$\times \exp\{\frac{1}{r}[(r-\mu)\ln(K) + \mu \ln(r-\mu) + r \ln(r)]\} \quad \text{for } \mu \geq 0$$

$$\lim_{\sigma \to 0} \overline{x}_{\mathrm{ps}}(\pi) \quad \text{not defined when } \overline{x}_{\mathrm{ps}} < \overline{x}_{\mathrm{c}} \qquad \qquad \text{for } \mu < 0$$

$$\lim_{\sigma \to \infty} \overline{x}_{\mathrm{ps}}\pi = \frac{(\alpha+1)(r-\mu)C}{\pi\alpha} > 0 \qquad (15.24)$$

Note that for $\mu = 0$ the strategic trigger equals the "Jorgensonian trigger" in the deterministic case, i.e., $\lim_{\sigma \to 0} \overline{x}_{\mathrm{ps}} = rK/\pi$.[19] When the profits are deterministic and have a negative growth rate, sleeping patents are suboptimal. Indeed, if profits are surely going to fall over time, it makes no sense to delay the investment once you have paid for the patent. Finally, when $\overline{x}_{\mathrm{ps}} \geq \overline{x}_{\mathrm{c}}$ we get

$$\lim_{\sigma \to 0} \overline{x}_{\mathrm{ps}}(\pi) = \frac{(\alpha\mu + r)(r-\mu)(C+K)}{\pi(r - \mu + \alpha\mu)} \qquad \text{for } \mu \geq 0$$

[19] rK is often called the Jorgensonian user cost of capital (see Dixit and Pindyck, 1994, p. 145).

$$\lim_{\sigma \to 0} \overline{x}_{ps}(\pi) \;=\; \frac{(r - \mu)(C + K)}{\pi} \qquad\qquad \text{for } \mu < 0$$

$$\lim_{\sigma \to +\infty} \overline{x}_{ps}(\pi) \quad \text{not defined when } \overline{x}_{ps} \geq \overline{x}_c \qquad (15.25)$$

The last statement results from the fact that when volatility is infinite, the patent will never be put to commercial use. Consequently, patents that are issued will sleep forever.

Figure 15.3D shows the effect of variation in the profit growth rate, μ. Both the first- and second-stage triggers are decreasing in μ: firms expecting a favorable profit trend will be willing to invest at a lower profitability level. As $\mu \to r$ and the discounted value of expected profits explodes, firms are even willing to grab the patent at a zero-profit threshold. They will, however, exploit the patent only at strictly positive profits. Indeed

$$\lim_{\mu \to r} \overline{x}_{ps}(\pi) = 0$$

$$\lim_{\mu \to r} \overline{x}_c(\pi) \;=\; \frac{(\sigma^2 + 2r)K}{2\pi} \;>\; 0 \qquad (15.26)$$

Finally, note that the behavior of the triggers as a function of the interest rate, r, is the mirror image of the case for μ: triggers are lowest at the point $\mu = r$, and then gradually increase with r.

15.4.2 Rate of Patent Exploitation

Newbery (1978) argues that social optimality requires that the acquisition of a patent be delayed until immediate introduction of the product innovation is worthwhile because the patent is costly and serves no positive social purpose while it is sleeping. An interesting question that then arises is how, and under what conditions, can a regulator ensure that inventions are put to commercial use as quickly as possible? Based on Proposition 7, we provide two possible answers to this question.[20]

One policy could consist of the regulator charging a patent fee, C^*, for which sleeping patents are ruled out and the exploitation of the patent is delayed. This twofold aim can be achieved by choosing C^* such that $\overline{x}_{ps} = \overline{x}_c \equiv \overline{x}^*$. Indeed, patent fees below C^* would lead to the socially undesirable situation of sleeping patents, while patent fees above C^* would delay the introduction of the innovation.

An alternative policy consists of the regulator charging a "refundable" patent fee, paid when the patent is issued but returned as soon as the innovation is put to commercial use. It is straightforward to see that there exists a patent fee, C^{**}, which leads to the fastest patent exploitation. Indeed, if the fee is negligibly small the invention will be patented almost instantaneously, but depending on the size of the exploitation cost, K, it may take quite a while before the product innovation will

---

[20] The policies described below illustrate how the sleeping patent phase can be eliminated, but do not intend to result in the most efficient outcome. The latter requires a rigorous welfare analysis that is beyond the scope of this chapter.

effectively be introduced (i.e., $\bar{x}_{ps} \ll \bar{x}_c$). As C increases $\bar{x}_{ps}$ will increase as well, but $\bar{x}_c(C)$ will decrease because the refunded fee will now subsidize part of the launching cost and thereby effectively speed up the introduction of the innovation.[21] For some value C^{**}, we ultimately obtain $\bar{x}_{ps} = \bar{x}_c(C^{**}) \equiv \bar{x}^{**}$, which corresponds to the fastest rate of innovation. Paradoxically, in this case the whole regulatory rule *appears* to be absent: the firm patents the invention, pays the fee, but gets it back immediately to cover part of its launching costs.

The following proposition derives the optimal nonrefundable and refundable patent fees, and characterizes the relative speed of innovation.

Proposition 8. *For $G(\pi) = (\pi/\pi_U)^\alpha$ and $\alpha > 0$, the nonrefundable patent fee that leads to the fastest patent exploitation is given by*

$$C^* = \frac{\alpha K}{(\alpha + \beta)(\beta - 1)} \qquad (15.27)$$

For this patent fee, the corresponding innovation path, $\bar{x}^*$, is given by

$$\bar{x}_{ps} = \bar{x}_c = \frac{\beta(r - \mu)K}{(\beta - 1)\pi} \equiv \bar{x}^* \qquad (15.28)$$

The refundable patent fee C^{**} leading to the fastest patent exploitation is given by

$$C^{**} = \frac{\alpha K}{(\alpha + \beta - 1)\beta} \qquad (15.29)$$

The corresponding innovation path, $\bar{x}^{**}$, is given by

$$\bar{x}_{ps} = \bar{x}_c(C^{**}) = \frac{\beta(r - \mu)(K - C^{**})}{(\beta - 1)\pi} = \frac{(\beta + \alpha)(r - \mu)K}{(\beta + \alpha - 1)\pi} \equiv \bar{x}^{**} \qquad (15.30)$$

The relative speed of exploitation is given by

$$\frac{\bar{x}^{**}}{\bar{x}^*} = \frac{(\alpha + \beta)(\beta - 1)}{(\alpha + \beta - 1)\beta} = \frac{C^{**}}{C^*} \qquad (15.31)$$

Which policy is preferable depends on the regulator's objective function. The first policy results in the regulator extracting surplus from the firm, which can be redistributed to society. The refundable patent policy does not imply a direct transfer of money, but ensures a faster availability of the innovation to society.

Figure 15.4 shows the impact of various parameters on the optimal patent fee (as a proportion of the exploitation costs, K) for the two regulatory policies, while Figure 15.5 plots the corresponding innovation paths, $\bar{x}^*$ and $\bar{x}^{**}$.[22] When there is

---

[21] The second-stage trigger is now given by $\bar{x}_c(C) = [\beta(r - \mu)(K - C)]/[(\beta - 1)\pi]$, i.e., the patent fee charged in the first stage subsidizes the exploitation costs of the second stage.
[22] The parameter values used in Figures 15.4 and 15.5 are $r = 0.03$, $\mu = 0$, $\sigma = 0.2$, $\alpha = 1$, $\pi = 0.3$, $\pi_U = 0.5$, $K = 4$.

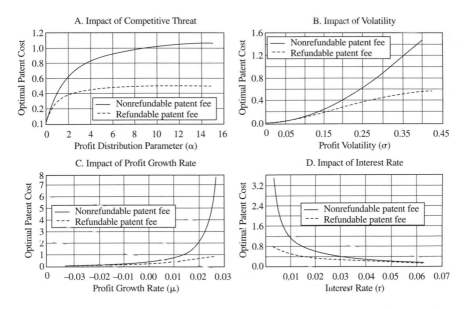

Figure 15.4 Sensitivity analysis of the relative optimal patent cost (C/K) to competitive threat (A), volatility (B), profit growth rate (C), and interest rate (D). The figure presents a sensitivity analysis on the optimal patent cost C (as a proportion of the commercialization cost K) for the nonrefundable and refundable patent fee policies, respectively.

no competition for the patent ($\alpha = 0$), both policies are identical and result in the absence of patent fees altogether. As competition intensifies, the optimal patent fee increases. In the nonrefundable patent fee case, this leads to a larger wealth transfer from the firm to the regulator, while in the refundable patent fee case the investment trigger gradually converges to the second-stage Marshallian trigger, $[(r - \mu)K]/\pi$, implying that the product innovation is bought and put to commercial use as soon as its discounted expected profits cover the exploitation cost, K.

Higher volatility delays the investment under both policies, but also leads to higher patent fees. The important difference is, however, that as $\sigma \to \infty$ the optimal nonrefundable fee, C^*, becomes unbounded (i.e., $\lim_{\sigma \to \infty} C^* = \infty$) while the refundable fee, C^{**}, is bounded by K (i.e., $\lim_{\sigma \to \infty} C^{**} = K$).

A lower profit growth rate reduces patent fees and delays investment. This accords with intuition: if the firm expects an unfavorable profit trend, it will want to pay for the patent only when profits are very high. Once it has bought the patent it will be reluctant to delay its exploitation, thereby reducing the likelihood of sleeping patents and consequently of high patent fees. A high interest rate, however, raises the investment threshold and decreases optimal patent fees. Indeed, a high interest rate raises the firm's opportunity cost and consequently the investment threshold. Furthermore, since it is expensive to let capital sleep when interest rates are high, sleeping patents are less likely to occur. Finally, whereas patent fees become unbounded in the nonrefundable fee case as $\mu \to r$, they are bounded by the exploitation cost, K, under the second regime.

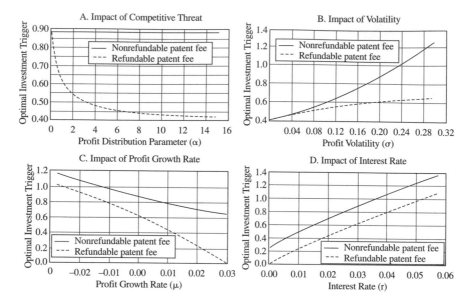

Figure 15.5 Sensitivity analysis of the optimal innovation path (investment triggers) to competitive threat (A), volatility (B), profit growth rate (C), and interest rate (D). The figure presents a sensitivity analysis on the optimal innovation path for the nonrefundable and refundable patent fee policies, respectively.

15.5 CONCLUSIONS

This chapter has derived the optimal investment timing rules for two ex ante symmetric investors who hold an option to invest in a two-stage sequential investment. The first investment stage consists of acquiring a patent on a product innovation. The firm that gets the patent then has an exclusive option to put the innovation to commercial use at any point in the future. We find that the optimal strategic trigger rule is stationary and strikes a balance between the option value of waiting to invest under uncertainty and the need to act quickly due to the competitive preemption threat. In particular, both the Marshallian break-even investment trigger and the trigger obtained by standard option valuation (under monopoly) are limiting cases of the strategic investment trigger developed in this chapter. When there is no threat of preemption, the strategic investment trigger coincides with the usual optimal option exercise trigger. The Marshallian trigger, at the other extreme, is obtained in a situation of extreme competitive preemption fear. The strategic investment option approach therefore unifies the standard option valuation approach with the net present value approach in a competitive environment.

The sequential structure of our model also allows us to analyze the sleeping patent phenomenon. It is found that low patenting costs in the first stage (as a proportion of the second-stage costs), high volatility, a high profit growth rate, low discount rates, and a low profit expectation lead to preemption where the invention is not immediately put to commercial use. When the fear of preemption is removed, there is no rationale for sleeping patents. Sleeping patents are not optimal either when profits are deterministic with a negative growth rate. On the other hand, when profit volatility is very large, patents can sleep forever. The strategic option trigger has some unusual features in the sleeping patent case, the most notable being that the trigger is a decreasing function of volatility.

We also suggest two regulatory policies to prevent sleeping patents. The nonrefundable patent fee policy results in the regulator extracting a surplus from the firm, while the refundable patent fee policy does not imply a direct wealth transfer but ensures a much faster availability of the innovation to society. We find that for both policies the optimal patent fee increases as competition intensifies. Interesting issues for further research are the introduction of ex ante asymmetry between the two firms (e.g., a powerful incumbent versus a possible entrant) and the possibility that a firm may leave the market after entry.

Appendix A

This appendix provides the proofs for propositions 1-8.

Proof of Proposition 1.   See Dixit and Pindyck (1994, pp. 323–326).

Proof of Proposition 2.   Proof is obtained by substituting Eq. (15.5) for $\overline{x}_{pm}$, and $[\beta K(r - \mu)]/[(\beta - 1)\pi]$ for $\overline{x}_c$.

Proof of Proposition 3.   The following important equalities will be used throughout the calculations:

$$1 - F_j(x|\hat{x}_t) = \frac{1 - F_j(x)}{1 - F_j(\hat{x}_t)} \qquad (15.A1)$$

$$f_j(x|\hat{x}_t) = \frac{\partial F_j(x|\hat{x}_t)}{\partial x} = \frac{f_j(x)}{1 - F_j(\hat{x}_t)} \qquad (15.A2)$$

$$\frac{\partial f_j(x|\hat{x}_t)}{\partial \hat{x}_t} = \frac{f_j(x)}{[1 - F_j(\hat{x}_t)]^2} \frac{\partial F_j(\hat{x}_t)}{\partial \hat{x}_t} = f_j(x|\hat{x}_t)f_j(\hat{x}_t|\hat{x}_t) \qquad (15.A3)$$

where $F_j(x|\hat{x}_t)$ and $F_j(x)$ are, respectively, the conditional and unconditional trigger distributions.

A. Derivation of $W_i(x_t, \hat{x}_t)$

It can be shown that W_i satisfies the following second-order partial differential equation (PDE):

$$r W_i(x_t, \hat{x}_t) = \mu x_t \frac{\partial W_i(x_t, \hat{x}_t)}{\partial x_t} + \frac{\sigma^2}{2} x_t^2 \frac{\partial^2 W_i(x_t, \hat{x}_t)}{\partial x_t^2}$$

$$\text{for } x_t \le \hat{x}_t < \overline{x}_{ips} \qquad (15.\text{A}4)$$

After applying the no-bubble condition as $x_t \to 0$, one obtains as solution for the value of the claim:

$$W_i(x_t, \hat{x}_t) = A(\hat{x}_t) x_t^\beta \qquad (15.\text{A}5)$$

The functional form for $A(\hat{x}_t)$ can be found by imposing the following boundary conditions:

$$W_i(\overline{x}_{ips}, \overline{x}_{ips}) = A(\overline{x}_{ips}) \overline{x}_{ips}{}^\beta = \left[V_i(\overline{x}_{ips}|\overline{x}_c) - C \right] \qquad (15.\text{A}6)$$

$$\frac{\partial W_i(x_t, \hat{x}_t)}{\partial \hat{x}_t} = f_j(\hat{x}_t|\hat{x}_t) \left[W_i(x_t, \hat{x}_t) - 0 \right] \qquad (15.\text{A}7)$$

The first condition gives the value of the claim when x_t hits the exercise point, $\overline{x}_{ips}$. The second boundary condition defines the behavior of W_i when x_t hits a new peak. It states that when $\hat{x}_t$ increases, there is a possibility [with probability $f_j(\hat{x}_t|\hat{x}_t)$] that the other firm will act, in which case the value of the claim jumps from $W_i(x_t, \hat{x}_t)$ to the payoff the firm gets in case it is preempted. The fact that the rival does not act when $\hat{x}_t$ increases is therefore good news and makes W_i increase with the amount expressed by the second boundary condition. We can rewrite the second boundary condition as follows:

$$\frac{\partial W_i(x_t, \hat{x}_t)}{\partial \hat{x}_t} = \frac{\partial A(\hat{x}_t)}{\partial \hat{x}_t} x_t^\beta \qquad (15.\text{A}8)$$

$$= f_j(\hat{x}_t|\hat{x}_t) \left[A(\hat{x}_t) x_t^\beta - 0 \right] \qquad (15.\text{A}9)$$

giving the following differential equation:

$$\frac{\partial A(\hat{x}_t)}{\partial \hat{x}_t} - f_j(\hat{x}_t|\hat{x}_t) A(\hat{x}_t) = 0 \qquad (15.\text{A}10)$$

The general solution for this differential equation is given by

$$A(\hat{x}_t) = \frac{B}{M(\hat{x}_t)} \qquad (15.\text{A}11)$$

where $M(\hat{x}_t) = \exp[- \int f_j(\hat{x}_t|\hat{x}_t) d\hat{x}_t]$, and B is a constant to be determined by means of the value-matching condition. Note that

$$M(\hat{x}_t) = \exp\left[-\int \frac{f_j(\hat{x}_t)}{1 - F_j(\hat{x}_t)} d\hat{x}_t\right] = \exp[\ln|1 - F_j(\hat{x}_t)|]$$

$$= 1 - F_j(\hat{x}_t) \tag{15.A12}$$

Finally, imposing the value-matching condition completes the specification for $A(\hat{x}_t)$.

B. Derivation of $\overline{x}_{ips}$

The first-order condition (15.11) can be obtained by differentiating W_i with respect to $\overline{x}_{ips}$. In what follows we show that the envelope $W_i(\hat{x}_t, \hat{x}_t)$ smooth-pastes at the exercise trigger, $\overline{x}_{ips}$, to the exercise line given by $V_i(x_t|\overline{x}_c) - C$. Smoothpasting of the envelope to the exercise line at $\overline{x}_{ips}$ requires

$$\frac{\partial W_i(\hat{x}_t, \hat{x}_t)}{\partial \hat{x}_t}\bigg|_{\hat{x}_t = \overline{x}_{ips}} = \frac{\partial V_i(\overline{x}_{ips}|\overline{x}_c)}{\partial \overline{x}_{ips}} \tag{15.A13}$$

or equivalently,

$$\frac{\partial W_i(\hat{x}_t, \hat{x}_t)}{\partial \hat{x}_t}\bigg|_{\hat{x}_t = \overline{x}_{ips}} = \left[V_i(\overline{x}_{ips}|\overline{x}_c) - C\right] f_j(\overline{x}_{ips}|\overline{x}_{ips}) \int_{\overline{x}_{ips}}^{\overline{x}_U} f_j(\overline{x}_{jps}|x_{ips}) d\overline{x}_{jps}$$

$$+ \left[V_i(\overline{x}_{ips}|\overline{x}_c) - C\right] (\beta/\overline{x}_{ips})$$

$$= \left[V_i(\overline{x}_{ips}|\overline{x}_c) - C\right]$$

$$\left\{\frac{\beta}{\overline{x}_{ips}} + \frac{f_j(\overline{x}_{ips})}{[1 - F_j(\overline{x}_{ips})]^2} \int_{\overline{x}_{ips}}^{\overline{x}_U} f_j(\overline{x}_{jps}) d\overline{x}_{jps}\right\}$$

$$= \frac{\partial V_i(\overline{x}_{ips}|\overline{x}_c)}{\partial \overline{x}_{ips}} \tag{15.A14}$$

Rearranging the last equality gives the first-order condition (15.11) for $\overline{x}_{ips}$.
QED

Proof of Proposition 4. When $h_j(x) = 0$, we get the nonstrategic case for which the trigger is given in Proposition 1. Let us now consider the case for which $h_j(x) > 0$.

Case A: $\overline{x}_{ps} < \overline{x}_c$. In this case the first-order condition (15.11) becomes

$$\overline{x}_{ps} = \left\{\frac{C[h_j(\overline{x}_{ps}) + \beta]}{A h_j(\overline{x}_{ps})}\right\}^{1/\beta} \tag{15.A15}$$

Taking the first derivative with respect to h_j, it is straightforward to show that $\overline{x}_{ps}$ is decreasing in h_j. Furthermore, as $x \to x_U$, it must be the case that $h_j(x) \to \infty$. Taking the limit and substituting for A using Eq. (15.2), we get

$$\lim_{h_j \to \infty} \overline{x}_{ps} = (C/A)^{1/\beta} = \overline{x}_{pm} \tag{15.A16}$$

where $\overline{x}_{pm}$ is defined in Eq. (15.5).

Case B: $\overline{x}_{ps} \geq \overline{x}_c$. In this case the first-order condition (15.11) becomes

$$\overline{x}_{ps} = \frac{[\beta + h_j(\overline{x}_{ps})](K + C)(r - \mu)}{\pi[\beta + h_j(\overline{x}_{ps}) - 1]} \qquad (15.A17)$$

Taking again the limit as $h_j \to \infty$ gives

$$\lim_{h_j \to \infty} \overline{x}_{ps} = \frac{(C + K)(r - \mu)}{\pi} = \overline{x}_{pm} \qquad (15.A18)$$

where $\overline{x}_{pm}$ is defined in Eq. (15.5). QED

Proof of Proposition 5. We evaluate the first-order condition [given by Eq. (15.11)] for the following two cases:

Case A: $\overline{x}_{ps} < \overline{x}_c$. In this case the first-order condition becomes

$$\left(-A\overline{x}_{ps}{}^{\beta} + C \right) h_j(\overline{x}_{ps}) + \beta C = 0 \qquad (15.A19)$$

or equivalently

$$\overline{x}_{ps} = \left\{ \frac{C\left[\beta + h_j(\overline{x}_{ps})\right](\beta - 1\}}{Kh_j(\overline{x}_{ps})} \right\}^{1/\beta} \overline{x}_c \qquad (15.A20)$$

Hence,

$$\overline{x}_{ps} < \overline{x}_c \iff \frac{[\beta + h_j(\overline{x}_{ps})](\beta - 1)}{h_j(\overline{x}_{ps})} < \frac{K}{C} \qquad (15.A21)$$

Case B: $\overline{x}_{ps} \geq \overline{x}_c$. In this case the first-order condition (15.11) becomes

$$\left(-\frac{\pi \overline{x}_{ps}}{r - \mu} + K + C \right) h_j(\overline{x}_{ps}) + \frac{\pi \overline{x}_{ps}}{r - \mu} - \beta \left(\frac{\pi \overline{x}_{ps}}{r - \mu} - K - C \right) = 0 \quad (15.A22)$$

or

$$\overline{x}_{ps} = \frac{(K + C)\left[h_j(\overline{x}_{ps}) + \beta\right]}{[\pi/(r - \mu)]\left[\beta - 1 + h_j(\overline{x}_{ps})\right]} \qquad (15.A23)$$

Hence,

$$\overline{x}_{ps} \geq \overline{x}_c \iff \frac{[\beta + h_j(\overline{x}_{ps})](\beta - 1)}{h_j(\overline{x}_{ps})} \geq \frac{K}{C} \qquad (15.A24)$$

QED

Proof of Proposition 6. Starting with the boundary condition, as $\hat{x}_t \to \overline{x}_U$ and patenting has not already taken place, firms of each type know that the other firm will almost certainly act in the next few instants. Consequently, the hazard of being preempted explodes. As we know from Proposition 5, this means that the option value of waiting is eliminated and that both firms act at the Marshallian trigger, $\overline{x}_{pm}(\pi)$, given in (15.5). Hence, $\pi_s(\overline{x}_U) = \pi_s[\overline{x}_{pm}(\pi_L)] = \pi_L$.

Substituting $h_j(x) = h_i(x) \equiv h(x) = [-xG'(\pi)\pi'_s(x)]/G(\pi)$ into the first-order condition (15.11), leads to the differential equation (15.18). Finally, applying L'Hopital's rule one can show that

$$\lim_{x \to \bar{x}_U} \pi_s'(x) = \begin{cases} -2\pi_L^2 \left(\dfrac{\phi K^{1-\beta}}{C} \right)^{1/\beta} & \text{for } \beta - 1 < K/C \text{ (i.e., } \bar{x}_U < \bar{x}_c) \\ & \qquad\qquad\qquad\qquad\qquad\qquad (15.A25) \\ \dfrac{-2\pi_L^2}{(C+K)(r-\mu)} & \text{for } \beta - 1 \geq K/C \text{ (i.e., } \bar{x}_U \geq \bar{x}_c) \end{cases}$$

Solving the differential equation subject to the boundary condition determines the solution, $\pi_s(x)$. QED

Proof of Proposition 7. Substituting the isoelastic distribution in the differential Eq. (15.18) gives

$$\pi_s'(x) = \begin{cases} \dfrac{-\pi_s(x)}{\alpha x} \left\{ \dfrac{\beta C}{\phi K^{1-\beta}[\pi_s(x)x]^\beta - C} \right\} & \text{for } x_t < \bar{x}_c \\ \dfrac{-\pi_s(x)}{\alpha x} \left\{ \dfrac{\pi_s(x)x - \beta[\pi_s(x)x - (r-\mu)(C+K)]}{\pi_s(x)x - (r-\mu)(C+K)} \right\} & \text{for } x_t \geq \bar{x}_c \end{cases} \qquad (15.A26)$$

Case A: $x < \bar{x}_c$. Introducing the change of variable $v(x) \equiv \pi_s(x)x$, gives

$$v'(x) = \frac{v(x)}{\alpha x} \left[\frac{\alpha \phi K^{(1-\beta)} v(x)^\beta - C(\alpha + \beta)}{\phi K^{(1-\beta)} v(x)^\beta - C} \right] \qquad (15.A27)$$

Inverting $v(x)$ and integrating both sides gives

$$\ln(x) = \ln(v) - \frac{\ln(v^\beta)}{\alpha + \beta} + \frac{\ln[-\alpha \phi K^{(1-\beta)} v^\beta + C(\alpha + \beta)]}{\alpha + \beta} + ct \quad (15.A28)$$

were ct is a constant. Redefining the constant and rearranging gives

$$\frac{x^{(\alpha+\beta)} v^{-\alpha}}{-\alpha \phi K^{(1-\beta)} v^\beta + C(\alpha + \beta)} = ct' \qquad (15.A29)$$

From Proposition 4 we know that

$$0 < \left(\frac{\beta K}{\beta - 1} \right) \left[\frac{C(\beta - 1)}{K} \right]^{1/\beta} < v(x) < \frac{\beta K}{\beta - 1} \qquad (15.A30)$$

Since the solution (15.A29) must be valid for all values of $\pi \subset [0, \pi_U]$, it must be the case that

$$v(x) \equiv \pi_s(x)x = \left[\frac{C(\alpha + \beta)}{\alpha \phi K^{(1-\beta)}} \right]^{1/\beta} \qquad (15.A31)$$

Case B: $x \geq \bar{x}_c$. Introducing the change of variable $v(x) \equiv \pi_s(x)x$, gives

$$v'(x) = \frac{v(x)}{\alpha x} \left\{ \frac{[v(x) - (C+K)(r-\mu)](\alpha + \beta) - v(x)}{v(x) - (C+K)(r-\mu)} \right\} \qquad (15.A32)$$

Inverting, integrating both sides and rearranging gives

$$\frac{1}{x} \left\{ \frac{v[(\alpha + \beta - 1)v - (C+K)(r-\mu)(\alpha + \beta)]}{\alpha + \beta - 1} \right\}^{\alpha/\alpha+\beta} = ct \quad (15.A33)$$

From Proposition 4 we know that $v(x)$ is bounded by

$$(C+K)(r-\mu) < v(x) < \frac{\beta(C+K)(r-\mu)}{\beta - 1} \qquad (15.A34)$$

Since the solution must be valid for all $\pi \in [0, \pi_U]$ it must be the case that

$$v(x) \equiv \pi_s(x)x = \frac{(C+K)(r-\mu)(\alpha + \beta)}{\alpha + \beta - 1} \qquad (15.A35)$$

QED

> **Proof of Proposition 8.** C^* can be obtained by solving $\bar{x}_{ps} = \bar{x}_c$ for C. Substituting C^* into $\bar{x}_c$ or $\bar{x}_{ps}$ gives $\bar{x}^*$.
> C^{**} can be obtained by solving $\bar{x}_{ps} = \bar{x}_c(C)$ for C. Substituting C^{**} into $\bar{x}_c(C)$ or into $\bar{x}_{ps}$ gives $\bar{x}^{**}$. QED

15.6 ACKNOWLEDGMENTS

I would like to thank the editors, Michael Brennan and Lenos Trigeorgis, and an anonymous referee for helpful comments. This chapter was originally a chapter from my Ph.D. dissertation at Cambridge. I would like to express special thanks to my supervisor, William Perraudin, and my examiners, Marcus Miller and Stephen Satchell. I also thank Richard Barker, Vicky Saporta, and Mike Scherer for helpful comments or discussions. Any errors remain my responsibility.

REFERENCES

Anderson, R., and C. Harris. (1986). A Model of Innovation with Application to New Financial Products. *Oxford Economic Papers* 38 (supplement), 203–218.

Baldursson, F. M. (1996). Irreversible Investment under Uncertainty in Oligopoly. Working Paper, National Economic Institute of Iceland, Reykjavik.

Beath, J., Y. Katsoulacos, and D. Ulph. (1989). Strategic R&D Policy. *The Economic Journal* 99, 74–83.

Brennan, M., and E. Schwartz. (1985). Evaluating Natural Resource Investments. *Journal of Business* 58, 135–157.

Dasgupta, P., and J. Stiglitz. (1980). Uncertainty, Industrial Structure and the Speed of R&D. *Bell Journal of Economics* 11, 1-28.

Dixit, A. (1989). Entry and Exit Decisions under Uncertainty. *Journal of Political Economy* 97, 620–638.

Dixit, A., and R. Pindyck. (1994). *Investment Under Uncertainty*. Princeton, NJ: Princeton University Press.

Fudenberg, D., R. Gilbert, J. Stiglitz, and J. Tirole. (1983). Preemption, Leapfrogging and Competition in Patent Races. *European Economic Review* 22, 3–31.

Fudenberg, D., and J. Tirole. (1985). Preemption and Rent Equalization in the Adoption of New Technology. *Review of Economic Studies* 52, 383–401.

Galbraith, J. (1952). *American Capitalism*. Boston: Houghton Mufflin.

Gilbert, R., and D. Newbery. (1982). Preemptive Patenting and the Persistence of Monopoly. *American Economic Review* 72, 514–526.

Grenadier, S. (1996). The Strategic Exercise of Options: Development Cascades and Overbuilding in Real Estate Markets. *Journal of Finance* 51, 1653–1679.

Harris, C., and J. Vickers. (1985). Patent Races and the Persistence of Monopoly. *Journal of Industrial Economics* 33, 461–482.

Harris, C., and J. Vickers. (1987). Racing with Uncertainty. *Review of Economic Studies* 54, 1–21.

Ingersoll, J., and S. Ross. (1992). Waiting to Invest: Investment and Uncertainty. *Journal of Business* 65, 1–29.

Kamien, M., and N. Schwartz. (1982). *Market Structure and Innovation*. Cambridge: Cambridge University Press.

Kulatilaka, N., and E. C. Perotti. (1998). Strategic Growth Options. *Management Science* 44, 1021–1031.

Lambrecht, B. M. (1998). The Impact of Debt Financing on Entry and Exit in a Duopoly. Cambridge: University of Cambridge mimeo.

Lambrecht, B. M., and W. R. M. Perraudin. (1994). Option Games. DAE Working Paper 9414, University of Cambridge.

Lambrecht, B. M., and W. R. M. Perraudin. (1996). Real Options and Preemption. Cambridge: University of Cambridge mimeo.

Lee, T., and L. Wilde. (1980). Market Structure and Innovation: A Reformulation. *Quarterly Journal of Economics* 94, 429–436.

Leininger, W. (1991). Patent Competition, Rent Dissipation, and the Persistence of Monopoly: The Role of Research Budgets. *Journal of Economic Theory* 53, 146–172.

Loury, G. (1979). Market Structure and Innovation. *Quarterly Journal of Economics* 93, 395–410.

Majd, S., and R. S. Pindyck. (1987). Time to Build, Option Value, and Investment Decisions. *Journal of Financial Economics* 18, 7–27.

McDonald, R., and D. Siegel. (1986). The Value of Waiting to Invest. *Quarterly Journal of Economics* 101, 707–728.

Miller, M., and L. Zhang. (1996). Oil Price Hikes and Development Triggers in Peace and War. *The Economic Journal* 106, 445–457.

Newbery, D. (1978). Sleeping Patents and Entry-Deterring Inventions. Cambridge: University of Cambridge mimeo.

Pakes, A. (1986). Patents as Options: Some Estimates of the Value of Holding European Patent Stocks. *Econometrica* 54, 755–784.

Reinganum, J. (1981). Dynamic Games of Innovation. *Journal of Economic Theory* 25, 21–41.

Reinganum, J. (1983). Uncertain Innovation and the Persistence of Monopoly. *American Economic Review* 73, 741–748.

Scherer, F. M. (1997). The Distribution of Profits from Invention. Cambridge, MA: Harvard University mimeo.

Schumpeter, J. (1975). *Capitalism, Socialism and Democracy*. New York: Harper & Row.

Smets, F. (1991). Exporting versus FDI: The Effect of Uncertainty, Irreversibilities and Strategic Interactions. Working Paper, Yale University, New Haven.

Smit, H., and L. Ankum. (1993). A Real Options and Game-Theoretic Approach to Corporate Investment Strategy under Competition. *Financial Management* 22, 241–250.

Smit, H., and L. Trigeorgis. (1997). Flexibility and Competitive R&D Strategies. Working Paper, University of Chicago, Chicago.

Spencer, B. J., and J. A. Brander. (1992). Pre-commitment and Flexibility: Applications to Oligopoly Theory. *European Economic Review* 36, 1601–1626.

Trigeorgis, L. (1996). *Real Options*. Cambridge, MA: MIT Press.

Vaughan, F. L. (1956). *The United States Patent System: Legal and Economic Conflicts in American Patent History*. Westport, CT: Greenwood Press.

16

Competitive Investment Decisions

A Synthesis

DOMINGO CASTELO JOAQUIN
KIRT C. BUTLER

This chapter provides a synthesis of work on competitive strategy. We combine elements of McDonald and Siegel's (1986) model of the investment timing decision of a monopolist with the strategic model of Dixit and Pindyck (1994) to develop a strategic investment model in which a firm has a competitive advantage over another. Competitive advantage is modeled here through asymmetric payoffs arising from differential costs. Allowing for asymmetric costs makes identification of the competitive equilibrium simpler and more intuitive, with the lower-cost firm entering first. Our model is a continuous-time version of the second stage of the discrete-time strategic model of Smit and Trigeorgis (1997), which also allows for unequal costs and managerial flexibility in output decisions.

16.1 INTRODUCTION

When faced with a now or never investment opportunity, the net present value (NPV) rule prescribes acceptance if the investment's NPV is positive. When there is an option to defer investment, one is effectively faced with a continuum of mutually exclusive projects indexed by their starting dates. In this case, the NPV rule recommends acceptance of the NPV-maximizing alternative. However, the optimal alternative need not be immediate investment. The pioneering works on real options by McDonald and Siegel (1985, 1986), Brennan and Schwartz (1985), Majd and Pindyck (1987), Pindyck (1988), and Dixit (1989) show that waiting can be optimal under uncertainty.[1]

When there is a threat of competition, each competitor's payoff depends on the actions of other competitors. This interaction can change the optimal timing

---

[1] The real options approach addresses precisely the problem of identifying the NPV-maximizing alternative in an investment opportunity set of mutually exclusive projects indexed by rules for exercising embedded options. One such option is the option to wait.

rules. Trigeorgis (1991) demonstrates in a continuous-time framework that a firm anticipating future competition at an exogenously determined time will invest earlier than if it does not face such competition. Dixit and Pindyck (1994, pp. 309–316) allow both competitors to strategically time their investments and come to qualitatively the same conclusion: optimal entry by the first investor occurs earlier than when there is no threat of competition. Dixit and Pindyck also demonstrate that because each firm's payoff is lower in a duopoly than under monopoly, the second investor will invest later than in the absence of competition.[2]

In this chapter, we synthesize work on competitive strategy. We build on McDonald and Siegel's (1986) model of the investment timing decision of a monopolist, as reformulated by Pindyck (1988), and on the strategic model of Dixit and Pindyck (1994) to develop a strategic investment model in which one firm has a competitive advantage over another. Competitive advantage is modeled here through asymmetric payoffs arising from differential costs. In most models of competitive strategy in a real options framework, costs are assumed to be zero or symmetric. For example, unit cost is assumed to be zero in the strategic timing models of Dixit and Pindyck (1994, pp. 309–316) and in Grenadier (1996). With symmetric firms, equilibrium is indeterminate and some random mechanism must be employed to select which of two identical firms will invest first. The introduction of asymmetric costs makes identification of the strategic equilibrium simpler and more intuitive: the lower cost firm enters first.

Asymmetric costs can arise from imperfections in the product and factor markets. Companies with privileged access to location-specific assets such as natural or manmade resources are especially well positioned to enjoy lower cost factor inputs. For example, De Beers of South Africa has dominated the global diamond industry in large part through its access to diamond mines on the African continent. Companies like Enron and Exxon are similarly driven to seek lower cost and preferably exclusive access to sources of natural gas and petroleum. Lower cost factor inputs can lead to higher revenues. For example, Wal-Mart grew into the world's largest retailer by becoming a cost leader in inventory control and product distribution. 3M Corporation grew from a sandpaper company into a world leader in applying coatings to a wide variety of backings, including photographic film, electronic storage media, and the ubiquitous 3M stick-em pads. Similarly, Honda used its core competence in small-motor technology to leverage itself into a globally competitive automotive giant.

We model asymmetric payoffs in the form of asymmetric costs in a one-good duopoly. We could just as well model asymmetric payoffs in firms facing symmetric costs but differentiated products that serve as imperfect substitutes. In this case, lower product demand imposes an indirect cost on the disadvantaged firm that must be overcome for the firm to generate the same revenues as the firm with higher demand. That is, the firm facing lower demand for its product would need to incur additional

---

[2] A strategic equilibrium changes entry in other ways as well. For example, Grenadier (1996) extends Majd and Pindyck's (1987) noncompetitive model of time-to-build to a symmetric duopoly context and demonstrates how initial conditions determine whether optimal investment occurs simultaneously or sequentially.

cost (e.g., in production, advertising, or distribution) to improve its product and generate the same revenues as its competitor. This indirect cost to the disadvantaged firm reduces profits in much the same way that a direct production cost reduces profits. The net result is the same in our strategic equilibrium whether competitive advantage is modeled in the revenue or in the cost structure: the firm with higher profits enters first.

To realistically model the strategic equilibrium, we allow firms to adjust their output levels in response to market entry by a competing firm. The strategic investment timing model of Dixit and Pindyck (1994, pp. 309–316) assumes a fixed level of output. This assumption is relatively harmless in modeling a monopolist because the output level can be chosen to be equal to the optimal monopoly output level. But fixing the output at just one level does not allow a duopolist to optimally respond to potential entry by a competitor through a combination of output and timing decisions.[3] The impact of varying output on project value and the timing decision can be significant because an otherwise irreversible investment will optimally be made earlier if the firm has the flexibility to adjust its output level. Introducing variable outputs in a strategic model thus allows us to more realistically characterize the resulting equilibrium.

Our model is a continuous-time version of the second stage of the discrete-time strategic model of Trigeorgis (1996) and Smit and Trigeorgis (1997). The second stage of their model allows for unequal costs as well as managerial flexibility in output decisions.[4] As is often the case, the continuous-time version has the advantage of making some important features of the model more analytically tractable than its discrete-time analog. In particular, a continuous-time model allows a more precise specification of the threshold prices at which each investor optimally enters. The continuous-time version also can most easily incorporate other results from the real options literature.

Our model begins with two domestic firms facing an investment opportunity in a foreign market. Each firm's investment yields a profit stream that depends on that firm's cost structure and output decisions and on whether the other firm has entered the market. Uncertainty is modeled in the exchange rate at which foreign currency cash flows are remitted to the parent firm. In this case, the value of the foreign investment depends on product demand, unit cost, the exchange rate, the timing of investment, and the actions of the competing firm in the foreign market.

The chapter proceeds as follows. Section 16.2 describes the investment opportunity that is exclusively available to two firms. Section 16.3 describes the value functions and identifies the threshold prices at which each firm optimally enters in the strategic equilibrium. This section also analyzes two important limiting cases

---

[3] For example, fixing the output level does not capture the fact that even for symmetric firms facing a linear demand, Cournot equilibrium outputs in a duopoly do not add up to twice the optimal monopoly output level.

[4] The first period of their model explicitly links production costs to R&D investment, whereas our model takes the cost differential as given. See Smit and Ankum (1993) for an early version of this model.

obtained by varying the cost of the higher cost firm.[5] Section 16.4 concludes the chapter.

16.2 THE INVESTMENT OPPORTUNITY

Consider two all-equity U.S.-based firms having the option to invest in a production project in a foreign country. The project requires an initial investment I denominated in U.S. dollars.[6] The output can be sold at time t at a unit price of P_t in the foreign currency, where P_t is obtained from the following inverse linear demand function:

$$P_t(Q_T) = a - bQ_T \tag{16.1a}$$

where Q_T is total industry output and a, b are positive constants. The instantaneous cost function (in the foreign currency) for firm j is given by

$$C_j(Q_j) = c_j Q_j \tag{16.1b}$$

where Q_j is the instantaneous output flow of firm j and c_j is a positive constant.[7]

We assume that one firm can have higher cost than the other. This cost differential reflects the competitive advantage of the lower cost firm in the factor and product markets. We indicate the lower cost firm by the subscript l and the higher cost firm with subscript h. Thus, $c_l < c_h$.[8]

In units of foreign currency, firm j's instantaneous profit at time t is given by

$$\pi_j(Q_j) = Q_j[(a - bQ_T) - c_j] \tag{16.1c}$$

Before the entry of another investor, the sole producer, say firm i, enjoys a temporary monopoly (m) with the following profit function in units of foreign currency:[9]

$$\pi_{im}(Q_{im}) = Q_{im}[(a - bQ_{im}) - c_i] \tag{16.2a}$$

---

[5] The first case is one in which the unit costs are equal, as in Dixit and Pindyck (1994, pp. 309–316). In the second case, the unit cost of the higher cost firm is so high that it is optimal for it to forego the investment opportunity altogether. In this case, the lower cost firm is effectively a monopolist and the problem reduces to that analyzed by McDonald and Siegel (1986).

[6] Henceforth, the U.S. dollar will be referred to simply as the dollar.

[7] The above demand and cost functions (with the quadratic cost term = 0) are the same as in Trigeorgis (1996) and Smit and Trigeorgis (1997). In the next section, uncertainty is introduced through the exchange rate at which the foreign currency cash flows are remitted to the parent firm.

[8] Differential costs could be determined endogenously through firms' decisions to invest in research and development. R&D can lead to competitive advantages in areas such as technology and technological processes, supply chain management, information systems, human resources, and organizational capital. This is the approach taken in the two-stage strategic model of Trigeorgis (1996) and Smit and Trigeorgis (1997). In their model, R&D investment in an initial stage influences the firm's competitive position in the second stage.

[9] The subscript m indicates a monopolist and the subscript d indicates a duopolist.

In this case, monopolist firm i maximizes instantaneous profit π_{im} by setting its output level to

$$
Q_{im} = \begin{cases} \dfrac{a - c_i}{2b} & \text{if} \quad c_i < a \\ 0 & \text{if} \quad c_i \geq a \end{cases} \tag{16.2b}
$$

Assuming $c_i < a$, firm i's maximum monopoly profit in units of foreign currency is therefore given by

$$
\pi_{im} = \frac{(a - c_i)^2}{4b} \tag{16.2c}
$$

When the competitor enters in a duopoly setting (d), the lower cost firm and the higher cost firm, respectively, have the following interdependent profit functions in units of foreign currency:

$$
\pi_{1d}(Q_1; Q_h) = Q_1\{[a - b(Q_1 + Q_h)] - c_1\} \tag{16.3a}
$$

$$
\pi_{hd}(Q_h; Q_1) = Q_h\{[a - b(Q_1 + Q_h)] - c_h\} \tag{16.3b}
$$

At (Cournot–Nash) equilibrium, we require each firm's output to be optimal given the other firm's output. The equilibrium output vector is obtained (simultaneously) by differentiating π_{jd} with respect to Q_j and equating to zero, yielding an equilibrium output level for firm j

$$
Q_{jd} = \begin{cases} \dfrac{(a - 2c_j + c_i)}{3b} & \text{if} \quad a - 2c_j + c_i > 0 \\ 0 & \text{if} \quad a - 2c_j + c_i \leq 0 \end{cases} \tag{16.3c}
$$

where $i, j = 1, h$ and $i \neq j$. Firm j's duopoly profit in units of foreign currency is given by

$$
\pi_{jd} = \frac{(a - 2c_j + c_i)^2}{9b} \tag{16.3d}
$$

The above output and profit expressions are the same as those in Trigeorgis (1996, Table 9.1, p. 293) and Smit and Trigeorgis (1997) (with $b = 1$).

The evolution of the entry game is divided into two stages. In the first stage, the first investor enters and enjoys a temporary monopoly in the market. In the second stage, the entrant's high profitability induces the entry of the second investor. The market is then shared by the two investors in perpetuity. As is typical in dynamic games, the problem is then solved by backward induction.

16.3 STRATEGIC TIMING DECISIONS

In this section we analyze, in turn, first the decision of the second investor to be a late entrant (given an earlier entry by the first investor), then the decision to be the first investor (given the possibility of later competitive entry), and finally the resulting equilibrium.

16.3.1 The Decision to Be the Later Entrant

We start the analysis by assuming that one firm, say firm i, has already invested in the project and the other, say firm j, is considering late entry with its production level set at the optimum duopoly output level Q_{jd} given in Eq. (16.3c).[10] The equilibrium profit is deterministic in units of foreign currency. However, the equilibrium profit in domestic currency (dollars) is risky since the exchange rate fluctuates randomly. In particular, we assume that the time-t dollar price X_t of one unit of foreign currency follows geometric Brownian motion of the form

$$\frac{dX_t}{X_t} = \theta \, dt + \sigma \, dz_t \qquad (16.4)$$

where θ is a constant (exchange-rate) drift parameter, σ is a constant proportional variance parameter, and z_t is a standard Wiener process. We assume that investing one unit of foreign currency in the foreign risk-free asset yields an instantaneous dollar income of δX_t, where δ is a positive constant.

The project can be seen as a derivative asset whose dollar value V_{jd} depends on the foreign-currency profit stream and on the current exchange rate X. By Ito's Lemma, the change in the value of the project satisfies

$$dV = \left(\theta X V_X + \frac{1}{2}\sigma^2 X^2 V_{XX} + V_t \right) dt + \sigma X V \, dz \qquad (16.5a)$$

where $V = V_{jd}$, $V_X = \partial V / \partial X$, $V_{XX} = \partial^2 V / \partial X^2$, and $V_t = \partial V / \partial t$. Thus, the following differential equation must be satisfied by the function V_{jd} in equilibrium:[11]

$$\frac{1}{2}\sigma^2 X^2 V_{XX} + V_t + (r - \delta) X V_X - rV + X\frac{(a - 2c_j + c_i)^2}{9b} = 0 \quad (16.5b)$$

Again, X denotes the current exchange rate, and r is the (assumed) constant domestic instantaneous risk-free rate. The last term on the left-hand side of Eq. (16.5b) is firm j's instantaneous duopoly profit in dollars [from Eq. (16.3d)]. Since the equilibrium duopoly output is settled in perpetuity, the value function depends on the current exchange rate but not directly on the current date. Hence, $V_t = 0$ and the solution to Eq. (16.5b) becomes

$$V_{jd}(X) = A_{jd}X^{\beta_1} + B_{jd}X^{\beta_2} + \frac{(a - 2c_j + c_i)^2}{9b}\frac{X}{\delta} \qquad (16.5c)$$

where A_{jd} and B_{jd} are constants to be determined from the relevant boundary conditions and β_1 and β_2 are, respectively, the positive and negative roots of the quadratic expression associated with the general solution to Eq. (16.5b) (e.g., see McDonald and Siegel, 1986, or Dixit and Pindyck, 1994, pp. 141–143):

---

[10] We assume that $a - 2c_h + c_l > 0$ so that equilibrium duopoly outputs are positive for both firms.
[11] This result follows from the standard replication argument of Black and Scholes (1973). It can also be derived using the consumption-CAPM as in Sick (1995) or by employing the risk-neutral valuation technique of Cox and Ross (1976).

$$\beta_1 = \frac{1}{2} - \frac{r-\delta}{\sigma^2} + \sqrt{\left(\frac{r-\delta}{\sigma^2} - \frac{1}{2}\right)^2 + \frac{2r}{\sigma^2}} \quad (>1)$$

$$\beta_2 = \frac{1}{2} - \frac{r-\delta}{\sigma^2} - \sqrt{\left(\frac{r-\delta}{\sigma^2} - \frac{1}{2}\right)^2 + \frac{2r}{\sigma^2}} \quad (<0) \qquad (16.5d)$$

Supposing that barriers to further entry exist so as to eliminate any threat of competition from other firms, both firms will choose to maintain the same level of output in perpetuity. The current dollar value of the project to firm j when both firms maintain the same level of output in perpetuity is given by the last term of Eq. (16.5c), which fully captures the value of the project to firm j once the other firm has already invested. That is, $A_{jd} = B_{jd} = 0$ for the second investor, whose value function reduces to

$$V_{jd}(X) = \frac{(a - 2c_j + c_i)^2}{9b} \frac{X}{\delta} = \frac{\pi_{jd}}{\delta} X \qquad (16.5e)$$

Thus, the dollar value of firm j as a duopolist is equal to the capitalized value of its perpetual, instantaneous foreign-currency duopoly profit flow times the current exchange rate.[12]

Suppose firm j has not yet invested in the project, but considers doing so at an optimal time by investing I. If the current exchange rate is X, then the net value of undertaking the project immediately is given by its net present value

$$NPV_{jd}(X) = V_{jd}(X) - I \qquad (16.5f)$$

The net present value of a commitment today to invest in the project at a future time when the exchange rate reaches $X_e \geq X$ is given by

$$NPV_{jd}(X_e; X) = E_x\left[\{V_{jd}(X_e) - I\} e^{-rT}\right] \qquad (16.5g)$$

where the random variable T indicates the first time the exchange rate hits X_e given that the initial exchange rate is X, and E_x is the risk-neutral expectation operator conditional on the current exchange rate being X. T is defined by

$$T \equiv T(X_e; X) = \inf\ (t \geq 0 : X_t \geq X_e, X_0 = X) \qquad (16.5h)$$

From Krylov (1980, Chapter 1) or Dixit and Pindyck (1994, pp. 315–316), we obtain

$$E_x\left[e^{-rT}\right] = \left(\frac{X}{X_e}\right)^{\beta_1} \qquad (16.5i)$$

with $\beta_1 > 1$ as given in Eq. (16.5d) above. Thus, the value of firm j's commitment today to implement the project when the exchange rate reaches X_e is given by

---

[12] Firm j's equilibrium duopoly profit π_{jd} is deterministic in the foreign currency, and is capitalized at the foreign risk-free rate δ.

$$NPV_{jd}(X_e; \; X) = \left[\frac{(a - 2c_j + c_i)^2}{9b} \frac{X_e}{\delta} - I \right] \left(\frac{X}{X_e} \right)^{\beta_1} \quad (16.5j)$$

Even though the NPV may currently be positive, the firm may be better off postponing undertaking the project. Postponement delays the investment expenditure. However, it also delays the flow of profits. The higher the exchange rate, the greater the opportunity cost (in dollars) of project delay. The firm is better off postponing project implementation until the exchange rate reaches $X_e(> X)$ if $NPV_{jd}(X_e; \; X) > NPV_{jd}(X) \equiv NPV_{jd}(X; \; X)$. Maximizing $NPV_{jd}(X_e; \; X)$ subject to $X_e \geq X$ yields the following optimal entry exchange rate X_{jd}^* for firm j as a second entrant:

$$X_{jd}^* = \frac{\beta_1}{(\beta_1 - 1)} \frac{9b\delta I}{(a - 2c_j + c_i)^2} \quad (16.5k)$$

provided $X_{jd}^* > X$. The following result follows from differentiating Eq. (16.5k), assuming an interior solution (and noting the fact that $\beta_1 > 1$).

Result 1. *The optimal entry exchange rate X_{jd}^* for firm j as a second investor is increasing in the required investment I, increasing in firm j's unit cost c_j, and decreasing in the first entrant's unit cost c_i.*

This result makes intuitive sense because the higher the required investment, the more cautious the investor is in initiating the investment. Also, the higher the unit operating cost (c_j), the less profitable the project becomes and so a higher cost firm would prefer to wait for the exchange rate to rise more before the project becomes attractive. Finally, the attractiveness of challenging an incumbent decreases with the incumbent's market power, which is greater the lower the incumbent's cost.

16.3.2 The Decision to Be the First Investor

Before entry of the competitor, the first investor enjoys a temporary monopoly in the market. The competitor will enter when the exchange rate hits X_{jd}^*, at which time the first investor becomes a duopolist. Thus, firm i's value as a first investor V_{if} is the sum of the value of its temporary monopoly position before time T and the value of its future duopoly position.[13] By a similar argument as in the previous section, the value function for firm i as a first investor V_{if} during the monopoly stage satisfies the following equation:

$$\frac{1}{2}\sigma^2 X^2 V_{XX} + V_t + (r - \delta)X V_X - rV + X\frac{(a - c_i)^2}{4b} = 0 \quad (16.6a)$$

where $V = V_{if}$, $V_X = \partial V/\partial X$, $V_{XX} = \partial^2 V/\partial X^2$, $V_t = \partial V/\partial t$. The last term on the left-hand side of Eq. (16.6a) is the dollar value of the instantaneous profit flow

---

[13] We use the subscript f in V_{if} to indicate a first investor.

for firm i as a monopolist [π_{im} from Eq. (16.2c)]. Since the value function depends on the current exchange rate but not on the current date, $V_t = 0$, resulting in the solution

$$V_{if}(X) = A_{if}X^{\beta_1} + B_{if}X^{\beta_2} + \frac{(a - c_i)^2}{4b}\frac{X}{\delta} \qquad (16.6b)$$

The last term of Eq. (16.6b) represents the current dollar value of the monopoly position when firm i has no option to exit and firm j has no option to enter (i.e., when the monopoly position is permanent). The first two terms represent the value lost from potential competition, with A_{if} and B_{if} determined from the relevant boundary conditions.

As the exchange rate declines, the dollar cash flows decrease and it becomes less likely that the competition will enter. As X approaches 0, we expect the impact of potential competition to vanish—the competitor will not enter at all. Hence, $B_{if} = 0$ (since $\beta_2 < 0$) and the value function reduces to

$$V_{if}(X) = A_{if}X^{\beta_1} + \frac{(a - c_i)^2}{4b}\frac{X}{\delta} \qquad (16.6c)$$

As the exchange rate increases and the project becomes more profitable in the domestic currency, it is more likely that the competitor will enter. In particular, when X rises to X_{jd}^* as given in Eq. (16.5k), it becomes optimal for firm j to enter as a second investor. At this time (T), the monopoly position ceases to exist and the first entrant becomes a duopolist. This yields the following value-matching condition:

$$V_{if}(X_{jd}^*) = V_{id}(X_{jd}^*) \qquad (16.6d)$$

where [see Eq. (16.5e)]

$$V_{id}(X_{jd}^*) = \frac{(a - 2c_i + c_j)^2}{9b}\frac{X_{jd}^*}{\delta} \qquad (16.5\,e')$$

Substituting Eqs. (16.6c) and (16.5e') into Eq (16.6d), it follows that

$$A_{if} = -\frac{1}{36}X_{jd}^*(a - 2c_j + c_i)\left[\frac{5a + 2c_j - 7c_i}{b\delta(X_{jd}^*)^{\beta_1}}\right] \qquad (16.6e)$$

Following the same argument used in deriving Eq. (16.5j), the value of firm i's commitment today to implement the project as the first investor (during the monopoly stage) when the exchange rate reaches $X_e \geq X$ is given by

$$NPV_{if}(X_e;\ X) = \left[A_{if}X_e^{\beta_1} + \frac{(a - c_i)^2}{4b}\frac{X_e}{\delta} - I\right]\left(\frac{X}{X_e}\right)^{\beta_1} \qquad (16.6f)$$

with A_{if} given in Eq. (16.6e). The usual optimization procedure yields the following optimal entry exchange rate X_{if}^* for firm i as a first entrant:

$$X_{if}^* = \frac{\beta_1}{\beta_1 - 1}\frac{4b\delta I}{(a - c_i)^2} \qquad (16.6g)$$

provided $X_{if}^* > X$. Differentiation yields the following result, assuming an interior solution.

Result 2. *If firm i is assured that it will not be preempted by its competitor, then its optimal entry exchange rate X_{if}^* as a first investor (during the monopoly period) is increasing in the required investment I and increasing in its unit cost c_i.*

Intuitively, if a firm is assured that it will not be preempted by its competitor, it would enter as a first investor at a higher exchange rate if it has a higher cost than the rate at which it would enter if it had a lower cost, i.e., $X_{hf}^* > X_{lf}^*$. Note that both firms cannot be first entrants at different preferred entry exchange rates. The entry profile (X_{lf}^*, X_{hf}^*) in which the lower cost firm enters at X_{lf}^* and the higher cost firm enters at X_{hf}^* cannot be an equilibrium since the higher cost firm would effectively be a second entrant. As a second entrant, the higher cost firm will maximize its payoff by entering later, at X_{hd}^*, the optimal entry exchange rate for the higher cost firm as a second entrant. We next turn our attention to the characterization of the equilibrium entry profile.

16.3.3 Equilibrium Entry

Two types of equilibria can arise in this duopoly situation: simultaneous entry and sequential entry. With simultaneous entry neither firm acquires a temporary monopoly position. Both essentially enter as second entrants. Because the payoff for a first entrant dominates that of a second entrant, it follows that both would choose to invest simultaneously only if the exchange rate is very favorable. More precisely, simultaneous entry at the current exchange rate X is optimal for both firms if X is greater than the optimal entry exchange rate for both firms as second entrants, i.e., if $X \geq \max(X_{hd}^*, X_{ld}^*)$ given in Eq. (16.5k). If this condition does not hold, then equilibrium will be characterized by sequential entry.

An outcome of the entry game with sequential entry is a triple exchange-rate zone $(X_l^*, X_h^*; X)$ characterized by the exchange rate X_l^* at which the first firm enters, the exchange rate X_h^* at which the second firm enters, and the current exchange rate X.[14] We refer to the firm with the lower entry exchange rate X_l^* as the first investor, and the firm with the higher entry exchange rate X_h^* as the second investor. To be considered as an *equilibrium entry profile*, we require (X_l^*, X_h^*) to possess the following properties:

1. The second investor's entry exchange rate X_h^* should be a best second-investor response to the first investor's entry exchange rate X_l^*.

2. The second investor should not prefer to invest earlier than the first investor. In other words, the first investor's entry exchange rate should be preemption proof.

---

[14] See also the discussion on demand zones in Smit and Trigeorgis (1997).

3. The first investor's entry exchange rate should be the best among all pre-emption-proof entry exchange rates.

4. The first investor should not prefer to invest later than the second investor.

Our main result below is that if the exchange rate is not too high, then the unique subgame perfect equilibrium is for the lower cost firm to enter first and for the higher cost firm to enter later.

Result 3. *Let the current exchange rate X be such that (a) $X \leq X_{lf}^*$; (b) $X \leq \hat{X}$, where $\hat{X} = \inf[X_1 : NPV_{hf}(X_1; X) > NPV_{hd}(X_{hd}^*; X)]$; and (c) $NPV_{lf}(X; X) \geq NPV_{ld}(X_{ld}^*; X)$. Then, in the subgame perfect equilibrium, the lower cost firm enters first at $\min(\hat{X}, X_{lf}^*)$ and the higher cost firm enters later at X_{hd}^*.[15]*

Example. Suppose that the investment project requires an investment of $I = 800$ million and the inverse demand function (in units of foreign currency) is given by

$$P_t(Q_T) = 50 - 5Q_T$$

[i.e., $a = 50$ and $b = 5$ in Eq. (16.1a)]. The marginal cost is $c_l = 20$ units of foreign currency for the lower cost firm and $c_h = 21$ units for the higher cost firm. The current exchange rate X is 1 dollar per unit of foreign currency. The riskless yield from holding a unit of foreign currency is $\delta = 0.04$. The exchange rate volatility is $\sigma = 0.20$ and the domestic risk-free rate is $r = 0.04$.

The payoff functions corresponding to an initial exchange rate of $X = \$1.00$ per unit of foreign currency are illustrated in Figure 16.1. The curves that are studded with open squares and open diamonds correspond to the payoffs of the lower cost firm, while those with the solid squares and solid diamonds correspond to the higher cost firm. The squares indicate a first entrant, while the diamonds indicate (a duopolist or) a second entrant.

From Figure 16.1 we see that if the lower cost firm has already invested, the higher cost firm will maximize its payoff at \$59.28 million (point B) by investing as a second entrant (solid diamonds in Figure 16.1) when the exchange rate hits \$3.67. At this exchange rate, the payoff to the lower cost firm of \$86.06 million as a first investor (open squares) coincides with its payoff as a second investor (open diamonds). For $X_e \geq \$3.67$, the payoff curve for the lower cost firm as a first investor coincides with its payoff curve as a second investor.

The equilibrium entry profile consists of the lower cost firm investing first at an entry exchange rate of \$1.03, and the higher cost firm investing second at an entry exchange rate of \$3.67. In this case, the payoff to the lower cost firm is \$175.69

---

[15] The proof is given in Appendix A.

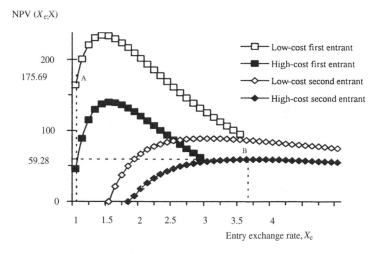

Figure 16.1. Equilibrium with sequential entry. NPV(X_e; X) is the Net Present Value of the commitment today to invest in the project at a future time when the exchange rate reaches $X_e \geq X$. The NPV curves that are studded with open squares and open diamonds correspond to the payoffs of the lower cost firm while those with the solid squares and solid diamonds correspond to the higher cost firm. The squares indicate a first entrant, while the diamonds indicate (a duopolist or) a second entrant. Given a current exchange rate of $X = \$1.00$, the equilibrium entry profile consists of the lower cost firm investing first at an entry exchange rate of $1.03, and the higher cost firm investing second at an entry exchange rate of $3.67. In this case, the payoff to the lower cost firm is $175.69 million (point A), while the payoff to the higher cost firm is $59.28 million (point B).

million (point A in Figure 16.1), while the payoff to the higher cost firm is $59.28 million (point B in Figure 16.1).

We now verify that this entry profile satisfies the four properties of an equilibrium entry profile.

1. As a second investor, the higher cost firm achieves the maximum payoff of $59.28 million by investing when the exchange rate hits $3.67.

2. The higher cost firm will have a payoff lower than $59.28 million if it invests at an exchange rate lower than $1.03 even if it is the first investor. Thus, it does not prefer to invest earlier than the lower cost firm. Hence, the lower cost firm's entry exchange rate of $1.03 is preemption proof.

3. The highest preemption-proof entry exchange rate for the lower cost firm is $1.03. If the lower cost firm invests at an exchange rate $X' > \$1.03$, then the higher cost firm will have an incentive to preempt. Payoff to the higher cost firm will exceed $59.28 million if it invests at any exchange rate greater than $1.03 but less than $3.67. On the other hand, the higher cost firm gains no advantage by entering at any exchange rate less than or equal to $1.03. Thus, the set of preemption-proof entry exchange rates for the lower cost firm consists of all exchange rates less than or equal to $1.03. Among these preemption-proof exchange rates, the highest payoff of $175.69 million is achieved at an entry exchange rate of $1.03.

4. The payoff to the lower cost firm will be less than \$175.69 million if it invests at an exchange rate greater than \$3.67. Thus, it does not prefer to invest later than the second investor. Hence, $(X_l^* = \$1.03, X_h^* = \$3.67; X = \$1.00)$ is an equilibrium profile.

It can be seen that the introduction of asymmetric costs makes identification of the equilibrium simpler and more intuitive in that the lower cost firm enters first. With symmetric firms, one has to rely on some random mechanism to select which of two identical firms will invest first. This situation can also occur with asymmetric costs, but only when the current exchange rate is high enough so that, compared to investing later as a duopolist, it becomes preferable for each firm to invest immediately as a temporary monopolist but not high enough to make it optimal for both firms to enter simultaneously as duopolists. In this case, we have the classic game of chicken in which both firms would want to be the first to enter. However, if they enter simultaneously, each firm would be worse off than if it had entered second. In our example, this occurs when the current exchange rate X is strictly between \$1.03 and \$3.00. In this situation, there are two pure strategy equilibria: (1) the lower cost firm invests immediately and the higher cost firm does not, and (2) the higher cost firm invests immediately and the lower cost firm does not. Without further assumptions, we cannot predict which of the two pure strategy Nash equilibria will occur.[16]

If the current exchange rate is greater than the optimal entry exchange rate for a firm as a second investor, then it is optimal for such a firm to enter immediately regardless of the entry decision of its competitor. Thus, if the current exchange rate is strictly between \$3.00 and \$3.67, the equilibrium consists of the lower cost firm investing immediately and of the higher cost firm investing later when the exchange rate reaches \$3.67.

If the current exchange rate $X \geq \$3.67$, then it is optimal for both firms to enter immediately. In this case, since entry is simultaneous, neither firm acquires a temporary monopoly position. Both essentially enter as second entrants. Simultaneous entry at the current exchange rate X is optimal for both firms if X is greater than the optimal entry exchange rate for both firms as second entrants, i.e., if $X \geq \max(X_{hd}^*, X_{ld}^*)$.

16.3.4 Limiting Cases

By varying the cost of the higher cost firm, we obtain two important limiting cases of our model: one in which the unit costs are equal, resulting in the model of Dixit and Pindyck (1994), and the other in which the unit cost of the higher cost firm is so high that it is optimal for it to forego the investment opportunity altogether, resulting

---

[16] A standard approach to this problem is to widen the choices by allowing mixed strategies. Another possibility is to cast the problem as a bargaining game in which the lower cost firm shares just enough of its temporary monopoly rent with the higher cost firm to induce the latter to postpone entry. The interested reader is referred to Fudenberg and Tirole (1991) and Rasmusen (1995) for a discussion of mixed strategies and the bargaining problem.

in the model of McDonald and Siegel (1986). The first limiting case occurs when $c_h = c_l = c < a$. In this case, our model reduces to that of Dixit and Pindyck (1994, pp. 309–316), except that the firm has the additional flexibility to adjust its output level. In this equal-cost case, all of our derivations and results continue to hold. But since each firm is both the higher and lower cost firm, we have to rely on some random mechanism to select which of the two identical firms will invest first in an equilibrium with sequential entry, as in Dixit and Pindyck (1994, pp. 309–316) and Grenadier (1996).[17]

The second limiting case occurs when $c_h > a > c_l$. In this case, the investment decision of the higher cost firm is quite simple: it will not invest at all, no matter how favorable the exchange rate becomes. Consequently, the lower cost firm acquires a permanent monopoly position. In this case, our derivations and results continue to hold with the entry exchange rate of the higher cost firm set at $X_{hd}^* = \infty$. The first term of Eq. (16.6c) drops out, resulting in the monopoly value function originally studied by McDonald and Siegel (1986) and reformulated by Pindyck (1989), with output set equal to the optimal monopolistic output level.

16.4 CONCLUSION

In this synthesis piece, we formulate a continuous-time version of the model of Trigeorgis (1996) and Smit and Trigeorgis (1997), extending the literature on continuous-time strategic timing decisions by allowing duopolistic firms to have different payoffs as well as flexibility in their choice of output levels. Variable output levels allow firms to optimally respond to entry by a competitor through a combination of output and timing decisions. This allows a more realistic specification of the threshold prices at which each investor optimally enters. Allowing for asymmetric payoffs makes identification of equilibrium entry simpler and more intuitive than the symmetric case.[18] This is an improvement over symmetric strategic models in which some random mechanism must be employed to select which of two identical firms will invest first.

We show that if the project is not yet very profitable, the unique subgame perfect equilibrium is for the lower cost firm to enter first and for the higher cost firm to invest second. The expected time before entry of the second investor is increasing in the amount of required initial investment and in the size of the cost differential between the two firms. By varying the cost of the higher cost firm, we can obtain two important limiting cases of our model: one in which the unit costs are equal, resulting in the model of Dixit and Pindyck (1994), and the other in which the unit cost of the

---

[17] Grenadier (1996) also uses the equal-cost, fixed-output structure of Dixit and Pindyck (1994, pp. 309–316). He extends the Dixit and Pindyck model by introducing the time-to-build aspect of Majd and Pindyck (1987).

[18] Here, we model asymmetric payoffs as asymmetric costs. Asymmetry could just as well be modeled in revenues or in profits. The important point in the model is that one firm has a competitive advantage that can be overcome by another firm at some cost.

higher cost firm is so high that it is optimal for it to forego the investment opportunity altogether, resulting in the model of McDonald and Siegel (1986).

Appendix A

This appendix provides a proof of Result 3. We need to show that $[\min(\hat{X}, X^*_{lf}), X^*_{hd}]$ satisfies the four properties of an equilibrium entry profile.

1. By definition, X^*_{hd} is the best entry exchange rate for the higher cost investor given that it is entering as a second entrant.

2. By definition of $\hat{X}$, $NPV_{hf}(X_1; X) \leq NPV_{hd}(X^*_{hd}; X)$ for all $X_1 \leq \hat{X}$. Hence, $\min(\hat{X}, X^*_{lf})$ is a preemption-proof entry exchange rate for the lower-cost firm as a first investor.

3. By definition, X^*_{lf} is the optimal entry exchange rate for the lower cost firm as a first investor if it is assured that it will not be preempted by the higher cost firm. Hence, entry at X^*_{lf} is the best preemption-proof entry exchange rate for the lower cost firm as a first investor if $\min(\hat{X}, X^*_{lf}) = X^*_{lf}$. If $\min(\hat{X}, X^*_{lf}) = \hat{X} < X^*_{lf}$, then we also have $\hat{X} < X^*_{hf}$ since $X^*_{lf} < X^*_{hf}$ by Result 2. Now $[dNPV_{if}(X_1; X)]/dX_1 > 0$ for $X_1 < X^*_{if}$, $i = 1$, h. It follows that $NPV_{lf}(X_1; X) < NPV_{ld}(\hat{X}; X)$ for $X_1 < \hat{X}$ and $NPV_{hf}(X_1; X) > NPV_{hd}(\hat{X}; X)$ for some $X_1 > \hat{X}$. Thus, there is no advantage to be gained by the lower cost firm by investing at an exchange rate lower than $\hat{X}$, but there is an incentive for the higher cost firm to preempt if the lower cost firm plans to invest at an exchange rate greater than $\hat{X}$. Hence, if $\min(\hat{X}, X^*_{lf}) = \hat{X}$, entry at $\hat{X}$ is the best preemption-proof entry exchange rate for the lower cost firm as a first investor.

4. Since $[dNPV_{ld}(X_2; X)]/dX_2 < 0$ for $X_2 > X^*_{ld}$ and, by Result 1, $X^*_{hd} > X^*_{ld}$, it suffices to show that $NPV_{lf}[\min(\hat{X}, X^*_{lf}); X] \geq NPV_{ld}(X^*_{ld}; X)$. If $\min(\hat{X}, X^*_{lf}) = X^*_{lf}$, then the optimality of X^*_{lf} and hypothesis (b) imply that $NPV_{lf}(X^*_{lf}; X) \geq NPV_{ld}(X^*_{ld}; X)$. If $\min(\hat{X}, X^*_{lf}) = \hat{X} < X^*_{lf}$, then hypotheses (a) through (c), together with the fact that $[dNPV_{lf}(X_1; X)]/dX_1 > 0$ for $X_1 < X^*_{lf}$, imply that $NPV_{lf}(\hat{X}; X) \geq NPV_{ld}(X^*_{ld}; X)$. QED.

ACKNOWLEDGMENTS

We are grateful to Michael Brennan and Lenos Trigeorgis (the editors) and an anonymous referee for very helpful comments. We alone are responsible for any errors or shortcomings.

REFERENCES

Black, F., and M. Scholes. (1973). The Pricing of Options and Corporate Liabilities. *Journal of Political Economy* 81, 637–659.

Brennan, M., and E. Schwartz. (1985). Evaluating Natural Resource Investments. *Journal of Business* 58(2), 135–157.

Cox, J., and S. Ross. (1976). The Valuation of Options for Alternative Stochastic Processes. *Journal of Financial Economics* 3(1/2), 145-166.

Dixit, A. (1989). Entry and Exit Decisions under Uncertainty. *Journal of Political Economy* 97(3), 620-638.

Dixit, A., and R. Pindyck. (1994). *Investment under Uncertainty*. Princeton, NJ: Princeton University Press.

Fudenberg, D., and J. Tirole. (1991). *Game Theory*. Cambridge, MA: MIT Press.

Grenadier, S. (1996). The Strategic Exercise of Options: Development Cascades and Over-building in Real Estate Markets. *Journal of Finance* 51(5), 1653–1679.

Krylov, N. (1980). *Controlled Diffusion Processes*. New York: Springer-Verlag.

Majd, S., and R. Pindyck. (1987). Time to Build, Option Value, and Investment Decisions. *Journal of Financial Economics* 18(1), 7–27.

McDonald, R., and D. Siegel. (1985). Investment and the Valuation of Firms When There Is an Option to Shut Down. *International Economic Review* 26(2), 331–349.

McDonald, R., and D. Siegel. (1986). The Value of Waiting to Invest. *Quarterly Journal of Economics* 101(4), 707-727.

Pindyck, R. (1988). Irreversible Investment, Capacity Choice, and the Value of the Firm. *American Economic Review* 78(5), 969–985.

Pindyck, R. (1989). Irreversibility, Uncertainty and Investment. *Journal of Economic Literature* 29(3), 1110–1148.

Rasmusen, E. (1995). *Games and Information*. Cambridge, MA: Blackwell.

Sick, G. (1995). Real Options. In R. Jarrow, V. Maksimovic, and W. Ziemba (eds.), *Finance*. Amsterdam: North Holland.

Smit, H., and L. Ankum. (1993). A Real Options and Game-Theoretic Approach to Corporate Investment Strategy under Competition. *Financial Management* 22(3), 241–250.

Smit, H., and L. Trigeorgis. (1997). Flexibility and Competitive R&D Strategies. Working Paper, Columbia University.

Trigeorgis, L. (1991). Anticipated Competitive Entry and Early Preemptive Investment in Deferrable Projects. *Journal of Economics and Business* 43(2), 143–156.

Trigeorgis, L. (1996). *Real Options: Managerial Flexibility and Strategy in Resource Allocation*. Cambridge, MA: MIT Press.

17

The Ship Lay-Up Option and Equilibrium Freight Rates

JOSTEIN TVEDT

In the classical lay-up decision of a shipowner, the choice of whether to operate a ship or to go into lay-up is primarily determined by the stochastic dynamics of the freight rate. In this chapter it is suggested that the flexibility to mothball production units itself influences the equilibrium dynamics of the price process. The industry equilibrium freight rate is affected by each shipowner's supply adjustments. Due to the lay-up option, the freight rate is bounded from below by the lay-up of the most efficient ship operators. In fact this aggregated effect on the equilibrium freight rate should be taken into consideration when evaluating the optimal lay-up policy in the first place.

17.1 INTRODUCTION

Investing in a ship to operate in the international transport spot market is a risky venture. Most markets for the bulk transport of commodities, such as coal, iron ore, grain, crude oil, and refined oil products, are characterized by a high degree of competition. As it may take between 6 months and several years from the time of first ordering a vessel until delivery, while demand for transport services fluctuates significantly, supply and demand often clear at freight rates that differ from the long-run average so that there is substantial volatility in the freight rates. In the short run, supply may not be able to adjust to unpredicted increases in demand with the result that freight rates may occasionally get very high. On the other hand, if there is too much speculative ordering of new vessels, freight rates may drop as new capacity is added, and can stay low for long periods until demand picks up or old vessels are scrapped.

The high volatility of freight rates implies that the flexibility to increase supply if freight rates are high or to decrease supply and costs if freight rates are low can have substantial value. This is particularly true for the flexibility to lay up a vessel. Mossin

340

(1968) discusses the optimal lay-up policy with an uncertain freight rate income. Due to the cost of laying up and taking the vessel back into trade, he finds that the threshold values for entry under uncertainty are higher than under certainty, and that the threshold for exit into lay-up is lower, i.e., there is a lag in optimal entry and exit. In Mossin's pioneering work on irreversible investment and optimal entry and exit under uncertainty, it is assumed that the freight rates follow a discrete random walk process. Dixit and Pindyck (1994) revisit the lay-up problem assuming that the freight rate follows a geometric Brownian motion. Their results are qualitatively equivalent to Mossin's, but they extend the analysis to include the question of optimal termination of the project by demolition and reentering by new building.

Laying up a ship in this context means to accept a small fixed cost from laying up in order to avoid potentially heavy losses from sailing in a market where freight rates are below operating costs. When a shipowner chooses to temporarily withdraw from the market, the aggregate supply falls accordingly. Short-term lay-up, long-term mothballing, or slow steaming due to unfavorable freight rates thus reduce total supply. Reentering and increased speed, on the other hand, increase supply. At the aggregate level, the shipowners' flexibility in the utilization of their vessels influences total supply and thereby the industry equilibrium freight rate.

This chapter illustrates how the ship operators, by exercising the option to mothball, influence the dynamics of the underlying stochastic freight rate process. The value of the flexibility to lay up depends on the ship operators' cost structure relative to the cost structure of the other suppliers in the market. That is, the flexibility to mothball is more valuable to the cost-inefficient than to the cost-efficient operators, since the freight rate seldom falls below the lay-up level of the cost-efficient operators.

The rest of the chapter is organized as follows. Section 17.2 discusses the lay-up option and equilibrium freight rates and Section 17.3 derives the value of a vessel with the lay-up option. The last section provides concluding remarks.

17.2 LAY-UP AND EQUILIBRIUM FREIGHT RATES

Assume that demand for shipping services at time t, Y_t, is totally inelastic to freight rates. This classical assumption for the shipping markets, going back to Tinbergen (1934) and Koopmans (1939), is a realistic characterization of the tanker markets, especially for the very large crude carriers for which the freight rate is a very small percentage of the end consumers' price of oil derivatives.[1] Demand is assumed stochastic, with incremental changes given by a geometric Brownian motion:

$$\frac{dY_t}{Y_t} = \hat{\mu}\, dt + \hat{\sigma}\, dz_t \tag{17.1}$$

where $\hat{\mu}$ and $\hat{\sigma}$ are the drift and standard deviation of the relative change of Y_t, and dZ_t is the increment of a standard Brownian motion.

---

[1] The model can easily be extended to the case of a demand with a constant elasticity, as in Dixit (1991). However, to reduce the amount of algebra, this path is not followed here.

Suppose the variable costs of operating a given vessel, i, are constant, c_i. These include fuel and crew costs as well as harbor and channel charges. We assume that each vessel provides one unit of supply.[2] If the freight rate is very low, the shipowner may consider laying up a vessel instead of continuing operating and paying the variable operating costs, yet certain costs must also be incurred during lay-up, mainly related to supervision, maintenance, and renting a sheltered harbor. Let the fixed cost of lay-up of vessel i be m_i. In addition, there may be costs related to taking a vessel in and out of lay-up.

If the effect of the entry and exit costs of lay-up is ignored, the freight rate that triggers both exit and entry, the lay-up level, $\bar{x}_i$, is equal to the cost of operating less the cost of lay-up, i.e., $\bar{x}_i = c_i - m_i$. The options to lay up or to reenter may be of substantial value if the freight rate is volatile and the entry/exit trigger, $\bar{x}_i$, is in the range of the freight rate fluctuations.

If all vessels have the same lay-up trigger, the freight rate will never go below this trigger. If it is optimal for one shipowner to mothball his vessel at $\bar{x}$, it will be optimal for all the other shipowners as well. Hence, the freight rate will never fall below the common lay-up level and, consequently, the option value of lay-up is competed away in equilibrium. This property is related to the discussion of the relation between real option triggers under monopoly and perfect competition by Leahy (1993).

In the maritime industry, however, it is fairly unrealistic to assume that all shipowners operate their vessels equally efficiently. Due to the long life of a ship, normally 25 years or more, together with technological developments and changing operational and environmental requirements, ships do not have the same cost structure and, hence, have different optimal lay-up levels. Let $\bar{x}_0$ be the exit and entry level of the most efficient vessel in the market when there are no fixed costs of entry and exit. $\bar{x}_0$ is also the lowest possible equilibrium freight rate level of the entire market, since below this level all vessels will be laid up.

From a microperspective, the entry freight rate level of a given vessel is determined by its variable operating cost less the lay-up cost. Denote the most inefficient active vessel in the market by j. Let the entry/exit freight rate level of vessel j be given by $\bar{x}_j = c_j - m_j = \bar{x}_0 + \beta\Theta^\phi$, where $\beta\Theta^\phi$ is the entry/exit level mark-up of the most inefficient active vessel, j, over the entry level of the most efficient vessel, and where Θ is the aggregate supply of shipping services, with $\beta > 0$ and $\phi > 0$ being constants. Let aggregate supply be a continuous function of the freight rate level.[3] A

---

[2] This is a simplification since vessels to some extent can adjust supply by slow steaming: high bunker costs and low freight rates may make it optimal to reduce speed and thereby restrict fuel consumption in order to maximize the voyage result. The hull and engine design of each individual vessel decides the potential for speed adjustment. Generally, older vessels have higher flexibility, although their overall fuel efficiency is lower.

[3] Vessels produce more than a marginal supply when they enter the market. The freight rate may rise to a level that induces entry, but as a new vessel enters, the freight rate falls, due to the more than marginal extra supply. Consequently, the real world supply adjustment process implies incremental steps in the freight rate each time there is a new entry/exit of vessels. However, as the number of vessels in international shipping is quite high, e.g., there are approximately 3500 units of crude and refined oil products tankers above 10,000

freight rate equal to the entry/exit level of the marginal supplier then implies that the aggregate inverse supply function, at time t, is given by

$$x_t = \bar{x}_0 + \beta \Theta_t^\phi \tag{17.2}$$

The freight rate will never go below the level of exit of the most efficient vessel, $\bar{x}_0$, and aggregate supply, Θ_t, is derived from entry of laid up vessels. Setting demand equal to supply, $Y_t = \Theta_t$, using the aggregate supply function in (17.2) and the dynamics of aggregate demand in (17.1), it follows that the change in the freight rate at time t is given by

$$dx_t = \mu(x_t - \bar{x}_0)\, dt + \sigma(x_t - \bar{x}_0)\, dZ_t \tag{17.3}$$

where $\mu = \phi[\hat{\mu} + \frac{1}{2}\hat{\sigma}^2(\phi - 1)]$ and $\sigma = \phi\hat{\sigma}$. It is interesting to note that the option to lay up vessels implies that the freight rate is bounded from below by the lay-up level of the most efficient vessel, $\bar{x}_0$.[4] Expression (17.3) shows the endogenous determined dynamics of the freight rate, which are given by the parameters of the demand function (17.1) and the inverse supply function (17.2). From (17.3) it follows that the integral representation of the freight rate at time τ, x_τ, given the freight rate at time t, is

$$x_\tau = \bar{x}_0 + (x_t - \bar{x}_0)\, \exp\left[\left(\mu - \tfrac{1}{2}\sigma^2\right)(\tau - t) + \sigma \int_t^\tau dZ_s\right] \tag{17.4}$$

17.3 THE VALUE OF A VESSEL WITH A LAY-UP OPTION

Since no analytical solution to the entry and exit problem exists if there are switching costs related to laying up or reentering, only the effect on the value of a vessel with costless entry and exit is studied below.[5]

At time t the shipowner maximizes the instantaneous profit rate, π_{it}. Given the option to lay up, the profit rate will be the maximum of the freight rate income less the variable operating costs and the fixed costs due to lay-up, i.e., $\pi_{it} = \max(x_t - c_i, -m_i)$, where the dynamics of the freight rate, x_i, are given by (17.3).

Using no-arbitrage arguments to determine market values and optimal behavior is well established when modeling markets for securities and storable commodities.[6] However, the freight rate is the price of transport services, which by nature cannot be stored. For transport services, the no-arbitrage arguments are less clear-cut and it

dead weight tonnes, the supply relation may reasonably be assumed to be fairly smooth at the aggregate level. Therefore, it is not unreasonable to approximate the aggregate supply function by a continuous function.

[4] $\bar{x}_0$ is reached only if $Y_t = 0$. It follows from (17.1) that this is an inaccessible boundary.

[5] See Brennan and Schwartz (1985) and Dixit (1989) for discussions of the effect of entry and exit switching costs. Note that an analytical solution is available by focusing on the lay-up decision of a unit of capacity, but to add the flexibility to choose optimal speed distorts the price linearity of profits, which substantially increases the complexity of the valuation problem.

[6] In this special case, with costless entry and exit, optimal behavior is independent of risk attitudes and follows immediately from maximizing instantaneous profits.

is necessary to apply equilibrium models that specify the risk attitude of the agents directly. In accordance with an equilibrium model approach, let the unit price of risk of the stochastic process x_t be given by λ. Further, assume that the risk-free rate of return r is constant. Then the value of the vessel and in particular the value of the option to lay up, given the prevailing freight rate, is easily derived using standard procedures (see, e.g., Dixit and Pindyck, 1994; Trigeorgis, 1996).

The cash flow generated by the vessel at time t is the freight rate, x_t, less the operating cost, c_i, if the vessel is operating. The cash flow is negative and given by the fixed cost of lay-up, m_i, if the vessel is mothballed. The optimal lay-up strategy in the case of no exit or entry costs is to lay up as soon as income less operating costs is more negative than the cost of lay-up. Let $\chi_{it} \in \{0, 1\}$ be an indicator variable taking the value one in the operating case and zero in the lay-up case. Under the certainty-equivalent probability measure Q, the value of vessel i is then given by the value function $\Phi_i(x_t)$:

$$\Phi_i(x_t) = \sup_{\chi \in (0,1)} E_t^Q \left[\int_t^\infty e^{-r(s-t)} \left\{ (x_s - c_i)\chi_{it} - m_i(1 - \chi_{it}) \right\} ds \right] \quad (17.5)$$

Between each change of state the value function must satisfy the following stochastic differential equation:

$$\frac{\partial \Phi_i}{\partial t} + \tilde{\mu}(x - \bar{x}_0)\frac{\partial \Phi_i}{\partial x} + \frac{1}{2}\sigma^2(x - \bar{x}_0)^2\frac{\partial^2 \Phi_i}{\partial x^2}$$
$$- e^{-rt}(x - c_i)\chi_i + e^{-rt}m_i(1 - \chi_i) = 0 \quad (17.6)$$

where $\tilde{\mu} = \mu - \sigma\lambda$ is the trend of $(x_t - \bar{x})$ under the certainty-equivalent probability measure Q. Let $\tilde{\mu} < r$. Intuitively, the change in the value function, given by the first three terms, must at any time equal the instantaneous cash flow, given by terms four or five. For the homogeneous terms of Eq. (17.6) let us try a solution of the form $\Phi = e^{-rt}g$ where $g = (x - \bar{x}_0)$. This gives a solution with the two roots

$$\gamma_k = \frac{-\left(\tilde{\mu} - \frac{1}{2}\sigma^2\right) \pm \sqrt{\left(\tilde{\mu} - \frac{1}{2}\sigma^2\right)^2 + 2r\sigma^2}}{\sigma^2} \quad \text{for } k = 1, 2 \quad (17.7)$$

where $\gamma_1 > 1$ and $\gamma_2 < 0$. The particular solution in the operating case is given by the expected present value of the cash flow from infinite operation; similarly, the particular solution in the case of lay-up is given by the present value of an infinite lay-up expense. The general solution in the operating case is thus given by

$$V_i^o = C_3 g^{\gamma_1} + C_2 g^{\gamma_2} + \frac{g}{r - \tilde{\mu}} - \frac{c_i - \bar{x}_0}{r} \quad (17.8)$$

where C_2 and C_3 are constants. In the case of lay-up, the general solution is given by:

$$V_i^l = C_1 g^{\gamma_1} + C_4 g^{\gamma_2} - \frac{m}{r} \quad (17.9)$$

where C_1 and C_4 are constants. The value of the option to lay up is negligible if the freight rate gets very high, and consequently the value of C_3 must be zero. Further, the value of the option to start operating is negligible if the freight rate is close to the lower bound $\bar{x}_0$. Hence, C_4 must also be zero.

At the trigger freight rate the value-matching and the high-contact conditions must hold. The value-matching condition says that the value of the state immediately before the change must be equal to the value immediately after the change. Since the optimal trigger implies that $\bar{g} = \bar{x} - \bar{x}_0 = c_i - m_i - \bar{x}_0$, the value-matching condition is

$$C_2(c_i - m_i - \bar{x}_0)^{\gamma_2} + \frac{c_i - m_i - \bar{x}_0}{r - \tilde{\mu}} - \frac{c_i - \bar{x}_0}{r} = C_1(c_i - m_i - \bar{x}_0)^{\gamma_1} - \frac{m_i}{r} \quad (17.10)$$

and the high-contact condition[7] is

$$C_2\gamma_2(c_i - m_i - \bar{x}_0)^{\gamma_2-1} + \frac{1}{r - \tilde{\mu}} = C_1\gamma_1(c_i - m_i - \bar{x}_0)^{\gamma_1-1} \quad (17.11)$$

Solving for the two constants C_1 and C_2 using Eqs. (17.10) and (17.11) finally gives the value of the vessel, at time $t = 0$, depending on whether the vessel is laid up or operating:

$$\Phi_i(x) = \begin{cases} k_1(c_i - m_i - \bar{x}_0)^{1-\gamma_1}(x - \bar{x}_0)^{\gamma_1} - \frac{m_i}{r} & \text{if } x < c_i - m_i \\ k_2(c_i - m_i - \bar{x}_0)^{1-\gamma_2}(x - \bar{x}_0)^{\gamma_2} + \frac{(x-\bar{x}_0)}{r-\tilde{\mu}} - \frac{(c_i-\bar{x}_0)}{r} & \text{if } x \geq c_i - m_i \end{cases} \quad (17.12)$$

where

$$k_1 = (\gamma_1 - \gamma_2)^{-1}\left(\frac{\gamma_2}{r} - \frac{\gamma_2 - 1}{r - \tilde{\mu}}\right) > 0$$

and

$$k_2 = (\gamma_1 - \gamma_2)^{-1}\left(\frac{\gamma_1}{r} - \frac{\gamma_1 - 1}{r - \tilde{\mu}}\right) > 0$$

For the lay-up case, $x < c_i - m_i$, the first term in (17.11) is the value of the option to restart operating in the future. The second term is the cost of infinite lay-up, i.e., the present value of future mothballing costs if reactivating is not an alternative. For the operating case, $x \geq c_i - m_i$, the first term is the value of the option to mothball in the future. The second and third terms represent the net present value of the expected infinite future cash flows from operating if lay-up is not an option.

By adding flexibility the decision maker must be at least as well off as without flexibility, and hence the option values in (17.12) above are always positive. The optimal strategy for the unit vessel is to lay up as soon as operating costs less the cost of lay-up are higher than the freight rate, that is $c_i - m_i = \bar{x}$ is the change-of-state trigger. In general, $c_i - m_i \geq \bar{x}_0$, with equality binding only for the most cost-efficient vessel in the market. Hence, the second factor of the option value terms is positive. Observe also that the option to lay up is of no value to the most efficient vessel, since the freight rate never falls below the lay-up level for this vessel. Consequently,

---

[7] See Dixit and Pindyck (1994) for a discussion of the high-contact condition.

the third factor of the option value terms is also positive, and the overall effect is a positive option value.

Evidently, the value of the flexibility to lay up for a given shipowner is closely related to the degree of cost disadvantage of the vessel compared to other vessels in the market. Relation (17.13) below shows the change in the value function from a change in the operating cost c_i:

$$\frac{d\Phi_i(x)}{dc_i} = \begin{cases} k_1(1-\gamma_1)(c_i - m_i - \bar{x}_0)^{-\gamma_1}(x - \bar{x}_0)^{\gamma_1} & \text{if } x < c_i - m_i \\ k_2(1-\gamma_2)(c_i - m_i - \bar{x}_0)^{-\gamma_2}(x - \bar{x}_0)^{\gamma_2} - \frac{1}{r} & \text{if } x \geq c_i - m_i \end{cases} \quad (17.13)$$

In the lay-up case, $x < c_i - m_i$, expression (17.13) is negative since $\gamma_1 > 1$ and all the other factors are positive. A high cost of operating implies that the relative attractiveness of staying mothballed increases and the value of the option to reactivate falls.

In the operating case, $x \geq c_i - m_i$, the first term in expression (17.13) is positive since $\gamma_2 < 0$ and the second term is negative. Higher operating costs imply that the downward potential increases if the lay-up option does not exist. Hence, the value of the flexibility to lay up increases. The negative term is due to the fact that the increased operating costs reduce the net present value of the expected future profits from operating. The overall effect on the value function is negative since the increase in the lay-up option value compensates only partly for the loss from higher operating costs.

The effect of an increase in the fixed cost of lay-up, m_i, has the reverse effect on option value, but a similar negative effect on the value of the vessel. In the lay-up case, an increased cost of lay-up increases the value of the option to reenter, but this increase in option value is more than offset by the increase in the net present value of the costs of infinite lay-up. In the operating case, a higher cost of lay-up decreases the value of the option to mothball. The overall effect of the increase in the lay-up cost is negative.

The effect on the value of a vessel of increased costs is negative, but the effect on the option value is determined by the change in the difference $c_i - m_i$. In this way the presence of the lay-up option moderates the effect on the value of a vessel of a change in costs.

From Eq. (17.2) it follows that the freight rate elasticity of supply is given by

$$\epsilon(x, \phi) = \frac{x}{\phi(x - \bar{x})} \quad (17.14)$$

Figure 17.1 shows the value of the option to mothball for different elasticities of supply.[8] A high elasticity of supply means that any decrease in demand is immediately met by a substantial lay-up of vessels such that a potential fall in the freight rate is limited. Hence, the value of the flexibility to mothball is low. A low elasticity of

---

[8] The graph is calculated for ϕ between 0.1 and 2.9, and with x and all the other parameter values fixed. The values are $x = 10$, $\hat{\mu} = 0.0005$, $\hat{\sigma} = 0.06$, $r = 0.01$, $\lambda = 0.01$, $\bar{x} = 5$, $c = 9$, and $m = 1$.

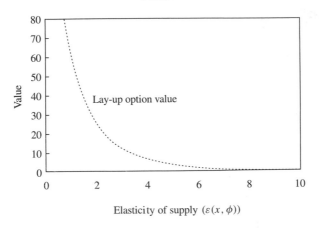

Figure 17.1 Value of the lay-up option as a function of the elasticity of supply, for a given freight rate level ($x = 10$).

supply implies that few vessels are laid up as demand falls and the freight rate is allowed to fluctuate significantly. In this case the value of the lay-up option is high.

Figure 17.1 is calculated by changing the value of the parameter ϕ in the inverse aggregate supply function (17.2). An increase in ϕ implies that the elasticity of supply, ε, falls and the volatility of the freight rate increases. Because of this the value of the option to lay up a vessel, as shown above, increases as the supply elasticity falls, i.e., as ϕ increases.

17.4 CONCLUSIONS

For practical valuation, a good description of the dynamics of the cash-flow process is vital when operating flexibility is present. For certain industries such as shipping, mothballing the production units at times of low prices is a valuable option. Individual shipowner decisions to lay up reduce total supply and restrict a potential fall in prices. This aggregate effect should be taken into consideration when valuing the individual production units. In particular, the option value of lay-up is restricted for the most efficient producer in the market. There is an option value related to mothballing a vessel, but this option is less valuable the more efficient the vessel is relative to the most productive units. Consequently, the difference in value between an inefficient and an efficient production unit is reduced when the lay-up option is taken into account.

As Lo and Wang (1995) point out, an improved specification of the price dynamics is important for a successful estimation of the parameters of a stochastic process. Erroneous estimation of the diffusion term may result in an incorrect valuation of flexibility. This chapter suggests an absorbing level above zero as a natural extension to previous models. For practical valuation and estimation, a mean reversion specification due to a long-run adjustment of capital should be considered. Bjerksund and Ekern (1995) and Tvedt (1997) provide some further insight in this regard.

ACKNOWLEDGMENTS

I thank Lars Mathiesen for useful suggestions. I also acknowledge very constructive advice from Michael Brennan and Lenos Trigeorgis (the editors) and an anonymous referee. This work has been partly carried out at the Norwegian School of Economics and Business Administration, Centre for International Economics and Shipping.

REFERENCES

Bjerksund, P., and S. Ekern. (1995). Contingent Claims Evaluation for Mean-Reverting Cash Flows in Shipping. In L. Trigeorgis (ed.), *Real Options in Capital Investment, Models, Strategies, and Applications*. New York: Praeger.

Brennan, M. J., and E. S. Schwartz. (1985). Evaluating Natural Resource Investments. *Journal of Business* 58(12), 135–157.

Dixit, A. (1989). Entry and Exit Decisions under Uncertainty. *Journal of Political Economy* 97(3), 620–638.

Dixit, A. (1991). Irreversible Investment with Price Ceilings. *Journal of Political Economy* 99(3), 541–557.

Dixit, A., and R. S. Pindyck. (1994). *Investment under Uncertainty*. Princeton, NJ: Princeton University Press.

Koopmans, T. C. (1939). *Tanker Freight Rates and Tankship Building*. Haarlem, Netherlands: De erven F. Bohn.

Leahy, J. V. (1993). Investment in Competitive Equilibrium: The Optimality of Myopic Behavior. *The Quarterly Journal of Economics* 108(4), 1105–1133.

Lo, A. W., and J. Wang. (1995). Implementing Option Pricing Models When Asset Returns Are Predictable. *Journal of Finance* 50(1), 87–129.

Mossin, J. (1968). An Optimal Policy for Lay-up Decisions. *Swedish Journal of Economics* 70, 170–177.

Tinbergen, J. (1934). Tonnage and Freight (translation of "Scheepsruimte en Vrachten"). *De Nederlandsche Conjunctuur* March, 23–35; reprinted in L. H. Klaassen, L. M. Koyck, and H. J. Witteveen (eds.). (1957). *Jan Tinberg: Selected Papers*. Amsterdam: North-Holland.

Trigeorgis, L. (1996). *Real Options: Managerial Flexibility and Strategy in Resource Allocation*. Cambridge, MA: MIT Press.

Tvedt, J. (1997). Valuation of VLCCs under Income Uncertainty. *Maritime Policy & Management*, 24(2), 159–174.

Index